Studying Your Community

ROLAND L. WARREN

STUDYING
YOUR
COMMUNITY

This Study was
Originally Supported and Published
by Russell Sage Foundation

THE FREE PRESS, *New York*
COLLIER-MACMILLAN LIMITED, *London*

6660I436

321066?

2,582,163

PUBLICATIONS OF RUSSELL SAGE FOUNDATION

Russell Sage Foundation was established in 1907 by Mrs. Russell Sage for the improvement of social and living conditions in the United States. In carrying out its purpose the Foundation conducts research under the direction of members of the staff or in close collaboration with other institutions, and supports programs designed to develop and demonstrate productive working relations between social scientists and other professional groups. As an integral part of its operations, the Foundation from time to time publishes books or pamphlets resulting from these activities. Publication under the imprint of the Foundation does not necessarily imply agreement by the Foundation, its Trustees, or its staff with the interpretations or conclusions of the authors.

For information, address:

THE FREE PRESS
A DIVISION OF THE MACMILLAN COMPANY
60 Fifth Avenue, New York, N.Y. 10011

Collier-Macmillan Canada, Ltd., Toronto, Ontario

Library of Congress Catalog Card Number: 55-7727

FIRST FREE PRESS PAPERBACK EDITION 1965

Introduction
to the Paperback Edition

CONTINUITIES AND CHANGES IN COMMUNITY STUDIES

IT IS CHALLENGING to have occasion to review a book and its reception and use over a decade of rapid change. The steady demand for *Studying Your Community*, published by Russell Sage Foundation in 1955, is an indication that it has been found useful by students, citizens, and professional workers who either alone or as part of a larger group wish to take a systematic look at some important aspect of their communities. Through this paperback edition the book will be made available to a wider reading public.

The many reviews of the first edition, particularly in journals designed for specific publics, such as those concerned with municipal government, education, religious activities, or industrial or welfare activities, perceived the book principally as a guide to their respective segments of the community rather than for "total" community studies. Although specifically and deliberately confined to the United States, large sections of *Studying Your Community* were translated into Spanish and put to use by an interdisciplinary study group consisting largely of officials from various governmental agencies in Puerto Rico, and proposals were made for translating it also into Italian and Japanese —proposals which, however heartening, did not seem advisable to implement.

Designed primarily as a practical guide to interested citizens, *Studying Your Community* is almost purely empirical, with only a most minimal sociological reference showing through here and there to provide focal points for various clusters of questions. This paucity of theoretical orientation imposed a rather weighty discipline on the author, and occasioned some feelings of guilt for spending so much effort on a book so singularly devoid of theoretical significance—and this in a field where theoretical conceptualization was much needed.

What, after all, is the nature and extent of the structured interaction which takes place in various localities and is given the name
"community?" One can hardly answer this question merely by pursuing the citizen's legitimate interest in the availability and quality of
facilities and services within his locality, important and desirable as
the inquiry may be.

Some years later, therefore, the author did attempt to compensate
for the lack of theory in the present book by taking a systematic theoretical look at the American community as a type of social system.
The outcome was *The Community in America,* published by Rand
McNally and Company in 1963.

Two Underlying Realities

Two points form the principal themes of that book, and both have
relevance to the present one. The first is that much social activity
occurs on the basis of propinquity—the bald fact of people living
together in the same locality. Notwithstanding the development of
special interest groups, the sense of identification with a national company or voluntary organization, the growing impact of federal governmental programs, the increasing urbanization with its alleged
concomitants of anonymity, impersonality, selective participation, and
the decline in importance of the immediate locality as a focus around
which major activities are organized, the clustering of people for residence and sustenance still has important meanings.

Further, recent research has cast grave doubts upon an earlier conception which proclaimed the decline of the importance of kinship ties
as a basis for significant social activity, outside the immediate nuclear
family. The extended family, with its important social functions, has
in a sense been rediscovered, largely within the decade since the publication of *Studying Your Community.* Likewise, the alleged decline of
"neighboring," the relative absence of meaningful relationships to one's
city neighbors, has been found to be highly exaggerated, and numerous
studies have pointed to the sturdy survival of this form of meaningful
social interaction based on propinquity.

The second major emphasis of that more theoretical book on the
American community also has direct relevance to this hopefully "practical" volume. It relates to a double set of relationships in which the
various units which make up communities participate—units such as
business establishments, government offices, schools, religious organizations, social agencies, and the like. When we look systematically at a

community we notice that these constituent units participate in two kinds of relationships. In one kind, they are involved in a *horizontal* relationship to each other, across the different sectors of the community. This relationship of community units to each other is often thought of in terms of community "cohesion" or "integration."

But the respective units of a community also participate in a different set of relationships—a set of *vertical* ties which relate them to organizations outside the community, often as subordinate parts of a larger organization. Such relationships are illustrated by the tie of the local branch-plant to the large manufacturing company with headquarters a thousand miles away, of the local post office to the U.S. Postal System, of the local church to its denominational headquarters, of the local health association to the national organization which charters it, of the local school to the state education department, and so on.

What makes the distinction particularly relevant to the present book is, of course, the fact that these vertical relationships are becoming stronger with the passage of time, as compared with the horizontal ones; and that for community units to be kept in an adequate functional relationship to each other, it now becomes increasingly necessary to plan for this, rather than to expect it to happen just in the free interplay of behavior among these individual units of the community. Hence, the chambers of commerce, the welfare councils and united funds, the councils of churches, the community councils, and other kinds of deliberate organization set up to bring the diverse aspects of communities into more consciously patterned relationship to one another. Yet, these coordinating efforts pale in significance as compared with the increasing significance of the ties to organizations beyond the borders of the community.

Recent Developments in American Communities

It is instructive to consider some of the important developments occurring during the past decade which relate to the efforts of citizens in studying their communities, as well as to changes in the communities themselves. The continued expansion of the population in areas surrounding cities both large and small is one such important development, as is the continued decline in the population of the centers of large cities. The process of suburbanization, with its attendant population shifts, continues to pose an awesome array of problems to those interested in today's communities.

Much more dramatic in its impact has been the rapid succession of events in the field of civil rights. Beginning with the Supreme Court decision of May, 1954, which provided a solid legal platform for racial integration in public education, a series of developments have precipitated both rapid movement and considerable conflict in this field, as the inexorable trend toward equal rights continues. One of the most significant aspects of this trend has been the ability of Negroes, joined by many whites, to organize—largely nonviolently—into a powerful force for continued implementation of the principle of equal rights.

The decade has been haunted by a development whose full implications are not even yet completely understood, but about which there is little doubt as to its vast repercussions for American communities. Automation has not only increased productivity; it has also brought about a shift in the demand for skilled labor and a rapid reduction of the comparative utility of unskilled labor. There is little doubt at this point that vast changes, both in the industrial employment pattern and in the indicated modifications in education and employment train- ing, are yet to have their full impact on American communities.

Related both to the problem of automation and to the race rela- tions problem has been the bold national program to combat poverty focused in the Office of Economic Opportunity, established by 1964 legislation. The sizable pockets of poverty, in both urban and rural settings, in some instances involving large sections of several states in regional depressed areas, have thus become the targets of systematic and massive programs. The "community action programs," which are a central feature of the federal strategy, are of particular importance in their requirement of systematic study of the extent and characteristics of poverty in the locality involved, and in their emphasis on involving the poor actively in helping to formulate and implement the programs.

Parenthetically, it is worthy of note that the program's official title uses the concept of economic opportunity rather than the negative con- cept of poverty. In this connection, it is interesting to observe the succession of terms employed in the past decade to denote some aspect of the poverty problem, such as multi-problem families, hard-to-reach families, hard core, culturally deprived, lower socioeconomic groups, and so on. Each term, significantly, was used originally as an attempt at a "neutral" or nonmoralistic designation, but in each case the term has acquired negative connotations and has become the target of attack as being somehow unfair or derogatory to the people whom the term was supposed to designate.

The Economic Opportunity program is a fairly dramatic example of a host of new federal programs which are important for concerned citizens of the community in a number of respects.

First, they offer an important stimulus for various communities simultaneously to attack specific social ills which can hardly be eradicated piecemeal, through the uncoordinated efforts of single communities.

Second, many of them establish a direct tie between a federal agency and the local community, often bypassing the state as an intermediate level of administration.

Third, like most grant-in-aid programs, they embody specific requirements to which the individual community must conform if it is to be eligible.

Fourth, they provide from federal sources a large proportion of the money needed to support the activity, thus making it possible for communities to engage in programs which would be difficult or impossible to finance with local tax money.

Fifth, many of these programs have as one of their requirements a systematic study of the community from the standpoint of data which are relevant to the specific purpose of the program.

Sixth, they constitute, of course, powerful tools which communities may use, if they wish and are able to organize themselves effectively, in attacking their local problems.

Finally, in their aggregate effect, there is little doubt that such federal programs are already making major impacts on the physical and social structure of American communities, and thus must be reckoned as one of the most important phenomena of our generation.

Even as *Studying Your Community* was being written, the Housing Act of 1954 was implementing a broad new concept of urban renewal, providing for a wider series of programs which went beyond slum clearance and redevelopment with a series of measures through which urban blight could be combated in its early stages, and neighborhoods could be protected from it, or if already deteriorating, could be rehabilitated rather than destroyed. But urban renewal, federal subsidies for low-rent housing, and other programs connected with the "physical" aspects of the community are only part of a much larger pattern of specific channels of federal assistance which have in the past decade been supplemented by massive programs in community mental health, mental retardation, transportation, juvenile delinquency, vocational rehabilitation, community planning for welfare, health services for the chronically ill, and a host of others. In fact, as Charles I. Schottland pointed out at the National Conference on Social Welfare in 1963, "today, more than one hundred separate Federal programs which relate to the general welfare of local communities are making an impact on local community organization through money grants, technical assistance, direct services, or a combination of these."

The fact that so many of these programs call for some type of *ad hoc* organization in the local community to engage in the development and policy-making functions is in itself a significant development, for among other things it involves the formation of a number of broad coalitions of agencies and organizations, each of which, though directed at a particular program, involves many different sectors of the community. The resulting ferment in community organization is making rapid changes in the more traditional modes of integrating structures.

The development of a plurality of community structures, each of which is engaged in planning on a topic which involves broad segments of the community, poses a significant problem for community planners. Take as an example the special planning bodies which have arisen in connection with the delinquency program, with the poverty program, with urban renewal, and with mental health—only four programs out of a much larger number which call for specific local citizens' planning bodies. Each of these problems has broad ramifications in the community, and the trend is toward acknowledging ever broader involvement of agencies and interests cutting across many fields. Are these planning bodies to develop and operate their programs in relative isolation from each other? If not, what form shall their interrelationship take?

Two obvious polar solutions present themselves. One is the development of a local "superagency" which would attempt to coordinate the efforts of these powerful planning coalitions. The other is to acknowledge that it is not feasible to attempt such global coordination through a special agency, and to hope for a degree of coordination through open channels of communication and joint consultation on matters of overlapping interest and responsibility. At present, although a few notable attempts have been made at some type of formal coordinative mechanism, the answer to this problem seems to be that of acknowledging the existence of a plurality of planning centers, each closely related to a specific federal or federal-state program and seeking some degree of functional coordination at federal, state, and local levels, without endeavoring to formalize this function in a single super-agency.

Another development of the past decade has been closely related to the proliferation of federally supported programs at the community level. This has to do with the whole concept of the function of the professional community organization worker, particularly in the field of health and welfare. It involves, basically, the relation of planning to consensus. Earlier conceptions of the role of the professional community organizer emphasized the importance of facilitating the process of goal-setting through the development of broad consensus of interested parties, and of working, at least in theory, toward broader and broader involvement of those who are interested, in the process of decision-making. The professional was thus not to lead in a directive way but rather merely to help broadly constituted groups to develop their own goals, policies, and programs, and to function within such broadly established areas of agreement.

This rationale has not been refuted or disavowed but a number of developments have occurred which have tended to make it less relevant to the situation in which community activities take place. First, there is increasing recognition that movement ahead in such areas as equal rights and integration can hardly wait for full consensus. The very issues which trouble the community are issues precisely because they involve different, often opposing, interests and different opinions as to how they should be resolved. In many cases, to wait for full consensus is to forestall effective action indefinitely, while problems grow ever more formidable. In this connection, social scientists have pointed out that the search for consensus is often essentially a conservative search, in practical application, simply because it deliberately avoids the moves which, though "controversial" in some quarters, are necessary if an effective approach to a particular problem is to be made. Thus, the positive value of controversy has received increasing attention in recent years.

Another related reason for the changing conception of the community organization process has been the very proliferation of planning centers mentioned above. If complete coordination of programs is waited for, nothing will get done. And with separate programs multiplying, the possibilities for effective coordination through formal structures become increasingly remote. The resolution of this situation seems to be the determination by individual planning bodies to go ahead, striving primarily for a modest degree of coordination within their own central programs, but not being diverted from action by the lack of total rational coordination with other programs. At the margins, where the lack of intercoordination produces special problems, these are then ironed out through negotiation, largely in the political arena, only when they become sufficiently intense to take on the proportions of a public issue.

But not all the forces are centrifugal. For example, one notes with particular gratification increasing communication between physical planners, housing planners, and health and welfare planners. The convergence is still minimal, yet it marks a definite step in a direction which is suggested in this book. There is every indication that the next decade will see a continuation and perhaps an intensification of the trend for professional personnel—as well as governmental officials and citizen leaders—to acknowledge their interrelatedness in these three fields and to communicate with each other on matters of overlapping concern.

Developments in the Behavioral Sciences

Finally, it may be of interest to note a few of the major recent developments in the behavioral sciences which have a bearing on community structure and processes. Unquestionably, the most noteworthy of these developments has been the marked interest and activity of behavioral scientists in the field of the distribution of social "power" within the community. The development is presaged by the reference on page 355 to Floyd Hunter's pivotal book, *Community Power Structure*. That book was hardly the first to point out the importance of the unequal distribution of power, or to suggest that power might not be exclusively concentrated among the holders of official positions, as indicated by the quotation from Louis Wirth on the same page. Nevertheless, in developing a method for locating the "power structure" and in devoting an intensive study to the distribution of power in one large city, Hunter precipitated a cascade of research projects on the distribution of power in various communities large and small, research conducted primarily by sociologists and political scientists. As a consequence, there exists today a vast body of research findings and a relatively highly developed and varied set of techniques available for the investigation of this important aspect of communities.

Another important development in the behavioral sciences has been the emergence of a growing number of political scientists who have made important contributions to our understanding of the processes through which community issues become resolved. Part of this contribution by political scientists has been made in the field of the distribution of power within the community. Generally speaking, although there are some important exceptions, political scientists in this field have tended to emphasize the plurality of power structures around different fields of interest and decision-making in the community, rather than seeing power as concentrated in a single structure. They have tended to investigate the distribution of power in connection with the actual exercise of power in decision-making on specific community issues, rather than approaching it from a purely reputational concept of who is believed to have power, and they have tended to emphasize the extent to which power is actually exercised by the holders of elective political office. Sociologists have likewise been active in the study of community power, but it is perhaps valid to say that they have not been so deliberately ranged on a specific side of these power "issues" as the political scientists.

Political scientists have made an increasingly important contribution in a closely related field, which is perhaps best described as that of specific studies of processes of political interaction in the community. The findings of Norton E. Long, Robert A. Dahl, and Edward C. Banfield are representative of the contributions made in this direction.* If there is any single conclusion to be drawn by people interested in studying their own community from the contributions of these and other political scientists, it is the close connection between party politics and the manner in which broad issues of social welfare are joined and resolved in American communities, particularly in the larger cities. The citizen genuinely concerned with his community can be hygienically "nonpolitical" only at the price of virtual ineffectiveness.

A development which is perhaps not so immediately accessible to the layman has been the growing elaboration of social system analysis and its application to communities. It is perhaps sufficient simply to note that adequate theoretical conceptualization in the field of community studies has been largely lacking—for example, in the question of what is really meant by the concept of a community, as distinguished from the local government. One way of conceiving the community is as a complex interrelated structure of interaction patterns, on the basis of which certain locality-relevant functions are performed. Sower and his associates, as an example, made very effective use of social system analysis in their study of a countywide self-survey of health conditions and services in a midwestern county; Lippitt and his associates used

* See Long, Norton E., *The Polity*, Rand McNally and Co., Chicago, 1962; Dahl, Robert A., *Who Governs*, Yale University Press, New Haven, 1961; and Banfield, Edward C., *Political Influence*, The Free Press, New York, 1961.

the concept of a social system in their analysis of the relationship of a consultant to a "client system" in the bringing about of planned social change, and included the community, along with the individual, the small group, and the formal organization, in the types of client system which they analyzed; the author's more theoretical work on the American community, mentioned earlier, constitutes an application of social system analysis to community phenomena. *

It would be remiss not to mention with gratification the growing interest of fellow behavioral scientists in the community as an arena of study and action. Investigators of the distribution of power within the community, though until recently largely indifferent to the total community context within which power distribution was being investigated, gave a much-needed impetus to social science research in the community field. The engagement of social scientists in applied research in health and welfare problems, itself a significant trend of the decade, led the investigators inevitably to an increased interest in the community context within which their special problems were being pursued. At the same time, the emergence of Community Development Institutes and of Centers for Urban Studies in many universities indicates a gratifying surge of renewed interest in the community as a form of human association. As a result of these and other developments, there is today a large reservoir of techniques of community analysis, through which a growing number of behavioral scientists and professional specialists can assist citizens in the making of rigorous and objective studies in their communities.

If knowledge is power, as Francis Bacon once asserted, then there is legitimate hope that the power which is to be derived from rigorous study of community phenomena, both for theoretical and for practical purposes, may somehow be enlisted for the enhancement of the values of community living. Royce's concept of the "the beloved community" may be sheer mysticism, but it represents an aspect of the entire matter which is not made any less relevant by the rapid changes through which American communities are now passing.

ROLAND L. WARREN

The Florence Heller Graduate School
for Advanced Studies in Social Welfare,
Brandeis University

---

* See Sower, Christopher, and others, *Community Involvement: The Webs of Formal and Informal Ties That Make for Action,* The Free Press, New York, 1957; Lippitt, Ronald, Jeanne Watson, and Bruce H. Westley, *The Dynamics of Planned Change,* Harcourt, Brace and Co., New York, 1958; and Warren, Roland L., *op. cit.*

Contents

Illustrations

XIX

I believe in the beloved community and in the spirit which makes it beloved, and in the communion of all who are, in will and in deed, its members. I see no such community as yet, but none the less my rule of life is: Act so as to hasten its coming.

JOSIAH ROYCE

Preface

IN PREPARING THIS BOOK, the author has been sensitive to certain pressures from different directions. On the one side, the professional sociologist looks over his shoulder to urge a much more scientifically rigorous methodology for community research. From a different angle, the people engaged formally in "community organization" in large cities may well feel that greater attention might have been paid to agencies, standards, and conventional community organization problems and procedures. Still another group, the "actionists," may be impatient with the time demanded in the seemingly useless cataloguing of factual material, time which might better go into improving obviously unacceptable conditions in the community.

But this book, like its predecessor, must remain a broadly conceived working manual of community study which, in seeking to satisfy in part the demands of all these groups, may succeed in completely satisfying none of them.

The immediate predecessor of this work, Joanna C. Colcord's *Your Community: Its Provision for Health, Education, Safety, and Welfare,* was originally published by Russell Sage Foundation in 1939 and went through three editions and many printings. It in turn had followed Margaret F. Byington's *What Social Workers Should Know About Their Own Communities,* a pamphlet first published by the Foundation in 1911.

The present book is designed to fulfill much the same need as its predecessor. The reason for a new book, rather than another revision of the earlier one, is largely one of orientation. *Your Community* grew out of a community study guide for social workers, and it has retained much of that early orientation. It now seems appropriate to think of a more varied group of citizens, both laymen and those professionally engaged in some branch of community service, to whose interests such a book may be germane. The result has been less emphasis on formal agencies and broader coverage in other respects. For example, more recent orientation or tools of analysis in intergroup relations, informal group processes, social class, and other such matters have been included in this book if only on an elementary level. In addition, the

XXI

new book takes into account the great need for orientation of the reader in survey procedures, providing, in addition to the chapters on different community topics, material on conducting the survey, both in its organizational and methodological aspects. In general, the thought has been to orient the community study process toward community "action" to a greater extent than its predecessor. Nevertheless, Colcord's *Your Community* has been of great use to the author as a resource book of proved usefulness in the community. Occasional specific questions have been taken over verbatim.

Many persons have read one or more chapters of this book or have otherwise been helpful. The author is especially indebted to Gordon Berg, Samuel W. Blizzard, Richard S. Childs, Nathan E. Cohen, Margaret E. Conrad, John P. Dean, Gunnar Dybwad, Lester J. Evans, Henry Fagin, John E. Gilmore, Shelby M. Harrison, Helen van O. Kerr, Merrill F. Krughoff, Robert D. Leigh, John Lobb, Leonard W. Mayo, John W. McConnell, James A. McLane, Arthur E. Morgan, Lawrence M. Orton, Joseph Prendergast, Mildred Rankin Rader, Albert N. Rogers, and Cyril G. Sargent. Although the book has gained by their suggestions, they are not responsible for any of its weaknesses.

Considerable aid was also given by Margaret M. Otto and Clarence M. Mitchell and the staffs of the libraries of the New York School of Social Work and Alfred University. The use of the quotation from Royce at the beginning of the book is an idea borrowed from Arthur Dunham.

R. L. W.

Studying Your Community

1. How to Use This Book

THIS BOOK IS A WORKING MANUAL for people who are interested in studying their own community in one or all of its aspects. It is designed for the layman but may be of help also to professional people, particularly in those aspects of the community not directly within their field of professional competence.

Even the most modest community survey is a venture in human relations. The processes involved in planning, organizing, and conducting a survey, as well as the different types of surveys which are possible, are considered in Chapter 18. In community survey work, there are many resources available to the investigator, such as the material in the federal censuses and in reference books of various kinds. In addition, there are certain methods of gathering facts which will be of service to the investigator. This material is taken up in Chapter 19. It is possible to gather and record all sorts of facts about a community without gaining sufficient comprehension of the intricate network of processes and relationships which constitute a human community. Chapter 20 is designed to supply some of this basic understanding of the "wholeness" of communities, as well as to point out certain underlying realities which often elude the investigator concerned only with specific answers to detailed questions.

The rest of the book is devoted almost entirely to chapters that help the reader to learn more about a particular aspect of his community. Each chapter consists of descriptive and interpretive text, as well as question outlines. In general, the text is designed to afford a framework of meaning for the questions. It does this by explaining some of the issues which are raised in the question outline, and occasionally referring to widely accepted standards for community appraisal. In this connection, frequent reference is made to various publications which will provide further background in the topic under consideration. Wherever possible and advisable, publications have been cited which are authoritative, readily available, and either free or relatively inexpensive. Publications which are out of print or otherwise inaccessible have usually been avoided. In order to con-

I

serve space, the references for further study listed at the end of each chapter do not repeat works which have been cited in the body of the chapter. In addition to consulting supplementary interpretive material, the reader may want to avail himself of the services of the various agencies which operate in one or another field relevant to community studies. A list of such agencies is appended to the book.

Each chapter explores the factual basis of the community and suggests organizational, planning, and action programs which may be undertaken toward community betterment in the aspect under consideration.

Even though the reader may wish to use the book for a survey of some one particular aspect of his community, such as mental health, housing, or recreation, the particular aspect to be surveyed should be related to the total community. The material from Chapter 2 will be a useful guide to community background data, no matter what special topic is being studied.

Several suggestions are appropriate to the use of the question outlines in the various chapters. The questions are designed to be as generally applicable as possible, and most of them apply to highly urban as well as highly rural communities. Since the purpose of this book is guidance in studying communities of all sizes, some questions are included which apply only to the largest communities, while others apply only to the smallest. For example, housing data available in the Census block statistics reports apply only to the larger cities. On the other hand, if you are studying a small village, questions about departments of parks and playgrounds, rapid transit systems, harbors, community welfare councils, museums, theaters, and such items may not be appropriate. A question on some particular practice in the school system may need answering only by a particular teacher at the community school, or it may need extensive investigation among the many schools of the large city.

Thus, the questions are designed to raise issues for further study. One question may perhaps need to be broken down into several parts, particularly in a large community, while in a smaller community, several questions may be combined into one. Many questions are usable in their present printed form. Others, however, will need to be reworded, expanded, or modified to fit the local situation.

To have developed each question into the extensive battery of information which the occasional reader may require would have given the book mammoth proportions. A little effort given to "pinning a question down" in terms of your community may be called for in some cases. For example, in the chapter entitled "Religious Activities," there is this question: "Do the churches lose many young people when they grow too old for the Sunday school, or do these young people go on into active participation in adult activities in the churches?" To answer the question thoroughly, it might have to be put into the following form and submitted to the appropriate official of each church:

Ten years ago, how many children aged 11 to 15 were enrolled in the Sunday school?

Of these persons, how many are now connected with the adult activities of the church as active members? As inactive members? As nonmembers who occasionally participate?

A comparison of the drop-outs between childhood and adulthood with those in an average group of adults during the same period would give an indication of whether such drop-outs are inordinately large, or merely represent the usual turnover in membership. Ordinarily, however, most questions will not require such reworking.

One other comment on the use of the question outlines is in order. Behind most of the questions lies a function of some sort. The important thing is the function, not the particular way the question is worded. Often, the function is performed by some agency specifically set up for the purpose, as in the case of child placement for adoption. Frequently, however, the function may be performed by many agencies, such as recreational opportunities within the school, within the family, at a recreation center, boys' or girls' club, or church. In some cases, one or several formal agencies will be involved in performing some function. In others, it may be performed within the family or neighborhood in an informal but effective way. Thus, there may be no elaborate detention facilities for juvenile delinquents in a small community, and yet there may be an excellent informal local arrangement through which the occasional delinquent who requires detaining (most of them do not) can be accommodated in a foster home.

The charts, maps, and other illustrations in this book have a double purpose. Their subject matter is related to the respective chapters where they are found, and serves to illustrate important points. In addition, these charts represent ways which the reader may employ to help illustrate key points in a survey report. Illustrations which make some complicated relationship more readily apparent, are helpful in aiding understanding and acceptance, as well as in making a community survey report more attractive.

It is suggested that early attention be given to Chapter 18. There the reader will be urged to consider whether the scope of the survey effort he has in mind is appropriate to the man-hours available for it. The temptation here, as in so many other aspects of life, is to bite off more than one can chew and thus endanger the whole effort as one becomes disappointed at not getting results quickly enough. In addition, Chapter 18 explores the relationship of fact-finding to action. It is pointed out that if the survey arises out of the concern of some group for a particular aspect of community life, it is perhaps more likely that some follow-up action will eventually result. Serious consideration should be given to the question of whether a voluntary group really wants to limit its objectives to pure fact-finding without giving considerable thought to what will be done with the facts once they are obtained.

Margaret F. Byington's advice given more than four decades ago in *What Social Workers Should Know About Their Own Communities* is just as appropriate today:

> Specific facts are more valuable than general impressions, and information is useful in proportion as it is concrete and quickly available. Whatever information is secured, therefore, should be (1) definite. For example, get the specific wording of laws when this is possible, not merely the general scope. It should also be (2) accurate. Simple, accurate statistics are better than elaborate, unreliable ones. If an estimate is the only possible answer to a question, so label it and give the basis of the estimate. "This law was violated twenty times last year" is much more convincing than "the law is often violated." When possible (3) compare the figures for a given city with those for other cities of the same size; this will show their real significance.

Finally, a word of caution is in order concerning evaluation. Whether and to what extent professional services in such fields as health, welfare, and education are adequate and of sufficiently high quality is a question on which the layman needs expert advice. At various places throughout the book, certain objective, often quantitative, standards of evaluation are included. These frequently give a specious sense of precision, and should be used only in a most tentative way. The best advice to citizens who believe that their survey has uncovered areas of deficiency is to get the help of a national agency operating in the appropriate field of interest. With the expert's professional evaluation available, the decision can then be made by local citizens, to whom belongs the final responsibility for the character of their own community.

2. Your Community: Its Background and Setting

TO BE PROPERLY INTERPRETED AND ADEQUATELY APPRAISED, the special topical material which is gathered in a community study should be considered in the broad perspective of community background and setting. The present chapter considers such underlying conditions as geography, transportation, the number and characteristics of the people, community history, local traditions, and community values. These conditions form the necessary backdrop for such special studies as recreational facilities, intergroup relations, education, or housing. For this reason, the reader who is interested in such a topical study, rather than a thorough study of all the different activities of the community, will want to make use of the present chapter as well as the one which takes up his special area of interest. Those who are making more inclusive studies will, of course, want to include this material as an integral part of their endeavor.

Geography and Transportation

In villages and cities, where man has done much to modify the natural environment, it is easy to overlook the importance of geographical factors in the development of community life. The presence of minerals in the earth, particular types of soil, the junction of rivers, natural harbors, or special scenic advantages may be of crucial importance in forming the community.

What people do with their natural resources is of equal importance. The development of previously unexploited resources often changes the character of the community in drastic fashion. This occurs not only in communities where gold or oil or a particular type of ore is discovered, but also where communities take advantage of natural scenic beauty or favorable climate to develop resorts.

Man's contribution to his own physical environment becomes increasingly important with the development of invention and technology. Mountains can be flown over or tunneled through; rivers or gulleys can be spanned

5

by bridges; canals can be built to connect natural waterways; warm, op-
pressive air can be air-conditioned.

Cities and villages, which themselves are influenced by the natural environment, become a part of the environment which influences the way people
live. Man-made cities, bridges, highways, railroads, air routes become as
much a part of the geographic setting of your community as the mountains,
rivers, mineral deposits, and climate.

Particularly important in the setting of your community are the transportation routes which lead into and out of it, and its proximity to other
communities of various types and sizes. It will depend upon larger cities
for more specialized goods and services than it can provide, and it in turn
will serve smaller communities at its own level of goods and services.

1. What is the nature of the countryside in which your community is located?
   Does it consist of plains, rolling hills, mountainous country, or wooded hills?
2. What is the average temperature in January?   July?
3. What is the average annual precipitation?
4. What kind of soil predominates in your locality?
5. How is your community located with respect to each of the following:

   Rivers   Canals   Principal highways
   Oceans   Railroad lines   Air routes
   Large lakes   Bus and truck routes

6. Does your community have any natural advantages, such as a good harbor,
   a beautiful lake-front, location at the convergence of two rivers, a healthful
   climate, or proximity to natural resources?
7. Has the topography of the land affected your community's location and development?
8. Do hills confine it within a valley?
9. Do rivers or other natural barriers channel its growth?
10. Is certain land within the community relatively unusable because of natural
    conditions such as cliffs, swamps, or steep hills?
11. Is the community you are studying delineated by any political or adminis-
    trative boundaries? If so, in which category is this political unit:

    Ward   City   Township
    District   Village   School District
    Borough   Town   County

12. What are the different "neighborhoods" in your community? (See Chapter
    19.)
13. How far is your community from the nearest city having a population of:
    1,000,000 or more? 100,000 to 1,000,000? 25,000 to 100,000? 10,000 to
    25,000? Under 10,000?
14. If your community is a large one, which villages or cities of various sizes
    are in its tributary area?

15. If your community is a small one, which cities serve it as the metropolitan center of the region? A cultural center? Center for hospital and medical services at various levels? Wholesale supplier? Shopping center? Transportation center?

16. What are the principal industries? (See Chapter 3.) Where do they get their raw materials? Where do they sell their products?

17. Are there commuting relationships involved in your community; if so, to or from what areas?

18. When people leave your community to visit a larger city for shopping or other purposes, to which city do they most often go?

19. From what area does your community draw people who come to get goods and services not obtainable locally?

20. Does the existence of certain transportation routes tend to link your community with certain other communities more than would otherwise be likely:

    Up-river or down-river   Up the coast or down the coast
    Along the valley   Along a principal air route
    Along a main highway   Along a main railroad line

The People of Your Community

The number and kind of people in a community have a great influence on the type of social living. In general, the higher the concentration of people in a given area, the greater the degree of specialization which must take place for them to subsist. High population density also usually means that people can be on only the most casual terms with other people in their vicinity, for there are more of them than one can know intimately. The fact that in a large population a person becomes practically anonymous when he leaves his door or his block does much to necessitate the various secondary controls on behavior which include complicated police systems and courts. The business of everyday living is carried on to a large extent with people whom one does not know.

The community becomes even more complex if it is made up of different kinds of people, whether the difference involves race, religion, national origin, or great extremes of wealth and poverty.

Most communities can expect a larger proportion of older people in their population as time goes on. Communities differ from each other in this respect, with small villages usually showing a higher proportion of older people than either the open country or the large city. At the other end of the age scale, the proportion of children is an important index. Just as old people may be more dependent economically, more conservative politically, and more susceptible to chronic illness, so children are also dependent economically, require school facilities, and in other ways confront the community with various needs.

The proportion of people 65 years of age and over in your community added to the proportion under 15 is a significant index, for it gives a rough idea of the people who are in age-groups usually economically dependent, as against those in the prime of life.

Usually there is a high sex ratio (number of males per 100 females) on the farms and in newly settled territory and among recent immigrant groups, while there is usually (though not always, particularly in industrial cities) a low sex ratio in the cities.

Growth in numbers is generally considered the sign of a healthy community. Nevertheless, city planners have pointed out for some time the advantages of taking care of additional population growth beyond a certain size through new cities rather than adding to the congestion of the older ones. The presence of more people in your community means, usually, more customers for the local stores, more workers for local industries, more people to pay taxes, but also greater city expenses for subdivision development, greater demand on municipal services, more children to be educated in the schools, and greater traffic congestion in the downtown area.

Ordinarily, city birth rates are not sufficiently high to balance the number of deaths. City population growth is therefore usually attributable to migration from the rural areas or (particularly in the past) from other countries.

21. How many people are there in your community?

22. What is the sex ratio? $\left(\dfrac{\text{Number of males}}{\text{Number of females}} \times 100 = \text{sex ratio} \right)$

23. If the sex ratio is not very close to 100 (equal number of males and females), what factors account for this?

24. What is the proportion of people in the various age-groups?

25. Specifically, what proportion of people in your community are under 15? 65 and over?
    How does this proportion correspond to that for the entire United States; for other communities of similar size?

26. How many people in your community live on farms?

27. How many people in your community are white, and how many nonwhite? Of the whites, how many are native and how many foreign-born? Of the nonwhites, how many are Negro and how many belong to other races?

28. Of all persons 14 years old and over in your community, how many are male? Female? Single? Married? Widowed or divorced?

29. What is the population per household in your community?

30. How many foreign-born persons are there in your community 21 years of age and older?

31. How many of these are naturalized?
32. How many foreign-born persons come from each country of birth?[1] (Information is available only for northern and western states.)
33. What is the population density of your community, or of its various parts?[2]
34. What was your community's period of most rapid growth of population? To what causes was it due?
35. How does your community's population compare with 1940?   1930?[3]
36. What is the rate of growth or loss of population of various parts of your community?
37. Is your community undergoing marked suburban growth?
38. How have the sex ratio and the age distribution of your community changed since 1940?   1930?[4]
39. Is your community growing as rapidly as the surrounding territory? The county?   State or section thereof?   Other communities of comparable size?
40. What is the birth rate in your community? How does it compare with other communities of similar size?

Local History

Your chief interest in the history of your community is probably to learn how your community came to be the way it is. More important than dates and genealogies and other historical minutiae will be the events and conditions which helped to mold your community. Did the opening up of the railroad tend to shift the downtown center away from the river? Did a particular wave of immigration drastically change the ethnic constitution of the people? Did the discovery of a new resource or the location of a new industry have a crucial effect on the economic organization of your community? These kinds of data will help you understand your community as it is today. The questions in the question outline are designed merely to suggest the type of thing to look for.

What you need to know may be already available in published histories of your community or county. A modest study may require little more than gathering the already assembled facts from one or several such histories.

Where historical material is not already available in the form required,

[1] All the preceding data are given for counties, urban places of 10,000 or more, metropolitan areas, and Census tracts in the *U.S. Census of Population: 1950*, vol. 2, chap. B; and many are given for urban places of 2,500 to 10,000 as well.
[2] Population density is the number of people per square mile. The Census gives this figure for counties, but you can compute it for your community by dividing its total population by the number of square miles it covers.
[3] Comparative population figures by decades are given in *U.S. Census of Population: 1950*, vol. 1, and in vol. 2, chap. A.
[4] Consult previous censuses.

or where a more ambitious effort is proposed in compiling a community's history, many of the following sources of information may be tapped:

I. SOURCES OF INFORMATION FOR LOCAL HISTORY

Library and general sources	Military records
Village, town, and city histories	Directories
County histories	Maps
State and regional histories	Atlases and gazetteers
Sociological material	Accounts of travelers
Family histories and biographies	Anniversary addresses and sermons
	Photographs and pictures

II. OTHER SOURCES OF INFORMATION

Old residents	Account books
Private letters	Keepsakes, heirlooms and relics
Diaries	

III. NEWSPAPERS AND PERIODICALS

IV. PUBLIC RECORDS

Census reports	County archives
Abstracts of title and title deeds	Town records
Surveyors' notes	State public records
Public school records	Pension bureau
Other public records	New planning agencies: national and state

V. BUSINESS RECORDS

VI. CHURCH RECORDS AND CEMETERY INSCRIPTIONS[1]

41. When was your community first settled? By what kind of people? Under what circumstances?

42. What different types of people have come to your community at different periods during its development?
Why did they come? How did they get along together?
What contribution has each group made to the culture of the community?

43. Are there any historical incidents in the relations of different groups of people in your community which have had a lasting effect upon their relations today?

44. What have been the principal events in the life of your community: opening of roads, railroads, canals; battles in connection with wars; floods, droughts, dust storms, blizzards; coming of new industries and methods of livelihood; visits by famous persons; or other events?

45. Have any of these events had a lasting effect which can be observed today?

46. What are the chief conditions, circumstances, resources, or factors of location, which determined your community's development to what it is today?

[1] This list of sources is quoted from the table of contents of the first 89 pages of Donald Dean Parker's *Local History:* How to Gather It, Write It, and Publish It, revised and edited by Bertha E. Josephson, Social Science Research Council, New York, 1944. Parker's book will be invaluable to the person or committee engaged in compiling a history of the local community.

47. What places in the vicinity are historical landmarks or have other historical interest?
48. What has been the influence of the natural environment (topography of the land, type of soil and mineral resources, location of rivers, bays, lakes, and so on) in shaping the development of your community?
49. What famous persons now deceased came from your community?[1]
50. What famous persons today either live in your community or have come from your community?[2]
51. What were the important steps in the economic (industrial) development of your community?
52. Where were the principal Indian trails, if any, in your locality?
    Compare a map of these trails with a map of highways and railroads today.
53. What was the pattern of physical growth of your community?
54. Can you find maps which delineated the community at different periods in its development?
55. Can you find old engravings or early photographs which depict conditions in various stages of your community's development?
56. Have there been any shifts in the major economic activities on which your community depends?
    When and why did these shifts occur?
57. What was the original form of local government?
58. What changes have there been in political boundaries, charters, governmental form, and so on?
59. What has been the history of political campaigning in your community?
60. Is your community politically a "one-party" town? What influence has this fact had on the level of honesty and efficiency of public service?
61. Have any popular movements swept through your community at one time or another? Revival movements? Political reform movements?
    Have there been any social reform movements such as prohibition, women's rights, and so on?
62. What has been the history of labor relations in your community?

Traditions and Values

Traditions are the customs, practices, bits of legend and folklore, and other material from your community's past, which are passed on by word-of-mouth and persist to affect social behavior in your community today. There are long-established ways of doing things and ways of looking at things in any community. These ways, along with specific bits of folklore and legend, go far in establishing the "tone" of the community, that in-

[1] *Dictionary of American Biography*, Index to vols. 1–20, Charles Scribner's Sons, New York, 1937, contains a list of birthplaces by state.
[2] See *Who's Who in America:* A Biographical Dictionary of Notable Living Men and Women, revised and reissued biennially by the A. N. Marquis Co., Chicago.

tangible quality which makes it different in spirit from other communities
of approximately the same size and situation.

Such traditions tend to become points of common reference to which
one can refer in finding his way. They are expressed in terms of "Well, we
don't do that sort of thing in this community," or "I remember when that
young businessmen's group wanted to try that out here back in the twenties.
They made a great hullabaloo, but nothing came of it," or "Ever since . . . ,
we haven't had much use for . . . ." (Supply the words "foreigners," Indians,
Yankees, Easterners, and so on). Similarly, legends and bits of folklore
are shared by people in the community and this common heritage from the
past gives people a sense of community solidarity—the time when the river
flooded, or what happened the day of the blizzard, or the day that the
explosives plant blew up.

Communities are likewise characterized by the things in which they are
most interested, the situations, or qualities, or conditions on which they
place high value. Some communities might place a great value on temper-
ance or individualism or "enjoying life" or educational activity or religious
activity or cooperation. These community values are hard to get at, and
without professional help, the answers you get concerning your community's
values are likely to be the least valid of any of the facts in your survey.
Nevertheless, the importance of the way people look at things, their values,
can hardly be overestimated.[1] These aspects of community life are particularly important as guides to the person trying to work with the community in any type of action program. Certain types of program may be
doomed from the start because they simply do not fit in with the dominant
values of that particular community. Furthermore, many a minor slip and
faux pas in human relations can be avoided if one is sensitive to local traditions and values.

63. Are there any attitudes or values arising from the nature of your community's
original settlers or from the conditions of early settlement which affect the
"tone" of your community?

64. Did later groups of arrivals to the community bring any new traditions
or values which affected community life and are discernible today?

65. Is your community generally characterized by one or more of the following:

Progressivism	Friendliness to strangers
Conservatism	Tolerance of different
Cooperation	peoples and beliefs
Internal conflict	Community-mindedness
Industriousness	Individualism
Lackadaisical attitude	Other characteristics

[1] An excellent discussion of values in American society can be found in Williams, Robin
M., *American Society:* A Sociological Interpretation, Alfred A. Knopf, New York, 1951.

66. What characteristics do you think your community rates most highly in the people it holds in esteem, the people of prestige:

Honesty
Industriousness
Generosity
Educational attainment
Patronage of the arts
Philanthropic activity
Industrial leadership
Athletic attainment
Musical, artistic, or
   literary accomplishment
Spirituality
Wealth

Political power
"Christian living"
Type of occupation
Location and type of residence
Family
Nationality
Holding of public office
Years of residence in the
   community
Community-mindedness
Other

67. Are there any special historical festivals, celebrations, or commemorations which give color and richness to your community's social life?
68. Are there any legends about local happenings which tend to be passed from person to person?
69. Are there any colorful customs which are practiced in your community either by some particular religious or ethnic minority or by the community as a whole?
70. From the following list of important American values, evaluate the relative emphasis which your community places on each one:

Freedom	Success	Happiness
Individualism	Education	Humanitarianism
Democracy	Science	Conformity
Practicality	Progress	Formal association
Material values	Patriotism	Religion

References for Further Study

Bogue, Donald J., *Structure of the Metropolitan Community:* A Study of Dominance and Subdominance. University of Michigan Press, Ann Arbor, 1949. This is a somewhat technical but highly informative work on the relation of the large metropolis to the various local communities in its metropolitan region. The thesis is maintained that this relationship is one of dominance by the metropolis.

Kinneman, John A., *The Community in American Society.* Appleton-Century-Crofts, Inc., New York, 1947. This is a good introduction to communities based upon the major topics of structure, people, institutions, organization, and functions.

Poston, Richard W., *Democracy Is You:* A Guide to Citizen Action. Harper and Bros., New York, 1953. The bulk of this book is devoted to "meetings and discussions" and "special outlines" in connection with the study of numerous aspects of the community. Particularly relevant are chapters on the character, population, and history of the community.

Sanders, Irwin T., *Making Good Communities Better.* rev. ed. University of Kentucky Press, Lexington, 1953. This book has a particularly lucid section on the way local values differ from community to community, and the importance of these differences in community study and action.

Other readings cited in Chapters 18, 19, and 20 are also appropriate.

3. Your Community's Economic Life

A COMMUNITY IS AN ECONOMIC TEAM. It provides means of producing goods and services and distributing them, both within its midst and in interchange with the rest of the world. The way in which it is organized does much to set the tone of the community and flavor the quality of daily living.

The Economic Structure of Your Community

Communities are differently situated as to the amount of money they can afford for schools, health facilities, leisuretime pursuits, food, clothing, housing, and government. There is considerable difference between a thriving small community with a sound, well-diversified economic base and one which lacks this advantage. Again, there is great difference between a community where there are few extremes of rich and poor and one in which the extremes are great. The type of industry likewise influences the tone of the community's daily life. A small mining town is different from a summer resort town, an agricultural trade center, or a transportation center. In another vein, some communities have a relatively stable economic base, while others, because of the type of industry which predominates, are particularly susceptible to the fluctuations of the business cycle. Communities depending on the tourist trade differ greatly in their type of activity and appearance as the number of tourists waxes and wanes with the seasons.

Regardless of such differences, communities can all be examined within a framework of certain basic facts. Some of the goods and services which people make use of within the community come from outside its boundaries, and money must be paid out of the community for these goods and services. Conversely, some of the goods and services produced within the community eventually go to people outside its borders, and for this, money is paid to people in the community. In addition, people within the community produce goods and services which are consumed within the community. Within the community, there is division of labor both to provide goods and services locally and to produce the things which "sustain" the community by bringing in the funds which the community needs.[1] So two basic questions underlying a community economic survey would be: What do we produce for ourselves? What do we give to and receive from the rest of the world?

A modern community therefore constitutes an economic team in which the various workers devote their effort in varying degrees to making available a particular type of goods or services for other people. Of course, some communities are too small to support a highly specialized commercial establishment such as a large department store, a hardware wholesale service, or a subway system. But communities are interrelated by lines of transportation and communication through which some larger communities become centers for distribution of goods and services for smaller communities. Examples are large wholesale establishments, department stores, and specialized medical and other services. On the other hand, grocery stores, gas stations, and similar establishments are located in even the smallest communities.

The following is an estimate of the number of families needed to support various types of retail and service establishment:[2]

Kind of business	Number of families needed to support
Appliance store	1,000
Auto parts and accessory store	1,800
Beauty shop	600
Bakery shop	2,400
Bookstore	12,800
Camera and photo supply store	12,300
Drugstore	800
Dry goods store	1,250
Furniture store	1,300
Gas station	500
Grocery store	250
Hardware store	1,100
Infants' and children's wear store	5,500
Jewelry store	1,750
Dry cleaning shop	1,300
Liquor store	1,100
Lumber and building supply	1,900

[1] Langer, Henry C., Jr., *Income and Spending as Reflected in Banking Transactions in the "Alfred Business Laboratory" for the Year 1947*, Alfred University Department of Business Administration, no date, mimeographed; and *The Pattern of Sustaining Employment*, Alfred University Area Study No. 4, 1948.

[2] Selected data from a table of "25 Businesses and Facts You Should Know About Them" incorporated in "Want a Business of Your Own?" *Changing Times: The Kiplinger Magazine*, vol. 7, May, 1953, pp. 10–11.

Men's wear store	2,500
Restaurant	300
Shoe store	1,900
Sporting goods store	5,400
Women's ready-to-wear shop	1,200
Women's accessory shop	4,600

Different economic enterprises in the community have different sized trade areas. Thus, a particular manufacturing company may cater to the world market; another enterprise may sell its products throughout the country, a whole region, a part of a state, a series of outlying communities, or to the people in the immediate vicinity of the trade center. For our purposes, however, in communities which are large enough to have wholesale establishments it is possible to distinguish between a wholesale trade area and a retail trade area. The former includes the communities served by the trade center, while the latter includes only the people who do most of their retail shopping in the trade center. Thus, the retail trade area is usually much smaller than the wholesale trade area.[1]

The importance of farm people within the trade area is often overlooked. The farmers and the people living in the trade center constitute an inter-related community (see Chapter 19). Farm people depend on the trade center for goods and services, and the trade center depends on their patronage. This applies not only to business enterprises but also to community institutions like churches, schools, and hospitals. Farm people usually produce some of the food which appears on the tables of people in the trade center. But in addition, they ship food elsewhere, thus getting the money with which to pay for the goods and services they receive at the trade center. An important question for the local community is how much of this farm income is spent along Main Street, as compared with mail orders and trade in other places.

1. What is the community unit you have chosen to study:

    | Living center (village, city, neighborhood) | Township |
    | Living center and retail trade area | County |
    | Living center and wholesale trade area | School district |
    | | Other |

2. Give a careful description of the boundaries of the community you have chosen for study.
3. List the factories and manufacturing establishments which are located in your community or employ people from your community, and in each case give the number of employees.

[1] These distinctions, though helpful, should not be pressed too far, for there is considerable overlapping, particularly when the trade areas are broken down by industry groups.

4. List other establishments or institutions which employ local people to perform some service that brings money into the community:
   State or federal hospital or other institution
   College, seminary, or other boarding institution
   Public schools
   Old-age home
   Departments of county, state, or federal government employing local people on civil service or other basis
5. List the wholesale distributors located in your community.
6. If there are no important types of wholesale establishment within your community, where are the establishments located which serve your community?
7. List the type and number of retail stores in your community:

Grocery	Dry goods	Clothing
Hardware	Appliances	Furniture
Stationery	Auto parts	Automobile dealer
Jewelry	Farm implements	Meat market
Ice cream and	Food	Variety (10 cent) store
confectionery	Vegetable	Gift shop
Liquor	Lumber and	Florist
Bakery	building supplies	Other
Drug	Shoe	

8. List the type and number of service stores in your community:

Dry cleaning	Hotel
Restaurant	Newspaper
Ice cream parlor	Undertaker
Tavern	Contractor
Shoe repair	Carpenter
Auto service station	Electrician
Laundry	Plumber
Recreational (bowling alleys,	Radio station
pool halls, theaters)	Insurance broker
Real estate agency	Other
Barber or beauty shop	

9. If any of the service establishments listed above are not available in your community, where do people obtain these services?
10. List the type and number of professional people in your community:

Physician	Chiropodist	Practical nurse
Druggist	Chiropractor	Teacher
Dentist	Osteopathic physician	Clergyman
Veterinarian	Lawyer	Other
Optometrist	Registered nurse	

11. In addition to those already mentioned, what types of establishment or industry bring income into your community: Mining? Construction? Transportation, communication, and other public utilities? Other?

12. How many farm people are there in your community's retail trade area?
13. What is the average income of farmers in your county?
14. How much income is received by your county's farmers from each of the following:

Vegetables	Livestock and livestock products,
Fruits and nuts	other than dairy and poultry
Other field crops	Forest products
Horticultural specialties	Other farm income
Dairy products	Nonfarm income[1]
Poultry and poultry products	

15. On what industries or particular market in the national economy is your own community's economic structure particularly dependent?
16. Which of your community's economic enterprises are absentee-owned?
17. Which of your community's industries are particularly susceptible to fluctuations of the business cycle?

   Which local industries are dependent upon the fortunes of some other industries outside the community?

   Which local industries are dependent upon government appropriations?
18. Which of your industries employ seasonal labor?

   How does this fact tie in with your community's economic structure?
19. Do your farms make use of extensive migrant labor?[2]
20. How many of each of the following types of cooperative are there in your community:

Consumer cooperative	Purchasing cooperative
Health cooperative	Marketing cooperative
Insurance cooperative	Other

21. If you had to classify your community according to its major economic base, into which category would you place it:

Manufacturing[3]	Dormitory
Industrial	Government center
Wholesale	Mining town
Amusement or health resort	Transportation center
Retail	Other
Diversified	

22. What organizations of industries exist in your community:

Trade associations	Employer associations
Personnel associations	Other
Industrial relations clubs	

23. What activities are carried on by the aforementioned organizations?

[1] See U.S. Census of Agriculture, vol. 1, part 2.
[2] For other questions on migrant labor, see Chapter 13.
[3] These classifications have been taken from the Municipal Year Book, 1950, International City Managers' Association, Chicago. In that publication each city in the United States with a 1950 population of 10,000 or over is classified and definitions are given for each category. See also p. 336.

Employment and Working Conditions in Your Community

Income and types of occupation. You will be especially interested in the number of people employed in various industries and occupations in your community. This will help you gain a picture of your community's economic effort. The latest Census reports afford extremely helpful data but, of course, these become increasingly out-of-date with every ensuing year since the most recent Census. The local state employment office will have later figures, but they may not be based on the same geographic area as the Census figures and they may be differently arranged. Inquire from this office exactly what types of information it has available for your purposes.

The importance of average wage earnings and cost of living figures merits some elaboration. High wage scales and full employment mean more money available for taxes, retail stores, private agencies, schools, and so on. Industries are coming to realize that low wage scales are not an unmixed blessing to them, for they are often accompanied by low labor productivity and poor community facilities. Nevertheless, some industries decide against locating in communities whose wage scales are thought to be too high. The changing American conception of the good life, the economic advantages of broadly distributed purchasing power, and the activities of labor unions have all tended to militate against the advantages of the "cheap labor" town. Wage rates must be considered in the light of cost of living to give a valid indication of a community's ability to buy what it needs and wants.

An important factor in living conditions is the presence of various types of cheap consumer credit, such as charge accounts, installment purchasing plans, small loan companies, commercial banks, or credit unions. You may want to investigate the availability and cost of various types of credit in your community.[1]

You will also want to investigate the number, types, and activities of cooperatives in your community in such fields as marketing, consumer's goods, and farm supplies.[2]

The income of farmers varies from time to time with market and weather conditions. This variation in farm income has an important effect in the community, as store owners, banks, tax collectors, and public welfare departments can readily testify.

Turning once more to industrial wage-earners, the activities of unions

[1] See Foster, LeBaron R., *Credit for Consumers*, rev. ed., Public Affairs Pamphlet, No. 5, New York, 1946.
[2] See *1952 Yearbook*, Cooperative League of the U.S.A., Chicago, 1952. This gives descriptions and statistics of various types of cooperative and includes a summary of recent developments in this field. For an exposition of the principles of cooperatives, see Casselman, Paul H., *Cooperative Movement and Some of Its Problems*, Philosophical Library, New York, 1952.

make themselves felt in the community through higher wages, a broader base of distribution of company income, and participation to various degrees in civic affairs. In many communities there is a growing sense of responsibility by management and by unions for the broader welfare of the local community. This often is reflected in successful contract negotiation which makes strikes unnecessary, and in participation in the health, education, and welfare activities of the community.[1] It used to be true that the two types of people who were underrepresented on civic boards and community enterprises were the farmers and the workingmen. This condition is gradually being changed.

Fair employment practice laws barring discrimination in employment because of race, religion, or national origin are in force in several states and cities. While it appears to be true that "you can't legislate attitudes," nevertheless various studies indicate that employment *practices* are amenable to legislative supervision, and fair employment laws have had considerable effect.[2]

24. Of all persons 14 years of age and older, how many are in the civilian labor force? How many of these are:

Employed   Unemployed
Male   Male
Female   Female[3]

25. How many of your community's employed persons are private wage and salary workers? Government workers? Self-employed workers? Unpaid family workers?[3]

26. How many employed persons in your community are in each of the following major occupation groups:[3]

Professional, technical, and kindred workers
Farmers and farm managers
Managers, officials, and proprietors, except farm
Clerical and kindred workers
Sales workers
Craftsmen, foremen, and kindred workers
Operatives and kindred workers
Private household workers

[1] See *Partners in Production: A Basis for Labor-Management Understanding*, prepared by the Twentieth Century Fund Labor Committee, assisted by Osgood Nichols, Twentieth Century Fund, New York, 1949; or the Public Affairs Pamphlet, No. 151, *Can Labor and Management Work Together?* which is based on it.

[2] See Chapter 15. For an analysis of the procedure in New York, which has a pioneer program in this field, see Rackow, Felix, *Combating Discrimination in Employment in New York State*, New York State School of Industrial and Labor Relations, Cornell University, Research Bulletin No. 5, 1949, and the annual reports of the New York State Commission Against Discrimination.

[3] This information can be found in the *U.S. Census of Population: 1950*, vol. 2, chap. B. For questions on employment of older people, see Chapter 13.

Service workers, except private household
Farm laborers, unpaid family workers
Farm laborers, except unpaid and farm foremen
Laborers, except farm and mine
Occupation not reported

27. How many employed males and females in your community are in each of the following industry groups:[1]

Agriculture, forestry, and fisheries
Mining
Construction
Manufacturing
Transportation, communication, and other public utilities
Wholesale and retail trade
Finance, insurance, and real estate

Business and repair services
Personal services
Entertainment and recreation services
Professional and related services
Public administration
Industry not reported

28. What is the income of your community's families by various income groups?[2]

29. What is the median income of your community's families?[2]

30. What percentage of your community's families and unrelated individuals have incomes under $2,000?[3]

31. What is the average value of the farms in your county?[4]

32. How many of your county's farm operators receive more than half of their income from sources other than sale of agricultural products?[4]

33. How many farm operators in your county are full owners? Part owners? Managers? Tenants?[5]

34. What is the dollar value of each of the principal farm crops or products (including livestock) produced in your county?[6]

35. Give the name and annual volume of business of local farmers' cooperatives.

36. How do weekly wage scales compare with other similar communities in your vicinity?

37. What sources of consumer credit are available, and how high are the interest rates?
What are the provisions of state legislation governing small loans?

[1] The answer to this question can be found in the *Census of Population: 1950*, vol. 2, chap. B, for counties, urban places of 2,500 or more, including standard metropolitan areas, and Census tracts in tracted localities. More recent figures on employment in your community may be available through the local state employment office.

[2] The answer to this question is available in the *Census of Population: 1950*, vol. 2, chap. B, for counties, urban places of 10,000 or more, including standard metropolitan areas, and Census tracts in tracted localities. For urban places of 2,500 to 10,000 corresponding figures are given for "families and unrelated individuals," but not for "families" alone.

[3] *U.S. Census of Population: 1950*, vol. 2, chap. B, gives data for all places over 2,500, including counties and metropolitan areas. "Unrelated individuals are persons (other than inmates of institutions) who are not living with any relatives."

[4] The answer to this question can be found in County Table 1 of the *U.S. Census of Agriculture*, vol. 1, part 2.

[5] See County Table 2 of the *U.S. Census of Agriculture*, vol. 1, part 2.

[6] See County Tables 4 and 5 of the *U.S. Census of Agriculture*, vol. 1, part 2.

38. How many workers were unemployed at the time of the most recent Census? How many of each sex were unemployed in the different major occupational groups?[1]
39. What percentage of the workers of your community are members of labor unions?
40. Which unions have the largest memberships in your community?
Is there a council or federation of labor unions in your community? What are its activities?
41. Which companies engage in collective bargaining with their employees?
42. What has been the nature of the history of union-management relations in your community?
Have there been evidences of bitter controversy?
How many strikes occurred last year? In which companies?
43. Are Negroes or other racial or religious groups barred from certain types of employment by law? By custom?
44. Is there a fair employment practices commission in your city or state which enforces nondiscrimination in employment? How effective is it?
45. Which labor unions admit Negroes and other minority groups or races on an equal basis?
Which unions maintain limitations prohibiting membership or limiting it to a certain "quota," either expressly or by unwritten law?
46. How do union wages compare with nonunion wages in skilled occupations? Semiskilled occupations? Nonskilled occupations?
47. To what extent do the various union leaderships appear to be sensitive to the wishes of the rank-and-file members?
48. To what extent do union organizations participate in health, education, and welfare activities through membership in community chest or similar bodies? Contributions? Civic activities of individual union leaders?[2]
49. Under the jurisdiction of what state district labor office is your community for purposes of inspection for compliance with labor laws?
50. How often does the inspection take place, and by whom; and what is its nature?
51. What employers give safety instruction over and above that which may be required by law?
What is the nature and extent of such instruction?
52. What is the rate of industrial accidents in your community; and what trends has it shown over the past few years?
53. What are the principal provisions of any laws governing working conditions as they relate to health and sanitation?
To what extent are the laws enforced?

[1] Answers are available for urban places of 10,000 or more, metropolitan areas, and counties in U.S. Census of Population, vol. 2, chap. B. Your local public employment office may be able to supply more recent figures.
[2] See Hart, Virginia, The Union-Community Handbook, University of Wisconsin School for Workers, Madison, 1946.

54. Are there any glaring needs for health, sanitation, or safety legislation voiced by local labor unions or disinterested citizens' organizations?
55. For each major employer, record the presence or absence of the following, and give a brief description:

Retirement pension plan	In-plant medical service
Union welfare fund contribution by employer	Profit-sharing plan
	Counseling service
Guaranteed annual wage	Company loans
Educational program	Death benefits
Paid vacations for wage-workers	Payroll savings or investment plan
Dismissal pay	Disability compensation
Free or low cost insurance	Other benefits

56. List, where appropriate, the number of employees served or covered in the programs listed above, the extent of company or employee contribution, the amount of benefit, and so on.
57. What special provisions in your state or municipal law designed to protect health, safety, or welfare govern the employment of children?[1] Women?[2]
58. How are these laws enforced in your community? By whom? How often are inspections made?
59. Is there a minimum wage law in your state? What are its provisions?

Personnel relations. Management and personnel practices in industry are in a state of rapid transition as newer findings from the field of "human relations" in industry are applied. Most communities contain in their industries a wide range of personnel practices varying from extremely backward to extremely progressive ones. While it is difficult to describe the newer developments in personnel administration in a few sentences, one may say that they arise from changed production conditions, they recognize new principles as a basis for dealing with various groups within the company, and they have developed new techniques for applying these principles of human nature to the changed production conditions which now prevail.

These changed conditions include the routinization and mechanization of many industrial jobs, the depersonalization of relations between worker and employer arising from the absence of the owner from the factory floor, the rise of powerful labor unions to equalize the bargaining strength of worker and management, and frequent conditions of full employment which have resulted in more than a decade of "tight" labor markets and at times made it difficult to recruit new workers or hold old ones if they became dissatisfied.

[1] See *Why Child Labor Laws*, rev. ed., Children's Bureau, Government Printing Office, Washington, 1954.
[2] See *Summary of State Labor Laws for Women*, Women's Bureau, U.S. Department of Labor, Government Printing Office, Washington, 1952.

The newer principles on which modern personnel practice is based have grown out of years of intensive research in such fields as social psychology, sociology, social anthropology, and labor economics, as well as specific studies of human relations in industry. These principles include the following:

Far from being the sole motivating factor, the economic motive in many situations may be secondary to such motives as the desire for prestige, status, or approval of one's group.

Attitudes are developed and maintained or modified in association with other people, and are intertwined with such motives as the desire for approval by one's group, the desire for high status, and so on.

Misunderstandings arise in the absence of adequate two-way communication.

Informal group affiliations may be as important in influencing behavior in the factory or office as the formal relations prescribed by the organization chart.

Workers do not leave their cultural background, their family problems, and their prejudices at the factory door, but take them right onto the factory floor where they continue to influence behavior.

Workers desire a sense of belonging, a feeling of participation in the company in which they work.

The attempt to build administrative practice on such principles has led to the development of many new techniques and to the new application of some old techniques. Included in these newer techniques are the following:

Use of opinion polls to assess employee reaction to new or prospective changes.

Training of supervisory personnel in informal techniques of leadership.

Providing for employee participation in decision-making wherever feasible.

Providing various types of incentive to increase labor productivity.

Development of various facilities, such as recreation programs, coffee breaks, and rest periods, to make the job pleasanter.

Development of scientific testing programs to place the worker in a type of work amenable to him and development of counseling services to help the troubled worker adjust to his difficulties.

Increased use of communication devices such as briefings, announcements, motion pictures, company journals, suggestion and "gripe" boxes, and so on, to facilitate understanding between various components of the industrial team.

Yet at the heart of the newer developments in personnel relations one finds not a system of "techniques" but a different conception of human motivation and a different type of atmosphere within which people of various groups relate themselves to each other. The change is from an attitude of "take it or leave it" to one of inducement and sympathetic understanding, from an authoritarian type of leadership to a democratic type, from a rigid formal structure to one which is patterned but not rigid.[1]

Your community is affected by the presence or absence of these newer personnel approaches in several ways. Its workers may be more satisfied, more willing to stay in the community. Management may be more community-minded, more eager to cooperate in improving community living conditions which in turn reflect themselves in worker productivity. Higher worker productivity through reduced absenteeism and conflict, and increased man-hour output will put your community's industries in a favorable competitive position in their attempt to gain a growing share of the national market.

60. What evidences are there of progressive personnel practices in your community's industries?
61. Which industries seem to have employees with high company morale? With high labor productivity? What factors contribute to their good record?
62. How familiar do industrial executives appear to be with recent developments in the personnel field?
63. What training programs in one aspect or another of "human relations" are available in any of your community's industries for top executives? Junior executives? Supervisors? Floor workers? Other workers?

Public employment offices. Public employment services function in every state in the union. These stand in various relationships to the state systems of unemployment insurance. In some states they are closely integrated, with both agencies occupying the same office. Your local state employment office will be able to give you important data as to employment conditions in your community.

At this point, you may want to turn to Chapter 10, which includes brief descriptive material and appropriate questions on unemployment insurance and workmen's compensation systems.

---

[1] The literature in the field of "human relations in industry" is growing rapidly. The following books exemplify the newer developments:

Chase, Stuart, *Roads to Agreement.* Harper and Bros., New York, 1951.

Dubin, Robert, *Human Relations in Administration.* Prentice-Hall, Inc., New York, 1951.

Gardner, Burleigh B., *Human Relations in Industry.* Richard D. Irwin, Inc., Chicago, 1945.

Hoslett, Schuyler Dean, editor, *Human Factors in Management.* rev. ed. Harper and Bros., New York, 1951.

Mayo, Elton, *Social Problems of an Industrial Civilization.* Harvard University Graduate School of Business Administration, Boston, 1945.

Roethlisberger, F. J., and W. J. Dickson, *Management and the Worker.* Harvard University Press, Cambridge, 1939.

Selekman, Benjamin M., *Labor Relations and Human Relations.* McGraw-Hill Book Co., New York, 1947.

See also the pamphlet by John Perry, *Human Relations in Small Industry,* Small Defense Plants Administration, Government Printing Office, Washington, 1953.

64. Is there a state employment service office in your community? If not, which regional office serves your community?

65. How many applicants for work were placed through this office during the past year?
   How did the number of placements compare with the number of applications? With the number of vacancies which employers listed with this office? With the number of referrals made by the office to fill the listed vacancies?

66. Are there any other employment services in your community, such as those operated by colleges, business schools, and so on?

67. How many commercial employment agencies are located in your community? What fees do they charge?
   What are the principal state laws governing their operation, and how adequate is the inspection?

68. What provisions are made in your community for employment counseling for high-school graduates and other young people seeking first employment? The handicapped? Aged? Other special groups?

69. Do local industries generally procure their employees through the Employment Service? Newspaper advertising? Hiring at gate? Recommendation by present employer? Other?

Your Community's Industrial Future

In the past few years there has been increased interest and activity on the part of local communities in studying the adequacy of their industrial base and the feasibility of its expansion. This development has resulted from the postwar expansion in business, the continuous economic stimulus of the defense effort, the growing movement toward industrial decentralization, and an increased realization of the importance of a sound industrial base if a community is to offer its citizens opportunity for an ample life.

The present section constitutes an outline of questions which will afford a factual basis for appraisal of the community's present industrial base and potentiality for future industrial development. The procedure for industrial development is beyond the scope of this book, but there is considerable printed material available[1] and the reader may also receive help from such state or federal agencies as the chamber of commerce, department of commerce, state university or industrial development commission, and so on.

[1] See, for example, *Start Now . . . A Community Development Program*, Kentucky Chamber of Commerce, Louisville, 1951; *How to Make a Local Area Trade Survey*, Chamber of Commerce of the United States, Washington, 1948; *Community Survival . . .*, University of Illinois College of Agriculture Circular 633, Urbana, 1949; and *Analyzing Opportunities for Expanding Business and Employment in Your Community*, U.S. Department of Commerce Field Service Office, San Francisco, 1950.

The trade area. The major areas for study in appraising your community's industrial future are the condition of the trade area, the condition and prospects of local industries, and the conditions which might attract or repel industries from outside the community. Within the local trade area, your community's merchants may or may not be offering the types of goods and services and shopping facilities which will attract customers to your town. If not, these people may be going to other communities or spending large amounts in mail order purchasing. The following questions will help to ascertain the extent to which the local trade area is being utilized as a source of mutual advantage for merchants and people in the area.

70. Is your trade center attractive?
71. Specifically, how does your trade center rate on the following features:
    Adequate parking space for shoppers
    Adequate public transit facilities both within the trade center and in the surrounding area
    Attractive appearance of storefronts
    Good variety of stores
    Stores well stocked with variety of merchandise at reasonable prices
    Courteous and prompt service by sales personnel
    Awareness of customer needs and willingness to stock desired items
    Sufficient advertising within potential trade area
72. Is there a retail merchants' association or other group that takes an active interest in improving the attracting power of the shopping center? What are its activities? Accomplishments?
73. Are there any types of professional service or facility which your community needs, such as banking facilities, legal service, and so on, whose presence might attract people to the community for other goods and services as well?
74. What particular lacks at the trade center cause people to go to surrounding communities for goods and services which might be made available locally?
75. Is it possible to find out the extent of the mail order purchasing carried on by people in your community?

Condition and prospects of present industries. In the effort by communities of all sizes to attract new industries, the industries presently located there are frequently given little attention. The occasional closing down or moving away of a local industry is a belated reminder of the importance of studying the fiscal soundness of the community's industries. It is usually easier to keep a local industry than to replace it with a new one if it dies out or moves elsewhere. Other communities would be glad to welcome some of your community's present industries.

76. What industries have been most successful in your community, and why?
77. What industries have failed in your community in the past 20 years, and why?

78. Are any of the following conditions working to the disadvantage of industries presently located in your community:
   Inadequate supply of the types of labor skill needed
   Recent history of bitter labor-management controversy
   Antiquated zoning laws
   Inadequate housing for employees
   Inadequate supply of water, gas, electricity, or other utilities
   Inadequate sewage disposal facilities
   Inadequate financial services
   Inadequate school and other community facilities
   Lack of cooperation by local government or citizens

79. Are any of the following opportunities for expansion of present industries or formation of new local industries appropriate to your community situation:
   Supplying parts to local industries, such as shipping crates, preassembled parts, or locally available materials
   Local processing of certain industrial items which are now being processed elsewhere
   Processing local resources and produce, through lumber mills, grist mills, frozen food and dehydrating plants, poultry processing plants
   Developing local resources, such as gravel pits, mineral deposits, timber resources
   Establishing of new retail, service, or wholesale establishments in the community
   Producing locally consumers' goods which are now being imported
   Developing possible scenic or other tourist attractions

80. Would research into possibilities for development or expansion of local industries be feasible in your community?

81. What are the possibilities for improving the income of your trade area's farmers and agricultural producers through the application of new crop techniques, advanced farming methods, or other resources?

82. What state agencies, public or private, can be of aid to the community in working toward the success of local industries?

Prospects for new industries. Communities often seek to attract new industries to provide for a gradual growth in population, to increase tax revenues, to provide job opportunities for unemployed residents, to balance local seasonal industries with new ones which will complement them, and to diversify the community's economic base. Too great a dependence on any one company or type of industry makes for an unstable economic base.

While new industry often has advantages, it usually brings with it associated problems. How can the community provide for increased school enrollment and greater burden on existing school facilities; greater traffic and parking problems; needed capital improvements or expansion in water, sewage, and other public services; additional housing facilities, trailer camps and attendant problems, and so on? Such problems call for close coordination in the planning for physical aspects of the community, industrial development activities, and health, education, and welfare programs.

The economic structure of your community may be weakened rather than strengthened by:

1. Speculative industries which would attract workers to the community only to leave them without employment if the venture fails.

2. Seasonal industries which do not fit into or complement the existing employment pattern and which might involve annual periods of widespread unemployment.

3. Industries which demand bonuses, tax concessions, free plant facilities, or other inducements beyond the community's ability to afford them.

4. Industries which would place an undue strain on existing obtainable sewage, water, and utilities.

5. Industries which are unwilling to become "members of the community," bearing their share of taxes, support of voluntary agencies, and interest in community betterment activities.

To complete the study of your community's economic life, you will want to consider the balance of various types of industrial pursuit in your community, the particular advantages and disadvantages which your community offers as an industrial location, and the community utilities, facilities, and other provisions which make it a desirable or undesirable place for industrial activity of various types.

83. What particular needs or disalignments are there in your community's industrial structure:
    Overdependence on a particular industry or company
    Recurrent seasonal layoffs
    Inadequate employment opportunities
    Other
84. What type of industry is needed to complete or balance your community's industrial foundation?
85. What special advantages does your community present for certain types of industry:
    Particular combination of certain types of labor skills
    Availability of some important natural resource or source of materials
    Proximity to industries which need certain products
    Favorable transportation facilities
    Low power costs
    Attractive living conditions
    Other

86. How does your community stand on each of the following basic industrial location factors:[1]

Location of production materials	Power
Labor	Water
Sites	Living conditions
Industrial fuel	Laws and regulations
Transportation facilities	Tax structure
Market	Climate
Distribution facilities	Other

87. What improvements in facilities are needed in your community:
    Better transportation facilities (port improvement, terminal facilities, etc.)
    Better utilities (cheaper or more ample gas, water, etc.)
    Better-equipped industrial sites
    Improvement of run-down appearance of shopping and business center
    Local government support of federal or state improvement programs (in highways, conservation, irrigation, etc.)
88. Which organizations in your community are most concerned with industrial development?
89. Which individuals or organizations are able to exercise important influence on community policy regarding your community's economic future?
    How is this influence exercised? To what ends?
90. Which, if any, of the following steps have been taken by your community to improve its industrial base:
    Organization of special industrial development commission
    Community advertising
    Assembling of a list of "prospects" for location in your community
    Contact with industrial "prospects"
    Formation of an industrial development corporation to develop or finance buildings or sites
    Engaging an industrial development consultant
    Enlisting the aid of power and railroad company industrial development departments

References for Further Study

The Economic Almanac, 1951–52. National Industrial Conference Board, New York. This handy fact book about the American economy includes several tables listing important economic data for various cities. Different

[1] For an elaboration of each factor, see *Basic Industrial Location Factors*, U.S. Department of Commerce Industrial Series No. 74, Government Printing Office, Washington. 1947. "The purpose of this publication is to aid local, state, and regional industrial development authorities and committees logically to assemble and present their area's industrial advantages."

tables cover different groups of cities. In general, if you live in a large city, you will find many important facts about its economy in this book.

Family Income, Expenditures, and Savings in 1950. U.S. Department of Commerce, Government Printing Office, Washington, 1953. For income, average family size, average number of earners per family, and other related information.

Monthly Labor Review, U.S. Department of Labor, Government Printing Office, Washington. This publication gives considerable information on wages, cost of living, and related material for various cities in different parts of the United States.

Morgan, Arthur E., *Industries for Small Communities.* Community Service, Inc., Yellow Springs, Ohio, 1953. The well-known champion of the values of small community living examines the industries of Yellow Springs, Ohio, as case studies in the relation of small industry to the community.

Roterus, Victor, and Max R. Bloom, *Community Development.* Business Information Service, Basic Information Sources, U.S. Department of Commerce, Washington, 1951. An excellent list of governmental and nongovernmental publications on "making community surveys, expansion of trade and industry, plant location, and planning and zoning."

"Survey of Buying Power," *Sales Management: The Magazine of Marketing.* This annual feature of the *Sales Management* magazine is replete with information on sales and marketing data, most of which are listed for "200 leading cities." If your community is one of the country's 200 largest cities, this will be a valuable annual source of information on effective buying income, retail sales, and other economic data about your community.

The W. E. Upjohn Institute for Community Research, *Full Employment in Your Community.* Public Administration Service, Chicago, 1947. This book is an extensive examination of the way a community can work toward and maintain full employment, including the organizational and action aspects of the effort.

Yaseen, Leonard C., *Plant Location.* Business Reports, Inc., Roslyn, New York, 1952. This authoritative book attempts to set up principles for scientific site selection, and methods for evaluating different communities. It also contains a helpful chapter entitled "Hints for Industrial Development Groups."

4. Government, Politics, and Law Enforcement

LOCAL GOVERNMENT IS RELATED to many aspects of community living. Yet local government in the United States is notoriously outdated and ill equipped to handle the complicated administrative problems of modern community life. It has been estimated that this country could eliminate half of its local governmental units and be better rather than worse off. Some students of local government recommend an even more drastic reduction in local units.[1]

Local Governmental Units

While outmoded boundaries and a multiplicity of governmental units have plagued the rural localities, political corruption and inefficiency have prevailed in the cities. As a result, Americans in their community living often pay overly high taxes for the services they receive, and they go without other services which would be possible and economical if their local governments were more suitable. "At the moment, there is probably less need for new research leading to the discovery of new techniques of political science than there is for the application of present knowledge and the broader extension of principles and techniques now generally understood by the well-trained."[2]

Health, welfare, education, recreation, housing, and other aspects of local government will be treated in the chapters devoted to those special topics.[3] The present chapter will confine itself to more central questions concerning the governmental and political structures and processes.[4]

[1] See Anderson, William, *The Units of Government in the United States*, Public Administration Service, Chicago, 1949.

[2] Jones, Howard P., "Citizen Groups, Tool of Democracy," *The Annals of the American Academy of Political and Social Science*, vol. 199, September, 1938, p. 177.

[3] There is an excellent outline of the functions of municipal government adapted from Bureau of the Census material in Hallenbeck, Wilbur C., *American Urban Communities*, Harper and Bros., New York, 1951, pp. 277 ff.

[4] Information is available in textbooks on local governments, in publications such as the *National Municipal Review* and *Public Management*, and in the *Municipal Year Book* (see page 336), as well as in your city charter, the state law governing your type of munici-

Some of the questions and interpretive material will not be pertinent to all studies, for they deal specifically with rural or urban governmental units. If one is studying a city or village or some other specific governmental unit, his task will be easier than if he is studying a metropolitan area or a village-farm community, where several different units of local government may be involved. Even so, a study of 397 cities uncovered and classified a total of 1,410 different governmental units such as counties, towns or townships, school districts, and various special purpose districts of many different types which overlay or provided services within the city area.[1] Similarly, in rural areas a person may find his village within a township, a county, a separate school district, and perhaps other special districts.

1. What units of government overlie your community:

Village	Special district	Park and recreation
Town or township	Flood control	Housing
County	Highway and bridge	Port and navigation
Borough	Sanitation	Fire
City	Health and hospital	Water
School district	Library	Other

2. Prepare a map of your community showing the different governmental units smaller than a county which overlie it. (Use different colored pencil for each set of boundaries so that they can be readily distinguished.)
3. Is the governmental unit you will principally study a village, borough, city, town, or township?[2]
4. Under what state law or special charter is the nature of your local government defined?
   Does it grant your local government adequate powers of home rule?
5. What powers are specifically designated to your local government?
6. What powers are specifically withheld?
7. What is the formal structure of your local government:

City structure	Village structure
Mayor-council type	Town or township structure
Council-manager type	
Commission type	
Other	

---

pality, local ordinances, annual reports, and other basic documents. Organizations such as the National Municipal League, governmental research bureaus, political science departments of universities, and the League of Women Voters can be of great help in their respective fields.

[1] *Governmental Units Overlying City Areas.* Bureau of the Census, Government Printing Office, Washington, 1947, pp. 4 ff. See also the Census Bureau publication *Governments in the United States in 1952.*

[2] Although your "community" may more closely correspond to a school district, or some other area, nevertheless your chief local unit (or units) of governmental services will most likely be one of those mentioned above.

Structure, Administration, and Functions

Turning to organizational structure, it is a widely recognized principle of municipal government that simplicity and clear definition of responsibility should prevail. All department heads should be directly responsible to the mayor or city manager. Where several administrative officials are elected independently, "buck-passing" is facilitated, since no one has sufficient authority to be held responsible for the administration of the municipal affairs. The same applies with council confirmation of administrative appointments. It tends to split responsibility and facilitate buck-passing.

You will perhaps be able to obtain a chart showing the organization of your local government. City governments vary in the degree to which they are organized for responsible administration and popular control. There are four general forms: the old weak-mayor–strong-council type, the commission plan (both of which are held in little esteem by political scientists and municipal government experts), the strong-mayor–council type, and the council-manager type.

The chart on page 37 shows the organization of the Greenwich, Connecticut, town government. Town government differs in structure from city government, as does one city government from another, but this chart will serve as an example of the manner of charting the structure of local government, and the reader can perhaps then proceed to chart that of his own local governmental unit, in case no such chart is already available.

A vehicle of great importance in the improvement of municipal government is the *charter commission*. "A charter commission, a distinctly American contribution to the art and practice of local government, is a body authorized by law, usually elected by the voters, that is set up for the sole function of drafting and submitting to the voters a new charter or revision of an existing charter."[1] One of the goals of the charter commission would be to make the local government more responsive to the people it serves. The National Municipal League lists several principles which should be incorporated into a city charter in order to improve popular control:

1. Majority rule
2. Short ballot
3. Ballots without party designations
4. Primaries without party designations
5. Separate municipal elections
6. Council elections at large
7. Proportional representation

[1] *A Guide for Charter Commissions.* rev. ed. National Municipal League, New York, 1952, p. 5. This publication has been an important source for the present chapter.

    8. Initiative, referendum and recall
    9. Access to public acts and records[1]

As modern community living grows more complex, people make more demands upon their government to provide services and agencies for dealing with the problems of everyday living. In subsequent chapters we shall see the manifold ways in which governmental activity has become an established part of community life. Local government, for example, has established or expanded functions in connection with planning and zoning, housing, safety, education, recreation, and so on through the list of chapter headings for this book. As these new functions and services become necessary or desirable, an important problem arises as to which agency of society—government, church, family, school, private associations, or business enterprise—should assume active responsibility for them.

Two facts are particularly worth noting in studying your community from this standpoint: One is the growing pattern of grants-in-aid through which smaller governmental units are extended funds by the state or federal government in order better to perform some desirable function. The other is the considerable variation among local governments in the functions they actually do perform. One city may sponsor a municipal mental health clinic, or youth recreation program, or hospital construction program, or low-rent housing project, while another may not. The same thing applies to units of government in rural areas, where one county may have a probation department, or a health department, and one village or township may sponsor a youth recreation program, or sell gas or electricity to its residents, and another may not.

With the multiplication of local government functions and the growing pattern of grants-in-aid, the county in most places outside New England is becoming increasingly important as the local unit for the performing of rural governmental services, whether they have to do with agriculture, conservation, health, mental health, or whatever. In urban communities, the city government is usually the important administrative unit for such programs.

    8. Secure or construct an organization chart of your local government. What are the major departments?
    9. Is there an executive head with clear responsibility, or is power distributed among independently elected officials?
    10. Are all department heads appointed by and responsible to the chief executive (mayor, city manager, and so on) of your local government?

[1] *Ibid.*, pp. 35–39. See also *A Model Direct Primary Election System*, and *Proportional Representation–Effective Voting*, 1951, both published by the League.

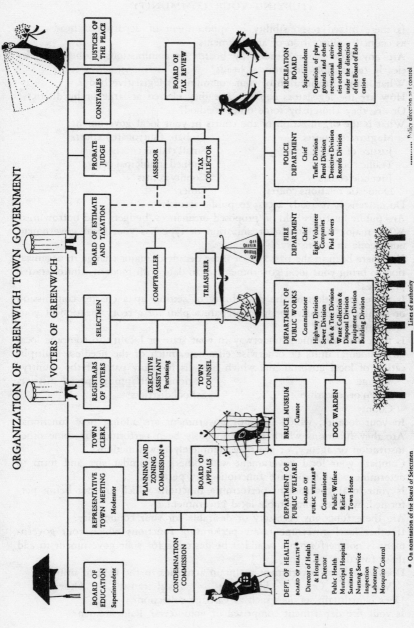

ORGANIZATION OF GREENWICH TOWN GOVERNMENT

VOTERS OF GREENWICH

BOARD OF EDUCATION
Superintendent

REPRESENTATIVE TOWN MEETING
Moderator

TOWN CLERK

REGISTRARS OF VOTERS

SELECTMEN

BOARD OF ESTIMATE AND TAXATION

PROBATE JUDGE

CONSTABLES

JUSTICES OF THE PEACE

PLANNING AND ZONING COMMISSION *

EXECUTIVE ASSISTANT
Purchasing

COMPTROLLER

ASSESSOR

BOARD OF APPEALS

TOWN COUNSEL

TREASURER

TAX COLLECTOR

BOARD OF TAX REVIEW

CONDEMNATION COMMISSION

DEPT. OF HEALTH
BOARD OF HEALTH *
Director of Health & Hospital
Director
Public Health
Municipal Hospital
Sanitation
Nursing Service
Inspection
Laboratory
Mosquito Control

DEPARTMENT OF PUBLIC WELFARE
BOARD OF PUBLIC WELFARE*
Commissioner
Public Welfare
Relief
Town Home

BRUCE MUSEUM
Curator

DOG WARDEN

DEPARTMENT OF PUBLIC WORKS
Commissioner
Highway Division
Sewer Division
Park & Tree Division
Waste Collection & Disposal Division
Equipment Division
Building Division

FIRE DEPARTMENT
Chief
Eight Volunteer Companies
Paid drivers

POLICE DEPARTMENT
Chief
Traffic Division
Patrol Division
Detective Division
Records Division

RECREATION BOARD
Superintendent
Operation of playgrounds and other recreational activities other than those under the direction of the Board of Education

* On nomination of the Board of Selectmen

* Policy direction and control
—— Lines of authority

Charts can be an aid in depicting complex administrative structures. A little imagination on the part of the artist often adds interest. SOURCE: *A Sound Town:* Summary of the Annual Report, Town of Greenwich, Connecticut, 1953.

11. Is there mixed responsibility in appointment of department heads, such as council confirmation of appointments?

12. Are any departments headed by boards or commissions, rather than by clearly responsible department heads?

13. What is the organization of your community's legislative body?
    How are the legislators chosen? Are they elected at large or by districts? Or are they chosen by some other method?

14. What is the organization of the courts in your local government:

Magistrates courts	Probate (surrogate) courts
Justice of the peace	Small claims courts
Traffic courts	Unified municipal courts
Juvenile courts	County courts
Domestic relations courts	Other

15. Do citizens have ready access to public records?

16. Are public hearings held on proposed ordinances, budgets, and borrowings?

17. What major revisions in organization or type has your local government undergone in its history?

18. Has there been in the past two or three decades a major change in organization to bring your local government up to date with modern administrative practices?

19. Is there indication of the desirability of setting up a charter commission or similar deliberative body to prepare a plan for a reorganization of your local government?

20. Is there any movement underway in your state or locality to combine local governmental units or otherwise eliminate much of the needless multiplication of local governments which prevails in many parts of the country:

Village	Various overlapping special districts
Town or township	School districts
County	

21. In your locality, which units of government are adding new functions? Are they functions which have previously been performed by some other institution or agency, or are they completely new functions?

22. Compare your local government with others of similar size and form to determine what respective functions they perform.
    Is your local government performing functions which are not being performed by other comparable local governments?
    Are these functions necessary or desirable for your community?

23. If other local governments are performing functions which your government is not performing, would it be desirable for your government to add these functions?

24. Does your local government maintain activities in the field of utilities:
    Water   Gas   Electricity   Local transit   Other

25. Does it maintain services such as garbage collection?

26. Is your fire department comprised of volunteers? Paid firemen?

27. Has any appraisal recently been made of the adequacy of your community's fire protection system and the efficiency of its personnel?
28. What fire protection rating has your community, and how does this affect fire insurance rates?
29. What is the extent of training programs for firemen?

Personnel

You will be concerned with whether your local government is recruiting the best personnel possible for the tasks it wants performed, and whether the working conditions are good, including such matters as salaries, sick leave, vacations, retirement and pension provisions, and promotion.

The merit system has been set up in many units of American local government to assure selection and promotion of civil servants on the basis of merit rather than politics or other considerations. A general principle is that top policymaking officials should be elected or appointed, while those who are employed to administer policy should be selected through the merit system. This may be accomplished sporadically in individual departments or comprehensively as a basic policy of the various branches of government under a general civil service law.

Local governments often hamstring their own efforts to secure the best possible people for certain positions by requiring that all applicants be legal residents of the locality for a stipulated length of time prior to the examination. Particularly in smaller units, this often needlessly limits the number of available applicants and makes it necessary to accept people of inferior ability simply because no one in the locality is qualified and would accept the position. As a result, local and state governments are increasingly eliminating arbitrary residence requirements for certain types of position where special ability is required.

It is coming to be realized that a government gets about what it pays for in its civil servants, and that salaries and working conditions should be commensurate with those available in other types of employment if people of character and competence are to be attracted to civil service positions.

30. Does your government have a merit system for the selection and promotion of nonpolicymaking employees?
   How is this system organized and administered?
31. Which positions in your local government do not come under civil service?
32. Which civil service positions entail residence requirements?
33. What provisions are there for retirement income (pensions, and so on) for government workers? Are they adequate? Equitable?
34. What provisions are there for sick leave, vacation, salary increments, and other working conditions of municipal employees?

35. In what departments of your local government are any of the following in operation:
    In-service training program
    Provisions for leave-of-absence for further training
    Lending library of departmental literature available to employees
36. Are salaries of elected and appointed municipal officials sufficient to attract people of ability and not to encourage income supplementing, such as graft, cut-backs, protection money, part-time jobs, and so on?
37. Are salaries of municipal employees comparable to those paid elsewhere for a similar level of ability and responsibility?

Expenditures and Taxes

The extent to which a local government can perform the functions which its citizens desire is limited by the amount of money it can raise through taxes and other means and the cost of the respective functions. The cost of governmental services is needlessly increased by inefficiency, corruption, and favoritism. It is also needlessly increased where government functions are expanded and multiplied beyond the desire of the citizens. It is a common characteristic of department and bureau heads to believe strongly in the value of their own activities and to feel that they should be greatly expanded. Careful appraisal by citizens' groups with expert counsel often substantiates the desirability of these aspirations, but often it does not.

Citizens' groups have therefore usually shown an understandable aspiration for economy in government. But economy alone should not be the decisive factor. Economies can be achieved, for instance, by across-the-board cuts of 10 per cent in budgets for all departments, but this policy would work havoc with many vital municipal services. The chief questions would seem to be what kind of community the citizens would like to make for themselves, what the appropriate role of their local government should be in such a community, and to what extent they are willing to back up their wishes with the necessary funds which come ultimately through taxes. From the tax standpoint the question is whether the various people in the community are paying their equitable share of the government's costs through the existing tax structure,[1] and whether the tax structure is satisfactory with respect to ease and economy of collection.

It can be seen that such questions call for specialized counsel; hence, the need for expert consultation, municipal research bureaus, and so on. Many sincere community-minded people are duped into a "crusade" for economy

[1] The main reliance on real estate taxes has been supplemented in recent years by the use of a sales tax which, like all taxes, has its own difficulties. Some cities like Philadelphia place an occupational tax on all wages or salaries earned in the city.

in local government under auspices which care less for the efficiency of local government services than for the lowest possible tax rate.[1]

Another question which alert citizens' groups will want to consider is whether the local community is taking advantage of existing grants-in-aid programs of state and federal governments. "By a grant-in-aid is here meant a payment made by a central to a local authority to defray part of the cost of a service administered by the local authority, usually subject to some conditions set by the central government, which may inspect and partially control the service and, if conditions are not satisfactory, withhold future payments of the grant."[2]

Federal grants to states for public assistance, general public health, hospital construction, public airport construction, school lunch programs, and housing projects are typically channeled through state auspices more or less directly to the localities. In addition, many other types of federal grants-in-aid are available to states, and money from these is in some instances administered at least in part under local auspices.

In addition to administering federal grant-in-aid funds, different states make various grants or shares of state taxes available to the localities under stipulated conditions. The following state-collected taxes may be shared with localities in your state: property taxes, income taxes, inheritance and estate taxes, poll taxes, severance taxes, sales taxes (motor fuel, alcoholic beverage, general), business license taxes, motor vehicle license taxes, and others. State aid in the form of shared taxes, grants-in-aid, and redistribution of federal grants may be allotted to localities for extremely diverse purposes. In addition to the chief grants for education, public assistance, and highways, state aid goes for aid to fire departments, health and sanitation, conservation, youth activities, county extension work, flood relief, civilian defense, flood control, veterans housing, unspecified purposes, and so on.[3] In some instances, more than half of the state's disbursements are to localities for one purpose or another and the average amount for all 48 states is one-third of total state expenditures.[4]

[1] If you are studying a city which had a population of more than 30,000 in 1940, the tabulation of comparative tax rates, which is an annual feature of the *National Municipal Review*, will be helpful. For all such cities, it lists important tax data, including the assessed value, the "per cent personalty," the actual tax rate as levied per thousand dollar assessed valuation broken down by city, school, county, state, and total, the estimated ratio of assessed value to true value in per cent, and the adjusted tax rate on one hundred per cent basis of assessment.

[2] Bittermann, Henry J., *State and Federal Grants-in-Aid*, p. 5, quoted in *Federal Grants-in-Aid*, Council of State Governments, 1949, p. 29.

[3] *State Aid to Local Governments*. Bureau of the Census, State and Local Government Special Studies. No. 28. Government Printing Office, Washington, 1948.

[4] See Stout, Randall S., *Recent Trends in State Grants-in-Aid and Shared-Taxes*, Pennsylvania State College, Bureau of Business Research Bulletin No. 36, 1948.

While such grants-in-aid warrant serious consideration by local citizens because they make possible considerable financial help in the development of local functions and services, citizens' groups should guard against the inclination to participate in them merely "to get state money."

38. In the past fiscal year how much revenue did your local government receive from each major source of income:

Property taxes	Fines	Grants-in-aid
Sales taxes	Fees and licenses	Shared taxes
Sale of property	Assessments	

39. Who assesses property for tax purposes? How are assessors chosen? What basis or method of appraisal do they use? Are they qualified to make equitable assessments?
Are the assessment officials thoroughly honest and immune from political influence or personal favoritism?

40. Are assessments for property tax purposes made on the basis of full value, or on a percentage of the full value? Are the assessments equitable?

41. What is the total value of tax-exempt property in your community?
Do individual tax exemptions appear to be justified? Are special tax exemptions offered to industry?[1]

42. For what purposes does your government receive income from the state:

Public assistance	Other purposes specified by the state
Highways	Unspecified
Education	

43. For what purposes does your local government receive money from the federal government, either directly or channeled through your state government?

44. How do your government's expenditures compare, department by department, with those of other similar localities?[2]

45. What is the financial indebtedness of your government?

46. Is there a legal debt limit imposed by the state? If so, how does your locality's debt stand in relation to this debt limit?

47. What interest is being paid on outstanding bond issues? How does this compare with interest rates paid by other comparable localities?[3]

Civil Defense

Your study of local government may extend to civil defense activities. If so, you will want to assure yourself that your community has an adequate

---

[1] For a more extensive outline of questions for a tax study, see *Local Tax Study*, League of Women Voters of the U.S., Washington, D.C., mimeographed.

[2] For each department or service, take the total expenditure for the past year and divide it by the number of people in that governmental jurisdiction. This will give the per capita cost, which will facilitate comparison with other communities.

[3] Questions on fiscal planning will be found in Chapter 5.

civil defense structure within the authority of the state and federal civil
defense legislation, that clear lines of responsibility are established, that
the various recommendations of state and national officials are given careful consideration, that adequate power to act in an emergency is given the
appropriate officials, and that desirable agreements for mutual aid in time
of catastrophe have been arranged with other governmental units.[1]

48. Has your locality set up an adequate civil defense program in accordance
with state and federal legislation?
49. Have appropriate local ordinances or resolutions been passed?
50. Does your mayor or chief executive have stand-by power in case of air
attack or other emergency?
51. Has your locality entered into reciprocal aid agreements with neighboring
localities on such factors as emergency medical aid, fire and police protection, and related needs?
52. How have the various departments of your local government been integrated
into the local civil defense structure?
53. To whom is the local director of civil defense responsible?

Political Organization

Behind the formal government in most communities is the "hidden government," the political party organizations which have no official governmental status but nevertheless exercise a crucial influence on the policies
and procedures of local government.[2] Political party workers are recruited
from various sources: Local jobholders and others who expect to get a job
through the support of the machine; interests which can rely on special
favor if they back the winning candidates; people whose illegal activities
demand "protection" from a sympathetic administration if they are to stay
in business; ambitious would-be politicians who are trying to work up the
ladder of the political party or of governmental office; people who simply
like to be "in on things"; conscientious community-minded citizens who
attempt to divert the party from selfish purposes toward communitywide
goals.

There are all too few of the last-mentioned group. One reason is the
apathy of many citizens who might be able to work for good government
within the political parties. Another reason is that all too often community-

---

[1] Read *Know Your Civil Defense*, League of Women Voters of the U.S., Washington,
1951, mimeographed. *A Checklist of Official Government Publications on Civil Defense*
is available free of charge from the Government Printing Office, Washington.
[2] Much of the material in this section is adapted from Fisher, Marguerite J., and Edith
E. Starratt, *Parties and Politics in the Local Community*, rev. ed., National Council for
the Social Studies, Washington, 1951. This short book is highly recommended.

minded citizens, though active, are oblivious to the actual political processes and hence expect the impossible. Still another reason is that honest, community-minded workers are often not wanted within the party organizations. They "get in the way," "upset the apple-cart," "ask embarrassing questions," and otherwise become thorns in the side of busy politicians who are anxiously going about their business of using the machinery of local government for their own and for their party's aggrandizement.

While superficially the rural areas often provide no such complicated picture of machine control as the big cities, nevertheless citizen apathy often leads to one-party government, to control by the "court house crowd," and the awarding of elective or appointive positions to political "hangers-on," "door-bell ringers," and others who work for the party.

There is tremendous pressure toward the misuse of political power in most governmental units of any size. Political party leaders, many of whom never run for public office, are in a strong position for the following reasons:

1. They control the distribution of government jobs, elective or appointive.
2. They often serve a useful function of helping the individual citizen through the web of government toward his goal (by a phone call to the appropriate official, etc.).
3. They often distribute largesse to the poor in a direct, over-the-barrel fashion without going through the "red-tape" of the welfare department.
4. They often influence the awarding of governmental contracts and concessions to business interests which have supported them.
5. Through their control over the police, the district attorney's office, and/ or the courts, they often ensure protection against arrest or prosecution to various illegal interests.

These circumstances do not make municipal political reform impossible, but they make it difficult. They also make it particularly necessary to "follow through" on reform movements, rather than relaxing when a particular objective (such as city manager plan, short ballot, or whatever) has been attained.

The merit system for the selection of nonpolicymaking governmental employees helps to remove government jobs from the patronage of the bosses, and to assure that merit, rather than political subservience, is the basis for selection and promotion. The short ballot, according to which only a relatively few officials are elected by the voters, the others being appointed, has come to be widely accepted in "good government" circles. It enables the voter to become informed of the merits of the candidates, and makes it more difficult for self-serving political machines to load the ballot with political favorites relatively unknown to the voters.

Primaries and Elections

Particularly in communities dominated by one major party, the primaries, by selecting the official party candidates, actually determine who will be elected. If the primary selections are left to the professional politicians, the voters on election day will be confronted with the choice between the machine candidate and the candidate who can best serve the interests of the rival machine. The fight for acceptable municipal officials is held in the primaries; or if the primary system is not used, in the party conventions; or in the circulation of petitions of nomination.

Closed primaries make it necessary for the voter to declare his party affiliation, and then he receives the primary blank for that party. For various reasons, individual voters, particularly if they are government workers, may not care to reveal their party affiliation, or may be pressured by this system into supporting the party in power even against their own better judgment. On the other hand, open primaries, which do not require statement and verification of political affiliation, enable voters from one party to "raid" another party's primary.

Some local governments use the nonpartisan primary, a system in which the candidates are usually nominated by petition and are listed on the ballot without official political party designation. This tends to minimize the influence of national political affiliation on purely local election issues.

A frequent impediment to the free use of the franchise is the system of registration of voters. Some adequate system of registration is necessary in order to assure that only qualified voters are allowed to vote and that there is no fraud in the voting. Permanent registration is particularly advantageous, for it is much more convenient for the voter, is economical and easy to administer efficiently, and makes it difficult to misrepresent or misuse the ballot. Signature identification of voters, used in 21 states, has been found to be highly effective in preventing fraudulent balloting.

The type of ballot used at elections may favor or hinder good voting practices. In the party-column (Indiana) type of ballot, the voter can vote the straight party ticket by marking only one cross at the head of the column or by pulling one lever on the machine. Such "straight ticket" voting assures the political machine a free hand in putting up people whose only qualification may be loyalty to the machine or a political debt which must be paid. In the office-group (Massachusetts) type, the names of the candidates are arranged according to the office for which they are running, and a separate mark must be made or lever pulled for each office involved. Such a mechanical setup favors discrimination in the choice of candidate for each office, rather than an indiscriminate voting of the straight party ticket.

Voluntary Citizens' Organizations

Citizens' good government organizations can be most effective if their effort is sustained, if the organization of local government is such as to encourage good practices and if it is sensitive to popular opinion.[1] But no governmental form, in and of itself, will assure efficient administration. "Thus, unfortunate experiences in a number of cities have taught the lesson that there are two aspects to the problem of local good government: the proper tools, in the form of an efficient governmental structure, and second, the sustained vigilance and participation of the citizens to keep the tools functioning properly."[2]

Often, however, citizen support of good government associations depends largely on sensational or spectacular issues and is highly sporadic. If the local machine can outwait these sporadic protests by independent citizens, it can usually move right back into the old political groove in a few years.

Often taxpayers' leagues and such organizations are simply aggregations of real estate interests and others whose prime goal is to keep taxes down regardless of the effects on governmental function. On the other hand, organizations such as the Citizens Union of New York City, citizens' organizations in Cincinnati and Seattle, and the local Leagues of Women Voters[3] in different communities of the country, although interested in economy, usually maintain some degree of balance between economy, efficiency, and improvement of governmental functions.

Fisher and Starratt give a helpful outline for influencing legislation by volunteer citizen groups:

> The various pressure techniques . . . fall roughly into four classes: first, study and investigation by the group in order to arrive at a program or series of recommendations; second, educating the membership of the group; third, educating the public concerning the issue; and fourth, pressure on governmental officials, both by members of the organization and by the public, through such tactics as group visits, letters, etc. A fifth class of techniques . . . would include activities engaged in by political parties as well as by a few citizen groups, namely, endorsement or nomination of candidates and active campaigning for these candidates.[4]

For a brief introduction to the possibilities of volunteer citizen action in

[1] See Childs, Richard S., *Civic Victories:* The Story of an Unfinished Revolution, Harper and Bros., New York, 1952.
[2] Fisher, Marguerite J., and Edith E. Starratt, *Op. cit.*, p. 100.
[3] See the following pamphlet study-guides published by the League of Women Voters: *Know Your Town Government*, 1949; *Know Your County*, 1946; and *Know Your State*, 1947.
[4] *Op. cit.*, p. 105. See also the pamphlet by Bond, Elsie M., *Methods of Securing Social Welfare Legislation*, New York State Charities Aid Association, 1941.

local government, read *Is Politics Your Job?*[1] and *Politics Is What You Make It.*[2]

54. What is the smallest unit of political party organization in your community:
 Precinct or election district   Town or township   Other unit

55. Does each party have a representative or committeeman (election district leader, precinct captain, district committeeman, and so on) in each election district? A committeewoman?

56. Does each party have a county (in New England, usually a town) committee? How is its membership determined?
 Is it made up of election district committeemen and women? Ward leaders? Both men and women?
 Are the members of the county committee chosen by voters at primary election? Local party conventions?

57. Is there a city committee for each party? A ward committee?

58. Is there a local political "boss"? Where does he get his power? How does he control votes?
 Have there been irregularities in the local government attributable to this "boss" and his machine?

59. What evidences are there of the following:
 Government jobs given out by boss as political rewards
 Government contracts given out to businessmen friendly to boss
 Favors to constituents (fixing parking tickets, and so on)
 Police protection to unlawful activities (gambling establishments, and so on)
 Gifts of food or other favors to the needy

60. What functions, in other words, does the boss perform which would remain unfilled if the boss were unseated?

61. In what local elections (below the state level) are citizens in your community entitled to vote:
 Village   Special district   City
 Town or township County   Other
 School district

62. When do these elections occur? Do they occur at the same time as state and national elections, thus encouraging a carry-over of state and national party politics to purely local issues?

63. How many people in your community voted in the last few elections of each type listed above? What percentage of registered voters? What percentage of qualified voters were these estimated to be?
 How did the number of voters compare with the number who voted at the last presidential election?

64. On primary ballots, is there only one candidate (the machine candidate) for each office?

[1] League of Women Voters of the U.S., Washington, 1946.
[2] Public Affairs Pamphlet No. 181, New York, 1952.

65. When are the primaries held in your community for the following:
    Federal offices   County offices
    State offices   Local municipal offices
66. For what offices is there nomination by petition?
67. Does your municipality have open primaries (voter need not reveal his political affiliation)? Closed primaries? Nonpartisan primaries?
68. Is there assessment of local office holders in your community?[1]
69. Does your state have a law requiring statements of contributions and expenditures for political campaigns to be made before the election? After the election?
70. What system is followed by your community in registering qualified voters:
    Personal periodic registration
    Nonpersonal periodic registration
    Permanent registration
71. Which type of ballot is used in your state? Is it the party-column type (Indiana)? Office-group type (Massachusetts)?
72. Does your state authorize voting machines? If so, does your local community use them? If not, why?
73. Are there any instances of violations of election laws in casting ballots:
    Booth not completely private
    Booth observed through mirrors, hole in ceiling, and so forth
    Other people entering booth than election inspectors assisting disabled voters
    Deliberate slowing down of balloting process to discourage voters waiting in line
    Distribution of literature or campaigning within prohibited area
    Tampering with voting machines by person other than legally authorized election inspector
74. Has your state an absentee voting law? What are its provisions for various types of election?
    How easy or difficult is it for a person to vote despite absence? How widely known are the provisions of this law?
75. Is there a taxpayers' league in your local community?
    Does this organization reflect a broad interest in progressive and economical government; or is it merely a device by certain groups to keep taxes down at all costs?
76. Does your community have a good government organization with a wide base of citizen support?
    Does it maintain continuous interest in the processes of government, or does it languish between periods of sporadic activity?
77. Is there a municipal research bureau or some other unit in your community

[1] Prohibited by federal and many state laws, but nevertheless goes on through a solicitation for "voluntary funds," without putting the actual amount requested in the letter of solicitation.

which makes studies of local government and presents the facts in understandable form to the voters?

78. Does your local government publish an annual report? If so, is it readable?
Does it include page after page of statistical reports which are practically
meaningless to the average citizen?
Are charts and diagrams used to help to tell its story?

79. How wide a distribution does this annual report have?
How many groups devote one or more meetings to a study of the annual
report?
How promptly is the annual report published after the close of the fiscal
year?

80. Does your local government make any attempt to inform the citizens as
to its various functions through the following media:

Schools	Mailings to the citizens
Pamphlets	Radio and television programs
Releases to the newspapers	Exhibits in schools, libraries, museums

81. Is there a citizens' organization in your community which concerns itself
with promoting good local government? To which of the following types
does it belong:

Municipal research bureau	Citizens' league
Citizens' council	Citizen charter committee
Taxpayers' association	Other

Crime and Law Enforcement

Law enforcement is a government responsibility, but the problem of crime
reaches beyond government to various aspects of American society, such as
the home and the school. Nevertheless, government is concerned with crime
directly in its law enforcement responsibility and secondarily in the tie-up
which often exists between organized crime, government officials, and
political parties. In this three-way relationship, the police, the district
attorney's office, and the inferior courts are highly vulnerable to corruption.
For decades, successive studies have shown this three-way tie-up to be present
in cities of different sizes in different parts of the United States. A recent
exposé is recorded in a report of the so-called Kefauver Crime Committee.[1]

Criminal activity has to a great extent become organized into large
syndicates involving numerous people each with his own specialized function to perform, much the same as in legitimate business. The leaders of
such activities hover on the fringes of respectability, and for reasons of
protection seek wherever possible to have the police and the courts on their

[1] See *Third Interim Report of the Special Committee to Investigate Organized Crime in
Interstate Commerce*, 82d Congress, 1st Session, Report No. 307, Government Printing
Office, Washington, 1951.

side. Needless to say many individuals and administrations have kept themselves scrupulously free of such entanglements.

While much crime is of this highly organized type, other types are largely outside this organized system, and have to do with sporadic acts committed by otherwise law-abiding citizens. Such individuals commit many types of crime against the person, including assault and murder, as well as crimes against property, like embezzlement.

Number and types of offenses. In connection with your study, it would be well to read some standard text on crime and criminals, such as *New Horizons in Criminology* by Harry Elmer Barnes and Negley K. Teeters,[1] *The Crime Problem* by Walter C. Reckless,[2] *Crime in Modern Society* by Mabel A. Elliott.[3] From the police department you can get records of offenses reported and arrests made. The courts can provide you with records of criminal cases, convictions, sentences, acquittals, and so forth.

For purposes of comparison, crimes in the United States are classified according to the uniform crime reporting system of the federal Bureau of Investigation.[4] For our purposes, the outline given below will be suitable. From it, you can construct a table, using the following headings for the vertical columns:

1. Petty Offenses
    Simple assault, petit larceny, trespass, vagrancy, breach of the peace and disorderly conduct (including prostitution), drunkenness, cruelty to animals, maintaining a nuisance, and violating liquor, traffic, gambling laws, or other local ordinances.
2. Serious Offenses
    (a) Offenses against the person (such as murder in its several degrees, conspiracy to kill or maim, robbery with violence, burglary, kidnaping, traffic in drugs and women, sex offenses other than prostitution).
    (b) Offenses against property (such as grand larceny, receiving stolen goods, fraud, forgery, embezzlement, extortion, arson, and malicious mischief).
    (c) Offenses against the family (such as nonsupport, abandonment, cruelty, neglect, impairing the morals of minors).
    (d) Offenses against government (such as perjury, bribery, malfeasance in office, counterfeiting, and violating election, internal revenue, and postal laws).

[1] 2d ed. Prentice-Hall, Inc., New York, 1951.
[2] Appleton-Century-Crofts, Inc., New York, 1950.
[3] Harper and Bros., New York, 1952.
[4] See the current issues of *Uniform Crime Reports*, Government Printing Office, Washington.

For the horizontal columns, the following are suggested:

Complaints entered   Arrests   Convictions[1]

82. Is your community one of the several thousand cities or towns which file regular reports with the Federal Bureau of Investigation?

83. Supply the information requested in the table for last year and for five years ago.

   What are the most frequent types of offense? What differences are apparent in the two sets of figures?

   How does the number of arrests compare with the number of complaints entered? Convictions?

84. If possible, plot addresses of either arrested or convicted persons.

   How does this map compare with other maps you may have made plotting health or housing conditions, juvenile delinquency, population density, and other relevant topics?

85. How do the numbers and types of offenses compare with those of other communities of similar size in your region?

86. Have any investigations of the relation of criminals to law enforcement officials and political parties been made in your community or region in recent years?

   What were the major findings? What steps have been taken to correct any abuses discovered?

Law enforcement officials. Local constables, police departments, county sheriffs, and in some cases state police and federal agents are all involved in detecting and apprehending suspected criminals. It is important that they be efficient, that they themselves obey the law as it concerns the civil rights and protection of suspected criminals, and that they be immune from corruption.

Questions on the police in their relation to juvenile delinquents can be found in Chapter 11, and in their relation to minority groups in Chapter 15. Procedures as to employment, promotion, working conditions, and so on, of municipal employees, considered earlier in this chapter, are relevant here in connection with the police.

87. What requirements and training are necessary for policemen?

88. Are policemen under a civil service system?

89. What agents of the law other than municipal police serve your local community; and what is their geographical area of jurisdiction:

   Constables   Sheriffs   State police   Others

90. Is there any in-service training program for police?

91. Have there been any evidences of "third degree" methods or other violations of civil rights of alleged offenders by the police?

[1] This table is taken from Colcord, Joanna C., *Your Community*, rev. ed., Russell Sage Foundation, New York, 1947, p. 40.

Conditions of detention. When a suspected criminal is arrested, he is generally given a preliminary hearing in an inferior court (justice of the peace, magistrate, and the like). Such courts have jurisdiction over cases involving minor offenses and punishments, but in the more serious offenses they can only conduct a preliminary hearing and order the person held. While awaiting trial, the offender is either held in the local jail or released on bail. Local jail conditions throughout the country are often intolerable. Less than a quarter of the 3,000 or so jails recently inspected by the federal Bureau of Prisons were approved. A visit to the local jail would constitute an excellent part of your study.

The decision whether or not to prosecute is often made by the district attorney, although the grand jury customarily decides whether or not the suspect is to be indicted, that is, charged with a crime, and with what specific crime he shall be charged. Where the decision is left with the district attorney, ordinarily an elective official, the broad latitude which this entails can be used to promote or obstruct justice.

92. How are inferior court judges (magistrates, police justices, and so on) selected?
93. Has your local municipal or county jail been inspected by the Bureau of Prisons? If so, was it approved? If not, why?
   In the local jail, are persons being held for trial kept separate from those serving sentences? Are males separated from females?
94. Are there adequate sanitary facilities? Is the food adequate?
   What constructive activities, if any, are available to inmates?
   If some responsibilities for self-policing are given to inmates, is the practice free of the cruelties sometimes perpetrated by these "kangaroo courts"?
95. Have any children been detained in the local jail during recent years? (See Chapter 11.)
96. How long do indicted offenders who are being held in jail pending trial have to wait before their trial begins?
   Are there any instances where people have been kept in jail an inordinately long time awaiting trial?
97. Does the district attorney make the decision whether or not to prosecute?
98. Does the district attorney ever agree to prosecute on a less serious charge if the offender will plead guilty to the lesser offense?[1]
99. Are all indictments for a serious crime handed out by a grand jury?

Criminal trials. Criminal law and the criminal courts still operate on the ancient principle of punishment rather than rehabilitation. That this system is inefficient in its function of protecting society is indicated by the fact that

---

[1] This practice is sometimes used to avoid long drawn out trials when there is a crowded court calendar, but it also lends itself to corruption.

the average length of stay in prisons is only about two years, and that there is a high rate of recidivism (repeated offenders). Hardened criminals must be released to society when they have served their sentence, whether or not they constitute a menace to public safety. On the other hand, offenders who might be released without any danger to society are kept unnecessarily and at high public expense, because the law says they must be "punished." Whether such punishment makes a hardened criminal out of someone who could have been rehabilitated to useful citizenship usually receives secondary consideration, if any at all.

The criminal trials, themselves, are typically conducted in an atmosphere of contest between the prosecuting attorney and the attorney for the defense. While several aids, such as probation work, adequate case histories, psychiatric examinations, and so on, are available to and being used by some courts, in others little use is made of them. As a result, people are often sentenced to prison who should be receiving psychiatric therapy, or are sentenced to punitive treatment when medical treatment is needed (as is true in the case of alcoholics and drug addicts).[1]

Since the basic goals of punishment and rehabilitation typically conflict, you will want to be forming an opinion, as you gather data in this part of your study, as to the relative importance of each goal—punishment and rehabilitation—in the trial and sentencing procedure.[2]

100. Does your state law make mandatory a thorough case study of the offender before he is brought to trial or before he is sentenced?
   If there is such a law, how regularly is it followed in the courts?
   Who makes such studies? Is it possible to obtain a copy of the outline used?

101. Is the physical and psychiatric examination of all indicted persons a regular part of court procedure?

102. What provision is there for legal counsel for those who cannot afford to hire a lawyer:
   Public defender
   Private voluntary defenders
   Lawyer appointed by court

103. What laws govern sentences for various types of crime in your state?
   To what extent are they flexible, providing maximum and minimum penalties, or in other ways leaving room for court discretion?
   To what extent do they provide for indeterminate sentences?
   To what extent do they provide for suspended sentences?

[1] See Orfield, Lester B., *Criminal Procedure from Arrest to Appeal*, New York University Press, New York, 1947.
[2] In many state juvenile court systems, the goal of rehabilitation is given primary importance (see Chapter 11). Although this practice is widely accepted, it is only beginning to spread here and there to adult criminal courts.

Probation and parole. Probation is a system according to which a convicted individual is released to the community under supervision rather than being punished with imprisonment or fine. Usually, there are special conditions of probation, including regular reporting to a probation officer or other designated person, avoiding association with certain individuals, seeking employment, and so on. Probation is granted by the court in cases where the release of the convicted person under these circumstances does not involve a danger to society, and where probation supervision rather than imprisonment gives promise of being a more constructive form of treatment in his case. Another feature of probation is its extremely low financial cost as compared with imprisonment. Probation, therefore, is an introduction of the principle of rehabilitation rather than punishment (usually the individual must serve a prison sentence at the discretion of the judge if he violates probation).

At this point you may want to consult *Probation and Parole in Theory and Practice:* A Study Manual by Helen D. Pigeon,[1] *Selection for Parole:* A Manual of Parole Prediction by Lloyd E. Ohlin,[2] or *Probation and Parole* by David Dressler.[3]

Adequate probation depends on a thorough understanding of its purposes by the judge, including an understanding of what type of person is most likely to benefit by probation, a competent probation staff adequately trained, and probation case loads which are not so heavy as to make the supervision largely perfunctory. Probation departments often perform the additional function of making case histories to be used by the court in disposing of the case.

Parole, on the other hand, is a system according to which people serving prison terms are released to the community under supervision of parole officers, rather than serving out the maximum amount of their sentences in prison. Parole systems apply chiefly to state and federal, rather than local penal institutions.

104. Does your local county or municipality have a probation department?
105. What are the requirements for probation officers?[4]
106. How many convicted offenders were placed on probation last year?
     For what types of offenses were these offenders convicted? (Use outline on page 50.)
107. How often must persons on probation report to a probation officer by mail? Personally?

[1] National Probation Association, New York, 1942.
[2] Russell Sage Foundation, New York, 1951.
[3] Columbia University Press, New York, 1951.
[4] Questions listed earlier in this chapter relating to civil service and other aspects of public employment are relevant here for probation workers.

108. What is the nature and extent of the casework carried on by probation officers?
109. What is the case load per probation officer?
110. In what proportion of cases has probation been violated in recent years? What has been done when violations have occurred?
111. Examine the reports of state correctional or penal institutions to which people from your community who are convicted of a crime are committed. What evidence do they reveal of medical care, psychological examinations, psychiatric treatment, educational and vocational courses, and so on?
112. How widely is parole used as a method of release from such institutions?

References for Further Study

There are many excellent texts in state and local government, some of which are listed below.

Anderson, William, and Edward W. Weidner, *State and Local Government in the United States.* Henry Holt and Co., New York, 1951.

Fisher, Marguerite J., and Donald G. Bishop, *Municipal and Other Local Governments.* Prentice-Hall, Inc., New York, 1950.

Gosnell, Cullen B., and Lynwood M. Holland, *State and Local Government in the United States.* Prentice-Hall, Inc., New York, 1951.

MacCorkle, Stuart A., *American Municipal Government and Administration.* D.C. Heath and Co., Boston, 1948.

Snider, Clyde F., *American State and Local Government.* Appleton-Century-Crofts, Inc., New York, 1950.

The following are recommended for consultation in connection with their respective topics of consideration:

Check-List on How Cities Can Cut Costs. International City Managers' Association, Chicago, 1949. This lists several hundred questions indicating possible methods of cutting operating costs without endangering quantity or quality of services. It is a useful device for an intensive study.

Compendium of City Government Finances in 1952. Government Printing Office, Washington, 1953. If your city had more than 25,000 inhabitants in 1950, this publication will yield much information on its finances and afford a basis for comparison with cities of similar size.

The following are recommended for groups interested in citizen campaigns for civic betterment:

The Citizen Association: How to Organize and Run It and *The Citizen Association:* How to Win Civic Campaigns, both published by the National Municipal League, New York, 1953.

Public Administration Organizations: A Directory, 1948. Public Administration Clearing House, Chicago, 1948. This directory describes more than 500 national organizations interested in the field of public administration and government improvement. It also lists nearly two thousand state, regional, and Canadian organizations.

Van Riper, Paul P., *Handbook of Practical Politics.* Henry Holt and Co., New York, 1952. A highly practical guide to the "ins" and "outs" of political campaigning.

5. Community Planning

PLANNING IN THE SENSE of anticipating and attempting to exercise some influence on the direction of future events is an important human process. Although planning by individuals, associations, corporations, and government departments goes on continuously, often it is uncoordinated and has undesirable consequences to the community which might have been avoided. The results of uncoordinated, piece-meal planning are apparent in most American communities, particularly the larger cities. Traffic congestion in the downtown section, inadequate space for parking, crowded bus routes, areas of deterioration and blight, inadequate space for parks and playgrounds, ugly waterfront sections, nuisances such as air and water pollution, poorly planned real estate developments which will be blighted in a generation, premature subdivisions, gridiron street plans unsuitable for residential neighborhoods, traffic hazards between children and their schools and playgrounds—these and similar problems arise in large part from the uncoordinated planning of the many individuals and agencies which make up the urban community.

The Need for Planning

In rural areas, also, results of inadequate planning are apparent. The construction of new, poorly planned residential developments fronting on heavily traveled highways, the depletion of the nation's soil, the countless dollars spent in maintaining town highways for only one or two persons on land which will not support a family to begin with, the pollution of streams, the marring of beautiful landscape with unsightly billboards, the deterioration of property values caused by mixed commercial, industrial, and residential land uses in many small villages—all these indicate that the need for planning is not exclusively an urban one.

But modern community planning involves more than an attempt to avoid the evils of unplanned, haphazard community development. It seeks definitely to guide community development toward positive ends.[1] Do the people of the community wish to keep it predominantly residential and commercial, discouraging manufacturing activities? Are more parks and playgrounds needed? Is it desired to build up the drawing power of the downtown shopping center? How large a concentration of population is desired within city limits? According to the way community people answer such questions, steps may be taken to work toward the goals which are indicated. Hence, one of the first steps in planning is to ascertain what kind of community the people desire. Occasionally, they want to keep things just as they are. But a pleasant community which "wants to stay the same" may wake up in ten or twenty years to find that it has in fact changed considerably, and in a direction which was not anticipated. Thus, while it is true that a community may do much to preserve its characteristic tone through generations, it usually must plan in order to do so.

Purposes for which community planning is undertaken frequently include the following:

Adequate community facilities

Favorable location of residential districts, commercial activities, and industries with relation to each other

School buildings, parks, playgrounds, and shopping centers well located with relation to residential areas

Adequate rapid transit facilities

Well-balanced economic base for the community

Adequate fiscal plans

A street and traffic system which permits the free flow of through traffic and avoids cutting up residential areas with through traffic

Adequate parking facilities

Adequate spacing of buildings

Controlled development of new real estate subdivisions

But all too often, planning for such purposes is likely to be piece-meal. The system of elementary and high schools is planned without reference to the system of playgrounds. Housing projects are planned without adequate attention to the community facilities on which their inhabitants will have to draw. New bridges or highways into the city center only add to the congestion rather than alleviating it. Predictions of future population are made without reference to industrial development plans. Ambitious com-

[1] For an introduction to various aspects of community planning, see Greer, Guy, *Your City Tomorrow*, Macmillan Co., New York, 1947; Breese, Gerald, and Dorothy E. Whiteman, editors, *An Approach to Urban Planning*, Princeton University Press, Princeton, 1953; and Anderson, William, and others, *City Planning:* A Selection of Readings in Its Theory and Practice, Burgess Publishing Co., Minneapolis, 1950. A highly elementary description of planning activities for smaller cities is Chapin, F. Stuart, Jr., *Communities for Living*, University of Georgia Press, Athens, 1941.

munity improvement plans are sponsored without an adequate conception of the way in which the money will be raised to pay for them. It can thus be seen that community planning activities require coordination if they are to be effective.

1. Is there any comprehensive body, public or private, which is charged with the overall responsibility for community planning in its broadest aspects?
2. Does this body help to coordinate in part or in whole the planning done in any of the following fields:

Health   Physical aspects of the community
Welfare   Recreation
Education   Fiscal planning
Industrial development   Other

3. Between which planning fields listed in the previous question is there coordinated planning activity?
4. What is the relationship of "community planning" to health and welfare planning and industrial development efforts in your community?
5. Which of the following examples of poor planning can be found in your community:

Extreme traffic congestion downtown
Inadequate parking facilities
Blighted (deteriorated) residential areas
Industrial nuisances, such as noise, air pollution
Inadequate park and play space
Ugly ribbons of commercial development along main highways
Poorly planned and poor quality suburban real estate developments
Others

Types of Planning

There are three major types of planning: industrial development (see Chapter 3), planning the physical aspects of the community ("city planning"), and health and welfare planning (see Chapter 17). There is no logical reason why three relatively distinct divisions of planning should exist. They have been separately discussed in this book not because their division is desirable but because they are likely to be so classified in the reader's own community. The fact that these types of planning go on relatively independent of each other usually operates to the detriment of the community. Occasionally, one sees a more comprehensive planning job being done by the planning board, or the welfare council, or the industrial development group, with the others operating in close coordination with it. This coordination was particularly noticeable in some of the postwar planning councils and is sometimes apparent in the community councils of smaller communities.

The present chapter is devoted chiefly to community planning as carried on by planning boards or commissions, or citizens' planning councils. The chief earmark of such planning is its official or semiofficial status, centered as it is in a formal planning board set up by the local government. But the attempt is here made to relate such planning to other planning activities, such as health, recreation, education, and housing.

Many communitywide or countywide rural planning activities occur which are not closely tied in with official planning bodies and which are considered in Chapter 17. Over and above these, there are certain rural counterparts of community planning which merit brief mention.

Rural land-use zoning has been introduced in a few states, notably Wisconsin. Its purposes are to encourage the distribution of people on the land in such a manner as to lead to efficient and economic maintenance of highways, school buses, and other community facilities, to preserve suitable land for recreational and forestry areas while it is still kept in private ownership, and to discourage use of submarginal land for agricultural purposes. *Soil conservation districts,* often on a county basis, have been set up in many of the country's counties in order to foster cooperation among individual farmers in conservation projects many of which require a consistent plan for a number of adjoining farms. These are set up in relation to the state and federal government. Various activities in the Tennessee Valley, notably the TVA *demonstration projects,* coordinate the activities of farmers in various sections, involving the joint participation of the TVA, the agricultural extension service, and groups of farmers.

Outside of these and similar programs, rural community planning is carried on by village and town and county planning boards in accordance with procedures described in this chapter.

Community planning has a long history. Many American communities today have advantages which were made possible by careful planning a generation or century ago. When the railroad passenger station is a place of beauty in an attractive setting, planning has generally been involved. The New England common and the village square testify to the foresight of earlier generations. Many small towns are fortunate in having an adequately wide Main Street because people of an earlier generation made it that way. There is perhaps nothing more paradoxical than a complacent citizen of a community which has many such advantages attributable to the foresight of earlier generations who says, "Planning will get you nowhere."

6. What special aspects of the physical layout of your community have resulted from careful planning many years ago:

Ample parking facilities   Attractive shopping center
Modern street pattern   Churches in prominent settings
Suitable park and playground space   Other

7. What problems are now growing in your community which will require careful planning for their solution:

Slums   Loss of industry to other communities
Blighted areas   Unsightly and slipshod suburban development
Traffic congestion   Housing
Parking problems   Slum clearance
Lack of playgrounds   Fiscal problems
Traffic hazards   Other

Planning Boards and Planning Processes

The governmental instrument through which community planning such
as is being considered here occurs, is the planning board or planning commission. This may be a village or city planning board, a town planning
board, a county planning board, or even a regional planning board comprised of one or more counties. The usual pattern is to have this board appointed by the mayor or governing body. Although state provisions differ,
most planning boards comprise between five and nine members. A frequent
procedure is for one or two of the members to be city officials, such as the
city engineer or commissioner of public works, and the others to be made
up of laymen in such fields as business, architecture, real estate, health,
education, and so on. This planning board or commission is responsible
to the mayor or governing body. It is usually empowered to engage a professional staff whose number and qualifications will vary with the size
of the community. Occasionally, particularly in the initial stages of its
work, it may be desirable to engage the services of a consultant.

One of its chief functions is to draw up a master plan, or community
plan. A quotation from recent New Jersey legislation will indicate the
broad scope of such a plan.

In scope the master plan may cover proposals for: (a) the use of land and
buildings—residential, commercial, industrial, mining, agricultural, park, and
other like matters; (b) services—water supply, utilities, sewerage, and other
like matters; (c) transportation—streets, parking, public transit, freight
facilities, airports, and other like matters; (d) housing—residential standards,
slum clearance and redevelopment, and other like matters; (e) conservation
—water, forest, soil, flood-control, and other like matters; (f) public and
semipublic facilities—civic center, schools, libraries, parks, playgrounds, fire
houses, police structures, hospitals, and other like matters; (g) the distribution and density of population; (h) other elements of municipal growth and
development.

The master plan may include in its scope areas outside the boundaries of the municipality which the planning board deems to bear an essential relation to the planning of the municipality. The studies in connection with the master plan shall be conducted wherever possible with the co-operation of adjacent planning agencies.

Such a plan does not have the force of law, but part or all of it may be enacted into law by the governing body of the municipality. Although there is widespread misunderstanding among laymen on this point, the plan must be highly tentative and highly general. For example, specific zoning ordinance provisions are too detailed and brittle to be included in the plan. Rather, zoning ordinance provisions should be formulated in accordance with the plan. The plan must also be subject to change.

Several instrumentalities are available to the planning board in carrying out its activities. Continuous *community survey work* involves the assembling of necessary facts from reports and data of other branches of the municipal government, and making specific studies to ascertain needed facts not already available. Such work provides the factual basis for planning. The *official map* is a document officially approved by the governing body which shows all public streets, parks, bridges, buildings, playgrounds, and other facilities as well as proposed streets, buildings, and facilities which are definitely planned for the near future. The master plan, or *community plan,* has already been mentioned. The planning board may or may not have considerable power in preventing municipal projects which do not accord with the plan, including power over too frequent and sporadic and uncoordinated amendment of the zoning ordinance. *Plat review* customarily gives the planning board the power to approve or disapprove plats for new subdivision developments, to assure that they meet established standards and conform to the community plan.

8. Has your community a planning board or commission?
9. Are there other planning boards or commissions which include your community:

    Town planning   County planning   Regional planning

10. What are the major provisions of the state law which authorizes such planning boards?
11. What are the major provisions of your local community ordinance, if any, setting up a planning board?
12. How many members serve on your planning board? Are any members *ex officio*?
    Are any members otherwise specified as to qualifications, occupation, and so on?
13. What are the specific functions delegated to the planning board?

14. What staff, if any, does your planning board employ:
    Full-time   Part-time   On consulting basis
15. What devices (instrumentalities, techniques) does your planning board utilize in carrying out its functions:
    Official map   Zoning
    Fact-gathering from official   Building codes
        reports and statistics   Plat approval
    Survey of community conditions   Other
    Community plan (master plan)
16. Does the community plan (master plan) seem to be rigid and inflexible, or is it constantly being developed, supplemented, revised, implemented?
17. Does your community have a zoning ordinance?
18. What is the relation of the community plan to the zoning ordinance?
19. Does your community plan include:
    Population forecasts
    Zoning and other land-use controls
    Housing plans
    Slum clearance and other redevelopment plans
    Public works and public facilities
    Transportation systems, including parking areas
    Rapid transit
    Water, sewage disposal, other facilities
    Parks and playgrounds
    Industrial site location
    Airports and other terminals
    Sites and plans for future public buildings
    Policies related to the desired future community character

The best planning practice goes beyond the drawing up and revision of a community plan. It provides constant encouragement of municipal officials and private interests to plan with reference to one another. It stimulates citizen interest, participation, and support of planning activities. And it seeks to achieve positive ends such as better neighborhood facilities, adequate outdoor recreation space, a desirable economic balance of residences and various types of industry, and a host of other matters.

While planning boards often have specific powers such as approving or rejecting plats for subdivision development[1] and in some instances have direct enforcement authority for zoning ordinances, the planning board's ultimate power comes from the extent to which different branches of government are willing to follow its advice and various citizen groups are willing to support it. Thus, it is important that the municipal legislative

[1] A *plat* is a plan for the development of an undeveloped tract of land. A *subdivision* is a tract of land divided into plots or streets for sale or development.

body understand the activities of the planning board, and that the various departments of the municipal government come to heed its advice. Otherwise, the legislature may amend the zoning ordinance all out of conformity with the "master plan" and the various governmental departments, which may be responsible in no way to the planning board, may disregard its plans at will. Both of these contingencies become less likely if a sincere attempt is made to consult these parties and keep them informed and if an informed citizenry supports the general features of the community plan.

20. Is fiscal planning closely integrated with "physical" planning in your community?

21. What is the relationship of your planning board to fiscal planning?[1]

22. Is there close coordination between planning processes in the various branches of municipal government?

23. Do the school board, industrial development committee, recreation department, and other branches use the same population forecasts in making plans, or does each group have its own?

24. Does your investigation of planning activity indicate that it is conceived by those involved as a rigid plan to be drawn up and carried out, or as a dynamic process in which plans are tentative, easily modified, supplemented with other studies, and so on?

25. Is there any marked attempt on the part of the planning board to encourage various governmental branches to cooperate with each other and coordinate their respective planning activities? What examples can you give?

26. Does your planning board's activity go beyond the remedying of existing community evils to planning ahead for the attainment of positive community goals?

27. Does your planning board make a constant effort to inform the city council or other governing board of its problems, activities, and accomplishments?

28. Does it maintain a close relationship to various branches of municipal government, offering its specialized facilities to help them with their planning problems?

Intercommunity Planning

Particularly in metropolitan areas, municipal boundaries are highly arbitrary. Many of the planning problems which arise involve more than one municipality. For this reason, county planning boards perform important functions in many metropolitan areas. They help to coordinate the activities of various branches of the county government.[2] Outside of California, they do not usually have zoning powers.

---

[1] See pp. 72–73 for other material on fiscal planning.
[2] See *County Planning*, Regional Plan Bulletin No. 83, Regional Plan Association, New York, 1953.

Just as planning problems sometimes cross municipal lines, they often cross county lines. Many states therefore have enabling legislation making possible the creation of regional planning boards for areas larger than a single county.[1]

Other methods of facilitating planning across municipal lines include joint planning boards, informal cooperation of separate planning boards, the creation of special purpose districts, and the consolidation of groups of municipalities.[2] Since control over real estate developments in neighboring suburban territory outside the municipal limits is essential to adequate city planning, many states grant their municipalities subdivision control jurisdiction over unincorporated territory within a specified number of miles beyond the city lines. Town planning in New England facilitates this process.

29. Is your municipality hindered in its planning activities by lack of jurisdiction over surrounding territory outside the city limits but which nevertheless presents problems to the municipality as the suburbs grow?

30. Is your municipality given some legal control over subdivision development within a specified distance from its legal boundaries?

31. Are there larger planning units with which your community has a functional relationship:
    Relation of neighborhood planning to city planning
    Relation of city planning to county and regional planning

32. Do the larger planning units help the municipalities organize planning programs? Do they offer technical assistance?

33. Do the larger planning units help the municipalities get together in planning on matters where more than one municipality is affected by the planning:
    In coordinating their zoning policies
    In highway planning
    In coordinating their economic relationship to each other (as where one municipality is more industrial, another more residential, and so forth)
    In organizing joint studies or other joint activities to advance their common concerns

34. Does the county planning board help to coordinate the planning of the various departments of the county government?

35. Is there a regional planning board? How broad or how narrow is its planning function?

36. Are there regional "authorities" which enable various branches of municipal,

[1] The neighborhood is still another level of planning activity. City planning usually places great stress on the neighborhood. An excellent booklet describing a carefully thought out neighborhood approach to city planning is *Berkeley Neighborhoods, 1950*, Berkeley City Planning Commission, 1950. (See Chapter 6.)
[2] Black, Russell Van Nest, and Mary Hedges Black, *Planning for the Small American City*. Public Administration Service, Chicago, 1948. This booklet, designed for cities of 50,000 or fewer, tells how to make a city plan and how to support and implement it.

county, or state government to get together in concerted development plans
such as transportation facilities:

| Bridges | Airports | Freight terminals | Other |
| Tunnels | Harbor development | Bus lines and terminals | |

37. Is there a "joint planning board" which coordinates some of the efforts of
two or more municipal planning boards?
How is it constituted? What are its functions?
38. How much informal cooperation and consultation takes place among the
members of planning boards in nearby municipalities?

Zoning and Other Land-Use Controls

In a democracy, there are definite limits beyond which people cannot be
forced to act even at the government's will. Nevertheless, some degree of
control must be exercised over individual citizen initiative if chaos is not
to result. One method of exercising control is through controlling land use.
The most prevalent form of land-use control is zoning. But there are others.
Building codes regulate the construction of buildings from the standpoint
of safety and sound construction principles. *Subdivision control* regulates
the opening up of new subdivisions and provides for adequate street plans,
sewage and drainage systems, and, in some instances, acreage for public
use.[1] *Multiple dwelling laws*, based on health and safety considerations,
govern specifications for the erection of tenement houses. *Subsidies* or special
concessions like *tax exemption* encourage certain types of land use. In addition, the interpretation of law in *individual suits* on grounds of nuisance
affords some degree of retroactive control. Finally, private agreements limiting land use, called *restrictive covenants*, may require the purchaser to agree
to certain conditions in the use of land, although the supreme court has
ruled against court support of racial covenants.[2]

"Zoning is the regulation by districts under the police power of the height,
bulk, and use of buildings, the use of land, and the density of population."[3]
It is upheld by the courts where the zoning regulations "have a substantial
relation to the health, safety, morals, comfort, convenience, and general
welfare of the community."[4] The earliest zoning districts were residential,

---

[1] A definitive work which sets standards for the development of new subdivisions is
Planning the Neighborhood, Public Administration Service, Chicago, 1948. A good booklet designed for New York State communities but having wide application is *Subdivision
Control: A Step Toward Better Communities*, State of New York Department of Commerce, Albany, 1946.
[2] For a good discussion of land-use control, see the chapter by Norman Williams, Jr., in
Breese, Gerald, and Dorothy E. Whiteman, editors, *Op. cit.*
[3] Bassett, Edward M., *Zoning*: The Laws, Administration, and Court Decisions During
the First Twenty Years. Russell Sage Foundation, New York, 1940, p. 45.
[4] *Ibid.*, p. 54.

business, and industrial, with each district including as permissible the uses of the preceding district. While such primary districting suffices for many communities, others, particularly large and complex communities, have found it desirable to segregate districts still further, often into local business districts, downtown business districts, merchandising districts, and so on. Similarly, industrial districts have been segregated for light and heavy industry, and residential districts have been segregated according to the number of dwelling units permitted in each building, the size of the plot, and so on. Recently, zoning has been employed to meet the problem of the location of trailer camps.[1]

Density of population may be regulated by limiting the allowable number of families per acre of land, or requiring a certain number of square feet of lot per family. Many planners consider such density control preferable to other, more rigid methods of land-use control. It is particularly important that rigid restrictions originally designed to govern one structure on one lot be liberalized to permit flexible design for multi-structured projects on large tracts.

High acreage zoning, for example two acres per plot, is often termed "economic discrimination" and frowned upon by many community planners. Others, however, feel that it is perfectly in conformity with the principle of "encouraging the most appropriate use of land" in some communities. More recently "architectural review boards" have arisen here and there to exercise some minimum influence over the exterior design and appearance of buildings in or near residential areas.

One difficulty in zoning is that often it must be superimposed on a land-use pattern including many nonconforming uses. The provision for retroactive zoning under suitable and fair conditions is gradually coming to be recognized, provided a fair amortization period is allowed. There is considerable agreement on the inadvisability of "spot zoning" of undesirable land uses in the midst of more restrictive zoning districts so as to legalize land uses which do not conform to the prevalent zoning pattern. Extensive practice of spot zoning soon vitiates the entire zoning effort.

Since sporadic and hastily conceived changes in the zoning regulations may have highly disadvantageous consequences, some planning boards are authorized to approve or disapprove such changes. Without such approval, an especially large majority of the municipal governing body is necessary to enact the change.

[1] See "Mobility—A New Aspect of Community Life," *Urban Land*, July–August, 1953. This is a brief but comprehensive review of the problems which trailer camps bring to communities and the measures available to cope with them. See also *Recommended Standards for Trailer Courts*, Housing and Home Finance Agency, Government Printing Office, Washington, 1952.

Zoning is essentially a negative method of land-use control, in that it helps to prevent certain kinds of use but does not assure positive use in the manner desired. Thus, although a particular area is districted for commercial use, this does not assure that commercial establishments will move in to saturate the area. Often, too much land is saved for commercial use, thus encouraging the wide dispersion of unsightly mixtures of residential and commercial uses throughout large areas.

Land-use control, like planning itself, is not only negative, but can also be positive. Slums may be cleared and rezoned; the city may acquire property for park or other public use, waterfront development projects for port facilities or for beautification and park space may be undertaken. For such purposes, land acquisition may take place through purchase, condemnation and excess condemnation, gift, exchange, foreclosure, reclamation, and lease.[1] A consistent, well-planned policy with respect to the handling of tax-default land may be an important tool in the gradual reshaping of land-use patterns to conform to the master plan.

39. Does your community have a zoning ordinance?
40. Is the zoning ordinance closely related to the master plan?
41. Has the zoning ordinance been revised in comprehensive fashion in the past ten years to keep up with new developments?
42. What agency is responsible for enforcing the zoning ordinance?
    How many individual enforcement actions were required last year and what were the results?
43. Is there a zoning board of appeals (board of adjustment)?
44. Procure a map of the zoning districts into which your community is divided.
    Into what types of district is your community zoned?
    Is your community "overzoned" for commercial or industrial uses?
45. In residential areas, what restrictions are there in regard to:
    Percentage of lot occupied by building
    Minimum lot frontage
    Number of square feet of lot per family
    Number of dwellings per acre
    Building set-back
    Other
46. Does your zoning map indicate an excessive use of "spot zoning"?
47. Does a lax interpretation of zoning ordinances in your community tend to make the zoning procedure ineffective and self-defeating?
48. Is there any plan for the gradual extinction of nonconforming uses?
49. Are there provisions in your zoning ordinance which discourage newer

[1] Lewis, Harold MacLean, *Planning the Modern City*. John Wiley and Sons, Inc., New York, 1949, vol. 2, p. 197. The two volumes of this work constitute an authoritative description of city planning from the standpoint of the city engineer.

building practices because they were formulated to fit now outmoded conditions?

50. Does your zoning ordinance provide for off-street parking facilities in connection with new apartment houses, commercial and industrial buildings?

51. Has your planning board the power to approve or disapprove changes in the zoning ordinance?

52. How does each of the tools of land-use control operate in your community:
    Building codes   Multiple dwelling laws   Restrictive covenants
    Subdivision control   Individual suits   Other

53. Has your planning board or similar authority the legal power to approve or reject plats for new subdivision development?
    What provisions must be met in order to obtain plat approval?

54. Is any provision for recreation space or other neighborhood facilities required in new subdivision development?
    Does the subdivider pay for new streets and utilities, or does the municipality pay for them?

55. Does the planning board attempt to guide new subdivision development into contiguous areas in order to economize on sewers, street construction and maintenance, and other facilities?

56. Does your planning board avoid the precarious device of premature improvement of possible residential land in order to attract building and residents?

57. Has your community a land-use policy which goes beyond merely negative restraints?

58. Are there activities in the following land-use fields:
    Slum clearance
    Land acquisition for parks and playgrounds
    Condemnation and excess condemnation
    Consistent plan for use of tax-default land
    Industrial site development

59. Are plans made well in advance for the acquisition of land for parks, schools, parking areas, and other community needs?

60. Is the device of the semiautonomous "authority" used in your community to accomplish various community objectives through its own bond issues, fees, and so forth:
    Housing authority   Transit authority
    Parking authority   Port authority
                                   Other

Some Special Planning Problems

A combination of developments has resulted in several interrelated problems facing most large cities and many small ones. These developments include the growth of the suburbs, the use of automobile, commuter train and bus transportation, and industrial decentralization. In their wake, these developments have left many problems. As more and more people have aggregated in metropolitan areas and around smaller cities, there has been a growth in congestion at the city center, with more and more people earning their living there. This has created an extensive traffic and rapid transit problem, with many remedial attempts at opening up new traffic arteries, merely resulting in a greater influx of passenger cars to the city center. This in turn has not only aggravated the already serious traffic problem, but has also created extremely difficult parking problems.[1] Noise, congestion, growth of commercial land use surrounding the city center, and the flight of many former residents to the suburbs have all contributed to a growing problem of blight in areas surrounding the city center.[2] The spread outward of nonresidential land use, increasing noise and congestion, and other factors contribute to slum areas characterized by high land values and poor housing facilities, and potential slums already showing signs of blight.[3] The extent of tax foreclosures indicates that the provision of low-cost housing on such centrally located land is beyond the ability of private initiative. If the slums are to be cleared and future blight prevented, drastic surgery is needed in the way of slum clearance and urban redevelopment. Out at the edges of the city, ribbons of commercial land use along the main highways create ugly fringe slums consisting of junk yards, used car lots, drive-in theaters, hot dog stands, cheap real estate developments, and similar blemishes on the landscape in every corner of the country.[4]

Permeating all these problems is the fact that most cities are in a desperate financial struggle to remain solvent. They are caught in a vicious circle where increasing problems such as those listed cause people to move to the suburbs, thus escaping the city's tax jurisdiction, depreciating land values within the city center, and adding to the city's cost for traffic, highway, parking, and other facilities. As shopping centers spring up outside city boundaries to cater to the suburbs, the business of the city's retail establishments is threatened, and their ability to pay taxes impeded. The

[1] See *Parking Manual:* How to Solve Community Parking Problems, American Automobile Association, Washington, D.C., 1946.

[2] For blight prevention and neighborhood conservation, an excellent booklet is Kayanan, A. C., *Neighborhood Conservation:* A Handbook for Citizen Groups, Regional Association of Cleveland, 1943. Somewhat old, the booklet is nevertheless unsurpassed in its presentation.

[3] See Chapter 6 for a consideration of housing problems.

[4] The steps which can be taken to avoid such pitfalls are clearly pointed out in a thick booklet entitled *Roadside Protection*, American Automobile Association, Washington, 1951.

fiscal problem becomes critical, and the need for greater coordination of policies not only within the city proper but within the whole metropolitan area becomes drastic.

This somewhat oversimplified account indicates some of the most knotty and widespread planning problems, particularly for larger communities. Just as the problems are interconnected, so are the remedial and preventive measures. None of the problems above can be adequately solved in piecemeal fashion. Some of the methods which go into a coordinated attack on these problems are land reclamation, slum clearance, urban redevelopment, peripheral parking, improvement of bus service, parking authorities, blight prevention, encouragement of dispersion of functions, better subdivision control, improved zoning methods, roadside control, intercommunity planning, capital improvement budgets, and progressive fiscal planning.

A question frequently raised by planners these days is whether planning for greater expansion of the city center makes sense under present conditions. Many city centers are losing their resident population. With industrial dispersion, suburban shopping centers, suburban residential centers, rapid transit, and increasing congestion problems at the city center, many planners renew the plea first widely developed by Ebenezer Howard[1] for a limitation on city size. According to his plan, population growth would occur through the "budding out" of new communities rather than the unrestricted sprawling growth of the metropolis. Planning boards must adopt a consistent policy, in solving their housing and slum clearance and parking and transportation problems, as to whether they want to encourage or discourage the expansion of the city center with its attendant congestion.

Occasionally an opportunity arises to apply the planning process to a proposed community before it has grown to accumulate the tangled web of problems described above. Examples of communities which have been built on a plan are Radburn, New Jersey; Garden City and Forest Hills, New York; Greenbelt, Maryland; and the other greenbelt communities.[2]

61. Does your community have a serious problem in traffic congestion?
62. Which of the following devices have been used to cope with the traffic problem:

> Prohibiting curb parking on certain streets so as to provide for another moving lane of traffic
> Rerouting traffic
> Restricting certain streets to one-way traffic
> Other

[1] Howard, Ebenezer, *Garden Cities of Tomorrow*. Faber and Faber, Ltd., London, 1945.
[2] For an authoritative account of such developments, see Stein, Clarence S., *Toward New Towns for America*, Public Administration Service, Chicago, 1951.

63. Have traffic counts and a thorough study with expert assistance been made of the traffic problem and possible measures to remedy it?
64. Are new traffic measures, highway and bridge facilities, and so on, adding to or reducing the problem of downtown congestion?
65. Is there a parking problem in the downtown area? What methods have been used to cope with it:
    Parking meters
    Commercial parking lots or garages
    Municipal parking lots or garages
    Requirements for off-street parking and loading facilities in new commercial and other buildings
    Limiting amount of permissible parking time at curb
    Parking facilities for commuter passenger cars at the edge of the city
    Other
66. Has your community a "parking authority"? What are its functions?
67. Are major highway routes which traverse your community zoned exclusively for commercial purposes, thus encouraging sprawling ribbons of mixed commercial and residential use, or are highway frontages zoned to conform to the land use of the district which they traverse?
68. Has your community experienced a rapid growth in suburban areas? Is this bringing fiscal problems to your community?
69. Has your community a highway authority?
70. Is there a roadside planning program? Are zoning and subdivision regulations designed to promote the best uses of roadside property?
    Are street patterns in new subdivisions regulated so as not to congest through highways with purely local traffic?
71. Are roadside uses restricted so as not to bring blight to surrounding residential districts?
72. Is there any public control over ugly and unsightly billboards and other uses of the land which mar the appearance of access highways and spread blight?

Capital Improvement Plan

Part of any well-developed community plan should be an adequate capital improvement plan. Briefly, this is a list of the capital improvements for various purposes—streets, parks, municipal hospitals, harbor improvement, sewage disposal, etc.—to be undertaken over a considerable period of years, with priorities attached as to the order of their importance and actual realization, and with a plan for raising money to finance them. A good capital improvement program is facilitated where there is central responsibility in municipal government, rather than independently elected department heads; where the proposed improvements are based upon sound studies of community needs rather than the whims or pet ideas of department commissioners, and where the fiscal planning is integrated with the capital improvement plan and both are related to other parts of the community plan.[1] As in other aspects of planning, there should be a reasonable balance between rigid inflexibility on the one hand and too frequent change and substitution on the other.

73. With what departments does your planning board actively collaborate in fiscal planning?

74. Has your community a capital improvement program? Is it tied in with the community plan?
   Are the projected improvements based on careful study of relative community needs?

75. Is there a practical plan for the financing of these improvements which is based on a sound study of sources of municipal revenue and the community's ability to pay?

76. Are some of the community's capital improvements financed through the creation of self-liquidating authorities empowered to launch bond issues in their own name, rather than being considered part of the municipality's public works?

77. Which methods are employed for financing individual projects: Special assessments against those who are principally benefited? General city charge? Both?

78. Is the length of bond issues realistically related to the nature of the projects so that the municipality is not saddled with debts whose amortization extends over too many years?

79. Which of the projects are on a "pay-as-you-go" basis?

80. In the capital improvement budget, have the following possibilities been considered:
   Raising the assessed valuations
   A municipal income tax
   Other possible sources of tax revenue
   State or federal aid
   Increasing the municipality's debt limit
   Use of short-term financing

Citizen Participation in Planning

Long experience with plans which never were adopted because they lacked citizen support has convinced most planners of the importance of keeping citizens informed as planning progresses, and going beyond that in bringing

[1] For an interesting brief account of the contrast between sound and unsound fiscal planning, see Walter H. Blucher's chapter on "Fiscal Programming" in Breese, Gerald, and Dorothy E. Whiteman, editors, *Op. cit.*

citizens into the planning process itself. Such citizen participation in planning usually takes place through a citizens' planning council.

A planning council is an unofficial or semiofficial body which is devoted to aiding and supporting the planning process but which has no governmental power whatsoever. It can be a purely unofficial association of citizens interested in planning, or it may be a semiofficial body made up of representatives of community services and planning bodies.[1] Such a council can represent a coordinated attempt to integrate the planning of economic development, health and welfare services, and city planning. A notable example is the Syracuse-Onondaga Post-War Planning Council, which was made up of representatives from the City Planning Commission, Council of Social Agencies, Chamber of Commerce, Syracuse Housing Authority, Safety Council, County Park and Planning Board, County Public Works Commission, and Agriculture Committee, as well as the general public.[2] Or it may be more narrowly confined to interest in the physical aspects of community planning.

In communities where official planning boards do not exist, one of the first activities of such a planning council is to work toward the creation by the legislative body of an official planning board.[3] It may also make preliminary studies, help the planning board get organized and secure personnel, publicize the activities and progress of the planning board, aid it in making studies which will be useful to it, help publicize and enlist citizen participation in determining the kind of community which citizens want, publicize and help gain support for various parts of the community plan as these are completed by the planning board, campaign for legislation or other municipal or private business action to put the plan into effect, exercise vigilance over weakening the zoning procedure through passing countless exceptions or removing basic provisions of the zoning ordinance, and so on.

Where a planning council can perform such functions and in addition coordinate planning in the economic development and health and welfare fields, it may represent the kind of coordinated, communitywide planning

[1] See *Action for Cities: A Guide for Community Planning*, Public Administration Service, Chicago, 1950, p. 77. This booklet is a broadly conceived guide for community planning employing a technique which was first tried in Corpus Christi, Salt Lake City, and Tacoma.

[2] See Bishop, Donald G., Wallace E. Lamb, Emily B. Smith, and Edith E. Starratt, *Community Planning in a Democracy*, National Council for the Social Studies, Washington, 1948, p. 18. See also "Syracuse Tackles Its Future," *Fortune*, vol. 27, May, 1943.

[3] For a helpful booklet on setting up the work of a planning board, see Morrow, C. Earl, *Planning Your Community: A Manual of Suggestions for Practical Community Planning*, Regional Plan Association, Inc., New York, 1945. Another helpful pamphlet for citizens interested in planning is *Your Stake in Community Planning*, National Committee on Housing, Inc., New York, 1944.

which is the promise of a sound, wholesome development for American communities of the future.

81. If your community does not have a planning board, through what state or private agency can you learn about the possibilities under your state law? Has an attempt been made in recent years to stimulate interest in creating a planning board in your community?

82. What citizens' organizations are there in your community which have planning as a primary function?

83. Is there any single community organization such as a planning council which coordinates citizen planning efforts?

84. How is the planning council constituted?

85. Are industrial development and welfare planning closely coordinated with the work of this planning council?

86. Does the planning council work in close coordination with the official planning board, housing authority, and any other municipal planning agencies in any of the following ways:

Making studies for the government planning agency

Helping to formulate policy

Helping to publicize the work of the planning board

Using its influence to get government agencies to cooperate with the planning board

Sponsoring or endorsing necessary legislation for specific projects, or campaigns for public approval of necessary bond issues, and so on

Sponsoring exhibits, institutes, and other public education activities related to planning

87. Do planning board members attempt to enlist public interest in planning and solicit suggestions from the public?

88. Do planning board members publicize their activities and seek to keep citizens informed on developments?

89. Does the planning board welcome interest by citizens' organizations in what it is doing, or does it discourage such interest?

References for Further Study

Bauer, Catherine, and others, *The Future of Cities and Urban Redevelopment;* and Ascher, Charles S., and others, *Urban Redevelopment:* Problems and Practices, University of Chicago Press, Chicago, 1953. These two volumes, under the general editorship of Coleman Woodbury, are part of the Urban Redevelopment Study of the University of Chicago. They constitute a definitive portrayal of the various aspects of urban redevelopment by a series of experts in the field.

Colean, Miles L., *Renewing Our Cities.* Twentieth Century Fund, New York, 1953. To assure vigorous, healthy growth for our cities, certain impediments to such growth should be removed and other positive planning measures introduced. This book shows how political, technological, and financial adjustments can further the process.

Sanders, S. E., and A. J. Rabuck, *New City Patterns*. Reinhold Publishing Corp., New York, 1946. Copiously illustrated, this book is a clear portrayal of its subject matter, which is that of analyzing urban redevelopment and "reintegration" using the metropolitan area as a base. Although somewhat technical, the volume is recommended to the layman because it is so well organized and clearly written.

6. Housing

THE HOUSING PROBLEM IN THE UNITED STATES is characterized by three important elements. There is a continuing demand for new housing caused by the increase in population, and there is a constant struggle to meet this demand. A second factor is the process by which residential sections become blighted and turn into slums at least as rapidly as the worst slums are cleared. Finally, new standards arise and conditions which seemed acceptable in earlier generations are no longer tenable. Examples are the outdoor privy and the backyard pump.

Construction of new dwelling units fails to keep pace with the increasing need for more homes. Outmoded zoning regulations, building codes, and building trades agreements militate against the economical use of new construction materials, procedures, and designs. Many people who need housing cannot afford the new homes which are being built. Local, state, and federal housing programs, while helpful, often violate important principles of sound community development and in any case are capable of meeting only a small proportion of the need.

The housing problem becomes most acute in the slum areas of large cities. Numerous studies indicate that the cost of slums is unbelievably high, both in human values and in dollar values. Slums have been found to contribute several times their share of juvenile delinquency, infant mortality, disease, crime, illegitimacy, prostitution and other forms of vice, and so on through a long list of human miseries. At the same time, the financial cost of slums is equally great. They have high rates of fire, need special police and court service, and they place inordinate strains on hospitals, jails, courts, probation services, welfare departments, and other services which perform the sorry task of coping with the human wreckage which slum conditions promote. Slums do not yield in tax revenue the cost of these and other municipal services. They are a costly "luxury" which neither modern social standards nor modern financial resources can afford to support.[1]

[1] See Rumney, Jay, and Sara Shuman, *The Cost of Slums in Newark*, Housing Authority of the City of Newark, New Jersey, 1946.

The problem of urban housing is more apparent, perhaps, but no more pressing than that of rural housing. In rural, as in urban housing, many of the units were first built long before the days of electricity, modern plumbing, central heating, and other modern comforts.

According to a survey prepared in 1945 by the Department of Agriculture Interbureau Committee on Post-War Programs, 2 1/2 to 3 million farm houses did not meet the standard of "decent, safe, and sanitary" housing. Recent investigations reveal that the quality of farm housing as a whole is considerably below the standards of non-farm housing.[1]

The inability of the private real estate and construction trades to cope alone with many aspects of the housing problem has led to various degrees of action by federal, state, and local governments. In the field of rural housing, the federal government has been active through such agencies as the Resettlement Administration, the now superseded Farm Security Administration, the Farmers Home Administration, and other federal agencies. At present, the bulk of federal aid for farm housing is supplied through loans, and in some cases contributions for the purpose of financing new housing or improvements, where suitable credit is not available to the farmer from other sources. Local communities do not enter the picture so directly as in the urban housing program, although local county committees cooperating in the Farmers Home Administration program are used to certify applicants for such housing loans and grants.

An important federal aid to housing is the insurance of loans made to private persons for building or repairing or improving their homes and for private rental housing. The loans are procured through a private financial institution and insured by the Federal Housing Administration. Such loan insurance encouragement is also given to privately financed nonprofit housing cooperatives. A somewhat similar program but with additional advantages is available to veterans through the Veterans Administration. But the most direct efforts of the federal government have been in the program of slum clearance and urban redevelopment, and low-rent housing, under the Housing Act of 1949.[2] State governments also take part in public housing chiefly through state housing authorities, state enabling legislation for local housing authorities, and state programs of low-rent and limited dividend housing.

---

[1] *The Local Community Job Under the Housing Act of 1949:* A Bulletin for Leaders of Local Community Groups. Housing and Home Finance Agency, Government Printing Office, Washington, 1949, p. 24.

[2] For a brief summary of federal activities in the housing field, write to the Government Printing Office for the leaflet *What the Consumer Wants to Know About Federal Government Housing Aids.* The 83d Congress drastically limited the federal government's low-rent housing program in the Housing Act of 1954.

Housing Conditions in Your Community

Much of the local community's concern with housing revolves around three questions: Is there enough housing? Is the housing adequate for healthy and wholesome living? Is the available housing well balanced for different income levels, family sizes, and personal tastes? A primary source of information concerning housing conditions is the *U.S. Census of Housing*, taken every ten years. Additional sources of already compiled data may be your local housing department or housing authority, real estate association, city planning board, citizens' planning council, council of social agencies, and Chamber of Commerce. In large cities, it is possible that the Bureau of the Census may have recently conducted a housing survey. Other special surveys or pertinent material may be available through your local college or university or some similar organization. Certain types of material are gathered and recorded by public utility companies, local health departments, and so on.

Public welfare and public health workers who have occasion to visit the more underprivileged homes may be able to give some good pointers on the location of substandard housing and living conditions. A walk through different sections of town, particularly those along the railroad, or behind the industrial district, or otherwise unfavorably located, may yield fresh impressions of different areas of need. In larger cities, housing authorities, or health, police, and fire departments can give valuable information, for poor health, crime, and excessive fires go along inexorably with poor living conditions. For areas in the surrounding countryside, county health or welfare workers can give valuable advice. Since the "rural slums" are not usually on the main highways, it is possible to have them in your own county and be completely unaware of them. If your county's farmers employ seasonal migrant workers, their housing facilities may afford a special area for concern, often overlooked because they do not confront the city dweller on Main Street. Housing for migrant workers is often unbelievably poor. (See Chapter 13.)

For background material on the subject of housing, read *The Future of Housing* by Charles Abrams,[1] *Breaking the Building Blockade* by Robert Lasch,[2] and *Two-Thirds of a Nation:* A Housing Program by Nathan Straus.[3] Two booklets, both of which are technical, afford standards against which local housing may be measured, particularly from the health standpoint. They are *An Appraisal Method for Measuring the Quality of Hous-*

[1] Harper and Bros., New York. 1946.
[2] University of Chicago Press, 1946.
[3] Alfred A. Knopf, New York, 1952.

ing: A Yardstick for Health Officers, Housing Officials, and Planners,[1]
and *Basic Principles of Healthful Housing.*[2]

In appraising the overall need for housing, population trends should be
kept in mind. Obviously, new housing needs will not be great in a community which is declining in size, although better housing may be a need.
"Doubling up" is an important indicator of overcrowding. Of course, some
dwelling units originally designed for large families may possibly be divided
up for smaller families (the average size of the household in the United
States has declined from 5.6 persons in 1850 to only 3.5 persons in 1950).
However, the fact is that doubling up typically occurs in the worst slum
sections and frequently involves the use of the same water, toilet, and other
facilities by several families. For example, in Chicago "From 1940 to 1950
there was a 50 percent increase in the number of dwellings without private
bath or toilet—the logical result of cutting apartments into small units
without installing sanitary improvements."[3] Hence, doubling up is a hint
that housing standards are deteriorating.

Many of the following questions can be answered with material from
volume one of the *U.S. Census of Housing,* for all urban communities of
2,500 or more population. Answers are not available by township or other
minor civil division, but are available by county. In addition, those studying
rural territory will find most of these questions broken down by the rural
farm and rural nonfarm portion of their county. For many of the larger
cities, block statistics and census tract figures are available in even greater
detail than the questions require. Chapter 19 of this book includes a brief
description of block statistics and Census tract figures. It is well to keep
in mind that Census figures are valid only for the year in which the Census
was taken.

1. How many dwelling units are there in your community? How many of these
   are owner occupied? Renter occupied? Vacant?
2. Of owner-occupied dwelling units, how many are occupied by whites?
   Negroes? Other races?
3. Of renter-occupied dwelling units, how many are occupied by whites?
   Negroes? Other races?
4. How many vacant dwelling units are there for rent or for sale?[4]
5. Is it easy or difficult to find a suitable dwelling in your community to purchase
   or to rent in the low-priced range? Medium-priced range? Upper-priced
   range?

[1] American Public Health Association, New York, 1945–1950.
[2] Rev. ed. Committee on the Hygiene of Housing, American Public Health Association,
New York, 1946.
[3] *Facts About Chicago's Low-Rent Public Housing.* Chicago Housing Authority, 1951,
p. 21.
[4] The Census term is "vacant nonseasonal not dilapidated, for rent or for sale."

6. Are there evidences of insufficient housing, such as doubling up, overcrowding, and so on?
7. How many building permits for new housing units were issued during the past year?
For what types of housing were these permits issued? Are they the types of housing for which there is the greatest need?
8. Which municipal government departments have a direct interest in housing construction in your community?
9. Which types of control are exercised over new housing construction:
   Zoning   Multiple dwelling law   Subdivision control
   Building code   Sanitary code   Architectural review
10. Do any of these controls operate needlessly to hamper new housing construction through:
    Costly but structurally unnecessary specifications designed to "make work" for the building trades
    Outmoded specifications which are holdovers from an earlier technological era
    Other unnecessary hindrances
11. If your community has a building code, when was it written? By whom is it enforced?
Has the code been amended to keep it up to date with present economical and sound construction practices?[1]
12. How do the requirements compare with those suggested by the Committee on the Hygiene of Housing[2] as to:
    Light, air, and ventilation   Structural provisions
    Fire protection   Proportion of building site
    Plumbing and drainage   to be left open
    Garbage and waste removal
13. What agency enforces these provisions in your community?
14. Does your state provide a uniform building code for municipalities? Is it kept up to date?
Has your community adopted this code?
15. How many violations were reported during the past year, and what was done about them?
16. Are there special groups with acute housing needs in your community:
    Low-income families   Veterans
    Certain minority groups Other
    Aged couples
17. What are the local estimates (by the housing department or authority or by local real estate boards) of the number and types of new housing units needed annually during the next few years?

[1] See Colean, Miles L., *Your Building Code*, National Committee on Housing, Inc., New York, 1946.
[2] See reference, p. 66.

18. Is new construction of the type and volume required being carried on to meet these needs?

Aside from the number of dwelling units is the question of their adequacy from the standpoint of health and wholesome living. Many data from the Census will give a good indication of the extent of certain inadequacies in the housing of your community. If your community is broken down by Census tracts or block statistics, it will be easier to locate the specific areas where inadequate housing is concentrated.

Overcrowding, inadequate facilities, dilapidation—these are the characteristic signs of the slum. That such conditions are not confined to the heart of the metropolis is indicated by the fact that overcrowding (as measured by the usual standard of more than 1.5 persons per room) is much higher for the rural nonfarm population than for the urban population. Overcrowding is most severe among nonwhite rural nonfarm renters, but both white owners and renters are more overcrowded in the rural nonfarm sections than in the urban.[1]

19. How many dwelling units are dilapidated?[2]
20. How many dwelling units either have no private bath or are dilapidated?[3]
21. How many dwelling units either have no running water or are dilapidated?
22. How many dwelling units do not use gas or electricity as a cooking fuel?
23. How many dwelling units have no:

Hot and cold running water	Central heating
Private flush toilet	Kitchen sink
Private bathtub or shower	Mechanical or ice
Electric lighting	refrigeration

24. How many occupied dwelling units have the following number of persons per room:

0.75 or less	1.01 to 1.50
0.76 to 1.00	1.51 or more[4]
	Not reported

25. How many dwelling units were built in the following years:[5]

1945 or later	1930 to 1939	1919 or earlier
1940 to 1944	1920 to 1929	

[1] See The 1950 Housing Situation in Charts: Based on Preliminary Results of the 1950 Census of Housing, Revised June, 1952, Government Printing Office, Washington, p. 23. This booklet is useful as a basis for comparing your community with the rest of the nation on various Census of Housing findings.
[2] "A dwelling unit was reported as dilapidated when it had serious deficiencies, was rundown or neglected, or was of inadequate original construction, so that it did not provide adequate shelter or protection against the elements or endangered the safety of the occupants." U.S. Census of Housing: 1950, vol. 1.
[3] Figures for this and the following question are available for all incorporated places and for unincorporated places of 1,000 to 2,500. These are an excellent, simple index of slum conditions.
[4] A rough measure of overcrowding is the "1.51 or more" category.
[5] Answers to the preceding questions are available in the U.S. Census of Housing for all

26. Are there areas of your community where there is a large concentration of undesirable housing as indicated by the answers to the preceding questions?

27. Are there other unhealthy or unwholesome features of these neighborhoods:
    Industrial smoke, gases, noises, odors
    Traffic or other street noises
    Traffic dangers to pedestrians
    Unprotected railroad crossings
    Unsafe or abandoned buildings or dumps which present a hazard to playing children
    Houses of prostitution, taverns, existing on residential blocks

28. How do these areas compare with the more desirable residential areas in such features as:
    Proximity to schools, playgrounds, and parks
    Width of streets and sidewalks
    Paving and repair of streets
    Lighting of streets
    Frequency of garbage and refuse collection
    Promptness of snow removal

29. Are there areas of lodging and boarding houses?
    Are such dwellings licensed? Inspected?
    Who inspects them, and according to what code?

A third consideration is whether dwelling units are available in balanced quantities for various income levels, types of structure, and location. Often, low- and middle-rent housing is not available in sufficient quantities. But in addition, there are the needs of those who prefer apartment house living, or single family living, or those who prefer to live within walking distance of the city center or out toward the periphery. Another consideration is that the size of the available dwelling units be appropriate to the proportion of families of different sizes.

30. How many dwelling units are there of each type of structure:

1 dwelling unit, detached	3 and 4 dwelling units
1 dwelling unit, attached	5 to 9 dwelling units
1 and 2 dwelling units, semidetached	10 dwelling units or more
Other 2 dwelling units	Trailers

31. How many dwelling units rent for the following monthly sums:

Less than $10	$30 to $39	$60 to $74
$10 to $19	$40 to $49	$75 to $99
$20 to $29	$50 to $59	$100 or more

32. What is the median monthly rent of dwelling units in your community?

___

places of 2,500 or more population, and in most cases for the rural farm and rural non-farm portions of each county.

33. How many single family structures are valued in each of the following
    categories:[1]

Less than $3,000	$ 7,500 to $ 9,999
$3,000 to $3,999	$10,000 to $14,999
$4,000 to $4,999	$15,000 or more
$5,000 to $7,499	Not reported

34. How many owner-occupied dwelling units are mortgaged? Not mortgaged?
    Not reported?[2]

Slum Clearance and Urban Redevelopment

In urban areas, the Housing Act of 1949 is the basis for a widespread
program including slum clearance, community development and redevelopment, and low-rent public housing.[3] The slum clearance program makes
financial aid available to local communities in the form of loans to acquire
land and prepare it for its new use and grants to help share whatever loss
the community entails between the price of purchase of the slum land and
the price of resale for its new uses. New uses for slum-cleared land must
be in keeping with an adequate community plan. "After the land is acquired, it may be sold, leased, or transferred for uses consistent with local
redevelopment plans. Redevelopment may include housing, industrial, business or commercial use, parks, schools, or public housing projects."[4] It
thus becomes possible for communities to rebuild whole sections of their
worst slum areas and put them to new use in accordance with a forward-
looking plan.

35. Has your state any enabling legislation which permits communities like
    your own to participate in the slum clearance and redevelopment program
    of the Housing Act of 1949?[5]
36. Does your state enabling legislation permit the following activities which
    are necessary if the local community is to participate fully in the slum
    clearance program:
    Specific enabling legislation for community slum clearance and urban
        redevelopment activities

[1] The heading for the Census table giving this information is "Value of Nonfarm Owner-
Occupied Dwelling Units, by Color, and Vacant-for-Sale Dwelling Units." Careful reading
of the "fine print" will avoid misinterpretation of the figures.
[2] Answers for all the foregoing questions except the last are available in the *Census of
Housing* for urban communities of 2,500 or more. Answers to the last question are available only for urban communities of 10,000 or more.
[3] See *The Relationship Between Slum Clearance and Urban Redevelopment and Low-
Rent Public Housing,* Housing and Home Finance Agency, Government Printing Office,
Washington, 1950.
[4] *The Local Community Job Under the Housing Act of 1949,* p. 5.
[5] The pamphlet *The Local Community Job Under the Housing Act of 1949* has been
used as a guide in formulating many of the questions in this and the following section.

Municipalities enabled to borrow from federal or other sources

Municipalities enabled to accept federal grants-in-aid

Municipalities enabled to make cash grants for local redevelopment undertakings

Sufficiently broad legislation to permit local land-use planning

No limitations on size of municipality which may engage in program

37. Has your municipality a duly authorized housing authority, or redevelopment agency, or department of the city government prepared to handle redevelopment work?

38. Are there any plans for slum clearance in your community at present? Are they such as to qualify for federal support?

39. Have they been made as an integral part of your community plan?

40. Are slum clearance projects now underway? In what stage is each project:

Slum area selected	Land acquired
Plans drawn	Buildings razed, streets changed,
Housing provided for displaced families	or other physical work done
	Land sold, leased, or.transferred
Plans approved by governing body	for new uses
Public hearing held	

41. Do redevelopment plans call for decreasing the density in tracts which will be put to residential use in the new land-use plan?

42. What plans have been made for rehousing any residents who will be displaced by slum clearance activity?

43. Will part of the cleared area be used for new housing? What income groups will it serve? What rents will be charged?

What community services will be needed, and how will they be provided?

44. What steps have been taken, in connection with slum clearance and redevelopment, to modernize and improve building codes? Modernize zoning ordinances? Modernize health, safety, and similar codes? Prevent the recurrence of slum conditions?

45. Are any individuals or companies engaged in demolition work in slum areas as a private venture in order to rebuild for residential or business use?

46. Are such private slum clearance activities made to accord with the desired land use for these tracts in the community's plan for future development?

Low-Rent and Limited Dividend Housing

The low-rent housing program under the Housing Act of 1949 includes both loans and contributions to local communities which meet certain requirements in order to help them develop low-rent housing projects. Such projects must be locally tax exempt, although local housing authorities may make payments in lieu of taxes up to 10 per cent of shelter rents. The local community must agree to eliminate unsafe or unsanitary dwellings equal in number to the newly constructed units within a period of five years, unless the site is declared to be a slum clearance area. There must be a local housing authority which determines the need, selects the site, cooperates with the federal Public Housing Administration, carries on construction work by means of contracts with private bidders, finances the project through sale of long-term bonds, and operates and administers the project. Federal Public Housing Administration loans are available for various purposes in connection with the projects, although privately subscribed loans are preferred. Annual federal contributions to the local housing authority are made in order to help it keep rents low.[1]

State and local governments have also been active for many years in the field of low-rent and limited dividend housing. State low-rent housing programs involve financial help to local housing authorities in financing low-rent dwelling units. Limited dividend housing is carried on by private capital, but the state exempts the company from all state taxes and fees in the venture and the local municipality may make some tax concessions. In exchange, the private company agrees to a limited return on the rental of the property, usually 6 per cent, and to the necessary inspection to assure the carrying out of the agreement. The housing is privately financed, and subsidized only through tax exemptions, but even so it is in a favorable position to charge moderate rentals for the medium-income group, which also often suffers from lack of adequate housing facilities at a price it can afford. Cooperative housing projects are also possible under this plan.

An important problem in large housing projects is that of adequate provision for community facilities, and the question of which facilities should be provided for the project alone and which for other citizens in the vicinity.[2]

47. Does state legislation enable your community to establish a local housing authority to participate in the federal low-rent housing program?
48. Is there a housing authority in your community? Is its area of jurisdiction a town? City? County? Group of counties?
49. Are copies of the local housing authority's annual report readily available? What is ascertainable from this document as to housing needs and the existing program of your local housing authority as well as its future plans for projects?
50. If your community does not have a local housing authority, is there a need for one?
51. Is there a need for a public low-rent housing program in your community?

[1] The low-rent housing program was drastically reduced and extended for only one year by the 83d Congress in 1954.
[2] An excellent checklist for detailed study of large housing projects is the "Engelhardt-Keller Check List for Enlightenment and Recreation in Relation to Large-Scale Housing Projects," in N. L. Engelhardt's article entitled "Interrelation of Schools and Large-Scale Housing," *The School Executive*, vol. 68, June, 1949.

Has any official study been given to this need?

What groups of people are involved? What neighborhoods are particularly affected?

52. Are any low-rent housing programs now underway?

Are they receiving financial or other help from your state housing authority? Are they participating in the federal low-rent housing program?

53. What facilities such as community centers, recreation rooms, nursery schools, health centers, craft rooms are available in the public housing?

54. What plans have been made for providing community services for the inhabitants of the housing project:

School	Playgrounds
Shopping center	Churches
Parks	Transportation facilities

55. Are these plans based on a procedure which would segregate low-rent tenants from other citizens in the vicinity in their utilization of local facilities?

56. What provisions are being made for people who will be displaced by the low-rent housing project but whose incomes are too high to qualify them for admission to this or other low-rent projects?

57. What rents are charged in the low-rent projects?

58. Has any study been made of what happens to people discharged from low-rent projects because their income has grown to exceed the permissible maximum? What happens to this critical group?

59. Are there any limited dividend housing projects in your community financed by private investors? Cooperative housing?

60. Which of the following stipulations must be met for a project to qualify for limited dividend housing:

Rents adjusted so as to limit returns

Periodic inspection

Stipulations against minority group discrimination

Other

61. What benefits does the company derive from limited dividend housing:

State tax exemption   Local tax exemption, full or partial   Other

62. In low-rent and limited dividend housing projects, has sufficient attention been given to the problems indicated in the following questions:

Are these projects increasing population density at the city center, or decreasing it?

Are they carefully integrated with other aspects of planning such as parking facilities, traffic congestion and traffic flow, availability of schools, playgrounds, postoffices, shopping centers, rapid transit facilities, churches, and so on?

An issue which comes up in public housing is the question of racial segregation. The federal housing policy is based on the "equal facilities" principle and thus permits segregation.[1] Various state and municipal ordinances make specific provision against discrimination of any kind in their public housing projects. Limited dividend housing often is based on the exclusion of Negroes. Occasionally, legislators, officials, and private companies are sincerely concerned about the injustice of discrimination, but fear possible social unrest and violence if the housing is made interracial. Frequently, this fear is a screen behind which the prejudiced may hide. Where it is genuine, a most useful pamphlet is *Open Occupancy in Public Housing: A Bulletin Based Upon Local Experience in the Administration of Federally Aided Low-Rent Public Housing Projects Occupied by More than One Racial Group.*[2] It includes an excellent bibliography. An instructive pamphlet on discrimination in housing is *In These Ten Cities.*[3]

63. Are any racial or religious groups barred from or discriminated against in connection with:
     Private housing developments
     Limited dividend housing developments
     Low-rent housing developments
64. In each instance, what is the policy within the specific housing project:
     Separate but equal housing projects for nonwhites
     Separate buildings within the same housing development
     No distinctions made whatsoever
65. Is there a state or municipal law, ordinance, or resolution specifically forbidding racial discrimination in specific types of housing projects?
66. Where interracial housing is provided, which of the following steps are taken:
     Consideration given to interracial nature of project in selection of the site
     Clearly defined and publicized interracial policy
     Conferences with staff
     Conferences with tenants
     Clear explanation of policies on occasion of application for admission
     Interracial staff
     Deliberate avoidance of racial "islands" in the location of tenants
     Care in the selection of tenants on the matter of interracial tolerance
     Specific provisions which terminate the lease because of disturbances by tenant, "including disturbances based on interracial intolerance."
67. What has been the experience of your community with respect to segregated or "integrated" housing?

[1] Recent Supreme Court decisions, notably that of May 17, 1954, outlawing segregation in the nation's public schools, indicate that the days of the "separate but equal" policy in housing may likewise be numbered.
[2] Public Housing Administration, Government Printing Office, Washington, 1953. The questions which follow are adapted from this pamphlet.
[3] Public Affairs Committee, New York, 1951.

Neighborhoods as Units of Housing

Housing is inseparably related to community planning in a number of ways. Much of the need for new housing stems from deterioration and blight caused by poor planning. For this reason, the slum clearance and urban redevelopment program involves extensive community planning before a project is approved.[1] Again, the opening of new subdivisions calls for careful planning in connection with the relation of the new subdivision to the rest of the community—its highways, transit systems, schools, hospitals, taxes, and so forth. The location of low-rent subsidized housing or limited dividend housing involves careful decisions as to whether to build the project near the city center or out toward the periphery, what to do with people who are displaced by the razing of the old structures, and what the demands of the new tenants will be on existing municipal services.

Community planning for housing has come to be based more and more on the "neighborhood unit" approach. As first outlined by Clarence Arthur Perry,[2] the neighborhood unit has six essentials:

1. *Size* . . . housing for that population for which one elementary school is ordinarily required. . . .

2. *Boundaries.* The unit should be bounded on all sides by arterial streets, sufficiently wide to facilitate its by-passing by all through traffic.

3. *Open Spaces.* A system of small parks and recreation spaces, planned to meet the needs of the particular neighborhood, should be provided.

4. *Institution Sites.* Sites for the school and other institutions having service spheres coinciding with the limits of the unit should be suitably grouped about a central point, or common.

5. *Local Shops.* One or more shopping districts . . . should be laid out in the circumference of the unit, preferably at traffic junctions and adjacent to similar districts of adjoining neighborhoods.

6. *Internal Street System* . . . the street net as a whole being designed to facilitate circulation within the unit and to discourage its use by through traffic.

Principles widely accepted and utilized include: elementary school, play area, and shops within walking distance; no through-traffic barriers between children's homes and their school and play space; street pattern which discourages through traffic; homogeneous character of neighborhood; adequate green space; streets roughly following contours.[3] Related in one way or another to the neighborhood unit concept are land-use controls such as sub-

[1] See *Community Planning:* Excerpt from Local Public Agency Manual, Housing and Home Finance Agency, Government Printing Office, Washington, no date.
[2] *The Neighborhood Unit.* Monograph I in vol. 7 of the Regional Survey of New York and Its Environs. Committee on Regional Plan of New York, 1929, pp. 34–35.
[3] See chart on p. 91.

division control; the design of multi-storied apartment projects, public or private (although these often violate the proviso for adequate shops, play space, and institutional services nearby); the "superblock" pattern of such planned communities as Radburn, New Jersey, and the layout of the green-belt communities of the Resettlement Administration.[1] Community planners are increasingly employing the neighborhood as the unit of planning, and neighborhood associations have grown up to give organizational structure to the local neighborhood.[2] Neighborhood blight prevention programs have been encouraged in Chicago with its Commission on Neighborhood Conservation, and by the Regional Association of Cleveland, which published in 1943 the useful booklet *Neighborhood Conservation:* A Handbook for Citizen Groups.

68. Has the neighborhood been used as a unit of planning in your community?
69. If possible, obtain from the local planning commission or housing authority a copy of a map which delineates the neighborhoods considered as units for purposes of planning.
70. Do the neighborhood delineations recognize such features as:
      Natural barriers, such as rivers, cliffs, swamps, and so on
      Homogeneous areas including much the same type of land-use pattern
      Historical neighborhoods with place names and strong local sentiment
      Administrative districts for which various figures are available
71. In new housing projects and subdivision developments, are the following features of neighborhood unit planning incorporated:
      Access streets designed to discourage through traffic
      Adequate arteries at the periphery of the neighborhood for by-passing
      Elementary schools and play space within walking distance
      Shopping centers at the periphery
72. Are subdivisions smaller than a "neighborhood" approved according to a plan whereby several together will constitute a functioning neighborhood with its local elementary school and other facilities?
73. Does your planning board or housing authority favor neighborhoods comprised of different income groups, types of houses, and so on, or does it favor fairly complete homogeneity in such matters?
74. Are any specific encouragement and help given to the development of neighborhood councils by official planning agencies or voluntary community organization agencies?
75. Does your planning commission engage in planning activities for neighborhood conservation, to help neighborhoods ward off blight and conserve the attractive features of the neighborhood?

[1] See Dahir, James, *The Neighborhood Unit Plan:* Its Spread and Acceptance, Russell Sage Foundation, New York, 1947. This pamphlet is out of print but it may be consulted in many libraries.
[2] For various physical specifications in neighborhood planning, see *Planning the Neighborhood*, Public Administration Service, Chicago, 1948.

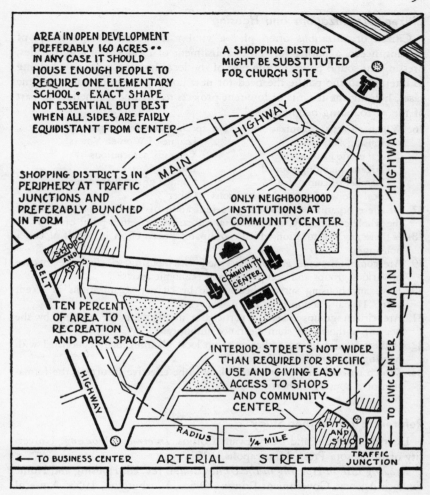

PERRY'S PLAN FOR THE NEIGHBORHOOD UNIT

Charts help to dress up a report, and in addition supplement such description as is given in the text. This chart illustrates the basic essentials of Perry's "neighborhood unit plan."

SOURCE: *The Neighborhood Unit*, Monograph I of vol. 7 of Regional Survey of New York, 1929.

Citizen Organizations and Housing

Citizen organizations often play a vital role in sponsoring surveys of housing needs, agitating for the establishment of local housing authorities, pressing for sound policy on the part of the local housing authority, helping to interpret to the public the need for new housing measures and, in some cases, helping the tenants of low-rent projects to become a functioning part of the surrounding neighborhood.

76. Which citizens' organizations have a special interest in housing:

Housing association	League of Women Voters[1]
Real estate association	Veterans' associations
Citizens' planning council	Labor unions
Chamber of commerce	Council of social agencies
Local property owners' associations	Other

77. Of these organizations, which give indication of working for the good of the whole community, and which take a narrow or selfish point of view?
78. Is there any organization which coordinates citizen effort in behalf of better housing?
79. Are communitywide groups concerned with housing widely representative of various groups and occupations and economic levels?
80. Have any housing surveys been made by citizen organizations in recent years? Has any action been taken as a result?
81. Are citizen groups asked to participate in planning for housing by the housing authority or slum clearance authority?
82. If there is no housing authority or no local planning body concerned with housing, is there a need for one?
83. Which citizens' groups are most likely to be effective in urging the formation of a housing authority?

References for Further Study

Deutsch, Morton, and Mary Evans Collins, *Interracial Housing*. University of Minnesota Press, Minneapolis, 1951.

Reading List on Housing in the United States. rev. ed. Housing and Home Finance Agency, Government Printing Office, Washington, 1953. A useful and comprehensive bibliography.

Straus, Nathan, *The Seven Myths of Housing*. Alfred A. Knopf, New York, 1944. This is a popular introduction to the function and promise of public housing programs. It is organized around seven "myths," or widely held misconceptions about housing, such as "The slum dweller creates the slums."

[1] See *Guide for Local Current Agenda Work on Housing*, League of Women Voters of the U.S., Washington, 1949, mimeographed.

7. Education

To the extent that education involves the transmission of various parts of the culture to new generations, it takes place in all social institutions and is by no means the exclusive prerogative of the schools. Three areas of contemporary life afford opportunities for such "education" which are believed to be at least as important as the school in their influence upon the facts, attitudes, and behavior patterns which the child acquires. These are the child's own play group, through which he acquires attitudes, manners of behavior, and a vocabulary not always completely acceptable to the school; the family, which has the child earlier, and longer, and in more intimate, sustained relation than any other institution; and the various means of mass communication, including radio, television, motion pictures, comic books, newspapers, magazines, and so on. As the child grows older, he is more and more likely to participate in the work of formal associations, clubs, and interest groups, which are important media of adult education.[1] The reason that schools are so often singled out for attention when education is discussed is that they are especially organized to fulfill this function, and great reliance is placed upon their effectiveness. This chapter is confined largely to the schools, especially the public schools, of your community.

The extensiveness of public school effort in the United States is indicated by the fact that there are approximately 25 million children enrolled in the nation's public schools who are taught by nearly a million teachers at a total annual expense of nearly six billion dollars.[2] American public school education extends to all regions and classes of people. Modern optimum standards call for universal free education not only through the high-school years but on into two years of college, institute, or other education at public expense for every child who is capable of benefiting by the experience. Despite these standards, there are many communities in which only a minority of children ever finish high school. Extreme variation in public

[1] See Chapter 14 for mass communication media and other forms of communication, and Chapter 16 for associations.
[2] These figures are as of 1950.

93

school facilities exists among communities in different parts of the country. Public education has moved rapidly in the past few decades, particularly in the direction of greater flexibility of curriculum, more attention to real life situations and needs, increasing concern for the personality development and social responsibility of students, and provision of specialized services in such fields as health, guidance, and vocational training. Nevertheless, as late as 1950 one-teacher schools comprised 44 per cent of the total schools, although, of course, not of the total enrollment. While it is extremely difficult for smaller schools to supply the multitude of specialized services which larger schools can supply, there may nevertheless be compensating advantages, which will be discussed later.

Perhaps one of the most important developments has been the trend, not without controversy, from the old-fashioned "subject-centered" school to the "pupil-centered" school, from strict conformity to self-expression, from "discipline" to "guidance." Before conducting your survey you may want to read such material as *How Good Is Your School? A Handbook to Help Parents* by Wilbur A. Yauch;[1] *The American High School:* Its Responsibility and Opportunity edited by Hollis L. Caswell,[2] and *High Schools for Tomorrow* by Dan Stiles.[3]

In conducting your study, you will be helped immeasurably by the fact that so many data about the schools are available in the regular reports made to the state education department. Your state or local department will be able to help answer questions about the education law, state aid, the administrative hierarchy, and so on. Occasionally, special studies in such fields as attendance, curriculum, placement, drop-outs, and other matters may have been made within the local school system and be available to you. In communities with more than one school, it will be necessary to gather facts concerning each of the schools. While in larger communities many of these may be available in the office of the superintendent of schools, a visit to each school may be necessary and in any case it is highly recommended. Sources of data will also include the annual reports of the board of education and special studies conducted by teachers associations or school study councils. In the reports of the state department of education you may be able to secure facts about other communities of similar size in the state with which you can then compare your own. From this source you may also obtain helpful pamphlet material. You will, of course, want to interpret the questions in the light of your own community size and characteristics. A largely agricultural community will have different school needs from

[1] Harper and Bros., New York, 1951.
[2] Harper and Bros., New York, 1946.
[3] Harper and Bros., New York, 1946.

a metropolitan community, although it should not be forgotten that approximately half of rural youth end up in the cities. Other community characteristics may likewise influence the school program.

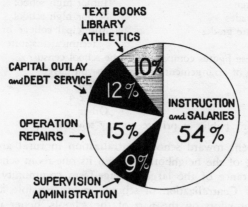

EXPENDITURES OF THE TENAFLY, NEW JERSEY, SCHOOL SYSTEM

Pie charts are helpful in showing the relative proportions of different items in the community budget, or in such aspects as education, health, and local government. The number of categories shown should not be so numerous as to be confusing.

SOURCE: *This Is Tenafly*, a "Know-Your-Town" study published by the League of Women Voters of Tenafly, N.J.

Structure and Administration

1. Under what state, county, or other education authorities does your local school system operate?
2. What is the organization of school administration in your local public school system—board of education, superintendent of schools, principals, and so on?
3. Are members of your community's school board chosen by election or appointment? If elected, how are they nominated? If appointed, by whom?
4. Is your school board politically dominated? Do the individual members have a record of sincere interest in public education?
5. Does your school board confine itself chiefly to making policy while delegating the execution of this policy to the superintendent of schools or other administrative officials?
   Or does the school board devote its entire time to routine or detailed matters, thus diverting attention from the important policymaking function?
6. Does the school board have the power to levy taxes?
7. How is the superintendent of schools chosen? What are his qualifications? Is his job relatively permanent, or subject to change in political party fortunes? Does he have tenure?

8. List the schools which are part of the public school system.
9. How many students are enrolled in each of the following levels in your community's school system:

Kindergarten	Junior high school
Primary grades	Senior high school
Intermediate grades	Municipal college or technical institute

10. How do these figures compare with the school census?
11. Which type of arrangement of grades do you have:[1]

K-8-4	K-6-6
K-6-3-3	K-6-2-4
	Other

12. Are there any public or private nursery schools?

The movement toward school centralization in rural areas reflects the gradual decline of the neighborhood with its one-room school and the increasing importance of the larger village-farm community as a basis for social services.[2] Centralization of schools makes possible a more efficient specialization of effort on the part of the schools, better paid and better trained teachers, more specialized services, wider course offerings, and many other benefits. Nevertheless, a number of educational leaders feel that it is possible to take centralization too far, and that there are important advantages to having the school, particularly the elementary school, in the local community. It is possible for the smaller school to keep in close touch with parents, adapt curriculum to individual needs, and be closely integrated into the local community life, but this takes imagination and initiative.[3]

13. Has your community a centralized school district on the high-school level? Junior-high level? Elementary level?
14. Does the centralized school district coincide roughly with a genuine community? (See Chapter 19.)
15. If centralized, what percentage of students come from rural areas?
16. Is there a movement underway for further consolidation at primary level? Secondary level?
17. Do you have a system of small neighborhood primary schools offering two, three, or four years in the elementary grades?
18. If you do not have a centralized school system, is there a movement underway to develop one?

[1] K is for kindergarten, the first numeral is for grade school, the other numerals for junior-senior high school. The combinations listed are the more frequent ones, but your community's pattern may differ.
[2] See Sanderson, Dwight, *School Centralization and the Rural Community*, Cornell Extension Bulletin 445, Ithaca, N.Y., 1940.
[3] See *Modern Ways in One and Two Teacher Schools*, Office of Education, Government Printing Office, Washington, 1951.

What reasons are advanced by those who favor it and those who oppose it? Is thorough consideration being given to the relation of the central school district to the local community?

19. If you do not have a centralized school system, how many high-school students come from "sending areas"?

Finance. In examining the cost figures of your school system, it should not be supposed that high costs in themselves necessarily imply either excellent school facilities on the one hand or extravagance on the other. There is, nonetheless, usually a positive relationship between expenditures and the quality of instruction supplied. The total current expenditure per pupil in average daily attendance for rural schools was $173 and for urban schools $206 in 1947–1948. In 1950–1951 the median figure was $219 for a sample of 259 city school systems of various sizes.[1] Figures from your own state may give you a more specific basis for comparison.[2] Nevertheless, it should be emphasized that comparative statistics on cost of education may be highly misleading unless one explores the possible differences in quality of school plant, personnel, and services. Your community's per pupil cost may be high, but so may be the quality of its program.

20. What is your community's figure on the following quantitative measures:[3]
    Average salary of the instructional staff
    Average length of the school year in days
    Percentage of total number of teachers who are men
    Number of pupils per teacher
    Percentage of pupils enrolled who attend daily
21. What is the local source of revenue for the school system?
22. Do your schools receive federal, state, or county financial aid?
    What proportion of the total revenue is raised by local tax? State sources? Federal sources?
    Which revenues are from earmarked taxes? General fund?
    What state or federal aid is specifically designated for particular functions:

    Vocational education   Guidance
    The handicapped child   Other
    Safety education

[1] See *Education in Rural and City School Systems*, Circular No. 329, Office of Education, Government Printing Office, Washington, 1951; and *Expenditure per Pupil in City School Systems, 1950–51*, Circular No. 337, Office of Education, Government Printing Office, Washington, 1952. The former is issued every few years, the latter annually.

[2] If you are interested in studying elementary education in a city's school system, read *Organization and Supervision of Elementary Education in 100 Cities*, Office of Education, Government Printing Office, Washington, 1949.

[3] These as well as certain other measures are given by state for rural and urban elementary and high schools of different sized communities of 2,500 up in *Education in Rural and City School Systems*.

23. What is the annual current expenditure per pupil? How has this figure varied in the past ten years?[1]

24. What percentage of total current expenditure is used for each of the following:[1]

Administration	Maintenance of physical plant
Instruction	Auxiliary school services[2]
Operation of physical plant	Fixed charges

The illustration on page 95 gives one possible way of presenting financial data about the schools in simplified fashion.

Physical plant. The physical plant of the school system is an important adjunct to the educational process. Many school buildings are outdated. While old buildings may be difficult to adapt to changing needs, the construction of new buildings affords an opportunity to review the function of the school, particularly as to the type of educational experience which is to be offered (for example, should seats be fastened down in rows or movable, should there be tables and chairs for small group study projects, etc.) and as to the role of the school in the community. In many localities, the school's function as a center of community activities is becoming increasingly important.[3]

25. For each separate school building in active use, list the following information:

Date of construction

Area of grounds

Method of heating, artificial lighting, ventilating

Ratio of window area to floor area

Type of desks and seats (adjustable, nonadjustable; fixed, movable)

Toilets and washrooms (adequate, sanitary, properly separated as to sexes)

Infirmary or first-aid room

School library

Guidance room

Shop

Laboratory facilities for science classes

Facilities for music, art, and so forth

[1] This question and the preceding are framed so as to facilitate comparison between your community and others through the use of national statistics. See, for example, *Expenditure per Pupil in City School Systems*, which groups cities in five classes, from 2,500 on up to the largest. The statistics are presented each year. You may want to break down some of these divisions still further; for example, instruction can be divided into salaries, textbooks, supplies, and so forth.

[2] It should be realized that certain items, such as transportation, vary tremendously from one school system to another.

[3] For a detailed instrument for the evaluation of school plant facilities, see McLeary, Ralph D., *Guide for Evaluating School Buildings*, New England School Development Council, Cambridge, Mass., 1952.

Audio-visual equipment
Facilities for training handicapped children
Sanitary drinking fountains, cafeteria
Space and equipment for outdoor and indoor games and play
Gymnasiums, swimming pool, showers, lockers
Faculty rooms
Cleanliness of halls and classrooms
Attractiveness, decorations, and so on

26. Does your community have a racially segregated school system officially? Unofficially, but nonetheless real?
Compare the schools for whites and those for nonwhites on the items listed above.[1]

27. Are there any schools in which overcrowding is a particularly serious problem?

28. Are you now utilizing rooms for classrooms which were not originally intended for this purpose?

29. Approximately how many pupils are there per classroom in the elementary school? High school?

30. Do any of the schools have two sessions (early and late)?

31. Is there a plan for the development of the physical plant of the school system in the next ten years or so:
New buildings, additions, playgrounds to be added
Old buildings to be renovated or discarded
What are the state provisions for aid on capital programs?

32. Is school planning functionally integrated with other aspects of community planning? (See especially Chapter 5, but also Chapters 3, 6, and 8.)

Teachers

On the quality of the teachers depends the value of the entire public school effort. While at various times and places in the past, teaching has often been thought of as a marginal occupation to be taken up in case other opportunities are not readily available, today's demands upon the teacher require high intelligence, considerable initiative, and careful training. Throughout the country, teachers are in short supply, largely because of the large salary differential between them and persons with equal training and ability in other fields. A high level of teacher competence usually requires careful recruitment, thorough preparation, good salaries, and acceptable conditions as to academic freedom, tenure, retirement, and such matters.

33. What are your state requirements for the certification of teachers?

---

[1] See Chapter 15 for material on integration in the public schools.

100

34. How many teachers in your community's public schools are not fully certified?
How do your teachers compare with those of other communities in this respect?
35. How many teachers have had each of the following amounts of post high-school training:

| Less than two years | Four years |
| Two or three years | Five or more years |

36. What measures are taken to assure the continuation of study by teachers who are especially in need of it?
37. Is there an in-service training program for teachers?[1] Does it include:

Orientation program for new teachers	Special help from visiting instructors
Study groups	Special workshops in mental health
Curriculum committee	
Workshops	Plentiful opportunity to attend conferences
Case conferences	

38. Are teachers encouraged to make suggestions and participate in planning courses, choosing textbooks, and other such matters?
39. How do salaries of your school teachers compare with those of similar communities in your state?
40. What is the minimum teacher salary established by state law? Local authorities?
41. What provisions are there in the school system for teacher and administrative:

Hiring	Leaves for further study
Tenure	Retirement
Promotion	Sick leave and maternity leave
Dismissal for cause	

42. Is there a professional organization of teachers in your community? What is its program? How many local teachers are members?
43. Are suitable students in your schools encouraged to become teachers?
44. Are teachers carefully selected with a view toward personal and social competence as well as academic qualifications? To what extent?
Do the teachers appear to be genuinely fond of young people?
Are there any teachers who are reported to be autocratic or unkind or otherwise undesirable in their attitude toward their pupils?
45. Are there pressures on teachers in any of the following:
Censorship of textbooks
Censorship of books and periodicals in school library
Pressure to avoid "controversial issues" in the classroom

[1] For a fruitful approach to in-service training, see Bard, Harry, *Teachers and the Community:* An In-Service Program in Action, National Conference of Christians and Jews, New York, 1952.

Attempts to introduce propaganda materials of special interest groups into the curriculum

Undue restrictions on the private conduct of teachers and other school personnel

46. Are teachers required to take a special loyalty oath in addition to the usual pledge to support federal and state constitution?

47. Has the school system a carefully thought-out policy for dealing with situations where a teacher's loyalty to his country is questioned?

Does this policy protect pupils from indoctrination under guise of education, and protect teachers from irresponsible charges and peremptory dismissal without a hearing?

48. Do the local citizens treat the teachers as people, accepting them in their homes as friends, or is the relationship entirely formal and professional?

Are teachers allowed to lead a "normal" personal and social life without undue interference?

Are they expected to participate in various community activities (Sunday school, charity drives, and like functions) *because* they are teachers?

Instruction and Pupil Participation

While the layman is usually not competent to evaluate the technical aspects of teaching methods, curriculum, and related matters, these things add up to such great importance that they can hardly be overlooked in a study of the schools. There may be people in the community or in the vicinity who have had sufficient experience and training to evaluate some of these matters, but one should beware of self-constituted "experts" who are most readily identifiable by their propensity to make unqualified statements about almost any aspect of public education. The National Education Association or state and local educational associations can be of help in supplying materials, criteria, and in some cases consultants, as can the United States Office of Education and your state education department.

49. Is a year of kindergarten available for every child in your community?

50. To what extent are different teaching methods used in the classroom:

Lecture	Demonstrations	Committee work
Recitation	Discussions	Visual aids
Projects	Reports	Auditory aids

51. To what extent do the various classes seek to utilize the community as an area for study or for service?[1]

52. Are there carefully planned assembly programs?

Is there a budget for professional speakers or entertainers? How large is the budget?

[1] See *How Children Use the Community for Learning*, Educational Bulletin, No. 6, Government Printing Office, Washington, 1953.

53. What is the extent of the school library facilities and services?
54. Are other factors than scholastic achievement considered in evaluating pupil progress?
55. Are pupils grouped according to their ability?
    Has the policy with respect to grouping or nongrouping been given critical appraisal recently?
    Is there any special provision for pupils who are slow learners?
56. What provisions are made for exceptionally bright pupils?
57. What provisions are there to encourage pupils with exceptional talents:
    Musical   Artistic   Other
58. What is the promotion policy on the elementary, junior high-school, and senior high-school levels?
59. In the following items, are your school's policies such as to serve the needs of all the pupils, both those who are not going to college and those who are, rural and urban:
    Diploma requirements   Promotion policies
    Standards of scholastic   Teaching methods
      achievement   Extracurricular activities
    Grading systems
60. To what extent does the curriculum appear to be "subject centered," and to what extent is it specifically adapted to the needs of your community's children in their various stages and directions of development?
61. What is the school's procedure regarding cases of individual misconduct? Under what circumstances is a child sent to the principal for disciplinary action? To the guidance department for counseling?
62. Who has the power of suspension and expulsion?
63. List the courses which are taught in your junior high and senior high school. Which courses are compulsory?
64. What proportion of courses are in such "practical" subjects as:
    Homemaking   Commercial subjects   Driver education
    Vocational agriculture   Shop   Family living
65. Do you have a work experience program?[1]
66. Is there a continuing program of curriculum improvement?
67. What curricular changes have been instituted during the past five years? Do they represent changes in the direction of making the school's efforts more flexible in meeting the needs of the pupils of your community?[2]
68. Is there adequate coordination in curriculum, guidance, and other matters among the different grade and school levels?

[1] Read Dillon, Harold J., *Work Experience in Secondary Education:* A Study of Part-Time School and Work Programs, National Child Labor Committee, New York, 1946.
[2] Read *Education Unlimited:* A Community High School in Action, Office of Education, Government Printing Office, Washington, 1951.

69. What proportion of your young people complete four years of high school? Go on to college or other advanced training? Leave your community for other reasons upon graduation? Remain in your community but seek work immediately? Take up farming?

70. How does your school curriculum provide for the needs of these diverse groups?

71. Are children of migratory workers in your vicinity enrolled in the schools? Are they taken care of in special classes or among the others?

72. What provision is made for the instruction of children who for any reason cannot attend school?

73. What extracurricular activities are available to students:

Clubs	Music	Craft and hobby work	Dances and "socials"
Athletics	Drama	Publications	Student government

74. What percentage of the pupils participate in each?

75. What proportion of those taking part are rural?

76. What provisions are made to transport rural students who take part in extracurricular activities?

77. Is there a vigorous intramural athletic program which attracts the great bulk of pupils?

78. In what ways does the extracurricular program provide training for citizenship in the adult community:

By offering opportunities for sharing responsibility

Through participation in community affairs

By fostering contact with community leaders, agencies, and so on

79. Do the pupils come from diverse economic, religious, or nationality backgrounds?

Do the pupils tend to group themselves in their social relationships according to their family's income, or religion, or national background?

80. What deliberate program, if any, does your school system have for fostering good relations among pupils of different cultural background?[1]

81. Are teachers sensitive to the varying social backgrounds from which their pupils come, and do they try to "meet the pupil where he is"?

Of particular importance is the safety education program of the school, both in regard to school matters and such matters as driver training and accident prevention.

82. Do your schools conduct periodic fire drills? Bus drills?

83. What units or courses in safety education are offered in your schools? On what grade levels?

84. Is a driver training course available in the public schools?

[1] See Kilpatrick, William H., *Modern Education and Better Human Relations*, Anti-Defamation League of B'nai B'rith, New York, 1949.

Special Services

The growth of special services, particularly in the fields of guidance and health, is an indication of the school's tendency to acquire new functions. Guidance is thought of as imparting vocational and educational information which enables the pupil to make a wise choice in these matters, while counseling emphasizes the development of his personality, and the emotional and other problems concerning which he may need some help. Both guidance and counseling reflect the complexity of modern life, with the number of possible occupations running into the thousands and requiring a specialist's knowledge, and the strain and stress of modern living making it increasingly desirable for young people to have expert counseling on personal problems.

In the field of health, such measures as are taken in large well-staffed school systems play an important part in reducing the sickness and death rates from communicable and other diseases, lengthening the average expectation of life, and training people to lead wholesome, healthy lives.

It is in such special fields as guidance and health services that the larger school systems are at a distinct advantage, for it is financially feasible for them to employ the necessary specialized personnel. In the smaller schools this is not the case. For example, high schools with from 10 to 99 pupils, comprising 31 per cent of the nation's public high schools, rarely employ specialized professional personnel.[1] But rural school systems have not yet fully explored all the means of pooling their resources to obtain at least part-time service in such fields as dental hygiene, school nurse service, guidance and counseling, and the rest.[2]

85. To what extent are the following types of personnel available in your school system:

Guidance counselor

School physician

School nurse

Dental hygienist

Attendance supervisor

Visiting teacher

Psychologist

School social worker

Remedial reading teacher

Special teacher for physically or mentally handicapped children

Other

86. How close is the cooperation among these special personnel, and between them and individual classroom teachers?

87. With what community agencies do these specialized personnel cooperate in individual cases?

[1] *High School Staff and Size of School.* Circular No. 317, Office of Education, Government Printing Office, Washington, 1950. p. 24.

[2] Read *Broadening the Services of Small High Schools*, Office of Education, Government Printing Office, Washington, 1948.

Guidance and counseling

88. Is there a guidance counselor available to each secondary school? Primary school? Full-time? Part-time?
89. Do smaller school units cooperate with other schools to share a trained guidance counselor?
90. What is the professional training of guidance personnel?
91. Are all individual students aided by the counselor in the selection of courses appropriate to their interests and abilities? If not, what percentage? Who helps the others?
92. To what extent does the guidance program involve counseling in the following fields:

    Vocational   Psychological
    Social   Educational

93. Do the guidance personnel report that they have insufficient time for any or all of the above-mentioned aspects of guidance?
94. How many pupils are there for each guidance counselor?
95. What testing devices are a part of the guidance program:

    Intelligence   Achievement   Personality
    Aptitude   Interest   Other

96. Are there exploratory vocational courses?
97. Are cumulative, centralized records for each pupil maintained in the school? How are they used in helping the pupil?
98. Does your program include follow-up services for out-of-school youth? How many students are interviewed annually?
99. Has any study been made of the percentage of high-school graduates who remain in your community? Of the college graduates who return to settle down in your community?
100. Do your school personnel have a guidance or mental health clinic available for referral of students in need of such service? (See Chapter 12.)
101. Are there any nonschool counseling services for youth available in your community in public employment offices? Social agencies? Elsewhere?
102. Is there a department of visiting teachers or school social workers? What professional training have these workers had? What are their functions?

Attendance and drop-outs

103. Who supervises attendance? What professional preparation has he (she)? What salary does he receive?
     Is the position full-time? Part-time?
104. What percentage of students are absent daily?
105. Is attendance thought of primarily as a disciplinary function or as a counseling function?
106. Is there a truancy problem in your community? What is being done about it?

107. What are the compulsory attendance ages in your state?

108. Have any recent studies been made of the drop-out situation in your schools?
    What do they indicate are the principal reasons pupils drop out?

109. What proportion of the high-school freshman class drop out before graduation? As a policy, are these students interviewed before they leave? What percentage have a record of academic failure? What percentage are rural students?

110. Is anything being done to try to prevent premature drop-outs?[1]

Health services and handicapped children

111. Are the health services in the school organized under one specific department with a well-planned overall program and competent staff?

112. Are careful physical examinations given to each pupil by a physician at least once a year?
    How many minutes, on the average, does each examination require?[2]
    What is done to follow up cases where remedial defects have been found or where action is otherwise indicated?
    Are parents informed of the need for corrective care? Are they helped in arranging for corrective care?
    Are parents invited to attend the physical examinations? Are they notified of the results of these examinations?

113. Are preschool physical examinations held with parents present?

114. Are preschool inoculation clinics held?

115. Are special x-ray or tuberculin tests given in the school system?

116. Are special eye examinations given? Hearing examinations?

117. Are special dental examinations given? What other dental hygiene services are available?

118. In each of the preceding cases, what is done about follow-up work where action is indicated?

119. Is there a full-time or part-time school physician?

120. Is there a full-time or part-time school nurse?

121. Is there a close working relationship maintained between health personnel, physical education teachers, guidance personnel, classroom teachers, and parents?

122. Is there effective coordination of the health program with related community services such as outpatient clinics, child guidance clinics, family physicians, and so on?

123. Is there special instruction in health and nutrition? At what grade levels? How much? By whom?

[1] Read Dillon, Harold J., *Early School Leavers:* A Major Educational Problem, National Child Labor Committee, New York, 1949.
[2] See also Chapters 12 and 13 for other health matters relative to the school.

124. Does your school have a hot lunch program?
125. What other services in connection with the health of school children are regularly available or are available when needed in your school system?
126. Do children with the following types of handicap follow the regular curriculum:[1]

Visual	Orthopedic
Auditory	Malnutrition
Speech	Emotional maladjustment
Heart diseases	Mental deficiency
Epileptic seizures	Glandular disturbances

127. What special provision is made for these children?[2]
128. Does your curriculum include any of the following types of special class:

Remedial reading	Hygiene
Sight saver	Physical therapy
Speech correction	Home teaching
Lip reading	Other

How often are these classes held? Are they available for children of all ages, or only during certain years?
129. Are rural children given the opportunity to benefit by such services as are available?
130. Does the guidance counselor give special attention to any adjustment problems of children with various handicaps:

Vocational planning	Performance of school work
Emotional adjustment	Social participation

131. What special provisions are made for slow learners?
132. What special help is available for emotionally disturbed children?[3]

The School and the Community

Developments have moved so rapidly in the field of public education in the past few decades that often school officials have failed to keep the public sufficiently informed on the newer trends and the reasoning behind them.[4] As a result, there is often confusion among parents and other community people as to what the schools are trying to do, and misgiving as

[1] Several helpful pamphlets on education and various types of exceptional children are published by the U.S. Office of Education and available through the Government Printing Office. See *Publications List* cited at the end of this chapter.
[2] For questions on community facilities and programs for the handicapped, see Chapter 13.
[3] See Chapter 12 for further questions concerning mental health and provisions for the mentally ill.
[4] See Scott, C. Winfield, and Clyde M. Hill, editors, *Public Education Under Criticism*, Prentice-Hall, Inc., New York, 1954; and Yeager, William A., *School-Community Relations*, Dryden Press, New York, 1951.

to whether the newer developments may not be undermining the values which they have come to associate with the public schools. Thus, questions often arise as to whether the schools are paying sufficient attention to teaching the "essentials," including spelling, reading, writing, arithmetic; as to whether the guidance program is not an expensive luxury; as to why magnificent new buildings should be necessary when the older generation had its training in one-room schoolhouses; and so on. Because the home is so crucially important in the education of the young, the schools need the informed cooperation of parents. For this reason, it is essential that parents understand what the schools are trying to do in general, and how this relates to their own children in particular.

133. Is there a parents' day or any similar occasion on which parents are especially invited to attend the school?
134. Are parents otherwise encouraged to visit the school?
135. Have school officials published recently a "handbook" for parents clarifying their rights, privileges, and responsibilities in relation to the school?
136. Does the board of education take various measures to interpret its problems, needs, and policies to the parents and citizens of the community?
137. What is the extent of citizen participation in:
    School board elections   Annual school meetings
    School budget hearings   Other school activities
138. Is there a coordinating council or committee for the improvement of education?[1]
139. Is it sponsored or actively supported by the school officials?
    How is its membership determined, particularly as to teachers? Administrators? Laymen?
140. Are its activities centered around curriculum and services to pupils? Teachers' salaries, standards, and so on? Ways in which the school may serve the community?
141. Is there a Parent-Teacher Association? What have been its principal activities in the past two years?

Largely because of misunderstanding of what the schools are trying to do, but also in part because of the excesses of some school systems in applying new insights into educational methods beyond the limit of their applicability, there have arisen here and there organizations definitely hostile to the existing school systems. While criticism is always chastening and no community service is above scrutiny, it has often been remarked that American education is the most self-criticized institution in existence; and purely negative, destructive criticism offers little hope for improvement. Often the hostility to the schools centers around alleged "un-Americanism," as

[1] See Hamlin, H. M., *Citizens' Committees in the Public Schools,* Interstate Printers and Publishers, Danville, Ill., 1952.

citizen groups come to fear the infiltration of "subversive" doctrines into the public school system.[1]

142. Have there been any groups organized with the specific purpose of attacking the schools?

143. Is the attack chiefly against teaching methods and curriculum; is it part of an "economy" drive; or is it centered on "subversive" tendencies in the school?

144. Have these groups brought their concerns before school officials and conferred with them on the difficulties as they see them?

145. Are these groups led by people who have a reputation for sincere civic concern and a forward-looking community point of view?

146. If the schools are the subject of attacks by such a group, are there other citizen groups that are seeking to present a balanced picture of the school situation to the public?

In many communities, schools are becoming virtual community centers through the active use of their facilities by various citizen groups. In addition, schools in some communities are leading the way in community betterment programs.[2] The assuming of new functions by the schools indicates their growing importance in American life. While some people feel that the schools often too hastily assume functions which they are unable to perform adequately, other people continue to press for the addition of new functions to the school's responsibility.

147. In which of the following ways does the school function as a community center:
   Sponsors active community improvement program
   Presents forum programs, concerts
   Carries on active adult education programs
   Makes auditorium, gymnasium, or classrooms available to civic groups free or for nominal charge
   Sponsors communitywide festivals, events
   Carries on educational or "art" motion picture program
   Serves as food canning or freezing center

148. In what additional ways does your school system contribute toward the recreational life of your community?

149. In what ways does the school engage in community service projects:
   Conducts surveys of various social conditions
   Organizes "tree-planting" and similar expeditions
   Participates in community "cleanup" day

[1] Read Hullfish, H. Gordon, editor, *Educational Freedom in an Age of Anxiety*, Harper and Bros., New York, 1953.
[2] See Cook, Lloyd A., *A Sociological Approach to Education*, McGraw-Hill Book Co., New York, 1950; and Olsen, Edward G., *School and Community Programs*, Prentice-Hall. Inc., New York, 1949.

Offers leadership facilities for community council or other community
   improvement work
Other

150. What new functions has the school system assumed in the past 20 years:
   Guidance   Religious training functions
   Community center work   Recreational functions
   Family life training   Driver training
   Health functions   Other functions

Adult Education

While most people think of adult education chiefly as evening classes
in the schools, more adult education takes place outside the schools than
within them. Perhaps the most extensive and effective adult education effort
in American society today is commercial advertising which appears in newspapers, magazines, and on radio and television programs. It is chiefly
through such communication media that Americans are kept abreast of
new developments in the scientific and industrial processes and products
of our culture. Such communication media reach more people with greater
frequency than do all the evening schools, libraries, and museums in the
country. (See Chapter 14.)

Another important adult education medium is the work of the Extension
Service of the United States Department of Agriculture, through which
various research activities are carried on at research centers in state universities, and county farm and home demonstration agents make available to
rural people the latest findings in various agricultural fields.[1] While this
service is somewhat differently organized in various states, nearly all rural
counties have an agricultural agent, and most of them have a home demonstration agent as well. Additional government sponsored adult education
activities include the extensive publishing activities of the Government
Printing Office (frequently recorded in this book), adult education activities
carried on through the vocational agriculture programs of the schools,[2]
and adult education training sponsored by the Veterans Administration.

On the national, state, and local scene various voluntary associations
carry on extensive campaigns in their respective fields of interest. Some
of the more important national agencies, many of which engage extensively
in adult education activities, are listed at the end of this book. Their local
affiliates, as well as other local organizations, add to the total effort.

[1] See Brunner, Edmund deS., and E. H. P. Yang, *Rural America and the Extension
Service*, Bureau of Publications, Teachers College, New York, 1949.
[2] See *An Evaluation of Local Programs of Vocational Education in Agriculture*, Office
of Education. Government Printing Office, Washington, 1949.

Many states encourage local communities through grants-in-aid to carry on adult education programs through the school system. This makes possible the familiar adult education classes. A newer trend in adult education is the trend to emphasize the dynamic processes which take place in the small group democratically organized, and to organize an increasing number of activities to engage in concerted action for community betterment.[1]

151. Which of the following educational methods are used in the adult education program of your community:

Community council	Forums
Survey	Classes
Citizen workshops, conferences, institutes	Other

152. Which organizations in your community carry on extensive adult education activities:

Health associations	Study clubs	Mental health associations, etc.
League of Women Voters	Labor unions	Other

153. What is the extent of the Agricultural Extension Service adult education activities among farm people? Is there an active farm demonstration program? Are there home demonstration activities?

154. What adult education courses have been offered in the past three years through the public school system? Which courses were not carried through to completion?

155. Do institutions of higher learning offer courses for laymen in various fields?

156. What activities do the churches carry on in the field of adult education? (See Chapter 9.)

157. What adult education efforts in your community center around family life education? Community improvement? Intergroup relations?

158. Is there a program of on-the-job or on-the-farm training for veterans?

Libraries and Museums

Libraries and museums are an important part of the educational effort of the community, serving both children and adults.

Although library facilities are often thought to be available in every community, one-sixth of the nation's counties have no public library service and more than 53,000,000 persons do not have "easy access" to books.[2]

[1] Read *Community Education in Action:* A Report on Community Organization and Adult Education, American Association for Adult Education, Cleveland, 1948.

[2] According to a study conducted by the New York State Library and reported in the *New York Times*, June 15, 1953.

The American Library Association has drawn up standards on the basis of which community libraries can be evaluated.[1] The modern trend seems to be to consolidate or otherwise affiliate small local libraries which are not sufficiently large for efficient operation. In this, as well as in establishing new library services, the county library plan is becoming increasingly widespread. This calls for one or more main libraries with community and school branches, smaller book deposit stations, and bookmobiles, with a circulation of books among the various units. Further, there is a distinct movement to make the library not only a place where books are available, but an agency which will reach out and touch people in the community through study groups, radio programs, audio-visual aids, cooperation with schools, churches, and so on.[2]

Museums, though not so common, are often found within effective traveling range of many communities. Here, too, a movement is afoot from the old-fashioned concept of a stuffy, uncomfortable place where people speak in hushed whispers toward a center of adult education and of various study activities.[3]

159. How extensive are the library facilities of the public school system?[4]

160. Has your community a public library service?

161. Do your community's library facilities meet accepted standards of library service for communities of its size?

162. Do your community's libraries constitute a coordinated system of community and school branches with additional services to outlying communities?

163. Is there a state library? What services does it provide to your school and community libraries?

164. Does your state have a law which encourages the formation of public libraries? What are its major provisions?

165. Is there a "county library" system in your county? Where is the county library located?

How many school branches are there? How many community branches and book deposit stations are there?

How many "bookmobiles" are operated in the county system?

What areas are still not served or do not have convenient access to county library books?

---

[1] See *Post-War Standards for Public Libraries*, American Library Association, Chicago, 1943, or the pamphlet *Standards and Planning for Public Libraries*, also published by the ALA.

[2] Read Carnovsky, Leon, and L. A. Martin, editors, *The Library in the Community*, University of Chicago Press, Chicago, 1944.

[3] Read Low, Theodore L., *The Museum as a Social Instrument*, American Association of Museums, New York, 1942.

[4] See *School Libraries for Today and Tomorrow:* Functions and Standards, American Library Association, Chicago, 1945.

166. Is there a regional library involving the cooperation of two or more counties?

167. If there is no county or regional library system, how many people in your community do not have "legal access" to library books?

168. Besides issuing books at the desk and performing the usual related work, which additional services does your library provide:
    Makes available library rooms for appropriate club meetings
    Sponsors lectures and discussions at library
    Sponsors exhibits by interest-groups in the community
    Conducts "great books" study program
    Conducts story hour for children
    Shows documentary and "art" films
    Operates a record library

169. How much per capita does your community spend for public library service?

170. Does your public library system have a governing board? How is it selected?

171. From what sources are revenues derived? Has the budget increased or decreased over the past ten years?

172. How many books are owned:
    Adult fiction   Children's books
    Adult nonfiction   Encyclopaedias and
                               reference books
    To how many periodicals does the library subscribe?

173. What is the per capita circulation of each type of book listed in the preceding questions?
    How does this compare with state figures, if available?

174. Has there been any recent pressure to withdraw certain books from the shelves because of their alleged "subversive" nature?[1]

175. What museums are within your community or within effective service radius of it:
    Art   Science   History   Industry   Other

176. Do museums carry on educational programs, sponsor the formation of study groups, offer lectures, or in other ways seek to become a vital part of the educational program of the community?
    Do they utilize radio and TV in reaching the public?

177. Do they cooperate with the schools in offering their facilities for special visits and lectures, or in other ways?

Private Schools

Private schools serve many functions. Sometimes they offer a denominational religious training program which would not be possible in the public

[1] For further questions relating to censorship, see Chapter 14.

schools. They may carefully select their student body on the basis of character, income, scholastic ability, religious affiliation, or the like. They frequently develop types of educational innovation which might be considered too unconventional by the taxpayers and parents in a public school district. The states exercise varying degrees of regulation, supervision, and control over such institutions, but in general they are allowed more flexibility in their programs than the public schools. Often, however, their programs are, in fact, rather conservative and old-fashioned. At their best an important function which they perform is that of blazing new trails in educational philosophy and methods.

178. What private schools are located in your community?
179. Under what auspices is each school operated? What is the approximate attendance of each?
180. How do their educational programs compare with those of the public schools?
181. What rating and reputation do these schools have?
182. What is the policy of your state department of education with respect to the supervision of private schools?
183. Do public and private school personnel meet together to exchange experiences or coordinate programs?

Higher Education

Institutions of higher education are extremely numerous in American communities. Various lists of different types of institutions are available from the United States Office of Education. Although such institutions are all under some kind of regulation by their state governments, perhaps the most important criterion of their acceptability is their accreditation by their respective regional accrediting organizations. If your local institutions are not so accredited, it is important to know why.

For people interested in community work, the local colleges offer excellent possibilities for aid and assistance. Many college departments in the social sciences are interested in being of service to the community. Thousands of students over the country are engaged in doing considerable work on term papers which often lack interest, purpose, and vitality. Cooperation of students, faculty, and local community leaders may provide a means of enriching the educational experience of the students, providing a "demonstration lab" for the social science departments, and being of service to the local community.[1]

[1] The continuous community study projects at Mount Holyoke, the Earlham College Program of Community Dynamics, and the Alfred University Area Study are examples of different types of contribution by the small college. Larger universities often have

In addition, through adult education classes, extension work, sponsoring of cultural events, and in other ways, higher education institutions can make a distinctive contribution.

184. Is there a community college offering two years of post high-school education to all students without cost?
185. Are there other types of higher educational institutions:
    Four-year liberal arts colleges
    Specialized colleges, professional schools, technical schools, etc.
    Universities
    What is the approximate enrollment of each?
    Are these institutions accredited by their respective accrediting agencies?
186. To what extent is there cooperation between secondary school and college personnel on admissions requirements? Student counseling records? Other matters?
187. Do pupils in your community have access to state scholarships, free tuition at the state university, and other financial aids to their higher education?
188. To what extent are deserving young students unable to attend college because of lack of economic means?
189. What studies of the local community have been made in such institutions?
190. What other types of community endeavor do they conduct?

References for Further Study

Handbook of Adult Education in the United States. Institute of Adult Education, New York, 1948. This is a comprehensive compilation of articles by experts on different phases of adult education.

Ivey, John E., Jr., and others, *Community Resources.* John C. Winston Co., Philadelphia, 1951. This book, written for school children, is an excellently planned and executed introduction to community planning and community organization. It should be in your school library if you want to interest students in the various aspects of their own community.

Kearney, Nolan C., *Elementary School Objectives.* Russell Sage Foundation, New York, 1953. A report on the work of the Mid-Century Committee on Outcomes in Elementary Education. It describes for educators, testmakers, and interested citizens the measurable goals of instruction in our American elementary schools.

Leigh, Robert D., *The Public Library in the United States.* Columbia University Press, New York, 1950. This is the general report of the public library inquiry which was made possible by a grant of the Carnegie Cor-

---

extensive research facilities, and in many instances are willing to cooperate in local community work.

poration. It constitutes an excellent report and appraisal of the function of the library in American society.

National Parent-Teacher: The P.T.A. Magazine. Published monthly September through June by the National Congress of Parents and Teachers, Chicago, Illinois. Especially helpful for laymen.

Publications List: United States Office of Education and Other Publications Relating to Education. This list is revised periodically, and available through the Government Printing Office, Washington.

School Life. Published monthly October through June for librarians, students, and laymen, this keeps people abreast of new developments, particularly of the activities and publications of the Office of Education. Government Printing Office, Washington.

"Trends in Postwar Adult Education." This is the theme of a special issue of the *Adult Education Journal,* for January, 1946, which describes newer developments in adult education programs. Other issues of this journal are also recommended.

8. Recreation

RECREATION IS ACTIVITY engaged in for its own sake. Playing the violin, playing baseball or golf, fishing, hunting, driving an automobile, doing craftwork are examples of recreational activities. A few people in our society find their daily vocation a sufficient source of enjoyment in itself and do not need other types of diversion. But however satisfying the day's work, most people seek a different type of activity for their leisuretime, if only for a "change of pace."

People find enjoyable in themselves activities which provide an opportunity to exercise their bodies in a pleasurable pursuit, set up a challenge for them to overcome, permit them to develop skills, call for their cooperation with other people, or tap their abilities for creative mental expression.

The increased leisuretime brought about by shorter working days raises the issue of whether this time will be used creatively (or better, "re-creatively"), or whether it will add up to hours of monotony. The new leisure presents an opportunity for more and more people to avail themselves of activities which formerly were available only to the "leisure class."

In the field of recreation, as elsewhere in our society, secondary agencies are stepping in to help the family adjust to changing patterns of family and community living. In the process, many recreational functions have been taken over from the family and neighborhood and placed in the hands of secondary groups and agencies.

Those facilities which are tax-supported and available to the general public either free or at a nominal fee are considered public recreational facilities. Public parks, playgrounds, and swimming facilities come most readily to mind. Yet the total recreational effort of the community extends far beyond these tax-supported facilities. Many communities have extensive recreational facilities and programs maintained by such agencies as churches, Y's, or community centers. Commercial recreational facilities also form an important part of the total recreational picture. The number of man-hours spent listening to radio, or watching TV or motion pictures may far outnumber those spent at park, pool, or playground. Finally, there are the many unorganized, informal activities which are usually carried on within small primary groups such as the family or friendship group. Thus, picnicking, card-playing, informal visiting, and after-school playing of children may loom large in the recreational picture.

There may be clear distinctions in your community between those activities which are part of the tax-supported public recreation programs, those which are business enterprises engaged in for profit, those conducted by private, nonprofit agencies, or those which have no such "auspices." However, most citizens think little of such differences, but spend their leisure in the activities which are available, which they know about, which they can afford, and which they prefer. Public recreation and private recreation should work in close cooperation and their services and facilities should complement and not duplicate each other. The goal is a system of wholesome recreational facilities equally available and not too expensive for all people. Actually, recreational facilities have usually grown up without sufficient planning, and often important groups in the population—minority groups, elderly people, poor people, teen-agers, newcomers, and so on—are neglected.

It is easy to confuse the process of recreation with the facilities available for it. Thus, the beautiful new school gymnasium may be idle except during school hours or when the "varsity" team is playing a home game. Certain generally agreed upon standards are available for various types of public recreational facility, and they offer some guidance as to the physical facilities and staff necessary for an acceptable program. Indeed, in scarcely any field of community endeavor is there such general agreement on detailed standards as in this public recreation field. But their usefulness is limited if the commercial and informal, unorganized types of leisuretime activity are not also taken into consideration.

A balanced recreation program in your community will provide ample facilities and occasion for both outdoor and indoor recreation for various age-groups. It will also take into account the type and quality of recreational opportunity available under commercial auspices, as well as radio, TV, newspapers, books, and such other commercially motivated leisuretime activities as reach into the home. It will not overlook other types of unorganized, informal recreational activities such as visiting back and forth, unorganized children's activities, and similar pastimes.

In making a recreation study, you will want to decide which of the following alternatives most closely suits your purpose and resources:

1. A study of municipally owned or operated facilities.

2. A study of all nonprofit recreational facilities generally available to the public.

3. A study of all recreational facilities and activities, including commercial recreation, private clubs, church activities, recreational programs of industrial companies, and so forth.

4. A study of the way people in your community spend their leisuretime. This would probably involve submitting to a representative sample of people an extensive questionnaire on the amount of time spent in each of the many possible leisuretime pursuits, supplemented by interviews and other techniques.

The present chapter affords an outline which is usable for any of the first three types of study.

Public Recreation

Facilities and programs. The National Recreation Association, which is the standard-setting agency in the public recreation field, recommends "a year-round program for all age-groups supported through public taxation, and conducted by trained leaders." The thought is that public recreation is a responsibility of government and that the burden for its support is distributed most equitably through the tax system. It should be year-round to meet year-round recreational needs, rather than confined to the summer, as many programs are. The fullest use of facilities is encouraged best by trained leaders who can help groups use their own resources and the public's facilities to the utmost.

Do not concern yourself unduly as to which department has facilities or conducts a program. It is the facilities and programs themselves which are of primary importance. Consider all the facilities and programs that are broadly available for public use. If school facilities are so available, this should be indicated; if they are not, include them in your list of public recreation facilities but make note of their limited availability. Many communities are learning to make wider use of their school recreation facilities.

If you are studying a small community, you will probably be able to consider it as a unit. In a small city of from 10 to 20 thousand, it may be advisable to consider both communitywide facilities and local neighborhood facilities, such as playgrounds or local small park areas. In cities large enough to have several districts, it may be advisable to confine your study to only one such district, with its constituent neighborhoods.

The relation of the immediate neighborhood within the large city to larger areas of the city is perhaps best illustrated through the progression from neighborhood playground to community playfield, or from local park or green space to communitywide park. Often, the local primary school district is a convenient and logical neighborhood to study, while the high-school district may correspond to the larger recreation district within the city. It is usually desirable to combine the elementary school playground with the neighborhood playground, and the high-school playfield with the community playfield.

Much the same principles apply to neighborhood planning for recreation as to neighborhood planning for schools, stores, or other facilities. More specifically, it is generally agreed that people should not be obliged to walk more than a half-mile to a playground, and even less in highly congested areas. Each playground should be designed to serve no more than 5,000 persons, and should vary in area from four to six acres. The neighborhood playground "is an area which affords a diversified play program for children from 6 to 14 and limited facilities for the use of young people and adults."[1]

The playfield is a larger area designed to serve a larger population than the small neighborhood. It is "an area developed for diversified recreation use primarily by young people and adults, although it commonly includes a playground for children." There should be one acre of playfield space and one acre of playground space for each 800 of the population. Playfields should be larger and less numerous than playgrounds, for they usually serve several neighborhoods.

1. Does your community's recreation program include a wide range of activities throughout the year? Does it include both indoor and outdoor facilities?
2. On a large-scale map of your community, locate and label each recreational facility, indoor or outdoor.
3. Are there substantial numbers of people more than a half-mile away from the nearest playground or playfield?[2]
4. How does your community conform to the following standards for public outdoor recreational facilities:

Total acreage of parks and recreation areas	one acre to each 100 population
Neighborhood playgrounds	one acre to each 800 population
Playfields	one acre to each 800 population
Baseball diamonds	one acre to each 6,000 population
Softball diamonds	one acre to each 3,000 population

[1] *Schedule for the Appraisal of Community Recreation*, National Recreation Association, New York, 1951, p. 8. This useful pamphlet sets forth numerous public recreation standards. Standards or quotations cited in the remainder of this chapter have been taken from this publication unless otherwise noted.

[2] For densely built-up neighborhoods, the National Recreation Association recommends a playground within a quarter-mile of all residents, but not farther than a half-mile. It recommends a playfield within a half-mile of all residents, but not farther than a mile. Less densely settled neighborhoods may have lesser needs.

CHILDREN NEED RECREATION AFTER SCHOOL HOURS. THEY NEED PLAYGROUNDS.

PLAYGROUNDS REDUCE STREET ACCIDENTS & CRIME:

	PLAYGROUNDS	CHILD DEATHS FROM STREET ACCIDENTS	ARRESTS OF CHILDREN UNDER 16 YEARS FOR VARIOUS CRIMES
A CERTAIN YEAR			
FOUR YEARS LATER			

Each symbol = 50 playgrounds   Ea. symbol = 100 deaths   Each symbol = 100 arrests

Source of data: Report of the New York Police Department - "Planning Cities"

PLAYGROUNDS DEVELOP CHILDREN'S INSTINCT FOR TEAMWORK THROUGH ORGANIZED GAMES:

YOU NEED NOT HAVE THIS ➡

· · · · · · YOU CAN HAVE ⬅ THIS

INFLUENCE OF PLAYGROUNDS ON CHILDREN.

RECREATIONAL NEEDS AND POSSIBILITIES

SOURCE: Kayanan, A. C., *Neighborhood Conservation: A Handbook for Citizen Groups*, Regional Association of Cleveland, 1943.

5. How many of the following items are provided as part of the recreational facilities of the community:

Playgrounds for various age-groups
Ball fields
Golf courses
Other game facilities
Tennis courts
Athletic fields with running track
Recreation buildings
Swimming pools or beaches
Skating, skiing, and other winter sports facilities
Picnic grounds with equipment

Roadside parkways with drinking water, toilet, and picnic facilities
Camping centers
Boating, canoeing, and fishing facilities
Bridle and bicycle paths
Zoo, arboretum, botanical gardens
Open-air theaters, stadiums
Bandstands or shells
Other special features

6. Which playgrounds or other outdoor recreation areas include shelter or field houses with toilets, lockers, or other facilities?
7. Are indoor recreational facilities such as recreation buildings, community houses, and so on available for public use widely distributed throughout the community and readily accessible to all neighborhoods?
How many such buildings include auditorium and gymnasium facilities, reading and game rooms, hobby rooms, general clubrooms, and other special rooms?
8. What other facilities such as those listed in the preceding question are available in other buildings in the community (churches, schools, etc.)?
How widely are such facilities used by the general public?
9. Is there an indoor swimming pool in the community? Is it available for use by the general public? Could it be made available by careful scheduling?
10. Which of the following activities are available in the public recreation program of your community (note, where appropriate, whether they are available the year-round, to both sexes, to various age and other groupings of the population, and accessible to various neighborhoods of the community):

Track and field athletics
Baseball
Softball
Soccer
Football
Touch football
Basketball
Field hockey
Ice hockey
Playground games
Free play activity

Volleyball
Horseshoes
Shuffleboard
Tennis
Paddle tennis
Badminton
Archery
Golf
Handball
Boxing
Wrestling
Water sports

Bowling
Hiking
Rollerskating
Pantomimes
Charades
Dramatic stunts
Storytelling
Story acting
One-act plays
Bicycling
Calisthenics
Gymnastics

Full-length plays	Social games	Paper craft
Local talent nights	Neighborhood parties	Woodwork
Puppetry	Metal craft	Nature study
Festival and holiday	Home gardening	Folk games and dances
celebrations	Community gardening	Social dancing
Community singing	School gardening	Interpretive dancing
Choruses	Nature hikes	Forums
Concerts and recitals	Nature games	Discussion groups
Glee clubs	Boys' club groups	Citizenship classes
Orchestras and bands	Girls' club groups	Camping
Music festivals	Painting, sketching,	Day camping
Toy symphonies	modeling	Picnicking
Christmas carols	Sewing	Hobby groups
Operettas	Reedwork	Others[1]
Oratorios	Leather craft	

11. Are the various activities in your public recreation program used extensively by the people of the community, with numerous recreation sessions well attended?

12. Is ample time devoted to the following activities:

    Active games and sports Social recreation and dancing
    Arts and crafts, drama, music General club and hobby
    Nature, gardening, camp activities
    and outing activities

13. Are there any teen-age recreation centers? What kind of program do they conduct? Under what auspices?

14. Is there opportunity for supervised dancing and social evenings?[2]

15. Are there youth hostels in your vicinity?

16. Are there county, state, or other parks within 50 miles of your community?

17. Does your community provide quiet park space for older couples and for mothers and nurses who have young children?

18. Are there Golden Age clubs or other special facilities for older people to come together for companionship, relaxation, and various activities? What activities are available within such programs?

    What other facilities and programs are there for older people?[3]

Recreational administration. You will want to relate your study of public recreation to such other community concerns as physical planning, health,

[1] This list is adapted from *Know Your Community:* Suggestions for Making a Study of Community Recreation Needs, National Recreation Association, New York, 1946. Some items are mentioned more specifically elsewhere in this chapter, but they are included in this list for ready reference.

[2] See *Youth Centers:* An Appraisal and a Look Ahead, Recreation Division, Federal Security Agency, Government Printing Office, Washington, 1945.

[3] Those interested in recreation for older people should read Williams, Arthur, *Recreation for the Aging*, Association Press, New York, 1953. See also *Recreational Activities of Ohio's Older People*, the March–April, 1952, issue of *The Ohio Citizen*.

safety, and education. The provision of parks, playgrounds, and other recreational facilities is an important concern of the city planning commission or similar body; and neighborhood planning for trade centers, school facilities, health facilities, and housing should all be purposefully coordinated. The planning commission should include in its master plan adequate facilities for public recreation and it should set aside adequate playgrounds and other facilities in plat maps for new subdivisions, for slum clearance programs, and so on. The relation of recreational needs to delinquency rates in various parts of the community should be explored. But it is now felt that public recreation is worthwhile in and of itself, and should be considered for its own intrinsic value rather than being "sold" to the public as a delinquency prevention program.

There should be an overall body which has responsibility for public recreation. This body may be part of the school system, or a separate recreation department, or a playground or park department, or a recreation commission or recreation board. Much will depend on the size of the community and its existing structure, as well as the state laws governing municipal activities.

Many communities have a policymaking commission or an advisory committee which concerns itself with the total community public recreation effort. This committee should be comprised of government officials representing each municipal department which undertakes a major recreation effort (parks, playground department) as well as officials whose responsibilities bear a close relationship to recreation (planning commission, housing authority, public school system, and so on). Provision is also frequently made for nongovernmental officials and leaders to participate in recreation planning through membership on or an advisory relationship to the commission or committee. Representatives of the commercial recreation field may contribute to a more inclusive and better coordinated leisuretime activities program if they are brought into the process of community planning for recreation.

The body responsible for public recreation should be given the following authority and responsibility:

1. To formulate policies and procedures.

2. To plan, promote, organize, supervise, and direct program services and operations.

3. To employ a qualified superintendent and other trained personnel.

4. To make agreements with the board of education and any other public or private groups for joint planning, exchanging use of facilities, services, and other matters for mutual advantage in providing a complete service in community recreation.

5. To present to the city governing body an annual budget adequate for operation and maintenance.[1]

19. Are users of public recreation facilities encouraged to offer suggestions for changes in the program to meet newly evolving interests and needs? How?

20. Is there a single municipal body specifically responsible for public recreation? Under what form of legislation was it established? If under the jurisdiction of a board, how are its members chosen?

21. Is the recreation program administered by one or more of the following, acting individually:

School board	Playground board or department
Park board or department	Other administrative agency

22. Is there a professionally qualified recreation director (the official title may vary) at the head of your community's public recreation effort?
Is his service on a part-time or full-time basis?

23. What additional staff members are there, such as supervisors of special activities, of specific playgrounds, recreation buildings; specialty teachers, hobby instructors, managers of special facilities like golf courses or tennis courts?
Are they paid or do they serve on a volunteer basis?

24. Are recreation personnel adequately trained and experienced for the positions they hold in your community?[2]

25. Are there provisions for the in-service training of recreation personnel?

Private and Semi-Public Recreation Programs and Cultural Facilities

Many organizations and activities are closely allied to public tax-supported recreation, for although they do not get their funds from this source, they are nonprofit ventures designed to be of service to wide groups of people at the cost of membership or a small fee. Many such agencies need additional funds which are obtained through private solicitations, income from endowments, or community chest participation. Scarcely a community is without some such activity, and often each community has many. Examples would be boys and girls clubs, Y's, settlement houses, Junior Grange, and so on.

Particularly in small communities, such agencies' efforts should be evaluated in terms of the participation of the groups served, since an inventory of special facilities may not show such widely known activities as Boy Scouts or Home Bureau.

[1] Brown, J. Lee, *Planning for Recreation Areas and Facilities in Small Towns and Cities*. Federal Security Agency, Government Printing Office. Washington, 1945, p. 44.
[2] The National Recreation Association has drawn up detailed standards for various positions in different sized communities. See *Recreation Leadership Standards*, or *Schedule for the Appraisal of Community Recreation*.

The public recreation effort and that of private organizations should be closely related. In a particular community, the Y, or a private settlement house, or some similar agency with indoor facilities may meet this type of community need, and the vital question in recreation planning is the extent to which these facilities are adequate to the total recreation needs of the community and can be made most widely available to the people in the community.

Various cultural activities such as forum groups, library or adult education study groups, choral societies, and similar organizations are most conveniently considered in this section. A few other activities are also included in this part of the study outline which might otherwise be considered under public or commercial recreation facilities.

26. What agencies and organizations carry on extensive recreational programs:
    Youth centers or boys clubs
    Settlement houses, neighborhood centers
    YMCA, YWCA, Catholic Youth Organization, Jewish community centers
    Boy Scouts, Girl Scouts, Campfire Girls, and so on
    4-H, Future Farmers
    Junior Grange
    Golden Age clubs
    Church activities (See Chapter 9.)
    Company recreation programs
    Union recreation activities
    Lodges and fraternal groups
    Private clubs emphasizing recreation programs
    Clubs, organizations, and interest groups (See Chapter 16.)
    Other clubs or activities

27. Which of the programs listed above are open for public participation? Which are restricted to "members only"?
    What are the numbers, ages, and types of persons included in the membership?

28. Which of the organizations listed above maintain extensive indoor or outdoor recreational facilities, such as tennis courts, gymnasiums, pools, auditoriums, meeting halls, craft rooms, summer camps?

29. Which of these organizations occasionally or regularly place any of their facilities at the disposal of the general public or for the use of other groups?

30. Which of these organizations provide specific activities listed on page 122?

31. Is there any neighborhood, age-group, or other group of people in your community in particular need of recreational services which are not available to them?
    If so, is there a group or organization which might take steps to help them acquire the needed facilities?

32. What recreational facilities are available in various institutions whose inhabitants are relatively isolated:

    County or city home   Jail   Children's home, etc.

33. Is there ample opportunity for creative expression in instrumental and choral groups such as:

    Church choirs   Community or school band
    Glee clubs and mixed choruses   Small ensemble groups
    Civic orchestra   Other

34. Is there a concert or forum series which brings outstanding artists or speakers or dance groups to the community?

35. Are the public library facilities adequate? (See Chapter 7.)

36. Does your local high school carry on an adult education program? Which of the following activities does it include:

    Classes in academic subjects   Class or sessions in music and art
    Classes in vocational training   Games and athletic activities
    Classes in hobbies and homemaking   Discussion groups

37. Is there a museum in or accessible to your community? (See Chapter 7.) What hours is it open?

38. Is there a "little theater" in your community which makes available worthwhile drama for community people?

    To what extent does it utilize local actors or "imported" talent?

    To what extent does it utilize amateur or professional talent for make-up, stage sets, lighting?

39. What schools, facilities, or professional teachers, and so forth, exist in your community which would help the developing young musician?   Artist? Writer?   Actor?

Commercial Facilities

Public recreation facilities rest on the principle that public operation and financing tends to assure an adequate and equitable distribution of facilities and of costs. Nevertheless, many types of recreational opportunity can be adequately provided under commercial auspices and conducted as a business for profit.

Such enterprises can be distinct boons to a community, and communities will do well, in planning their further development in the recreation field, to consider the part which commercial recreation may afford. Under certain conditions, commercial swimming pools, ski-tows, concert halls, motion picture theaters, athletic stadiums, and spectator sports add to the richness of recreational opportunity in the community.

Nevertheless, commercial recreation has come under wide criticism for two principal reasons: the passive nature of much commercial recreation and the lack of responsibility to uphold basic esthetic and moral standards. The first criticism is that leisuretime spent in active participation in games or creative expression is more truly re-creative than sitting passively and watching or listening to the performance of others. Thus, it is maintained that it is much more desirable to participate in plays, choral groups, or amateur athletics than to be entertained by professional movie stars, singers, or athletic teams. Many commercial recreational activities are of the type which discourage, rather than encourage, active participation in wholesome activities and the individual becomes a passive spectator slumped in his seat in a motion picture theater, or at the professional ball game, or in his lounge chair watching television. This criticism does not apply to such important active commercial recreational opportunities as bowling alleys, golf courses, swimming pools, and tennis courts.

Concern has also been widely expressed at the type of production which is portrayed on the motion picture or television screen. It is pointed out that esthetic standards are kept purposely low with the idea of appealing to the lower emotions of great masses of people, and that worthwhile human dramas are often boiled down to an insipid and stereotyped formula in order to show success in the box office or in the radio listening poll.

Finally, some establishments present recreational surroundings with a background conducive to crime and sex immorality. Thus, the pool parlor may be the hangout of adults engaging in activities on the fringe of legality and who often encourage young people into delinquent behavior patterns. Sex immorality may be encouraged by the type of entertainment at roadhouses or night clubs and the availability of "hostesses" and other women who are either hired or allowed to offer intimacies for financial or other rewards.

The reader may want to assure himself that everything possible is being done to bring various types of pressure, through law, regulation, or public opinion, to bear on such establishments, and to assure in general that the commercial recreational facilities are meeting as honestly as possible the standards of wholesome recreational experience.

40. List every establishment under each of the following types:

Amusement park	Ski tow	Vaudeville
Penny arcade	Bowling alley	Motion picture
Bathing beach	Pool room	"Art theater"
Swimming pool	Commercial gymnasium	Burlesque
Commercial	Ice skating or roller	Drive-in
golf course	skating rink	Radio
Tennis court	Theater	Tavern
Riding academy	Legitimate	Dance hall

Cabaret, night club,	Baseball	Bingo establishment
roadhouse	Wrestling	Circus
Excursions	Basketball	Traveling carnival
Spectator sports	Horse racing	Other
Boxing	Hockey	
Football	Juke parlor	

41. If possible, secure figures on the amount your community pays each year for each type of commercial recreation.
42. How do these figures compare with figures for various programs and facilities for public recreation?
43. What "holes" in the commercial recreation program need to be filled through publicly sponsored recreation programs?
44. In the case of each commercial establishment mentioned above, answer the following questions where appropriate:
   Are there state laws or local ordinances governing the conducting of such an establishment? If so, are they satisfactory and are they adequately enforced?
45. Do any of the establishments constitute an environment which is morally undesirable for the community in general or for its young people in particular?
46. Is the establishment a place where individuals and groups whose attitudes toward law enforcement or morality are undesirable, seem to congregate?
47. Are there any establishments which for the above-mentioned or other reasons constitute a detriment to the community?
48. In case the establishment is undesirable, is there a possibility of improving the situation through the passage of new laws or the enforcing of existing ones, or through negotiation or various types of pressure brought to bear by citizens' groups?
49. Which of the establishments listed above constitute a distinct asset to the welfare of the community by providing a wholesome type of recreation which is not being provided by public recreational facilities?
50. Have any steps been taken, formally or informally, to bring the commercial establishments into active cooperation with the communitywide recreation program?
51. Are there instances of undesirable commercial recreational facilities which could be improved by setting up facilities for the same activity under public auspices and control?
52. What types of wholesome recreational facility does the community lack, and what types might be supplied by the encouragement of a commercial establishment?
53. What is your state law or local ordinance with respect to various forms of gambling? How adequately is it enforced?
54. What is the rate of arrest for intoxication? Drunken driving? Disorderly conduct?

130 · STUDYING YOUR COMMUNITY

Informal Activities

Not everyone wants to spend all his leisuretime in supervised recreation. As mentioned earlier, probably the majority of leisuretime activity is spent in informal, unorganized pursuits. Such pursuits go across all lines arbitrarily separating public, agency, and commercial recreation. An afternoon spent in the park involves making use of public facilities, though probably not of a supervised activity program. Similarly, an evening spent at home at a hobby which was originally learned at a neighborhood center is part of the unsupervised program, as is attendance at the local commercial theater or listening to the radio. Public, agency, and commercial recreational facilities and programs can be thought of as supplements to the spontaneous employment of leisuretime by individuals and intimate family and friendship groups.

Because of their informal nature, many such activities are difficult to track down. Certain activities can be evaluated quantitatively if a little ingenuity is used. One can ask for the average daily number of admissions to parks, theaters, the number of pleasure-car licenses issued in the community. From various sources one may be able to get the number of radio or television sets owned. One can find from the alcohol beverage control board or similar governmental agency the number of liquor licenses issued and possible figures on the consumption of alcoholic beverages in public places.

Unless special studies have been made, other types of data may be obtainable only through a sample study of how people use their leisuretime. Only in such ways will information be obtainable on how many vegetable gardens there are and how many hours are spent taking care of them, how much neighborly visiting takes place, how often family members play games together, and other appropriate information.

55. Through observation, interviews, sample studies, or other appropriate means, make a rough estimate of the extent of such informal, unorganized types of recreational activity as the following:

Unorganized street play of children

Exchange of visits for card playing (bridge, canasta, etc.) by individual couples

Informal "bridge clubs," "coffee klatches," "poker sessions"

Swimming in nearby unsupervised brooks, lakes, rivers or in home swimming pools

Boating

Picnicking

Backyard "cooking out"

Painting, singing, or playing a musical instrument

Other creative activities in the home

Home hobbies

Gardening

Walks

Vacation trips	Home motion pictures
Camping	Automobile excursions
Fishing	Home table tennis or other
Hunting	game facilities
Skiing and skating	Home game rooms
Listening to the radio	Soda store sessions
Watching TV	Tavern and bar sessions
Reading books, newspapers	Other
Playing records	

56. What implications for the community's public recreation program arise out of the pattern of home recreation activities?
57. In what ways does the public recreation department encourage informal recreational activities at home or in private groups?

Planning the Community's Recreation

It is probably easier to get results from a voluntary citizen program in recreation than in any other aspect of community need. Small communities may find it difficult to provide adequate facilities for a child guidance clinic or for hospital care, but the cost of recreation need not be prohibitive.

Often facilities are at hand, but simply call for wider use. Thus, the school playground may be used for a summer recreation program. A school or other public building may be used for adult recreation activities. Needless duplication of school and adult facilities is both costly and undesirable. Some cities make it a deliberate policy to acquire park or playground acreage adjacent to school properties and cooperate to administer it as a multi-purpose area.

Often a public recreation program is initiated by voluntary citizen effort and private funds, later to be taken over as a public responsibility by the municipality after the program has proved its worth and attracted sufficient voter support.[1] In some states, certain grants-in-aid are available to municipalities to help pay the cost of approved recreational efforts. Frequently the program starts as a summer recreational activity for children and then grows into a year-round program for both children and adults.

Studies such as that outlined in the present chapter are essential to assure an adequate plan for community recreation. Such a study should include not only recreational needs,[2] but also the community's background and

[1] There are many projects which a small town committee can undertake in order to start specific recreational activities or to develop recreational facilities. A helpful mimeographed pamphlet describing many such possibilities is *What Can We Do in Our Town?* National Recreation Association, New York, 1953.

[2] In addition to the study outline in this chapter, see the following study guides published by the National Recreation Association: *Schedule for the Appraisal of Community*

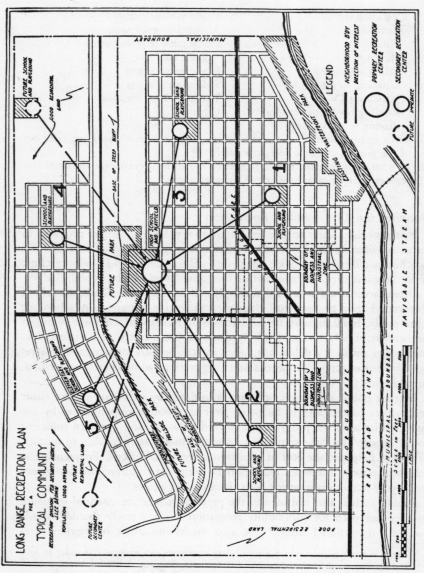

MAP ILLUSTRATING A LONG-RANGE RECREATION PLAN

SOURCE: *Planning for Recreation Areas and Facilities in Small Towns and Cities*, Federal Security Agency, 1945.

something of its resources, population characteristics and trends, city government structure and financing, housing, city planning activities, industrial development plans, and special problem areas such as delinquency and traffic accidents.

A comparison of community recreational facilities can be made with standards established by the National Recreation Association.[1] Plans can be built around existing facilities. A list can be made of things which are considered most necessary and desirable, establishing a priority for some things over others. The future development of the community can be anticipated in this section of the effort. Such a plan is most valuable if it is accompanied by a detailed plan for raising the money for capital development and for administering the program. Provision should be made for its continued current financing on an annual basis. State enabling legislation may govern park boards, playground and recreation boards, and utilization of school facilities. Special ordinances may be necessary in order to put the program in effect. However, your state legislation may permit a municipality to act in such endeavors without a special ordinance.

Essentially the same process applies to larger communities. There, however, the task is more likely to be one of coordinating the efforts of existing park departments, recreation departments, or playground boards with each other and with private agencies and commercial facilities to make better use of present resources as well as planning for needed additions. The plans may include a long-range program for acquisition of land for parks or playgrounds or for the acquisition of indoor community recreation centers.

The work of already existing health and welfare councils or city planning councils or other broad community planning agencies should be studied. It is possible that such a body may be the logical one to sponsor the program, rather than setting up a completely independent organization for recreation alone.

58. Is there an organization, widely representative of volunteer citizens and municipal officials, whose principal function is continuous planning for recreation in your community?

59. Has a major study of community recreation resources and needs been made in the past ten years?

Was any action program initiated as a result of this study?

Are the proposals made still being carried out, or is the study now "history"?

Recreation, 1951; *Know Your Community:* Suggestions for Making a Study of Community Recreation Needs, 1946; and *New Neighbors in Your Community:* Community Recreation Score Card. The last named is a leaflet with a brief set of questions.

[1] See *Standards for Neighborhood Recreation Areas and Facilities*, 1944, and *Schedule for the Appraisal of Community Recreation*.

60. Are there advisory committees or citizen commissions that help plan the recreational endeavor of the appropriate municipal agencies (park department, recreation department, and so on)?
61. Is there any organization whatsoever that takes the overall, community-wide view on recreation—public, private, and commercial?
62. Is there regular administrative provision for close coordination of efforts of the school board, park board, housing authority, planning commission, or other groups concerned with recreation?
Have the preceding groups drawn up agreements on acceptable standards for future recreational facilities?
63. Are recreation agencies well represented on welfare councils, planning councils, community councils, or similar bodies?
64. Is the public recreation program closely related to the school's recreation instruction so as to facilitate carry-over from school to public facility?

References for Further Study

Butler, George D., *Introduction to Community Recreation.* rev. ed. McGraw-Hill Book Co., Inc., New York, 1949. This is a standard text in the field of community recreation. Like most texts, it confines itself largely to public recreation programs.

Danford, Howard G., *Recreation in the American Community.* Harper and Bros., New York, 1953. This text in public recreation is particularly noteworthy for its direct, interesting style. Questions at the conclusion of chapters form useful outlines for community study. It is largely oriented toward the city and urban recreational needs and programs.

Isaacs, Reginald R., "Educational, Cultural and Recreational Services," *The Annals of the American Academy of Political and Social Science,* vol. 242, November, 1945.

Williams, Jesse F., and Clifford L. Brownell, *The Administration of Health and Physical Education.* 3d ed. W. B. Saunders Co., Philadelphia, 1946. Community recreation overlaps in many places the health and physical education programs, of which this is a standard text.

9. Religious Activities

ORGANIZED RELIGION is the system of organizations and practices through which religious activities are usually channeled. It is the purpose of this chapter to explore those religious activities which have an impact on the daily life of the community, rather than to define the religious experience as such. In studying the religious activities of a community, it is well to keep in mind what it is that organized religion actually provides, and how it affects the community.

1. Organized religion provides a place of worship and association. This includes the church buildings, parish houses, and so on.

2. It provides opportunity for group worship and other religious expression, such as prayer, hymn singing, reading of holy scripture, and administering of sacraments or other rites.

3. It has its own social structure, including leaders and officials who are in various relationships to the members.

4. It provides recreational enjoyment. This may be closely connected with a religious interest, such as a passion play, a hymn sing, or the playing of games based on Biblical events; or it may be less closely connected with strictly religious concerns, like holding a dance, or presenting a show, or providing a place to play bingo.

5. It provides educational experiences. These may be confined to the study of religious scriptures, or may extend to considering a religious orientation toward any of life's activities. Parochial schools, seminaries, and other church-sponsored educational institutions are devoted specifically to the church's educational function.

6. It often performs health and welfare functions. A number of churches minister to the needs of their own congregation, and many through denominational organizations support in part or in full health and welfare activities which serve nonmembers.

7. It often influences the social process. It may, through its teachings, be an influence for change or stability in its community. It may take a definite stand on various types of social legislation, or on various topics of

great current concern. Through its own orientation to race, class, and nationality differences it may strengthen or weaken such cleavages in the local, national, and international community.

8. In these and other ways, organized religion strengthens or weakens the effort of local people to fashion the type of community to which they aspire.

Number and Types of Churches

In American communities religious association takes place predominantly in churches,[1] most of which are organized into national religious bodies. There are some 260 different religious bodies in the United States.[2] Their large number is chiefly a result of the splitting off of sects which has characterized Protestant church bodies since the Reformation. The various Protestant religious denominations represent extremely wide divergencies in doctrinal belief and community concern.[3] Important differences of belief are also found within the same denomination and even the same congregation. This is true of the difference between those who take the Bible to be the literal word of God (fundamentalists) and those who accept the validity of modern science over the Bible on matters where they differ (modernists), and in other matters relating to traditional or liberal attitudes toward theological and social issues.

Different church bodies are much less numerous within Roman Catholicism, the Orthodox Church, and the Jewish religion. Because doctrinal differences are often of relatively minor nature, and because often much larger differences of opinion exist within congregations or denominations than between them, many Protestants feel that some degree of cooperation, if not consolidation, should be attempted. Councils of churches working on the local or state level combine the efforts of various Protestant denominations in certain types of work. For the whole country, the National Council of the Churches of Christ in the U.S.A. is the most important and inclusive coordinating body.

Particularly in rural areas, different patterns of cooperation or consolidation of local congregations have arisen. Among these is the *nondenominational community church*, which is not affiliated with any denominational

[1] The term "church" will be used throughout to include any organization for worship, including synagogues, "companies" of Jehovah's Witnesses, "monthly meetings" of the Society of Friends, and so on.
[2] *The Yearbook of American Churches*, 1953, p. 251. (See "References for Further Study" at end of chapter.)
[3] Not all denominational differences are exclusively matters of doctrine. See, for example, H. Richard Niebuhr's *The Social Sources of Denominationalism*, Shoe String Press, Hamden, Conn., 1954. Reprint.

body. Somewhat similar are the *affiliated* churches, which maintain a loose connection with a denominational body in order to have some source of supervision and of ministers as well as a mission outlet, but which remain substantially independent. *Federated churches* are combinations of formerly different congregations which maintain their previous denominational ties but meet together on the local level. Another type is the *denominational community church*, which, in accordance with the cooperative decision of other denominations, is accorded an exclusive field in the community, usually with the proviso that it broaden its terms of membership and that it minister to the whole community. In the *larger parish* type of organization, churches share their ministerial or other staff personnel, with perhaps one in charge of the worship services, another in charge of pastoral work, and so on.[1]

In larger communities, denominational boards attempt to coordinate the location and programs of their churches, and there is some cooperation in this respect among the various denominations.[2]

Something over 50 per cent of the population have some religious affiliation. Perhaps only half of these nominal members are active and regular participants in the religious activities of their respective churches.

1. List by denomination[3] the names of the churches in your community.
2. How many members does each church have? In each case, how is the term "member" defined?
3. What is the average weekly attendance at church services?
4. Which churches are increasing and which are decreasing in membership?
5. Divide the population of the community you are studying by the number of its churches. How many people are there per church in your community?
6. How does total church membership compare with total population?
7. What indications are there of "overchurching" or "underchurching" in your community?
8. Are there instances of nondenominational churches? Affiliated churches? Federated churches? Denominational community churches? Larger parish organizations?
9. To what extent is there interdenominational cooperation in planning for the community's church needs?

[1] Kolb, John H., and Edmund deS. Brunner. *A Study of Rural Society*. 4th ed. Houghton Mifflin Co., Boston. 1952, pp. 375–377. The chapter entitled "Religion and the Rural Church" is recommended for those who are interested in familiarizing themselves with the structure and problems of America's rural churches.
[2] *Comity Report* by H. Paul Douglass is "an intensive study of urban comity practices reported by the Committee on Cooperative Field Research." See also *Churching the Community Cooperatively*. Both of these are pamphlets published by the National Council of the Churches of Christ in the U.S.A.
[3] For convenience, the term "denomination" will be used throughout to designate a specific religious affiliation, such as Baptist, Presbyterian, Roman Catholic, or Jewish. "Church" will be used to designate a local congregation of worshippers.

Church Location, Population Shifts, and Economic Groups

A plot map of the different churches in your community, showing their denomination, may reveal interesting relationships between the location of the churches and the people they serve. Sometimes there are indications of the adaptation of church location to nationality group and income level.

The movement of people into and out of various sections of the community since the building of the existing churches may result in a geographic distribution of churches which does not correspond to present community needs. The development of new real estate subdivisions or the rapid increase in population of certain sections of the community may place great strains upon existing church facilities there. The problem is particularly accentuated when the religious affiliation of newcomers is not the same as that of existing church facilities. On the other hand, gradual changes in the types of people inhabiting certain areas of the city may result in some churches finding that many of their former members have moved away.

In the more rural areas, the decreasing number of farmers has led to a reduction in the number of people served by open country churches. The development of the automobile and improved roads has made it possible for farmers in formerly remote places to travel to town in only a few minutes. This leaves many open country churches without a reason for being, and quite a number of them have died out. Nevertheless, in many places the rural churches are still distributed largely on a neighborhood basis, while other neighborhood institutions such as the school and various stores have "moved" to the village center.[1]

In order to maintain a thriving Sunday school, a well-attended church service at least once a week, active organizations for adults and children, and an adequate physical structure, a certain minimum size of congregation is necessary. The presence of too many churches cuts down the number of people on which any church can draw. Nevertheless, it should be pointed out that pure size or other quantitative measurements do not always get to the root of the matter. In some communities, sentimental attachments to the small, neighborhood church may enhance the experience of church membership and participation and give the individual a sense of close identification with his church which may not be experienced by the member of a larger congregation.

Occasionally, the regional denominational bodies of the various churches cooperate in giving some overall planning and direction to the question of which churches shall be closed and which new churches shall be established.

[1] See Hoffsommer, Harold, "The Relation of the Rural Church to Other Rural Organizations," *Social Forces*, vol. 20, December, 1941. See also Blackwell, Gordon, *The Church and the Community in the South*, John Knox Press, Richmond, 1949.

Such interdenominational cooperation, or "comity arrangements," make possible a more effective church-population ratio, and eliminate the excesses of interdenominational rivalry.

While churches typically encompass people from more than one income level, the proportion of various income groups in the congregation often varies from one church to another. Although there appears to be a significant variation among national church bodies in the social and economic status of their members,[1] it is impossible to predict for a particular community which congregation will have the greatest proportion of members of low or high socioeconomic status. Adroit questioning of clergymen and community leaders will sometimes indicate whether and to what extent there is a division of church affiliation according to income and social status.

Racial discrimination in religious worship still remains strong in many parts of the United States. Even in places where such discrimination is not the official policy, Negroes and other nonwhites are given little encouragement to attend certain of the churches.

10. On a map of your community plot the different kinds of churches in different colors according to denomination.
    Are certain denominations concentrated in certain sections of the community? Is there a preponderance of any one denomination?
11. Has the growth in church membership kept pace with the growth in the population of your community?
12. Are population shifts affecting the type of people who constitute the congregation of the individual churches?
13. Which churches are overburdened because of a great growth of population in their vicinity?
14. Are there new real estate developments or neighborhoods of rapidly growing population which currently do not have sufficient churches?
15. What new churches have been established in your community since 1936?[2]
16. Are any attempts now being made to establish new churches in your community?
17. Has there been an influx of people whose usual denomination does not have a church in your community? Is there a plan to form one?
18. If your community is decreasing in population, how is this affecting the churches?
19. Are any churches in your community experiencing a decrease in membership because of movements away from the neighborhood in which the church is located?

[1] Pope, Liston, "Religion and the Class Structure," The Annals of the American Academy of Political and Social Science, vol. 256, March, 1948.
[2] See p. 152 for a brief description of the Census of Religious Bodies: 1936. Because this Census was last taken in 1936, that year provides a bench mark against which to measure change in religious organizations in your community.

20. What churches have died out in your community since 1936?
21. How many churches in your community have changed their location since 1936? In what direction have they moved? What reasons are given for these changes in location?
22. Which if any churches in your community include preponderantly high-income people in their congregation?
23. Which churches in your community include preponderantly middle-income people in their congregation?
24. Which churches in your community include preponderantly low-income people in their congregation?
25. Which churches in your community include a cross-section of the people in your community?
26. Do some churches discourage certain types of people from attending?
27. In general, what relation do the churches of your community bear to the high, low, and middle-income groups of your community?

Buildings and Equipment

Physical structures vary all the way from imposing cathedrals to churches or meeting houses which have been made over from former dwellings, and mission-type "store-front" churches. Church edifices have hardly kept pace in recent years with the imposing new public school buildings in many communities. This is particularly noticeable in rural communities where school centralization has taken place. In their religious education programs the churches often find themselves at a disadvantage when compared with the schools on such matters as attractiveness of rooms and adequacy of equipment. In recreational facilities, most churches likewise have nothing comparable to the school gymnasium or swimming pool. However, in perhaps no other segment of community activities is a description of the effectiveness of institutions according to their physical and statistical characteristics likely to be as misleading as it may be in the case of religious activities.

28. Would you rate the general appearance of each of your community's churches as high, medium, or low in structure? Maintenance?
29. Does the appearance of the churches correspond to the general economic and social conditions of the neighborhood where they are located?
30. Would you say that in general the churches in your community present a better appearance than the schools? Other public buildings? The theaters? Business establishments? Factories?
31. How are the churches situated with regard to the following facilities:

Kitchen and eating facilities
Facilities for dramatic productions
Rooms for large meetings
Rooms for church school
Facilities for indoor athletics and games
Rooms for other social activities

32. Can you determine how the annual budgets of your community's churches compare with other community expenditures, such as for schools, theater admissions, alcoholic beverages?
33. Which churches, if any, provide transportation to church services and meetings for those who need it?

Services for Worship

The central function of the church is worship. One church service a week would seem to be a basic minimum for such worship activity, but some small rural churches without a resident minister do not even meet this modest standard. On the other hand, some churches hold several services on Sunday as well as others during the week. Catholic churches may hold masses every day. Protestant churches often hold prayer meetings on Sunday evening or sometime during the week. Many of the manifold activities which take place particularly in some of the larger churches have strong worship components, such as Bible study groups, some young people's groups, and similar activities. Sunday schools, confirmation classes, Hebrew schools, and other types of religious training activity for the young involve worship activities. Still other activities have less direct relation to the worship function.

Most religious faiths would probably agree that the worship services are the most vital aspect of religious endeavor, but at the same time that the quality and intensity of the religious experience in such services are extremely difficult to appraise in a community study.

34. How many churches in your community are unable to hold at least one service each week?
35. Which churches hold more than one worship service each week?
36. What types of service are held (Sunday morning worship, mass, vespers, prayer meetings)?
37. Do the churches individually or jointly hold special services to observe such occasions as Mothers Day, Thanksgiving, Rural Life Sunday, Brotherhood Week, World Day of Prayer, Mental Health Week, Independence Day, Memorial Day?

Clergymen

A few church bodies, such as Christian Scientists, do not have an ordained clergy. Some small Protestant churches of the fundamentalist type may have the barest minimum requirement for their clergy, and indeed no special formal training of any kind may be required. Nevertheless, the amount and quality of formal training, both in college and theological seminary, are considered to be appropriate indices of the competence of the clergymen of a community.

As with other types of professional people, the more effective and successful clergymen tend to gravitate toward the large cities with their large churches and large congregations. Many dedicated clergymen out of principle remain in the rural areas where they feel their leadership is needed. Nevertheless, small rural churches are often a refuge for retired ministers or for those whom their denominational boards consider unable to take the responsibilities of a larger church. In general, the larger the church, the more competent ministry it can afford. Perhaps fortunately for the poor churches, such "competence" is usually measured in terms of popularity, congeniality of personality, oratorical ability in preaching sermons, and effectiveness in organizing various church and community groups, rather than in terms of basic religious qualities.

A high average age of the clergymen in the community may raise a question as to whether its paid religious leadership is on the whole able to reach the minds and loyalties of its young people.

Particularly appropriate for those interested in community work is the question of the extent of community participation and leadership among the clergy. In many communities, leadership in civic affairs is expected of the clergy, but such effort takes time away from the concerns of the individual congregation. Congregations and clergymen both differ on the proportion of effort which they think clergymen should devote to the work of their own church groups and to worthwhile activities in the larger community.

There is extreme variation among clergymen in the amount of personal counseling which they do, their individual competence to do it, and the special training they have had for this type of activity. Most theological seminaries are paying increasing attention to the need for such training, as are various national church organizations.

It is generally agreed that wherever possible a church should have a full-time resident minister. Actually, one minister may serve two or even three or more churches, particularly in rural areas. Churches which are so small as not to be able to afford a full-time minister are not likely to have as many organizations and activities as do the larger ones. Often, the total church effort in such small churches without a resident minister comprises little more than the Sunday service.

38. List the clergymen attached to each church in your community who are employed by that church full time. Part time.
39. What is the average age of clergymen employed by the churches in your community?
40. What churches do not subscribe to the idea of an ordained ministry?

41. List other paid officials attached to each church in your community:
    Director of religious training   Religious teachers
    Organist or choir director   Recreation leaders
42. What is the average length of time the clergymen have been with their present congregation?
43. How many years of formal education have they had?
44. How many of them are college graduates as well as graduates of a theological seminary?
45. What salary do the clergymen receive? How do their salaries compare with those of other professions?
    Does their salary include residence? Living expenses? Automobile? Other items?
46. Would you say that most of the clergy are active and cooperative in civic projects?
47. What clergymen are represented in important posts in community activities, such as members of boards or committees of health, welfare, recreation, or educational agencies?
48. Which clergymen carry on extensive counseling activities? How well trained and capable are they in such activities?
49. Is there a ministers' association in your community? How often does it meet? What are its principal activities?
    Which clergymen belong to this organization, and which clergymen do not?
50. Do clergymen cooperate actively with physicians, social workers, and other professional people?
51. What do clergymen give as the chief problems confronting their churches in your community?

Church Organizations

Church units are variously organized in the United States. Roman Catholic churches are organized on a hierarchical principle with authority from the top downward, and there is no such democratic control over the selection of clergymen, order of service, and other matters as exists within many Protestant churches and Jewish congregations. The largest number of churches are Protestant. The typical Protestant church organization provides for an ordained clergyman who is the spiritual leader and to a varying extent the administrative leader. Responsible for the spiritual guidance of the church is an elected board of elders, or deacons, and having charge of fiscal matters is an elected board of trustees. There may be some type of executive or advisory board made up of the heads of various organizations within the church.

Most churches have numerous subsidiary organizations. The organization most frequently found within the church is probably the Sunday school.

Parallel to this religious training and worship organization are confirmation classes and other special types of study groups. Other organizations within the church are youth groups, young adult groups, men's clubs, women's clubs, Bible classes, and missionary groups. The church may also contain groups which are almost entirely recreational, such as athletic teams and dramatic societies. Out further toward the periphery of the church's activities are certain groups that may not be religious in orientation and may not be confined to the membership. Boy Scout troops are an example.

Fichter has suggested an outline for the organizations of the urban Catholic parish which is useful in classifying activities within the Catholic churches, in particular, and with certain modifications, within the Protestant and Jewish congregations.

1. *Liturgical groups* which assist in the religious services, such as Acolyte Society, Choir, Ushers.

2. *Socio-spiritual groups* "organized . . . for the primary objective of sanctification," such as Children of Mary, Sodalities, Junior and Senior Holy Name Societies, etc.

3. *Educational groups,* including Parents' Club, Confraternity of Christian Doctrine, etc.

4. *Ameliorative groups,* doing "corporal works of mercy," such as St. Vincent de Paul and Daughters of Mercy.

5. Primarily recreational groups, Boy and Girl Scouts, sports teams, and related adult committees.[1]

Often, an all-inclusive type of organizational program is desired by the individual churches and considered a sign of a healthy and thriving congregation. However, the needless proliferation of activities and organizations not essentially religious in character may add to the difficulties of an already "over-organized" community which has more organizations than it can afford to keep going. Here, as elsewhere, churches find their part in the overall community organization, and some degree of coordination and avoidance of wasteful duplication is desirable. (See Chapter 17.)

While such information as the average weekly Sunday school attendance, the size of the men's club, or the number of church athletic teams is easy to gather and relevant to the church's functions, statistics alone do not measure the intensity of the spiritual experience.

52. To what extent are church policies determined by the local congregations?

53. What is the structure through which congregational control, where present, takes place?

[1] Fichter, Joseph H., "Conceptualizations of the Urban Parish," *Social Forces,* vol. 31, October, 1952, p. 46.

54. For each church, check the following activities:
   a. Sunday school
   b. Adult Bible study group
   c. Men's club
   d. Women's club
   e. Young people's club
   f. Young adults' club
   g. Missionary society
   h. Training classes for teachers, group leaders
   i. Church library
   j. Facilities for motion pictures, slides, etc.
   k. Lecture or forum program
   l. Concerts
   m. Church choir
   n. Dramatics program
   o. Church open daily for devotion
   p. Church office open daily
   q. Annual every member financial canvass
   r. Bulletin or calendar issued weekly[1]

55. Which churches have special organizations in the recreational field, such as basketball teams, bowling leagues, softball teams, or similar groups?
56. Do any of the churches sponsor Boy Scouts or other such organizations?
57. Can you find examples of the churches making available to nonaffiliated groups the use of their meeting places?
58. What activities do the church organizations sponsor which draw families together for worship, recreation, or social service work?
59. Is leadership of various church activities widely dispersed or is it concentrated in the hands of small "ruling cliques"?
60. Are church organizations burdened with factional disputes between conflicting cliques, or does harmony prevail?
61. How do the quarters which are used for Sunday schools compare with the classrooms in the public schools?
62. How does the quality of instruction in the Sunday schools compare with instruction in the public schools?
63. Are the Sunday schools carrying on a vital program of religious education, or a perfunctory one?
64. Do the churches lose many young people when they grow too old for the Sunday school, or do these young people go on into active participation in adult activities in the church?
65. Is there any type of program of religious activity or instruction in connection with the public schools?
   Are the rights and sensitivities of religious minority groups or of nonreligious citizens being respected?
66. Is there any program of after-school religious instruction, such as Talmud Torah schools or confirmation classes?
67. How many vacation Bible schools operate in your community?

[1] The last few items are taken from much longer lists of activities available in Douglass, H. Paul. *How to Study the City Church*, Institute of Social and Religious Research, New York, 1928; and Sanderson, Ross W., *The Strategy of City Church Planning*, Institute of Social and Religious Research, New York, 1932.

68. What parochial or denominational schools are to be found in your community?
69. How do the parochial schools compare with the public schools? (See Chapter 7.)
70. Is there a denominational college in your community? What contribution, if any, does it make to the religious life of the community?
71. If your community has a boarding school or college, is there a definite effort made to acquaint the students with the religious activities available to them in the community?
72. Has your community any of the following organizations:

| YMCA, YWCA | Knights of Columbus | Other similar |
| YMHA, YWHA | Jewish community center | organizations |

Interfaith Relations

There is a historical background of hostility and misunderstanding in the relations of Protestantism, Catholicism, and Judaism. Basic doctrinal differences as to the status of Jesus, the scriptures, the church, and the clergy have caused much friction in times past. Increasingly, an attitude of tolerance of doctrinal differences has arisen. The different religious faiths do not minimize their doctrinal differences, but have learned to get along with each other despite these differences. This process of interfaith cooperation has been aided by the search for common areas of basic values on which the major faiths largely agree, and by the experience of interfaith cooperation in various types of social endeavor in the community.

Occasionally, matters of doctrinal differences lead to obstructions in cooperative action. An additional source of disagreement concerns the performing of religious functions, such as praying, scripture reading, and celebrating religious holidays in the schools. Still another area on which improvement in interfaith relations has been found difficult is the status of parochial schools, and whether they shall have access to tax money, whether tax-supported transportation of pupils to parochial schools shall be instituted, and so on. Practices in such matters vary from state to state. Another area of tension is that of interfaith marriages.

There is a growing pattern of cooperation among the Protestant churches, and to a lesser extent among the three major religious branches, Catholics, Jews, and Protestants, on stands taken on public issues, social work in the community, and other secular matters considered germane to religious concern.

73. Has your community any of the following organizations:

| Women's Christian Temperance | Alcoholics Anonymous |
| Union | Catholic War Veterans |

       Jewish War Veterans   Other religious organizations not
       Fellowship of Reconciliation   based in a single church

74. Is there a federation of church women?

75. Is there a council of churches? What are its activities? Which churches belong to it?

76. In general, do the various religious groups work together well in the community, or do they work at cross-purposes?

77. Are there any indications of tension or conflict between people or groups of different religious affiliations?

78. Have the past ten years seen progress toward better interfaith understanding?

79. Is there in your community an agency or committee to foster interfaith understanding and cooperation, such as a branch of the National Conference of Christians and Jews?
    What is its program? Do the individual churches cooperate with it?

80. What interfaith projects have been carried out in your community in recent years:

    Union services   Joint action with respect to legis-
    Forums on interfaith relationships   lation or social issues
    Fund-raising drives   Interfaith celebration of Christian
    Cooperative radio program series   and/or Jewish holidays
    Religious census   Other

81. Do the clergy carry on an "exchange pulpit" program?

82. To what extent do church congregations visit back and forth for various services or social functions?

83. Do the clergymen themselves maintain a sympathetic and tolerant attitude toward the beliefs of other religious organizations in the community?

84. Have the clergymen in your community ever taken joint action for anything? What?

85. Are sermons ever devoted to bettering the relations between people of different religious faiths in the community?

86. Do the churches take an active part in pointing out violations of civil rights, fair play, or sympathetic understanding?

87. Do the churches maintain a vocal ministry against segregated housing, discriminatory employment policies, and other violations of equal treatment to all groups?

88. What attitude predominates in each church toward interfaith marriages?

89. What estimate would you make of the effect of the churches on the following types of intergroup relations:

    Interracial   Between the older generation
    Interfaith   and the younger
    Between people of different   Between "oldtimers" and newcomers
      nationality backgrounds   Between townfolk and rural people
    Between employers and employees   Other

90. Is there extreme competition for new members among the churches?

Does such competition ever engender hostile attitudes or derogatory charges?
91. In general, how would you appraise the total impact of religious organizations on intergroup relations in your community? (See Chapter 15.)

Religious Action in the Community

While some churches confine themselves to the religious and secular interests of their own members, others are more active in community matters
and in being of service to nonmembers.

On the local level, particularly in larger communities, churches may singly
or in combination support various types of professional social work activity.
Examples would be such institutions as children's homes, homes for the
aged, hospitals, and such agencies as neighborhood centers, recreational
centers, city mission activities, and family societies.

The churches may also carry on types of social endeavor which involve
participation in matters of community concern, such as educational programs in family relations, mental health, race relations, international relations, industrial relations, and various social problem areas; activity in
support of progressive health and welfare legislation and administration
on the local level; cooperation in conducting surveys of various aspects of
the community; provision of meeting places or supervision for clubs, youth
groups, and other recreational organizations; cooperation with other agencies
in health and welfare, including participation in the activities of the health
and welfare council; cooperation with the police, schools, courts, and other
agencies in the prevention of delinquency and in other correctional problems; recruiting capable volunteer religious leadership for community boards,
committees, and service groups; and providing leadership for new constructive developments in the way the community faces its problems.

Individual clergymen may act as chaplains in hospitals or prisons; afford
active skilled volunteer leadership for worthwhile community projects; visit
appropriate officials or citizens to admonish them about injustices; form
close professional cooperative relationships with physicians, school teachers,
social workers, and other professional people, and in general be interested
and alert citizens with a special contribution to make by virtue of their key
positions in the community.[1]

Various churches, through their own national denominational organizations, support many widespread activities beyond the local community. Part
of this activity is in connection with church missionary work, either domestic or

---

[1] Many of the activities listed in this section are taken from Shelby M. Harrison's paper
entitled *A Strategy for Protestants in Social Welfare*, distributed in mimeographed form
by the National Council of the Churches of Christ in the U.S.A.

foreign. Domestic missionary endeavor includes work with migrant workers, Indians, and various underprivileged groups. Foreign missionary work includes, in addition to the strictly religious program, church schools, colleges, hospitals, research and industrial projects, and other activities in the health, welfare, and recreational fields. In addition, the churches frequently cooperate with other national agencies to further international understanding, or mental health, or rural life, or any number of various activities. There is hardly a field of human need in which some active church group cannot be found.

92. What programs of the churches indicate that they are a vital force for love, sympathy, and mutual understanding in your community?
How could they become more vital in this respect?

93. Do the churches take the leadership in developing programs of community betterment?

94. Are your churches alert to further such programs as the mental health movement, the fight against venereal disease, the betterment of interracial relations, the improvement of housing, and similar endeavors?

95. Do the churches cooperate actively with various social agencies?

96. What social work programs are maintained by your churches in the local community:

Settlement houses or recreation centers	Health clinics
	Institutions for children, the
Summer camps	handicapped, the aged
Child guidance clinics	Social casework agencies
Counseling services	Other
Hospitals	

97. Which of the programs listed are available only to members of the church or denomination which sponsors them, and which are available to all people who need the service, regardless of religious affiliation?

98. Which of the social endeavors of the churches in your community are devoted to:

Alleviating misery	Prevention
Rehabilitating those who need help	Positive community improvement

99. Which churches perform a function as a center of neighborhood or community activities?

100. Which churches take a responsibility for improving social conditions in their neighborhood or community? Examples?

101. Which churches have lay groups, such as sisterhoods, brotherhoods, St. Vincent de Paul Societies, sodalities, and so on, that carry on benevolent activities among the congregation? Do they serve members and nonmembers as well?

102. Is there a Federation of Protestant, Catholic, or Jewish health or welfare agencies? What are its activities?

103. In what ways do the churches depart in their actions from the way of love and mutual respect which they profess?

104. To what extent does each church indicate a primary preoccupation with its own problems of organization, management, budget, and so on; and how much energy does it have left for worship and good works?

105. Do the churches have active programs to promote international understanding and peace?

106. What attitude do the churches take toward individuals who are conscientious objectors on religious grounds? On purely secular grounds?

107. Do clergymen make a definite attempt, either in their sermons or on other occasions, to help the people apply the teachings of their religion to the daily problems which confront the local community?

108. Are the churches bearing a message which seems vital and worthwhile to large numbers of youth?
What criticisms do young people make of their churches?

109. To what extent are the churches providing means of wholesome association of different people, over and above the purely religious functions?

110. Do you notice groups of people lingering on the church steps and passing the time of day after services?

111. Do you notice that weddings and funerals are the occasions for people who have not seen each other in a long time to renew their acquaintances?

112. Are the various groups in the churches actively seeking out people who may have a special need for the type of association and fellowship available in the churches, specifically newcomers? Strangers? Migrants? Transients? People who are alone in the community?

113. Are older people encouraged and made to feel that they are wanted in the various church groups?

114. Are there provisions for transporting older people who might participate in church activities if such transportation were available?

115. Do older people who are lonely or confined to their own homes, nursing homes, and so on, receive visits by members of one church group or another?

Changes in Functions

Health, welfare, educational, and recreational functions in earlier times were performed chiefly by the church. While many of these functions have split off from their religious sponsorship, some of them are still carried on in part by church groups. Examples would be hospitals, care of the poor, parochial and Sunday schools, church pageants, dances, entertainments, and athletics.

It is interesting to note the functions which the churches take up or discard in one or another period of history. In our own times, noticeable changes are taking place in the functions which churches perform, and out of these changes the role of the church in the community is continually redefined.

Thus, many churches are assuming adult education functions which a few decades ago were performed, if at all, under secular auspices. Public education in international relations, in industrial relations, and in connection with various social problems are illustrations. From the family, the churches are borrowing certain counseling and family life training functions.

At the same time, some functions are being transferred in part to the schools. Much of the recreational program for youth in rural communities is gradually becoming absorbed by the schools. The care of the needy has been largely taken over by social work agencies, public and private. Indeed, many of the functions formerly performed by private, chiefly religious charitable endeavor, have been taken over by various governmental units to the extent that it has been alleged that the old practice of "tithing" has been supplanted by the income tax.

116. What functions have been taken up by the churches in your community which were formerly carried on in part or in whole by:
   The family   The government
   Public schools   Other agencies in the community
   Commercial recreation agencies
117. What functions which were formerly carried on in part or in whole by the churches are now being carried on by:
   The family   The government
   Public schools   Other agencies in the community
   Commercial recreation agencies
118. From what agencies in your community do the churches appear to be taking on new functions?
119. To what agencies in your community do the churches seem to be giving up functions?
120. For each item in the following list, record which churches are increasing and which are decreasing their activities:
   Counseling   Adult education
   Family life training   Athletics
   Economic assistance   Recreation
   Health care   Center of community activities
   Education   Devotional and worship services

Some Aids to the Church Survey

The research departments of local, state, or national church councils and denominational groups may have published studies of the religious institutions of your community. In a city large enough to justify a survey, the council of churches may be able to offer invaluable assistance in the religious aspects of a community study. Indeed, it is questionable whether a study of any magnitude should take place without the active participation and support of the council of churches. For modest inquiries, the council of churches may be able to supply all the information which the study requires. For the more extensive studies, the council is not only a source of liaison with the various church groups, but also may be able to participate actively in the study. It should be kept in mind that some religious bodies, of which the largest is the Roman Catholic Church, do not as a matter of policy participate in the council of churches, and information or support in a study must be sought directly.

In addition to what the council may do, or in the absence of a council, certain sources of information will prove particularly helpful. One such source is the city directory, if there is one. This will list the names of the churches, but may leave out smaller religious groups which meet in homes, store-fronts, and so forth. H. Paul Douglass' *How to Study the City Church*[1] will afford invaluable advice to those desiring to make more extensive studies of a city's churches than that which is outlined in the present chapter.

For cities which numbered 25,000 or more inhabitants in 1930, volume one of the *Census of Religious Bodies: 1936*[2] is a fruitful source of information concerning the churches in that year. It supplies statistics on the total number of churches, church membership, membership by sex, number and value of church edifices, financial information, and Sunday school figures. It also gives the breakdown by denominations for much of this information. These figures can form a bench mark for measuring changes which have taken place in subsequent years and thus discovering the trends. For example, it is possible to determine which denominations have shown the greatest growth in number of churches, and which have declined. Membership figures can also be compared with the 1936 figures. Such gains and losses might then be compared with population changes in the past two decades (see section "Using the Census," page 328). Religious leaders may be able to help in interpreting the changes which are found.

For surveys of rural churches, a basis for comparison is afforded in H. Paul Douglass, "Some Protestant Churches in Rural America: A Summary and Interpretation."[3] He reports on a series of studies including a total of 1,231 churches predominantly in rural territory. Below are some of his findings:

[1] See footnote, p. 145.
[2] Bureau of the Census, Government Printing Office, Washington, 1936.
[3] *Town and Country Church*, no. 58, January, 1950.

Average membership	186
Ratio of attendance to membership	43.6%
Average Sunday school enrollment	114
Average ratio of benevolences to congregational expenditures	27.0%
Churches which are growing	39.9%
Churches which are stationary	19.4%
Churches which are declining	40.7%
Churches without any youth organization	More than 3 out of 10
Churches served by nonresident ministers	3 out of 10
Churches with either nonresident ministers or part-time pastoral care	54.5%

A similar summary of urban church studies, "Some Protestant Churches in Urban America," also prepared by H. Paul Douglass, was published in the January 21, 1950, issue of *Information Service*, National Council of the Churches of Christ in the U.S.A., New York.

Considerable material can be obtained from diocesan or other denominational headquarters as to the churches in any particular community. Church yearbooks and directories are fruitful sources of data. Still other types of information will have to be obtained directly from the churches involved.

References for Further Study

Abrams, Ray H., editor, "Organized Religion in the U.S.," special issue of *The Annals of the American Academy of Political and Social Science*, vol. 256, March, 1948. An excellent survey of organized religion in the United States with specific articles by experts on such topics as Characteristics of American Organized Religion, Religion and the Class Structure, The Churches and Social Problems, and many others.

Fichter, Joseph H., *Dynamics of a City Church:* Southern Parish. University of Chicago Press, Chicago, vol. 1, 1951. This book investigates "the religious supernatural activities of the parishioners of St. Mary's (a southern parish) in so far as they could be externally observed and measured. . . . Each major religious function of the parish is measured against the 'ideal' set forth in the teaching and legislation of the Catholic Church."

Hallenbeck, Wilbur C., *My Community, My Church, and Me!* Friendship Press, New York, 1938. "A handbook for guidance of groups concerned with making sociological studies of urban institutions in their community setting."

Hunter, Edwin A., *The Small Town and Country Church.* Abingdon-Cokesbury Press, New York-Nashville, 1947. This little book treats many of the problems of American rural communities with particular reference to the role of the church and of the rural community pastorate in community betterment.

Landis, Benson Y., editor, *The Yearbook of American Churches*. Sowers Printing Co., Lebanon, Pennsylvania, published annually. A definitive source of up-to-date information on the Protestant denominations. Among other data, this book includes a list by communities of such organizations as councils of church women, local councils with voluntary leadership, and field organizations with paid leadership. Contains an extensive directory of social, civic, and religious service agencies.

Lindstrom, David E., *The Methodist Church and the Rural Community*. Board of Missions and Church Extension of the Methodist Church, New York, 1948. This pamphlet gives the recommendations of a national committee on such topics as Business, Labor, Health, Education, Organizations, Race and Class, Recreation, Social Welfare, Government, Rural-Urban Relations, and Christian Leadership.

Randolph, Henry S., *A Manual for Town and Country Churches*. Board of National Missions, Presbyterian Church in the U.S.A., New York, 1947.

Smith, Rockwell C., *The Church in Our Town*. Abingdon-Cokesbury Press, New York-Nashville, 1945. This book is a deliberate attempt to apply the concepts of rural sociology and economics to the concerns of the rural church. It describes different aspects of rural community living and relates them to the church's function.

The American Jewish Yearbook. Jewish Publication Society of America, Philadelphia, published annually. Contains various articles about recent developments in Judaism as well as a directory of Jewish federations, welfare funds, and community councils, listed by state and city.

The City Church. Bimonthly publication of the Department of the Urban Church, National Council of the Churches of Christ in the U.S.A. This is an interesting journal of events and items of interest to urban church people.

The Official Catholic Directory. P. J. Kenedy and Sons, New York, published annually. Authoritative compilation of facts about the Roman Catholic Church. Among other data it gives by communities the names of churches, as well as the names of schools, the number on the staff, and so on. It also includes the names of pastors and other priests.

10. Social Insurance and Public Assistance

RECENT DECADES have seen an extensive multiplication of agencies, laws, and programs designed to be of aid to families in many different ways. Some of the programs for the family are under private agencies, but an increasing number of them have come under government auspices in the past generation.

The increased participation of government agencies in programs which minister to the welfare of individuals and families is a reflection of basic changes which are occurring in community living. (See Chapter 20.)

The economics of family living is complicated by the dependence of increasingly large numbers of people on large, impersonal companies for employment. Remote markets in various parts of the world and the exigencies of the "business cycle" at home often affect the individual's opportunity to earn a living. At the same time, it becomes more difficult for family, neighborhood, and community to care for their members in times of need. Families are smaller in size and there are fewer close bonds between relatives, movement around the country frequently keeps families uprooted, local neighborhood strength often wanes as people become absorbed into the larger community, and even communities and whole states and regions vary in their ability to care for the families that are in economic need.

Under these circumstances, two large fields of economic assistance to families have grown up. One is based on the insurance principle, which combines "saving for a rainy day" and "spreading the risk." The other is based on a system of federal, state, and local cooperation in caring for the nation's needy. It is often thought that the latter is appropriate only to times of economic depression and mass unemployment, but there is continuous financial need by many families and individuals. The two largest items in the welfare budget of most communities are old-age assistance and aid to dependent children, both of which are relatively stable items having only limited variation with the business cycle. Each of these programs makes payments to more than two million persons even in relatively prosperous years.[1]

Economic need may arise as a result of old age, unemployment, illness, death, broken homes, accident, feeblemindedness or other handicaps to economic self-sufficiency.[2] In addition, sheer size of family may be a cause of economic need, a fact which is acknowledged in some systems of differential payment that recognize family size as a pertinent factor. Family size influences size of payments in various public assistance programs as well as in the armed services, a few private industries, and in some school systems.

Social Insurance

The various social insurance programs are designed to meet the economic need of the individual or family which is caused by unemployment, industrial accidents or illness, death of wage-earner, medical expenses, and retirement due to old age. Of course, such provision for individual families also lightens the burden which communities would have to face in caring for these people if they were not already provided for through social insurance programs. As long as American values include the idea that no family should be allowed to starve, and that certain minimum provisions for health, shelter, and family living should be provided for those who need them, social insurance provides in some fields a convenient way of preparing for such need before it arises, often with the individuals, themselves, contributing and thus sharing in the responsibility. While such programs are available through government agencies, there are many insurance benefits available through the employer or through union and employer jointly. For each of the social insurances except unemployment insurance, there is in most communities a strong industry-related private plan, especially in pensions and health insurance.

Unemployment insurance. An important type of social insurance is unemployment insurance. All states have unemployment insurance programs, under provisions of the Social Security Act which make it advantageous to do so. Benefits are distributed through public employment offices or other agencies approved by the federal government. Within the wide limits defined by the Social Security Act, your own state law governs which workers

[1] For current figures on these and other social security programs in your state or the country as a whole, see the "Annual Statistical Supplement" to the *Social Security Bulletin,* a monthly bulletin of facts and figures about the social security program, Government Printing Office, Washington. The Annual Statistical Supplement usually appears in September.

[2] For background, read Miles, Arthur P., *An Introduction to Public Welfare,* D.C. Heath and Co., Boston, 1949.

are covered, what the qualifications for benefits are, and how much shall be paid out, and for how long. Unemployment insurance and workmen's compensation laws typically do not apply to all enterprises, but only to those which employ a certain number of workers. Often other groups are excluded from benefits, such as employees of religious, charitable, and government agencies. Your local unemployment insurance office can give you material describing your state law as well as descriptive figures on the benefits paid to workers in your community.

1. Which office receives claims, interviews claimants, and establishes eligibility for unemployment insurance benefits in your community?
   In what relationship does this office stand to the public employment service?
2. How many different workers received unemployment insurance benefits at some time during the past year?
3. According to your state law, which types of workers are covered by this program?
4. What percentage of payrolls is paid by employers for unemployment insurance?
   Which employers must by law participate in this plan?
5. How do workers qualify for benefits?
6. How much do unemployed workers receive each week as a maximum? For how many weeks?
7. Does the number of weeks of benefit vary with past earnings?
8. Does the amount of payments vary with the number of the unemployed worker's dependents?
9. How long is the waiting period before benefit payments begin?
10. What specific provisions disqualify a worker from benefits?
11. Do local businessmen's associations and labor unions take an active interest in the administration of unemployment insurance?
12. How does the merit rating or experience rating formula of your state law affect employers in your community?

Workmen's compensation. Workmen's compensation laws in every state are designed to compensate the worker or his family through medical care and cash benefits in case of his injury or death "arising out of and in the course of employment." State laws vary as to which occupations are covered, what the benefits are, how long they will last, and so on.[1]

13. Which office determines eligibility for benefits for injured workers in your community?
14. How many workmen or workmen's families received compensation payments during the past year?

[1] See *How Good Is Your Workmen's Compensation Law?* Bulletin 70 of the Division of Labor Standards, U.S. Department of Labor, Government Printing Office, Washington, 1944.

SERVICES TO INDIVIDUALS AND FAMILIES

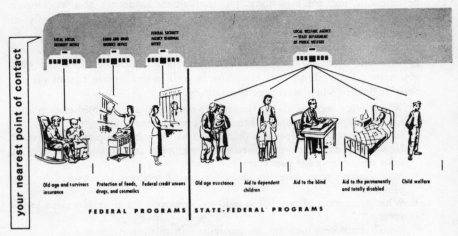

SOURCE: *For You and Yours,* Federal Security Administration, 1952.

15. What types of employment are covered by your state workmen's compensation law? Are certain types of workers such as the following excluded:
    Farm workers   Employees of charitable or religious
    Domestic workers   organizations
                                         Other
16. Must all employers covered by the law participate in a workmen's compensation insurance plan: Public insurance program? Commercial insurance program? Either?
17. Are any injuries specifically excluded that are due to:
    Employee's intoxication   Employee's gross negligence
    Employee's willful misconduct   Other
18. Are payments based on the employee's wages at the time he was injured?
19. Are there maximum and minimum limits to the amounts paid?
20. What limitations are made on the number or duration of the payments, or on the maximum regular allotment?
21. Is there any limitation on the time or total cost of the medical care furnished to injured employees?
22. Is your state one of the few in which benefit payments are made for unemployment caused by sickness or injury even though not related to the worker's occupation?
    If so, how do these provisions operate? How financed? By whom administered?
    How is eligibility for benefits determined?

THROUGH FEDERAL SECURITY AGENCY PROGRAMS

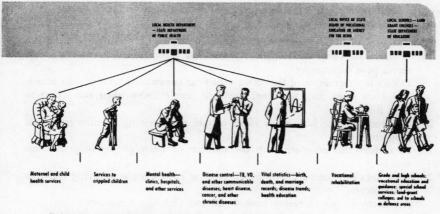

The local offices are usually your best point of contact for these services. State headquarters are generally located in the capital city. See the first page for a list of the parts of the Federal Security Agency through which the Agency carries on its share of the partnership and maintains connecting links with your State and community.

Old-Age and Survivors Insurance. A program of particular importance to old people in the community is Old-Age and Survivors Insurance. This is a program to which workers, employers, farmers, and some self-employed people contribute. It affords a retirement income to an individual who has worked long enough in a "covered" occupation to become insured under the program, and to his widow or other specified survivors at his death. The retirement age is 65. The vast majority of people employed in paid civilian work in the United States are earning credits toward this retirement income at any one time. This program is operated directly by the federal government, with no participation by intermediate governmental units such as state and county. The Bureau of Old-Age and Survivors Insurance operates six area offices, approximately 480 field offices, and about 1,800 stations where regularly scheduled services are maintained.[1] The 1954 Revision of the Social Security Law sets maximum monthly benefits at $108.50 for a retired worker, $54.30 additional for a wife or for a dependent husband, up to $200 for a widow with two or more children.

Old-Age and Survivors Insurance should not be confused with Old-Age Assistance, which is distributed only in case of need. The OASI is a retirement pension financed out of payroll deductions and employer contributions,

[1] See *Social Security in the United States,* Department of Health, Education, and Welfare, Government Printing Office, Washington, 1953.

while Old-Age Assistance is a type of public assistance to the needy aged, financed out of federal, state, and local tax money. Nevertheless, the two are related in that many more old people would be in need of Old-Age Assistance were it not for the OASI program. (See Chapter 13 for a further consideration of older people as a special group.)

23. Where is the office of the Bureau of Old-Age and Survivors Insurance which serves your community?
    Does a representative of this office visit your community on a regular schedule? How often does he come? How do people know when and where to meet him?
24. Can you find out how many older people are receiving benefits from this program today?
25. How does this compare with the number of older people in your community?[1]
26. How does this compare with the number of older people receiving Old-Age Assistance?
    Are many people receiving both OASI and Old-Age Assistance?
27. How many people in your community are now working in covered occupations and accumulating credits in the OASI program?
    How does this figure compare with the total number employed in your community?
28. What are the levels of OASI benefits actually paid in your community?
    In terms of budgets for elderly couples published in the *Social Security Bulletin,* are these benefits adequate?
29. Are there any groups that are not covered by the OASI program?
    Is there any special provision made for their retirement income?[2]

Health insurance. Another widespread type of economic need which is amenable to the social insurance principle is that caused by sickness and the cost of medical care. In this field, there is much less governmental participation, largely because of strong opposition on the part of the American Medical Association. Four states have provided for disability payments for those who because of injury or illness are unable to work. In another vein, the Farm Security Administration until 1946 provided a plan whereby its low-income borrowers organized into a prepaid medical program. Rural health cooperatives are flourishing in various parts of the country. They are usually based on a voluntary prepayment plan for medical care. In addition, commercial insurance companies offer individual policies which

[1] See the *Census of Population,* vol. 2, sec. B. For comparability be sure the figures refer to the same geographic area. Also, keep in mind that the Census figure is for 1950.
[2] Both federal employees and railroad workers have their special retirement programs, as do employees in some state and municipal civil service systems, but in many states public servants also participate in OASI.

pay specified benefits for specified types of sickness or injury, often including not only payments for medical care, but also family income payments during the illness or disability.

Nevertheless, the bulk of insurance against illness comes in the privately operated voluntary nonprofit prepayment plans for hospital expenses such as Blue Cross and similar plans for surgical expenses such as Blue Shield, and in individual commercial policies. A notable development has been the writing of health provisions into collective bargaining contracts. A growing practice is for such industrial programs to purchase insurance from existing nonprofit organizations such as Blue Cross and Blue Shield.[1]

30. What voluntary hospital or surgery prepayment programs exist in your area?
31. In each program, who is eligible to participate?
32. What is the monthly cost?
33. What are the benefits?
34. How many people in your community are enrolled in such programs? What proportion of the total population?
35. How many hospitals participate? How many physicians?
36. Which industries have health insurance programs?
    Are these industry-operated, or do they purchase insurance from existing nonprofit plans?
37. What provision is there for hospital and surgical expenses in the case of those who cannot afford to participate in these voluntary prepayment programs?
38. Can you find out the extent of policies with private commercial companies which sell individual insurance providing payments for medical care and/or income during illness?
39. Do these policies permit cancellation by the company at the close of any annual period, thus leaving completely unprotected those who may fall prey to a chronic disease?

Public Assistance

Public assistance is financial aid or service provided at public expense by a government agency for persons or families who are in need. Need is defined differently in each state, but it usually means less income than a minimum subsistence budget requires for an individual or family unit. The term "public assistance" corresponds roughly to what laymen mean by the word "relief." While public assistance seems to be a simple thing, it is actually rather complex, consisting of a number of different types of allot-

[1] See Chapter 12, particularly pp. 219ff.

ments for specific types of need, sometimes called "categories," usually supplemented by a residual type of "general assistance" or "home relief" for needy people who are not eligible under one of the special categories. These various types of public assistance are set up differently as to the degree of federal, state, and local financing and supervision as well as eligibility, maximum payments, and so on.

Types of public assistance. Since the days of the Elizabethan Poor Laws there has been an unbroken tradition of recognition by local government of an obligation to afford a basic minimum of food, clothing, and shelter to those in need. Subsequent developments have involved decreasing use of the "almshouse" or "poorhouse" as the sole means of providing for aid to the needy, and an increase in programs of assistance to people in their own homes and an increase in cash payments rather than payments in kind. There has also been a decrease in the stigma placed upon need as unemployment has come to be caused increasingly by impersonal economic forces; a growing acknowledgment of respect for the individual relief recipient as a human being, and an increasing emphasis on the desirability of helping the individual become restored to self-sufficiency wherever possible. This last principle is usually in opposition to earlier punitive attitudes toward those receiving public aid or private "charity."

Gradually, particular types or "categories" of need came to be singled out for special consideration other than commitment to the "poor house." These types of special need, or "categories," have become an integral part of public welfare administration in the United States. As the characteristics of an industrial society became more pronounced, there developed the need for organizing certain aspects of the public assistance program on a wider base than that of the local municipality. Thus, state governments and the federal government came to participate in limited fashion in one program or another. The Great Depression created a situation in which not only individual families were unable to care for their needy members, but whole communities and even whole states lacked the means necessary to meet the economic need. A series of federal relief programs was therefore instituted, and a plan was developed for a system under which public assistance could remain in the hands of states and municipalities, but the cost could be in part equalized through federal grants-in-aid to the states and through state grants-in-aid to the local communities. This resulted in the Social Security Act of 1935, with subsequent amendments, which, among other programs such as OASI and unemployment insurance, set up a system of grants-in-aid for such categories as Aid to the Blind, Old-Age Assistance, Aid to Dependent Children, and later Aid to the Permanently and Totally Disabled. It also provided for grants-in-aid for state programs of maternal and child health, services to crippled children, and various child welfare services.[1]

State programs of public assistance are thus aided by federal grants-in-aid. In contrast, no federal grants-in-aid are made for "general assistance," a residual category of public assistance to recipients who are found to be in need but who are not eligible under one of the special "categories." Such programs are financed exclusively by the states and localities. In the case of the categories, some states operate their public assistance programs directly, with branch offices in counties or regions of the states, while in others the municipalities (counties, towns, or cities) operate the public assistance programs. Since considerable autonomy is left with the individual states and in the case of many states with the individual municipalities, there are many different types of setup for the local administration of public assistance. Sometimes all programs are coordinated in one agency. In other cases, various agencies administer one part or another of the program. An early task for the citizen interested in studying public welfare facilities will be to determine the administrative setup for the various public assistance programs in his community or in the welfare district or county of which his community is a part.[2]

Certain principles, some fairly recent, others which have been developing for centuries, are associated with progressive public assistance standards: (1) Prevention of dependency should be effected wherever possible. (2) Where this is not possible, restoration of the recipient to self-sufficiency should be an important goal. (3) Meanwhile, it helps neither the recipient nor society to stigmatize him as a pauper; rather, his self-respect should be preserved and encouraged, for it is important if he is not to develop an attitude of dependency on others. (4) Even in cases where restoration to self-sufficiency is not possible, the client should be treated with respect and understanding. (5) Public assistance clients should be helped by trained social workers rather than politicians. (6) Eligibility for assistance should depend on objective impartial standards and be free of favoritism or political pressure on the recipient. These and other principles are based on the acknowledgment of the extreme importance of the family in our society and of public responsibility for maintaining the family intact wherever possible.

An overall consideration is that although the cost of public assistance

[1] For a description of how these programs operate, see Social Welfare Administration in the United States of America, Federal Security Agency, Government Printing Office, Washington, 1950; and Social Security in the United States, Department of Health, Education, and Welfare, Government Printing Office, 1953.

[2] See Characteristics of State Public Assistance Plans, Federal Security Agency, Government Printing Office, Washington, 1950.

is great, the cost of neglecting it may be greater—greater in terms of sickness, future impoverishment, delinquency, unrest, and loss of respect for humanitarian values in our society.

40. What agency or agencies administer public assistance in your community?
41. Which types of public assistance are now available in your community:

Aid to dependent children	General assistance (home relief, etc.)
Aid to the blind	Veteran assistance
Aid to the disabled	Work relief
Old-age assistance	Other

42. Which agency has responsibility for each type of public assistance?
43. Is the public assistance agency a city, town, or county agency? A local branch of a state agency?
44. To what extent is each type of public assistance supervised by the appropriate state department?
45. How is the local welfare commissioner chosen?
46. Does the local public assistance agency have a local citizen welfare board? How is this welfare board chosen? What are its functions?
47. How many caseworkers and case supervisors are engaged in the local public assistance program?
How many of these have had professional social work training? How much training?
48. Are all public assistance workers hired on the basis of civil service examinations, or are they political appointees or electees?
If under civil service, what qualifications are necessary for each type of position?
49. How do salaries compare with the qualifications desired? With salaries paid in comparable communities? Are they such as to attract competent staff?
50. Are there provisions for in-service or other training of caseworkers?
51. Where is the public assistance office located? Is it pleasant and attractive?
52. Are there places where clients may be interviewed inconspicuously and without unnecessary distraction?
53. Is there a waiting room with sufficient seating space and with adequate toilet facilities?
54. How many persons are at present enrolled as recipients of one type or another of public assistance in your community?
55. How many were enrolled a year ago? Five years ago?
What significant changes have been taking place in public assistance enrollments?
56. Make plot maps of the residences of recipients of different types of public assistance.
Are they spread evenly throughout the community, or do they concentrate in certain localities?[1]

[1] Different states and municipalities have different policies with respect to making avail-

57. If there is no work-relief program at present, are there any plans for one in case of widespread economic need?

58. What is the maximum, minimum, and average grant under each of the public assistance programs?

59. Does each program have its own independent basis for assistance allotments, or are the maximum and minimum figures the same for all programs?

60. Under each program, what is the basis for allowance for the following items:

| Food | Shelter | Light | Medical care |
| Clothing | Heat | Transportation | Other |

61. What proportion of public assistance grants are made in cash payments? In goods such as food and clothing? In voucher payments (a purchase order on a particular store)? In work-relief wages?

62. What was the total expenditure of your community's public assistance services during the past year?
How much of this amount was reimbursed by federal and state funds?

63. How many persons were served and what was the total expenditure in each type of public assistance?

64. How are the federal government's contribution and that of the state and the local welfare district determined in the four federally assisted categories of public assistance:

| Aid to the blind | Aid to the disabled |
| Aid to dependent children | Old-age assistance |

65. What other types of public assistance are there? What proportion of the cost of these programs is borne by your state and what proportion by your locality?

66. Do all public assistance programs use the same standard budget in determining needs?

67. Are the names of relief recipients publicized? In what way?
Does this procedure cause hardship in individual cases?
Is there any basis for the widely held belief that such publicity discourages unscrupulous persons from applying for relief?

Eligibility requirements. An important aspect of public assistance work is the definition of what constitutes need and the determination of individual cases of need for such assistance. This is customarily done through setting eligibility standards which must be met by any applicant in order to receive assistance. Such standards should be simple so as to be easily explained and understood. They should also be nondiscriminatory. A widely accepted method of determining need utilizes a standard minimum budget for the family involved, and then compares this with the family's resources

---

able to the public the names and addresses of relief recipients. However, most such departments will make such information available for bona fide survey or research purposes, and where the anonymity of the relief client will be protected.

and income. If the minimum budget exceeds the funds available to the family, public assistance is indicated for the balance.

Two knotty questions are: What should be done in the case of property? and What should be required by way of support by relatives? It is often found that restoration to self-sufficiency is hindered if all available assets must be summarily wiped out before public assistance is granted, yet the public must be protected from unnecessary expenditures in cases where the assets of the applicant are inordinately large. Likewise, forcing the relatives to contribute to support may create as many problems as it solves. Yet most Americans are unwilling to give up completely the idea of responsibility of various relatives for each other. With so many people on the move in this country, outmoded residence requirements, or "settlement laws," are a great hindrance to the administration of public assistance, and work real hardship in numerous cases.[1]

68. What is the basis for eligibility under each of the public assistance programs:
    Economic need   Citizenship or residence requirements
    Age requirements   Other
69. What specifically must applicants do in order to qualify for various types of public assistance:
    Register with public employment agency if employable
    Dispose of or deed over personal property
    Sign a "pauper's oath"
70. What specific types of people are excluded from public assistance:
    Workers who are on strike
    Employables who refuse any type of employment
    People who have retained any personal resources
    People who have any earnings, however inadequate
    People receiving social insurance benefits, even though inadequate
71. Are the conditions of eligibility under each public assistance program stated as clearly and simply as possible?
72. To what extent are relatives required to support the needy person? Which relatives? How does this policy operate in practice?
73. Is there provision for emergency grants in cases of immediate need pending more thorough examination of eligibility?
74. What provisions are there for appeal by those who believe their cases have been handled unfairly?
75. Are there needy persons who cannot qualify for any type of public assistance? Why not? Does this indicate needed changes in eligibility requirements?
76. In the case of a person who is eligible for public assistance, trace the steps which he must follow to procure it, from the first inquiry at the public assist-

[1] See Falk, Myron, *Settlement Laws:* A Major Problem in Social Welfare, American Association of Social Workers, New York, 1948.

ance office until the first grant is made. (Initial interview, formal applications, declarations, investigation, determination of budget, determination of payment, issuing of payment, and so on.)

77. Do applicants for public assistance receive courteous and understanding service throughout this procedure?

78. Is adequate casework service available to those clients who have troubles which may be a cause or result of the economic need, such as family disagreements, neglect of health problems, inadequate budgeting, and so on?

79. Is the caseload for each public assistance worker small enough to permit such casework?

80. Are public assistance recipients referred to other agencies in the community when they need types of service not available through the public assistance programs?

81. In each type of public assistance, how often is a regular checkup made to be assured that the recipient is still eligible?

82. How often are home visits made in each type of assistance?

83. Is a constant attempt made to see that people who are employable get work and thus leave the relief rolls? How is this accomplished?
Is there a close working arrangement with the public employment office?

84. Is there a close working relationship with other public agencies in the community? Which agencies?

85. Has there been any attention given to ways in which prevention of dependency may be emphasized rather than merely aiding those who have already become dependent?

Public homes. Many years ago, the public almshouse was thought to be the principal answer to problems of individual dependency. As the idea of "outdoor" relief came to prominence, it was thought better to aid people in their own homes rather than relegating them to an institution. Nevertheless, in some special types of difficulty, institutional care is still indicated: for example, people who cannot handle a budget or make their way in the daily life of the community; older people who need special types of care; children with certain problems, and so on. The old almshouse was at its worst a deplorably depressing institution. Modern public homes can be pleasant and wholesome and still be economically operated. Nevertheless, certain public domiciliary institutions, among them many of the nation's county homes, are unbelievably shoddy. Citizens interested in the welfare program can benefit by a tactful visit to their public homes.

86. Does your local community operate a public home (city home, county home, and so on)?

87. What types of people are served by the public home?

88. Does the home meet satisfactory standards as to quality of administration? Space per resident? Quality and amount of food? Availability of work and

recreation experience? Cleanliness? Fire escapes and other safety precautions?

89. Are visitors welcome to inspect the public home at any reasonable time?

90. Does your local public welfare department give assistance in meeting hospital or medical expenses in the case of families that are otherwise self-sufficient but that are unable to meet the special expenses of sickness?

91. Is care in the following types of institution provided where necessary? Under what conditions? In which institutions?

Hospitals and infirmaries	Temporary shelters
Nursing and convalescent homes	Children's institutions
Homes for the aged	Detention care shelters for children
Public homes	Other

92. What services are available to people with various types of handicap, such as blindness, deafness, physical disability, and so on?[1]

When you have finished answering the preceding questions, give your estimate of how your community's public assistance program measures up in terms of the following questions:

93. In general, is public assistance administered in a constructive manner respecting the rightful claim of needy persons to such aid, or with a punitive and disapproving attitude designed to humiliate and shame those who have become dependent?

94. How does your answer to the foregoing question relate to the desired goal of restoring public assistance recipients to full self-sufficiency as early as possible?

Related voluntary agencies. Side by side with various types of public assistance to the needy, various voluntary agencies have for many centuries assumed responsibility in the maintenance of the needy. Gradually, public assistance programs have come to outshadow these private endeavors in the field of care for the dependent. Voluntary agencies have come to concentrate their principal services in other fields than that of financial assistance. (See Chapter 11.) Nevertheless, some types of voluntary agency still issue financial assistance either to supplement public allotments where these are insufficient, or to make public allotments unnecessary, or to meet certain types of need for which public assistance does not adequately provide. Examples are the local welfare effort of certain churches, the Red Cross, the Salvation Army, special financial assistance extended by certain family agencies, and so on. These efforts all supplement the public assistance programs, and so are treated here.

95. What voluntary agencies offer financial assistance to those in need in your community?

[1] See Chapter 13.

96. Do such grants involve the services of a trained caseworker, or are they limited simply to financial help?

Citizens and the Welfare Department

Public welfare policies affect favorably or unfavorably the lives of many citizens of the community. In addition, public welfare is one of the largest expenditures in the cost of state and local government. Yet there is relatively little citizen interest or participation in welfare programs. Where it is present, such interest and participation may take several forms.

In many states, the municipalities or welfare districts have local welfare boards which determine specific matters of policy and, in some instances, even review cases. Such a setup, though it often opens the door to political pressure and to unprofessional policies in the administration of welfare, nevertheless assures a certain degree of local autonomy and control over the welfare department, and is a source of interpretation of policies and problems to the public.

In some states, statewide organizations of citizens with a primary interest in social welfare have made outstanding records of support of economical and progressive welfare standards. Two examples are the New York State Charities Aid Association and the Public Charities Association of Pennsylvania. Local citizen groups affiliated with such statewide organizations are sometimes particularly effective. In various parts of the country, local community councils interest themselves in welfare as in other phases of community living. However, this is often only one interest among many and is not uniformly displayed.

In the cities, councils of social agencies are engaged in providing a means for interagency cooperation and coordination of effort. (See Chapter 17.) Composed as they are of lay people and professional workers, these agencies form an effective medium for the reflection of the attitudes of local community people in relation to the public welfare effort.

In recent years there have been concerted attacks on the local public welfare programs in various places by citizens' economy organizations as well as rural interest groups. These often take the form of sponsoring "investigations" by private management consultants. Such investigations are seldom objective but are usually designed from the start to "prove" that welfare costs are too high, that programs should be cut back, and so on. Where there is a lack of organized and informed citizen opinion on welfare problems and programs, communities are particularly vulnerable to such onslaughts. Lack of information by the public is often caused in part by the lack of desire or the inability of welfare officials to publicize adequately the why's and wherefore's of their program.[1]

97. Is there an organization in your state which has local affiliates that take an active interest in furthering economical and progressive welfare standards?
Is there a branch in your community?

98. Is there a local group which keeps itself informed on welfare matters and interests itself in improving services?

99. Does it send representatives to budget hearings?

100. Does it invite members of the city, town, or county governing body to its meetings?

101. Does it keep in close touch with the commissioner of public welfare?

102. Does the welfare council or the welfare department carry on an active program of helping to inform the public about welfare policies and procedures?

103. Has the welfare council or any other group made a survey of public assistance programs in recent years?[2]

104. Are there any organizations in your state or in your locality engaged in combating the whole welfare program as such?

105. What organizations in your community have at least a secondary interest in welfare, or can be expected to interest themselves in one aspect or another of the welfare program?

106. To what extent are any of the following methods used in helping inform the public of welfare activities:

News releases on current programs
Radio talks, discussions, dramas, etc.
Television broadcasts

Pamphlets or other publications
Speeches to various organizations
Institutes, forums, workshops

107. Is any attempt made to acquaint the public with the costs, financial and otherwise, of not maintaining an adequate public assistance program?

References for Further Study

Buell, Bradley, and associates. *Community Planning for Human Services.* Columbia University Press, New York, 1952. The results of an intensive study of four types of social problems in St. Paul, Minnesota—dependency, ill health, maladjustment, and recreational need, and their interrelations.

Fink, Arthur E., *The Field of Social Work.* rev. ed. Henry Holt and

[1] See Baker, Helen Cody, and Mary Swain Routzahn, *How to Interpret Social Welfare: A Study Course in Public Relations,* Russell Sage Foundation, New York, 1947; and *Telling the Welfare Story,* State Charities Aid Association, New York, 1950. The latter is designed specifically for volunteer welfare groups.
[2] For further treatment of such surveys, see Chapters 18 and 19.

Co., New York, 1949. This gives a broad introduction to the various branches of social work in both public and private agencies. Case illustrations introduce the reader to the way people with particular problems are helped in various agency settings.

Freeman, Lucy, *Children Who Never Had a Chance*. Public Affairs Pamphlet No. 183, New York, 1952. This pamphlet describes for the layman the operation of the program of aid to dependent children, and clears up many misconceptions about it.

Haber, William, and Wilbur J. Cohen, editors, *Readings in Social Security*. Prentice-Hall, Inc., New York, 1948. A book of readings by experts in the various aspects of social security, including public assistance and social insurance programs.

Howard, Donald S., *The WPA and Federal Relief Policy*. Russell Sage Foundation, New York, 1943. A definitive study of the country's experience with work relief under the WPA program.

Landis, Benson Y., *Rural Welfare Services*. Columbia University Press, New York, 1949. A very readable book which outlines in rather elementary fashion the various welfare services available in rural America.

McConnell, John W., and Robert Risley, *Economic Security:* A Study of Community Needs and Resources. New York State School of Industrial and Labor Relations, Cornell University, Ithaca, 1951. This pamphlet reports the results of a study of the community needs and resources for economic security in Elmira, New York.

Stroup, Herbert H., *Social Work:* An Introduction to the Field. American Book Co., New York, 1948. A discussion of the different types and settings of social work, including public assistance and social insurance programs.

11. Aids to Family Living and Child Welfare

MODERN LIVING CONDITIONS make the family less and less an independent unit, more and more a unit which depends on many other institutions and agencies for its everyday living. Businesses and farms supply work and income; the schools provide guidance services, vocational training, family life education; public and commercial recreation establishments provide leisuretime opportunities; and so on. Thus, in a more or less literal sense, every aspect of the community is related to family living, and the study of the community is actually a study of the way families seek and find patterns for survival and wholesome living through various community institutions. Nevertheless, there are certain types of agency and activity which are especially related to the family in that they work directly in the field of strengthening the family, preventing family breakdown, or helping individual families to overcome the difficulties they already face. Such special aids to family living, including those more specifically concerned with child welfare, are the subject of this chapter.[1]

Before considering these special aids to family living, some basic information about families in your community should be obtained. The first question below is answerable from the latest Census, Volume 2, Chapter B, as well as in Census tract reports:

1. Of all persons 14 years of age and older in your community, how many are single; how many are married; and how many are widowed or divorced—both male and female?
2. In your state what is the legal age for marriage with parental consent? Without parental consent?
   Under what circumstances, if ever, are exceptions made? Who authorizes them?
3. Are secret marriages allowed? Who authorizes them?
4. What special requirements must be followed before a marriage license may be issued (venereal disease test, and the like)?

[1] For background on the American family, see Burgess, Ernest W., and Locke, Harvey J., *The Family: From Institution to Companionship*, 2d ed., American Book Co., New York, 1953; and Baber, Ray E., *Marriage and the Family*, 2d ed., McGraw Hill Book Co., New York, 1953. There are many other good books available on this topic.

5. What types of people are declared ineligible for marriage?
6. Is racial intermarriage forbidden? If not, do any special requirements apply?
7. Is there a waiting period between the time of application and the issuance of a license? How long?
8. In your community where do civil ceremonies for marriage usually take place? Are the surroundings pleasant and dignified?
9. Is common law marriage permitted in your state?
10. Under what legal circumstances in your state may a marital relationship be terminated by divorce? Annulment?
11. How many divorces and annulments were there in your community in each of the past five years? (Keep in mind that people often migrate for a divorce.)
12. If the courts involved are not "family courts" (see page 177) are there any provisions for social investigations and attempts at reconciliation?
13. What special study and follow-up is given to the welfare of children affected by the dissolution of a marriage?

Services to Strengthen the Family

In recent years, increasing attention has been given to programs designed to help assure the formation of strong families and to strengthen family living in general, as distinguished from giving special help to families with serious problems. The development takes many forms, including adult education classes, family life education in the regular public school program for children, marriage and family counseling services, child study groups, and "family checkup" programs of various family agencies. Outstanding in the development of this positive approach toward strengthening the family are the National Council on Family Relations, which brings together professional workers engaged in various fields connected with family living, and the Child Study Association of America, which works more directly with parents themselves, as well as with professional workers. In addition, many family service agencies which offer casework service (see page 174) also engage in this type of general program.

14. Is there a program of family life education in the schools?
    Is it conducted by special teachers in special courses, or diffused throughout the curriculum?
    If conducted by special teachers, what training have they had for this type of instruction?
15. Are family life education programs available through the public adult education program, or under the auspices of the Y's, or of family agencies, or of various other voluntary associations?
    What are the qualifications of the instructors?

How many persons have attended such courses, lectures, discussions, workshops, or other activities in the past five years?

16. Is there a marriage counseling service which engages in premarital counseling? Counseling of married couples on marital conflict situations? Sex adjustment difficulties? Sterility? Legal questions? Other matters?
Are counseling services available in connection with any of the activities listed in the preceding question?

17. What are the qualifications of the counselors? Do they belong to the American Association of Marriage Counselors?

18. What special activities such as the following are available which help to strengthen family living:
"Ladies Day Out" programs of the Y's
Well-baby centers
Nursery schools with parent education programs
Other

19. Is there a birth control clinic (planned parenthood center)? Is it a member of the Planned Parenthood Federation of America?

20. Is there a legal aid society? Is it a member of the National Association of Legal Aid Organizations?
Do family casework agencies refer to it those families that it can best serve?

21. Is there a travelers aid service? Is it conducted by a private family agency; or is it a special agency conducted for this purpose?
Does it have a paid, professionally trained staff? It is a member of the National Travelers Aid Association?

22. Is there a family consultation center, however titled, which makes available the professional consultation of psychologists, sociologists, clergymen, doctors, lawyers, and other professional persons but does not engage in casework?

Family Casework

While in the normal course of living most families are able to cope with their problems with a minimum of special help beyond that provided by school, church, government, and family life agencies, sometimes circumstances arise in which families do need such special assistance. One type of help needed may be financial assistance, which is now ordinarily administered by public assistance programs. But there are often other types of problems on which a family may require help. Perhaps there is an unruly child concerning whom the parents need counsel. Perhaps there is a problem of vocational adjustment, inability to budget adequately, difficulties caused by sickness, the desire to adopt a child, a legal dispute in which the family needs legal advice, marital friction, or the like. Family casework agencies are set up specifically to help families with such problems. Social casework is a process which involves more than the solving of the immediate problem, however. It involves working with people in their interrelationship, helping them develop skill in solving their own problems, helping them develop sufficient integration and resourcefulness so that they will no longer need agency help. It is this careful, skillful help based on a thorough analysis of the individual family situation and oriented toward helping the family members develop more steadfast relationships toward each other as they work out their particular problem which distinguishes family casework from the aid, counsel, service, or advice offered by others.

Family casework is often the special activity of a family casework agency (family society, family welfare society, and so on). However, casework services to families are also available through other auspices, such as the social service department of a hospital, the school social worker or visiting teacher, the casework available in child guidance clinics, the probation service, and so on. Within the public welfare field, casework in the sense described above is sometimes available in connection with the public child welfare services. It is also increasingly available through qualified private practitioners. In addition, of course, much family counseling is performed by teachers and school principals, clergymen, physicians, lawyers, and so on.

A voluntary family casework agency is usually devoted primarily to offering professional casework services to families that need them. Such agencies typically receive a major part of their income from the community chest, are governed by a lay board and administered by a specially trained and experienced executive. A number of caseworkers are employed, headed by one or more case supervisors. As an adjunct to their work, there may be specialized professional personnel, such as physician, psychiatrist, lawyer, either employed full time by the agency or retained on a consulting basis.

Smaller cities and villages do not ordinarily have this type of family case-work agency. Casework and counseling services must therefore be looked for in connection with school, public assistance, probation service, or various types of service performed by such professional people as clergymen and physicians. In rural communities, the public assistance and child welfare divisions of the public welfare department (county, town, or whatever) are often called upon for services which in a city would ordinarily be rendered by a voluntary family agency.

In any event, the principal question is what sort of help is available to families with various types of problem, and how competent is that help. Sometimes, even where comprehensive casework service is available, individual families either out of ignorance or preference consult friends, employers, shop stewards, or other people, rather than trained social caseworkers. One study reported the local druggist and bartender performing important counseling functions even though there were many professional agencies available.[1]

23. Which of the following types of agency are available in your community for families with problems:

Family casework agency	Child guidance clinic
Voluntary child welfare agency	Marriage counseling agency
Public child welfare service	Other professional casework agency

24. In addition to, or in the absence of, such professional casework services as the aforementioned, to what extent do troubled families avail themselves of professional people who do not necessarily have special training for counseling in family problems:

Physicians	Lawyers
Clergymen	Other professional people
Teachers and principals	

25. Can you determine the extent to which families avail themselves of commercial counselors whose training and methods do not meet accepted professional standards of casework practice:

"Advice to the lovelorn" editors
Radio programs which "solve" family problems over the air
Self-appointed "experts" who advertise their services in pulp magazines
Others[2]

26. If you live in a large city, consult your classified telephone directory for a listing of "psychologists."
Who may list himself as a psychologist in your state?

27. Is there a family casework agency?

28. Is it a member of the Family Service Association of America?

29. How many families did it help directly in the past year?

30. Has it a paid staff with special preparation and experience in family casework?

31. Are there specialized personnel available in legal counseling? Psychiatric service? Home economics? Other?

32. Can you get some idea of the relative frequency of the different types of problem encountered by this agency:

Conflict between various family members	Delinquency, desertion, crime, etc.
Economic problems	Employment problems
Mental health problems	Health problems
Legal problems	Other[3]

[1] Koos, Earl L., *Families in Trouble*. King's Crown Press, New York, 1946.
[2] Read Lee R. Steiner's *Where Do People Take Their Troubles?* Houghton Mifflin Co., Boston, 1945.
[3] This outline includes the types of problems most frequently encountered in a study cited in Fink, Arthur E., *The Field of Social Work*, rev. ed., Henry Holt and Co., New York, 1949.

33. Is there a separate family agency serving Jewish families? Protestant families? Catholic families?
    If there is such an agency, give in each case the answers to the foregoing questions.

While not strictly a social work agency itself, the "family court," in those communities where one exists, often gives aid and counsel in helping to work out family difficulties, in addition to enforcing the law where the rights of any members of the family are being infringed. In addition, such a court often has access to casework, medical and psychiatric services, and so on. Like the children's court, it constitutes a move in the direction of considering the social and psychological factors involved in human relationships, as well as the purely legal ones.

34. Is your community served by a family or domestic relations court? What is its jurisdiction over family problems?
35. What specific relationship has the court to cases of juvenile delinquency? Nonsupport, neglect, abuse, and so on? Divorce? Annulment?
36. How is the judge chosen? Is he especially qualified in family matters?
37. To what special professional services does the court have access, and how regularly are such services utilized?
38. What cooperation exists between the family court and the various social agencies in the community?
    How often and under what circumstances are referrals made or agencies consulted?

Social Services for Children in Their Own Home

Contemporary child welfare practice is based on recognition of the importance of the family as the basic social institution. Thus, casework practices are designed to strengthen the family, rather than to supplant it. The basic thought is not to do something for the family, but to help the family do it for itself. Only in those instances where because of death or other factors the family is broken up, or where special circumstances warrant placement of a child outside the family, is this done, and even then only as long as is necessary.

There are many services offered by different agencies of society for children in their own homes, including those performed by the schools, the churches, public health nurses, and so on. In the preceding chapter, the Aid to Dependent Children program was mentioned as part of the public assistance program. It warrants further consideration here. The ADC program, as it is called, is designed to give public support to needy children who are living with parents or relatives but are deprived of normal support because of death, absence, or incapacity of either parent. This enables the child to remain in his own family and makes unnecessary the unfortunate "farming out" of children to institutions, foster homes, and elsewhere when the home environment is suitable except for the economic need.[1]

Child welfare services of one type or another are available in every state, but the local organization of such services varies. Usually it includes public and voluntary agencies working with different degrees of intensity in the various programs. A frequent pattern includes a child welfare division within the local welfare department but separate from the public assistance program. In the more populous areas, various voluntary child welfare agencies work in the field of casework, institutional or adoption placement, or actual operation of children's institutions. In addition, departments of health, education, and other branches of state or local government participate in different child welfare programs.[2]

The need for child welfare services in the individual family may involve any one or combination of such difficulties as the following: behavior problems of the child, sickness or other incapacity of one or both parents, delinquent behavior of the child, the need for homemaker service, parental neglect or abuse, unmarried parenthood, marital conflict, special handicaps of the child, health problems, and so on. In making your study, it is well to keep in mind that several different agencies may be of help in any or all of these problems in your community.[3]

39. What is the extent of the Aid to Dependent Children program in your community?[4]

40. What social agencies in your community offer various child welfare services to children in their own homes: Public agencies? Voluntary agencies?

41. Which public or voluntary agencies give service to parents who face difficulties in the form of behavior problems of their children? Is there a fee for such service?

Is such service available to all who need it? If not, what restrictions are placed upon such service?

42. What casework service is available where family problems endanger the welfare of the children in the families involved?

[1] See Freeman, Lucy, *Children Who Never Had a Chance*, Public Affairs Pamphlet No. 183, New York, 1952.

[2] Read *A Healthy Personality for Every Child:* A Digest of the Fact Finding Report to the Midcentury White House Conference on Children and Youth, Health Publications Institute, Inc., 1951. Read also the section on child welfare in the latest edition of the *Social Work Year Book*, published by the American Association of Social Workers, New York; and *Child Welfare at the Crossroads*, Children's Bureau, Government Printing Office, Washington, 1949.

[3] See Davis, Annie Lee, *Children Living in Their Own Homes:* Social Services Provided Through Child Welfare Programs, Children's Bureau, Government Printing Office, Washington, 1953.

[4] Chapter 10 includes many questions on the various forms of public assistance, including ADC.

43. Is "homemaker service" available where the sickness or temporary absence of the mother might otherwise necessitate the breaking up of the home?[1] Is such service available to all economic groups, with appropriate charges, or is it limited only to the economically dependent or to some other restricted category?
44. Is there a "day care" program for children of working mothers?[2] Under what inspection, if any, does it come?
Are there professionally trained social workers on the staff? Is there a charge for this service?
What special circumstances are required for acceptance of the child in the day care program?
45. What special programs of health care for mothers and children who need it are available in your community?
46. What special social services are available to handicapped children in your community? (See Chapter 13.)
47. How many handicapped children are now receiving special services of any type?

A special problem is that presented by unmarried parenthood. Frequently the mother is young enough to come under the child care program, but in addition the welfare of her child is involved. Since many of these mothers come from underprivileged homes, adequate prenatal care is often a problem. Serious casework problems may be presented by the parents' attitude toward the unmarried mother, the question of the paternity of the child, the question of possible marriage to the child's biological father, the girl's adjustment to her own pregnancy, the problems of the confinement period and adequate care in childbirth, the problem of whether or not to place the child for adoption, and so on. Frequently the behavior of the unmarried mother is but a symptom of underlying emotional difficulties which require extensive casework.[3]

48. What is the usual procedure in cases of unmarried parenthood which come to the attention of the child welfare workers?
49. How many unmarried mothers received casework service from child welfare organizations in your community last year?
50. What percentage of children of unmarried mothers are retained by the mother? Are given up for adoption? Receive other disposition such as institutional placement?

[1] See *Practices in Homemaker Service*, Children's Bureau, Government Printing Office, Washington, 1951.
[2] See *Standards of Day Care for Children of Working Mothers*, Children's Bureau, Government Printing Office, Washington, 1942. For special day care provisions for children of migrant farm workers, see Chapter 13.
[3] Read *Services for Unmarried Mothers and Their Children*, 1945, and *Maternity Homes for Unmarried Mothers: A Community Service*, 1946, both published by the Children's Bureau, Government Printing Office, Washington.

Are the rights of unmarried mothers protected, particularly with respect to custody of the child?

51. What provision is made for prenatal, natal, and postnatal medical care in the case of unmarried mothers?

52. To what extent are unmarried mothers helped with the basic psychological or social problems which led to their unmarried motherhood?

53. What is the legal status in your state of children of unmarried mothers with regard to their right to claim paternity? To bear father's name? To claim support? Inheritance?

54. Do birth certificates expose a child to unnecessary stigma by revealing that the child was born out of wedlock?

The children's court typically exercises jurisdiction over families in safeguarding children from neglect, abandonment, abuse, and immoral home background. Because of the importance attached in our society to the child's right to live in his own home with his own family, the child is seldom removed from his own home unless the situation is extremely deleterious to the child's welfare. Citizens often protest that the children's court does not act quickly enough in cases of excessive punishment, cruelty, and so on. Nevertheless, the courts are usually loath to act unless the situation is extremely critical. In some states another function[1] of the children's court is to engage in adoption proceedings.

55. Under what circumstances does your state law permit the removal of a child from his own home because of undesirable circumstances in that home?

56. Is a thorough investigation by competent personnel made before such legal action is instituted?

57. If a child is removed from his own home, what provision is made for the child's nurture and upbringing?

58. What action short of removal of the child is open to the court in cases of neglect, abuse, and so forth?

59. What is the procedure in cases of nonsupport?

60. In what other ways does the children's court exercise a protective function over the welfare of children?

In some communities there are voluntary citizens' organizations which have as a primary function the protection of children from neglect, abuse, cruelty, or immoral conditions. Occasionally these organizations receive special recognition and are delegated special police or other powers by law enforcement agencies.

61. Does your community have a children's protective association (society for the prevention of cruelty to children, or other name)?

[1] Functions which have to do with juvenile delinquency will be considered later in this chapter.

62. Is it a member of the Child Welfare League of America?
63. What are its functions?
64. How many children were in its custody during the past year?
65. What special relationship has it. to the police? Children's court? Other legal authorities?

Child Placement and Adoption Services

In any community, situations may arise in which it is deemed advisable to remove a child either temporarily or permanently from his own home and place him elsewhere. Often this is done by relatives who take care of the youngster for a few days while his mother is in the hospital, or while his parents are out of town or are otherwise unable to care for him. The great majority of such cases never reach the attention of a child welfare agency, although there is considerable concern as to whether such placements with relatives are always in the child's own best interest.

In many instances where a family is temporarily unable to care for the child, the relatives are unwilling or unable to perform the service. Such a child may be placed temporarily with a foster family, either for a sum of money or free, or he may be placed temporarily in a children's institution until his family is once more ready to receive him. In some cases he may be placed permanently in a foster home or children's institution.

Sometimes the child is legally eligible for adoption and there are parents who would like to adopt him. Adoption is a legal process which gives the child the same legal status as though he were the natural child of his adoptive parents, and which terminates any special legal relationship between the child and his natural parents. This does not occur in the placement of a child in a foster home or in a children's institution.

Foster home placement has grown with the increasing conviction that a child's own home is usually the best place for him, and that if this is not possible, the next best is a foster home. Such placement involves certain generally accepted principles.[1] While foster parents are entitled to remuneration, they should not take children primarily as a source of income. Aside from this qualification, there is no reason why families of extremely moderate means, as well as more well-to-do families, may not make perfectly desirable foster families. Families should not require foster children to do any more work than they would expect of their own children. Foster children should be treated just like the other children of the family. Foster children often come from disturbing home situations, and hence need

[1] See Day, Gladys D., *Home Finding:* The Placement of Children in Families, Children's Bureau, Government Printing Office, Washington, 1951.

parents who are especially discerning. Children placed in foster homes should be visited regularly to assure that they are receiving proper care.

66. Do social work agencies report that the placement of children with relatives in your community presents a special child welfare problem? If so, in what respect?
    Are there suggestions as to what might be done about it?

67. Does your state law provide for licensing and inspection of all boarding and foster homes for children whether maintained by agencies or individuals, whether remuneration is given or not, and regardless of the child's age?

68. What agencies engage in foster home placement in your community?

69. Are they members of the Child Welfare League of America?

70. How many children were in foster homes last year, by age and by sex? How many of these resulted from court commitments? Voluntary applications by relatives?

71. What qualifications are required of foster parents?

72. What is the monthly allotment for a child in foster home care?

73. Is there a reported shortage of satisfactory foster parents?

74. How are foster parents recruited?

75. Is there a program of training for foster parents?[1]

76. How often are children placed in foster homes visited by the placing agency?

77. Is there constant case review to see if the children's own families are now ready to receive them again?

78. Is casework with the children's own families carried on with a view toward helping them arrive at the point where they can once more take the child?

79. Is careful casework undertaken to help prepare the child for his placement in a foster home, to help him adjust to his foster home, and to help him prepare, where appropriate, for return to his own home?

80. Is there evidence that foster parents are kind and competent?

81. Do teachers or other persons with whom foster children come in contact regard them in derogatory terms, such as "welfare children," and so on?

82. Is any child-caring agency equipped to provide emergency care for short periods where no foster home placement is available?

Adoption is a legal process which changes the legal parenthood of the child. For several reasons adoption has come to be charged with emotional content in recent years. One is that there is a great demand by childless couples for suitable young infants to adopt. Such couples are understandably impatient to effect the adoption, once their decision to adopt a child has been made. However, careful adoption work takes many months, and sometimes extends over more than a year from the time a couple applies to an agency to adopt a child until the time when it receives a child. Since the agency is concerned primarily with safeguarding the interests of the child,

[1] See *Step by Step:* A Guide for a Program to Help the Foster Parents in Your Community, New York State Charities Aid Association, New York, 1952.

and only secondarily with the interests of the natural and adoptive parents, some couples are rejected by the agency because of their unsuitability. For these and other reasons, many couples have turned to other methods of procuring a child for adoption. A common practice is for a physician or lawyer to act as intermediary. In many instances, unscrupulous individuals engage in procuring children for adoption for a sum of money, often as high as a thousand or more dollars. While this is against the law in most states, nevertheless, a "black market" for babies exists. Where babies are procured through the "black market" or through the "grey market" of well-intentioned intermediaries, grave dangers to the future welfare of the child and also of the adoptive parents may be involved. The child may be found to be subnormal in intelligence, or to have physical handicaps which had been overlooked, or to have hereditary characteristics making him visibly different from his adoptive parents, or to have inherited diseases. The adoptive parents may not be realistic about the obligations they are incurring with the legal adoption of a child. They may look upon the child as a source of satisfaction for selfish needs rather than with generous love.

One reason "agency placements" take so long is that the child is thoroughly studied as to physical and mental characteristics, and the adoptive parents are likewise studied, so that the child may be placed in a home where he is most likely to receive a desirable kind of care and love. Nevertheless, approximately half of the children placed for adoption with nonrelatives are placed without the aid of agency study.[1]

83. What are the provisions of your state law governing adoption?[2]
84. Is there a waiting period after adoption placement before the adoption is certified as official by the court?
85. How many children were adopted in your community during the past year? Of these, how many were placed with relatives? Of the adoptions by nonrelatives, how many were agency placements?
86. Do agencies report having certain types of children who are legally free for adoption but are difficult to place?
87. Do applications by childless couples for a child to adopt tend to be confined to requests for children under two years of age?
88. Is there indication of a "black market" in your community, where a fee is paid for finding a child for a couple to adopt?
89. What provisions are there to protect the true parent from a hasty decision to give up the child?
90. Is any attempt made by child placement and other agencies to acquaint the

[1] See Perlman, I. Richard, and Jack Wiener, *Adoption of Children, 1951:* A Statistical Analysis, Children's Bureau, Government Printing Office, Washington, 1953.
[2] See *Essentials of Adoption Law and Procedures,* Children's Bureau, Government Printing Office, Washington, 1949.

public with desirability of agency placement and with the reasons why this sometimes takes many months?

91. In the case of agency placements, are thorough studies made of the physical and mental characteristics of the child?

92. Is a thorough study made of the situation, personality, and motives of prospective adoptive parents?

93. Does the agency give casework service to help all three parties to adjust to their situation—the child, the natural parent or parents, and the adoptive parents?

While the modern trend is to provide children with the opportunity for family living wherever possible, there are certain circumstances where institutional placement is called for. This is often the case with: older children, who do not always adjust well to foster family placement; children needing special types of attention for mental or physical illness or handicaps; children who for some reason have not been able to adjust well to foster family care; children committed to a training school as a result of serious patterns of delinquency; groups of brothers and sisters who are to be kept together; children who need temporary shelter where foster homes are not readily available and who will soon be returned to their own homes.

A newer type of institution which is receiving increasing attention is the children's institution designed for emotionally disturbed children.[1] Another development is the "small treatment home." Operated by foster parents under agency supervision, such a home is often established in an ordinary city residence and has many features of family living.

In keeping with the emphasis on the values of family living, children's institutions are coming to simulate family relationships in many ways. One of the more important trends is the cottage system, wherein relatively small groups of children live in a separate dwelling under the care of "cottage parents."[2]

94. Under what circumstances do local social agencies suggest institutional care for children?

95. How many children from your community were in each type of institution during the past year:

Children's home	Institution for the mentally retarded
Correctional institution	Institution for the mentally
Institution for the handicapped	disturbed
(blind, cerebral palsied, etc.)	Other

For each such institution serving your community obtain the following information:

[1] Reid, Joseph H., and Helen R. Hagan. *Residential Treatment of Emotionally Disturbed Children:* A Descriptive Study. Child Welfare League of America, New York, 1952.

[2] For background, read Hopkirk, Howard W., *Institutions Serving Children*, Russell Sage Foundation, New York, 1944.

96. Under what auspices is the institution operated?
97. Is it a member of the Child Welfare League of America?
98. What are the charges, if any?
99. Is it restricted to a particular religion, race, and so on?
100. What provisions are there for its inspection and regulation by state or local authorities?
101. What are the conditions under which a child is accepted for care?
102. What steps are taken to return the child to family living where desirable and possible?
103. What provisions are there for the child's religious development?
104. What provisions are made for the child's education?
105. What provisions are there for recreation and participation in community clubs, sports, and so on?
106. Does it utilize the cottage system of residence?
107. Is follow-up care given to children dismissed from the institution?
108. Do local child welfare agencies report the lack of a particular type of institutional care for children?

Juvenile Delinquents

In a recent year an estimated 350,000 children of both sexes were brought before the juvenile courts of the United States because of delinquent behavior. Nearly three times as many, approximately a million, were dealt with by the police. Some studies show that approximately half the children who come to the juvenile courts today will later be convicted of a serious crime as adults. Apparently the program of treatment of juvenile delinquents is not highly effective.[1]

The problem of the "cause" of juvenile delinquency is a knotty one. Despite much public misunderstanding, sociologists agree that no one single factor causes juvenile delinquency. Rather, each case results from a whole configuration of circumstances which may be different from the next. Nevertheless, certain general conditions are found to be associated with high rates of delinquency, and much practical experience has been gained in preventive and treatment programs. For background, read *Juvenile Delinquency* by Paul W. Tappan;[2] *The Juvenile in Delinquent Society* by Milton L. Barron;[3] or *Understanding Juvenile Delinquency*.[4]

As in many other social problems, prevention is coming to be emphasized

---

[1] These and many other facts about juvenile delinquency are brought together in an informative little pamphlet prepared by the Children's Bureau entitled *Some Facts About Juvenile Delinquency*, 1953, available through the Government Printing Office, Washington.
[2] McGraw-Hill Book Co., New York, 1949.
[3] Alfred A. Knopf, New York, 1954.
[4] Children's Bureau, Government Printing Office, Washington, 1949.

as more desirable than cure. Both are needed, but authorities agree that much human and financial waste may be avoided by giving more attention to programs of prevention. Delinquency feeds on some of the very conditions which would be considered problems even if they did not contribute to delinquency: poverty, poor housing, disorganized neighborhoods, inadequate recreational opportunities, poor parental care, broken homes, and so on. Thus, the better a community is constituted with respect to these conditions, the less likelihood of a serious delinquency problem. It may sound trite, but it is important to realize that delinquency cannot be coped with effectively as a problem isolated from the general life of the community. Effective delinquency prevention is thus tied to a program of general community improvement.

As a specific program, delinquency prevention involves certain measures and facilities designed to identify individuals and groups of children who are particularly vulnerable to delinquency and to give them special preventive consideration which will help them adjust along law-abiding paths. Such groups may include groups of children in neighborhoods with high delinquency and crime rates, children who are truants or who drop out of school early or who do not adjust well to the school social situation, children in homes characterized by conflict, or criminal behavior; children from broken homes, and so on. Such classes or categories of children may be of special concern. In addition, of course, there are the children whose actual behavior shows signs of maladjustment which, if left unchecked, may result in delinquency.

109. What areas in your community contribute the greatest proportion of juvenile delinquents?[1]
110. How do these areas compare with the rest of the community in respect to the following items:

Housing
Recreational facilities
Income
Crime rates
Sickness rates

Physical appearance of neighborhood
School attendance rates
Public assistance rates[2]

111. If possible, make a plot map of the incidence of delinquency in various sections of the community.

[1] There are several different ways of measuring the rate of delinquency. One is to base it on police records of those apprehended; another, on referrals to the juvenile court for delinquency; another, on dispositions of the court. Each method has its disadvantages. Most important of all is to use the same measure whenever a comparison between two places or times is made.
[2] For further material on each of these subjects, consult the appropriate chapter of this book.

How does this compare with plot maps made in connection with other chapters of this book?

112. What special attention is being given within the school system to develop curricula and special programs which will be more attractive to children who might otherwise become truants, early drop-outs, or behavior problems in the school?

113. What is school procedure for dealing with children whose behavior indicates that they may develop into patterns of delinquency?

114. Is there a child guidance clinic available for referral of children with serious emotional and behavior problems?

115. To what extent do the schools, churches, and other youth-serving agencies make use of the child guidance clinic as a resource?

116. What is being done in neighborhoods in which there is an acknowledged problem of lack of adequate, wholesome recreational facilities?

117. Is there a Police Athletic League which seeks to build up desirable relations between children and the police and which provides recreational opportunities for underprivileged children?

118. What social group work agencies—settlement houses, neighborhood centers, and so on—are there with trained personnel to which disturbed youngsters may be referred for wholesome recreational experience under trained professional care?

119. Have any special methods been developed, or are any special testing devices used in the schools or elsewhere for the "screening" of children who may be particularly vulnerable to delinquency?

120. What follow-up is given in the case of those whom the screening reveals to be potential delinquents?

121. Are there any youth councils, youth bureaus, or other publicly sponsored organizations of youths which deal with the problem of the overall adjustment of youth in the community?

In the treatment of juvenile delinquents, two factors are of utmost importance. One is somewhat intangible, having to do largely with attitudes. Professional practice in dealing with delinquents has long since recognized the need for considering delinquency from the standpoint of therapy rather than punishment. Punishment as such all too often has the effect of intensifying the child's emotional maladjustment, setting him apart as different from other children, and increasing his antagonism to the school, the police, or "society" in general. Once treatment is considered most important, then the question becomes not "What has this child done and how much punishment does he deserve?" but rather "What circumstances have led to this child's delinquent behavior and how can society's resources be brought to bear in helping the child to adjust to his problems in a law-abiding or nondelinquent way?" The juvenile court system in many states is at least a partial recognition of this change of attitude.

The other important factor is the availability and quality of personnel and facilities for dealing with the delinquent. These can be grouped into the following: police, juvenile court, probation services, detention facilities, training school or other institution. In addition, a child guidance clinic is often available.

Children and the police

122. Do your community's policemen receive instruction in handling juvenile delinquents as part of their basic training?[1]
123. Is there a separate unit or officer within the police department designated for work with juveniles?
    Are such personnel specially selected as to personality and other qualifications?
    What training have they had for this work?
124. Do such personnel help to acquaint other police personnel with special problems and procedures in dealing with juveniles?
125. Are law enforcement agencies represented on coordinating councils, youth councils, youth boards, or other communitywide organizations planning services for children and youth?
126. How many juveniles have come to the attention of the police during each of the past five years because of alleged delinquent acts?
127. Of these, how many did the police take to juvenile court?
128. In instances where the police do not refer a child to the court, how often, if ever, do they consult with the child's parents, school authorities, religious adviser, recreation organization, welfare or health agency?
129. What procedure is there for notifying the parents when a child is apprehended?
130. In general, do the police tend to treat delinquent children as children who are in trouble and who have problems, or do they treat them as young "criminals"?

The juvenile court. Although most states have juvenile court laws, provisions of the law and practices under the law vary widely. The National Probation and Parole Association publishes *A Standard Juvenile Court Act.* The reader will perhaps want to see how his own state law compares with this. The Association has also drawn up a relatively simple outline which constitutes a rough "measuring rod" for any juvenile court. Its ten items include: exclusive jurisdiction over children, an understanding judge, private

[1] This and many of the following questions on juvenile delinquency are adapted from *Recommended Standards for Services for Delinquent Children* and *What's Happening*

hearings, pleasant offices, good detention care, clinic facilities, probation services, trained staff, adequate records, and community coordination.[1] In some states other laws make special provision for "youthful offenders," young people who are too old to come under the protection of the juvenile court law but for whom special consideration in treatment is nevertheless given on the basis of their youth.

131. Does your state have a juvenile court law? If not, what court considers children's problems?

132. What age-group of children is covered by your state's juvenile court law? How does your state law define a juvenile delinquent?

133. For what offenses or reasons connected with delinquency can a child be brought before the juvenile court?

134. Is the juvenile court separate from other courts?
Does it have jurisdiction over all cases involving juvenile delinquency and nonsupport?

135. Is the anonymity of the juvenile delinquent guarded both from harmful publicity and from the criminal records?
Is the actual court procedure more like an informal hearing than a trial?
Is the general public excluded from juvenile court hearings?

136. Do children appearing before the court have the right to legal counsel?

137. Is a thorough study made of the child's situation before the court hearing? Does the judge make use of this report? Does the court keep accurate records of the proceedings?

138. Under what circumstances does the judge:
Dismiss a child with only a warning
Handle a case informally, without any notice of it appearing in his statistical report
Place a child on probation to a probation officer
Place a child on probation to his own parents or some other adult
Place a child on probation to the welfare department
Refer a child to a psychiatric clinic
Place a child in a foster family
Commit a child to a training school or other public or private correctional institution

139. How many times was each of these actions taken during the past five years?

140. Is the judge's decision in the case of a child adjudicated delinquent based

---

to *Delinquent Children in Your Town?* Children's Bureau, Government Printing Office, Washington, 1953. The latter is a more intensive schedule of questions than is possible within the space limitations of the present chapter. These pamphlets are part of a series prepared for the Children's Bureau by the Special Juvenile Delinquency Project. Others are *Some Facts About Juvenile Delinquency* and *Helping Delinquent Children,* both published in 1953.

[1] See *The Juvenile Court Steps In,* a pamphlet prepared for the NPPA by Marjorie Bell, no date.

on treatment in the best interests of the child, or is it based on punitive considerations?

141. Which types of service are not available to your juvenile court:
    Psychiatric   Medical
    Psychological   Foster care
    Casework

142. Does the juvenile court cooperate with other agencies in the community which offer services to children?

143. How many children were brought before the court in each of the past five years for reasons of delinquency?
    How many of these were referred by police? Parents? Schools? Others?

144. For what offenses were how many children referred each year?

145. How many delinquency cases received each of the following types of dispositions in the past five years:
    Dismissed   Committed to public or
    "Warned"   private agency or person
    Placed on probation   Committed to an institution
                                        Other

146. How many children appeared more than once before the court for delinquency during the past five years?

147. Is there a competent, professionally trained probation service available to the juvenile court?

148. Is the probation service part of the children's court organization, or does it consist of workers from some other organization, such as welfare workers, adult probation department, and so on?

149. Has the probation officer a bachelor's degree with a major in social sciences? A master's degree from a school of social work? Other?

150. Is the probation service under the civil service system?

151. Does the probation service make social and psychological investigations of alleged delinquents?

152. Is the probation service empowered to try to adjust some problems without bringing them before the court?

153. What is the usual procedure in probation supervision?

Detention facilities. Most children who are to appear before the juvenile court can well remain in their homes until the hearing takes place. Where this is feasible, it is better for the child and more economical for the community. In some instances, however, where the home background has been found to be one of cruelty or immorality or where for other reasons it is not in the child's best interests to return, he can be placed in a foster home or children's home. Where there is likelihood that the child may commit a further delinquency if released, it may be necessary to detain him in secure custody. Best practice has long since recognized the undesirability of detaining children in local jails and lockups where they may come into contact with hardened criminals or other influences deleterious to their welfare. Nevertheless, the Children's Bureau reports that for the 2,500 children's courts in the country there are only some 174 detention homes. Of course, it is often possible to find a suitable foster home in which the child can be detained, particularly in rural districts where the population is too sparse to make a detention center feasible. Nevertheless, an estimated 50,000 to 100,000 boys and girls are locked up in jails each year on the authorization of children's courts or other law enforcement agencies. Needless to say, the experience of being put in jail is a traumatic one for many children.

154. Is there an agency in your state which encourages or provides the establishment of suitable detention centers on a regional basis?
155. Are counties or other suitable local units in your state permitted to establish detention centers on a joint basis?
156. Under what circumstances are children detained for the court in foster homes?
157. Are children ever detained in jail in your community?
158. Is your community served by a detention center?
159. If so, how does it stand with relation to the following items:
    Secure custody but as pleasant looking as possible
    Sympathetic and understanding supervision
    Provision for bathing, clothing, feeding, medical attention
    Constructive program of school work and supervised recreation
    Provisions for studying the child's personality and background
    Provision for spiritual counsel where requested
    Other professional services, such as psychiatric, where needed
160. Is every effort made to keep the detention period as brief as possible by scheduling frequent hearings of the children's court?
161. Is a children's court order necessary to place a child in detention or release a child from detention?

Training schools. Conditions in the training schools which accept delinquent children from your community are particularly important for several reasons. Since the institution has the child 24 hours a day, there are few influences to counteract the impressions made by the training school. Furthermore, in the nature of the case, the training school does not present a normal environment but rather surrounds the already disturbed child with other children, many of whom have committed more serious delinquencies. The training school is typically a last resort, the device used by society when all others have failed. Unfortunately, many young boys and girls are committed to training schools each year who need not have been if there were adequate facilities in their own community to care for them—probation service, child guidance clinic, casework service. Sometimes the youngster is committed to a training school when his needs, if sufficiently ascertained, would have rather indicated an institution for the mentally disturbed or deficient. For these and other reasons, conditions in the training schools are especially important.[1]

In conducting your study, you will want to keep in mind an important question: Do the conditions I am investigating operate to help the child toward rehabilitation as a normal participant in regular community living, or do they hinder this process? The child should be introduced to the life of the institution in such a way as to make his transition as easy as possible. The day-to-day life should be designed best to serve the child's rehabilitation, and provision should be made for his return to the larger community as soon as his situation will permit and under the most felicitous circumstances possible.

162. How many children were committed to training schools for boys or for girls from your community during each of the past five years?

163. What are the names and locations of such institutions?

164. Are there any children so committed whom the judge would not have committed if there had been adequate facilities to care for them in their own community?

165. Does the number of children in each institution exceed the recommended maximum of 150?

166. Does the training school have a cottage plan of residence with a maximum of 30 children to each cottage?

167. Is special attention given to orienting the child to his new institutional situation and making his adjustment as easy as possible? How is this done?

168. Are all pertinent case materials, results of medical and psychological tests, and other such information forwarded with the child so that the training school may use them to help the child as much as possible?

169. Is periodic review made of the progress of each child in the institution and are plans for his treatment modified where the situation indicates?

170. Does the training school have the services of a clinical team of one or more psychiatrists, psychologists, and social workers?

171. Is there a full-time psychologist for every 150 children? Full-time social caseworker for every 30 children?
Does the institution have the regular services of a physician?

172. Who determines how long each child shall remain in the institution? What is the average length of stay in the institution?

173. What recreational opportunities are available in the training school?

[1] For a popularly written account of one observer's description of various training schools in different parts of the country, see Albert Deutsch's *Our Rejected Children*, Little, Brown and Co., Boston, 1950. The second part of this book is a popular introduction to the problem of juvenile delinquency.

174. While at the institution, do the children participate in school, recreational, religious, or other services of nearby communities?
175. How regularly does the training school keep in close touch with parents? Under what circumstances and how often may children make home visits?
176. What types of disciplinary measures are taken in cases of misbehavior?
177. How do the school facilities, curricula, and programs for the children in the training schools differ from those in a regular community school?
    What special facilities are there? What deficiencies are there as compared with ordinary schools?
    Do the training school teachers meet the usual standards of certification?
178. What provisions are made for the religious training of the children in their own faith?
179. Are training school personnel included in the civil service system?
180. Is there an in-service training program for cottage parents and other personnel?
181. What specific preparations are usually made for the return of a child to his own community?
    What contacts are made with the local community?
    Do records of the child's tests and accomplishments accompany him for the use of school officials in the local community?
182. In the case of a child who leaves the training school to seek employment, is employment counseling or job procurement service available?
183. Do children released from training school benefit from follow-up service? Of what does this service consist? Is it staffed by professionally trained social workers?[1]

Citizen Action for Family and Child Welfare

Citizen action on behalf of family and child welfare takes many forms. In some communities a public welfare committee may take a lively interest both in the public assistance and in the child welfare efforts of the public welfare department and such private agencies as exist. Community councils occasionally pay particular attention to the needs of families and children. In larger communities welfare councils have this interest as one of their major areas of activity. Youth commissions or committees, variously titled, are often active in a broad field of youth betterment work with more or less of a direct eye on prevention of juvenile delinquency and a strong emphasis on adequate recreational opportunities for the different age-groups. In some cases these are composed exclusively of adults; in others, practically exclusively of youth. In many communities both youths and adults work together in planning adequate youth programs and youth facilities. Co-

[1] See Clendenen, Richard, *After the Training School—What?* Children's Bureau, Government Printing Office, Washington, 1950.

ordinating councils, particularly active in California and the Middle West, are organizations primarily concerned with general programs of delinquency prevention but which range far afield as they find various aspects of community living related to the delinquency problem. (See Chapter 17.)

In addition to such organizations as those mentioned above, veterans organizations, service clubs, and similar groups often have committees which concern themselves with some aspects of family and child welfare or delinquency prevention.

184. What organizations in your community have as their primary interest the furthering of agency services to strengthen the family or to contribute to child welfare?
    Are they affiliated with state or national organizations?
185. Has any survey been made in recent years of family and child welfare services?
186. What organizations in your community have delinquency prevention as their primary activity? One of their important areas of interest?
187. Under what auspices, if any, are the various youth serving agencies, public and private, brought together to consider communitywide programs in behalf of children and youth?
188. Does your state have any legislation which furnishes grants-in-aid or in other ways encourages local communities to provide opportunities and conditions designed to help reduce the problem of delinquency?
189. To what extent has your community taken advantage of such legislation?

References for Further Study

Applegate, Melbourne S., *The Boy in Court*. Public Affairs Press, Washington, 1953. This helpful book is designed specifically for parents of children who get into trouble with the law. It is written in terms which the layman can understand, and shows both an understanding of the complex problems involved and a spirit of sympathetic concern for those who must face them.

Gruenberg, Sidonie M., and others, *Our Children Today:* A Guide to Their Needs From Infancy Through Adolescence. Viking Press, New York, 1952. Experts in various aspects of child study present current knowledge in their fields. The book is a sort of inventory of what has been learned about children.

Paradise, Viola, *Toward Public Understanding of Casework:* A Study of Casework Interpretation in Cleveland. Russell Sage Foundation, New York, 1948. Typically, the general public does not understand the philosophy underlying social casework or its methods and objectives. This book considers the problem of promoting such public understanding.

Programs of the Federal Government Affecting Children and Youth. Interdepartmental Committee on Children and Youth, Government Printing Office, Washington, 1951. This report describes various federal programs affecting children and youth.

Young, Pauline V., *Social Treatment in Probation and Delinquency: Treatise and Casebook for Court Workers, Probation Officers, and Other Child Welfare Workers.* 2d ed. McGraw-Hill Book Co., New York, 1952. This book constitutes a handbook for various social workers and officials working with delinquents. It provides excellent background material for those interested in pursuing the subject of the treatment of delinquents in their communities.

See also the titles listed at the end of Chapter 10.

12. Health

NOWHERE DOES THE DYNAMIC NATURE of American communities show itself so plainly as in the field of health care. There are many important trends, some of which may be more noticeable in your community than others. One of the most important is the growth of the total health effort. It involves a complex web of physicians, nurses and other medical personnel, hospitals, clinics, medical schools, commercial and nonprofit medical insurance programs, pharmaceutical manufacturers, salesmen, pharmacists, and so on. The total expenditures for health services in a recent year were estimated at between 10 and 11 billion dollars.[1] One aspect of this development is that technological devices in the field of medical care have made it more difficult for the individual citizen to pay his medical bills and for the individual physician to set up and carry on his routine practice without direct access to hospital or other sources of expensive diagnostic and treatment equipment.

In a different vein, the fight against communicable diseases has been largely won, although not completely, and the chronic diseases have moved into the limelight as the number one health problem. Associated with this change is the gradual aging of the population, so that a larger proportionate amount of medical care must be given to older people. Still another development has been the widening concept of illness and more specifically the rise of the field of psychosomatic medicine. Not only do physicians often state that over half the people who come to them have problems which are largely psychological, but half of the nation's hospital beds are for mental patients.

These and other important developments have led to many changes within the field of health care. Group practice by physicians has been steadily rising, as have voluntary hospital and surgical expense insurance plans and health prepayment plans.

Perhaps of more lasting importance than any of the other changes is

---

[1] *Health Insurance Plans in the United States.* 82d Congress, 1st Session, Report No. 359, Part 1. Government Printing Office, Washington, 1951, p. 1.

the one which is most intangible: the broadening scope of medical concern. This involves increasing recognition of the psychological, mentioned above, and also a growth in stress placed on social factors; a tendency to consider the whole family rather than the individual as the basic health practice unit; a tendency to emphasize prevention wherever possible; and the emerging concept of the hospital not only as a place for sick patients but as a community health center. With this expanding scope and importance of medicine in American life, the field of health care becomes the concern not only of specialized medical personnel but of the layman who benefits from the total impact of the program and, in the last analysis, pays the bill.

Although notable advances have been made in the health field, these benefits have not been evenly distributed. There is tremendous variation in different parts of the country in health personnel and facilities. Indexes of health care, such as infant mortality rates, show great differences among the states. Access to adequate health facilities varies not only by geographic region and by income, but by race as well. Negro life expectancy is several years lower than that of whites.

Health Background Factors

It is important to exercise care in choosing the geographic area in which you plan to study health conditions, and to understand its place in the surrounding region of health care facilities. The American Medical Association has divided the whole country into local "medical service areas" for the purpose of study and planning.[1] These typically include part or all of several counties. Many counties have a public health department which carries on active public health programs. Such counties are best considered a single unit when studying public health conditions. From another standpoint, there are the "service areas" of the various general hospitals, as well as the regional organization of various hospitals in relation to a primary medical center, and so on. Your local health officer or representative of the state department of health, or your county medical society may be able to help you in determining the most judicious area for you to study.

Certain background conditions are important in understanding the health care situation in your community. For example, the proportion of children and old people, respectively (Census categories "under 15" and "65 and over"), will have a bearing on the type of medical need. The location of the community with respect to trade and service areas will have a relation

[1] See Bulletins 94 and 94A. See also Mountin, Joseph W., and Clifford H. Greve, *Public Health Areas and Hospital Facilities:* A Plan for Coordination, Public Health Service, Government Printing Office, Washington, 1950.

to local hospital facilities and their service areas, and both will be related to nearby hospital facilities as centers offering or receiving more specialized services. The degree of rurality of the community may have an effect on the number of physicians who wish to practice there. Sanctioned customs with respect to medical practice may influence the total health effort. For example, in some communities there is ready referral for psychiatric treatment whenever indicated, while in other communities there is little tradition of referral for such treatment. The income and standard of living of the people have also been found to have a bearing on health care and the use of health facilities.

Since different aspects of the community such as welfare program, recreation, and education each in its own way is related to health care, it is important that a general health survey be rooted in its community setting by depicting these other aspects. In this process, material from other chapters will be found helpful. Certain facts about your community may be even more closely related to health care—for example, housing conditions as reflected by overcrowding, dilapidation, and lack of plumbing facilities.

In attempting to arrive at a general picture of the quality of health care, you will be helped by certain indexes which are believed to be particularly important in reflecting more or less directly local health conditions. Among the best of these are the infant and maternal mortality rates. Others are the rate of stillbirths and the proportion of births in hospitals as opposed to births elsewhere.[1] The size of various rates of sickness (morbidity rates) is important but difficult to ascertain because such rates are poorly recorded in most communities. The tuberculosis rate is particularly indicative in that since this disease can be largely controlled by man, a high rate indicates possible neglect of modern control methods widely available to American communities.[2] Accident rates, infant mortality rates, proportion of births in hospital, maternal mortality rates, and per capita expenditures for public health, to be considered later, are also important indices to community well-being.

1. What is the amount per capita spent by your health department?[3]

[1] Birth and death rates give the annual number of births and deaths, respectively, per 1,000 population; specific death rates give the number of deaths from specific diseases per 100,000 population; the maternal death rate gives the annual number of deaths due to maternity per 1,000 live births; the infant mortality rate gives the annual number of deaths under one year per 1,000 live births; and the fatality rate gives the proportion of cases of a disease resulting in death.

[2] In various vital statistics, it is wise not to rely on the rates for any single year, since the year chosen may be highly atypical. This is particularly true of infectious diseases, but applies also to other statistics. At least three years, preferably five, should be combined in comparing different rates.

[3] This figure is fairly easy to compute if your community coincides with a health district, such as a city or county, which is the effective local health unit. Otherwise, important

2. If you can obtain data on selective service rejections for reasons of ill health or disability, what are the most frequent types of disability?

   Can any inference be made from these reports as to needed health services in your community?

3. Is the health of your community especially affected by local geographic or climatic conditions, such as periods of extreme heat or cold, dry spells, dampness, fog, and so forth?

Health Personnel

The key word in health personnel throughout the country seems to be "shortage." The increase in numbers of health personnel has not kept up with the increasing demand for them. Ever greater demands are placed on existing physicians, dentists, nurses, and other health personnel by more exacting and more widespread health practices. In addition, many health personnel serve in institutions, medical, dental, and nursing schools, the armed forces, and so on, and thus are not available for general practice. Particularly in rural areas, there is a lack of general practice physicians and specialists. Some of this is to be expected, for since health facilities of the larger medical centers serve whole regions of a state, one would expect to find a concentration of professional personnel there. However, there is a dearth of medical personnel in the rural areas beyond what can be accounted for by the regional services offered by large cities.

Some small communities have engaged in concerted efforts to attract one or more physicians. They have pooled their resources to provide a small clinic or health center, or to provide housing (lack of which is often a deterrent), or to provide certain types of equipment, or to guarantee a minimum annual income.

As with physicians, so with other personnel. Nurses and dentists are in short supply. A host of auxiliary technologies have grown up around the field of medicine and health care. In many areas there is a lack of such auxiliary medical personnel as laboratory technicians and physical therapists.

A growing problem caused by increased specialization among physicians is the impairment of the traditional personal relationship of long-standing acquaintance between physician and patient, and the "fragmentation" of the patient into the component parts served by each medical specialty.

The number of people needed to support specialists in the various medical specialties can be estimated only roughly, subject to modification according

local public health services may come from different levels of administration. The most thorough source of comparative data in recent years shows a median figure of 92 cents. However, for larger communities, the median was $1.05 and for smaller 88 cents. See *Health Practice Indices, 1947–48*, American Public Health Association, New York, 1950.

200 STUDYING YOUR COMMUNITY

to the situation of the individual community, medical traditions, proximity of larger communities with many specialists, and similar items. Here are some rough figures merely to give an approximate idea:

Specialist	Number needed to support
Internal medicine (diagnostician)	At least 10,000
Fully qualified surgeon	10,000
Fully qualified obstetrician	15,000 to 20,000
Ear, nose, and throat	15,000
Roentgenologist	60,000
Pathologist	100,000

"A community of 20,000 to 25,000 population could expect to have 18 to 20 active practitioners of whom 3 to 5 would be qualified specialists— an internist, a surgeon (possibly two), an ear, nose and throat specialist and an obstetrician."[1]

4. How many physicians (M.D.) serve your community in private practice? In other capacities, such as public health, institutions, industrial medicine, and so on?[2]
5. What medical specialists are available in your community, and in what numbers?
6. What medical specialties are not represented by a practicing specialist in your community?
7. Where do people in your community most often go for specialist services not available in the local community?
8. Is there a shortage of physicians in your community? If so, what has been done to attract more physicians?
9. Is there a shortage of service in any particular medical specialty? Is the community large enough to support a specialist in this field?
10. Are any special advanced training facilities available to physicians in your community? To what extent do physicians take part in such training programs?
11. Do any physicians in your community engage in group practice, whereby various physicians own together various expensive pieces of equipment and collaborate in diagnosis and treatment of the individual patient?
12. How many registered professional nurses are there in your community?[3] Practical nurses? Midwives?

[1] *Measuring the Community for a Hospital.* American Hospital Association, Chicago, 1945, p. 15.
[2] Consult the *American Medical Directory*, published by the American Medical Association. Where possible, try not to include in your count physicians who have retired or who are not practicing for other reasons.
[3] See your state or local nurses' association, or local nurses' registry, where available. Your state has a list of registered nurses. Typically, not all qualified nurses are actually available for nursing service, for some devote their full time to their family, or have retired because of age, or for some other reason.

13. Are licenses required for all nurses, professional and practical?
14. Is there a shortage of nurses available for hospital service? Private duty?
15. How many dentists are there in your community?
16. Is there a local dental society?
17. Is there a shortage of dentists?
18. How many of each of the following are available in your community:

Druggists	Anaesthetists (exclusive of
Dental hygienists	physicians)
Dieticians	Physical therapists
Laboratory technicians	Other auxiliary medical
X-ray technicians	personnel

19. Is there a critical shortage of any particular type of health personnel? If so, what is being done to recruit them?
20. How many osteopaths are listed in telephone or other directories of your community? Chiropractors? Other types of practitioner?
21. What laws govern the licensing of persons who treat people's health or who sell glasses, drugs, and so on?

Hospitals

Several developments in the field of hospitals are important to keep in mind as you study your community's hospital service. Diagnostic facilities and equipment of the local hospital are becoming more and more important to the general practitioner. Best advantage of medical progress can be taken only if local community general hospitals are allied with larger hospitals with extensive specialized equipment in some sort of regional hospital organization. This is now proceeding in some states through the encouragement of regional organization of hospitals around major medical centers. Hospital bed shortage, though eased by federal grants-in-aid for hospital construction, is still a problem, often accentuated by the presence in hospitals of people who would not need to be there if other chronic care facilities were available in the community. Home care programs, through which the facilities and personnel of the hospital are "brought to" the patient who can therefore be released much earlier from the hospital, if home conditions warrant it, show promise of relieving some of the strain and being more conducive to convalescence.

The idea of the hospital as the place only of the sick person has definitely been superseded, as more and more communities come to develop hospitals which provide laboratory, educational, and other services for well patients and in other ways function as "health centers." Hospitals for the tuberculous, for mental patients, and for certain other types of long-term illness have become increasingly a government concern. Indeed, general hospitals of all types make up slightly less than half the country's hospital beds. (Thus, in considering the number of beds per thousand, one should be clear whether one means general hospital beds, hospital beds of all types, and so on.) For the country as a whole, the total hospital beds per thousand is about ten.[1]

In studying your community's hospitals, you will want to consult the list of hospitals approved by the Joint Commission on Hospital Accreditation as well as the annual report on hospital service in the *Journal of the American Medical Association*. These should be available through local physicians or health officials, or through the public library.

22. How many hospitals are located in your community? Of these, how many are general and how many are special purpose (mental, tuberculosis, and so on)?
23. Which hospitals are nonprofit? Proprietary? Government?
24. For each hospital how many resident physicians and interns are on the staff? How many graduate nurses? Student nurses?
    What is their weekly schedule of hours on duty?
25. For each public hospital, which types of personnel are covered by civil service? Which types are not covered?
26. Is there a social service department? What qualifications have the staff?
27. What rates are charged by each hospital? How do these rates compare with the actual cost of care?
28. Are rates adjusted according to the income of the patient?
29. What is the rate of payment by public agencies for hospitalization of their clients?
    What agencies authorize hospitalization of clients at public expense?
30. Where do people go for hospitalization when hospital facilities in the local or nearby community are not adequate to meet the special requirements of their sickness?
31. How many general hospital beds are there in your community for each 1,000 population?[2]
32. Is there a shortage of hospital beds in your community?
33. Has there been new hospital construction in recent years? How many beds?
34. Are plans underway for expansion of hospital facilities in your community?
35. What kind of ambulance service is available? How is it paid for?
36. Which of the following specialized facilities are available in each of your community's hospitals:

[1] *Building America's Health*, vol. 1 of the Report to the President by the President's Commission on the Health Needs of the Nation. Government Printing Office, Washington, 1952, p. 23. This volume is a well-written summary of health conditions throughout the nation.
[2] The figure for the country in 1950 was 3.2 acceptable general hospital beds per thousand population, but it varied by states from 6.4 for Montana to 1.9 for Arkansas. The Hill-Burton program uses the standard of one general hospital bed for roughly every 220 persons.

Physical therapy facilities
and personnel
Laboratory facilities and
personnel

Diagnostic x-ray
Therapeutic x-ray
Oxygen tent
Incubator

37. Is each hospital fully or provisionally approved by the Joint Commission on Hospital Accreditation (formerly, by the American College of Surgeons)? If not, why?

38. Which hospitals in your community have a lunch bar or cafeteria? Library? Nursery? Chapel?

39. Which of the following is available in your community's hospitals:[1]

System of referral to public
health nurses
Home care programs
Psychiatric service
Rehabilitation programs

"Rooming in" provisions in
the maternity section
Bloodbank service
Medical library

40. Do any hospitals act as health centers in any of the following ways:
Contain doctors' offices
Provide public educational courses, films, etc.
Place auditorium at disposal of citizen health institutes
Provide meeting rooms for health organizations

41. Which hospitals have outpatient departments?

42. Which of the following services are provided in outpatient departments:
Well-child care
Prenatal advice or expectant mothers' and fathers' classes
Laboratory services for ambulatory patients

43. Do any hospitals refuse admission to Negroes or other groups? If so, what alternative provision is made? Are facilities equal?

44. Can you get an estimate of the number of hospital beds which would become available if earlier release from the hospital were made possible through the following measures:
An extension of nursing and convalescent homes
An extension of home care
Other provision for care of the chronically ill

Public Health Services

Public responsibility for many health functions has long been recognized. An example of such a long-standing community responsibility is that of communicable disease control. Although methods have changed, the now largely outmoded "Quarantine" sign is an indication of the centuries-old activity of the community in the public health field. A whole series of other

[1] See *It's* YOUR *Hospital and* YOUR *Life!* Public Affairs Pamphlet No. 187, New York, 1952.

functions have come to be associated with the public health program, and, of course, this expansion of adequate health functions has been one factor in man's conquest of the communicable diseases and in the gradual lengthening of the average life span. A brief listing of these functions will serve to sketch out broadly the field of public health and to form an outline for this section of your health study. However, as in all dynamic fields, there is considerable variation from community to community, and changing developments often lead to the inclusion of new functions:

Records and vital statistics	Public health nursing
Sanitation	Maternal and child health
Laboratories	Communicable disease control
Health education	Chronic disease control

Other items could be added. Examples are nutrition, rehabilitation, industrial hygiene. Although there are important public health functions on the state and national level, those listed above cannot be adequately performed except as they operate in the community itself, being based in a local health district comprising one or more counties, or in a municipality such as a city or populous township. Some 40 million Americans are without full-time tax-supported public health services in the local community.

In order to carry on the major public health services in acceptable fashion, the following standards are considered a *minimum* by authorities in the field:

Type of health personnel	Number of people served
Medical health officer	50,000
Public health nurse	5,000
Sanitarian	25,000
Health educator	50,000
Clerk	15,000

Adequate services by such staff would call for an annual expenditure per capita of about $1.50 each year as a minimum.[1] But in 1950 the average per capita expenditure for preventive local health services was only 96 cents while in 12 states it was less than 50 cents.[2] While there will be considerable local variation, it is also usually agreed that a population of at least 50,000 is necessary to support an adequate public health program, and that populations under this number receive only spotty service as a general rule. They are therefore not recommended as a base for a local public health department except where the population is extremely sparse. Nevertheless,

[1] *Planning for Health Services:* A Guide for States and Communities. Public Health Service Bulletin No. 304, Government Printing Office, Washington, 1950. This booklet is an invaluable guide for citizen groups.
[2] *Building America's Health*, p. 36.

59 out of every hundred health departments serve units of fewer than 50,000 persons. Federal funds are available to states in developing their local public health programs, and the states in turn offer support to local districts. Thus, the entire cost of local public health services is not usually borne solely by the local tax unit.

A frequent procedure is to have a local physician act for a small unit like a township as a part-time "health officer," charged under the state health law with certain functions. But the small municipality is not a feasible unit for such public health functions as communicable disease control, public health nursing, and education. The functions which are performed under this plan are often highly perfunctory. Seldom are effective disease prevention programs possible. As the American Medical Association has put it, "the survival of the part-time general practitioner as the local administrator of a health department cannot be encouraged by the medical profession or be recommended to the tax payer as the best his money can buy in public health."[1]

The American Public Health Association publishes an *Evaluation Schedule: For Use in the Study and Appraisal of Community Health Programs*, as well as an instruction booklet entitled *What's the Score?* which tells how to use it. The annual report of your local health department will be most useful at this point in your study.

Some public health services are often carried on by nontax-supported agencies, in cooperation with public health officials. The outline of questions in this section is designed to cover such services, as well as those covered by a public health department. In making a local study, it will be well to record which type of agency performs which service.

45. Is there a local board of health? How is it selected, and what are its functions?
46. What tax-supported public health department operates in your local community:

| State-operated public health district | City public health district |
| County or multi-county public health district | Other |

47. Which hospitals, clinics, or other such facilities does your health department maintain?
48. What supervisory, service, or regulatory functions does the state health department perform in your community?

[1] From a resolution quoted in *Your Neighbor's Health Is Your Business* by Albert Q. Maisel, Public Affairs Pamphlet No. 180, New York, 1952, p. 29. This is an interesting, simplified description of the services of local health departments.

49. What private organizations perform public health functions in your community?
50. Do they work in frequent consultation with public health officials?
51. What public health workers function in your community in either public or private agencies:

    Medical public health officer   Health educator
    Public health nurse   Rehabilitation officer
    Sanitary engineer or other   Clerk
      (milk) sanitarian   Other

52. How do your local public health personnel compare with the standards quoted on page 204 for local health departments?
53. Does your local health department fill out and send in the APHA's *Evaluation Schedule?*
54. How does your community compare with others on the various public health indices tabulated in *Health Practice Indices?*[1]

Records and vital statistics. An important function is that of maintaining records and vital statistics. Records of the spread or decline of a particular disease; of the outbreak of a contagious disease which calls for countermeasures in order to prevent an epidemic; records of the chief causes of death; which diseases are becoming more important, which are declining; and birth and death records—such information, when assembled by districts, gives health officials the knowledge they need in order to plan adequately for preventive programs. Some common forms of records are birth reports, death reports, and communicable disease reports. Certain diseases, because of their extremely contagious nature or because of their public health importance, are required to be reported by the physician who encounters them or by the family in which the disease occurs. This permits immediate public health action where such is called for, and also gives an idea of the rate of illness from any particular disease (often called morbidity rate). These supplement the death rates from particular diseases which are compiled from information given on death reports.

55. What provision is made for the local registration of births and deaths?
56. What specific diseases are reportable by law?
57. Are compilations of local vital statistics and morbidity rates made and published by your local health department?
If not, are such reports about the communities of your state published and made available by your state health department?

Sanitation. In an adequate public health service, various systems of inspection are set up to assure that minimum sanitary requirements are being maintained in the community. Inspection should be frequent and thorough

[1] American Public Health Association, New York.

enough to ensure proper enforcement. In many places, both in large and small communities, important sanitary measures are neglected because of the lack of an adequate law, the lack of adequate staff for systematic enforcement, or other reasons.

Sanitation work is not only a matter of enforcing adequate sanitary codes, but also one of education and collaborative effort between health officials and private citizens, businesses, and institutions of one sort or another. Often, adequate sanitary measures work to the direct economic benefit of the individual, as where food spoilage is prevented through adequate refrigeration or packaging, or where farmers can gain a higher price for milk with a low bacteria count, or where the more efficient use of fuel in industrial plants effects fuel savings as well as decreasing air pollution.

You can procure from the federal Public Health Service material which will give you standards to use as a basis of comparison for your own community on many of the sanitary measures referred to below. Information on various aspects of your community's public sanitation program can probably also be obtained from the appropriate state and local health officials.

58. Is there a public water supply? What is the source of this water? How is it treated? Is it filtered; are chemicals, fluorides added, and so on? Is the water hard or soft?

59. Is the supply ample? Have there been shortages in recent years?

60. Is the public water supply approved by the appropriate state health authorities?

61. Is provision made for regular inspection by state or local officials?

62. How often and by whom are samples analyzed?

63. Have there been any unsatisfactory reports of analysis of samples or inspection of facilities in the past few years? If so, what has been done in each case?

64. Have any illnesses in the past few years been attributed to the water supply?

65. Has the question of adding fluorides to the water for dental health been considered in recent years? By what groups? With what results?

66. How many houses are not tapped into the municipal public water supply?

67. Are private water supplies inspected? How often? Is such inspection mandatory?

68. What is done in the case of unsatisfactory results in the test of a private water supply?

Laws differ in various states and communities in their provision for milk and food inspection and for inspection of eating establishments.

69. What local or state ordinances govern the sanitary inspection of milk and dairy products which come into your community?

70. What agency issues permits for milk distribution in your community? How many permits were refused or revoked in the past five years?
71. Must herds be inspected periodically for tuberculosis? Brucellosis (undulant fever)?
72. Must barns, milk houses, milk transportation vehicles, pasteurizing, processing and bottling plants be inspected?
73. Is the sale of bulk milk (unbottled) at retail permitted in your community?
74. Must milk in restaurants be served from individual bottles?
75. What percentage of the milk supply is pasteurized?
76. How often and by whom, and at what stage of milk distribution are sample tests made of the milk which comes into your community as to bacteria count? Butter fat content? Other items?
    What standards must be met in such tests?
77. What special inspection provisions are made for dairy products such as cheese, ice cream, and so forth?
78. What local or state ordinances provide for the inspection of various types of food sold at retail?
    What local food inspection procedures are carried out?
79. What special sanitary regulations govern the sale of prepared food in your community?[1]
80. Is there any difference in the provisions for boarding houses, restaurants, taverns, soda fountains, snack bars, and so forth?
81. Must food-serving personnel be especially licensed?
82. Must special provisions be made for washing facilities for restaurant workers, patrons, etc.?
83. By whom and how often is the inspection of restaurants and other eating establishments carried on?
84. What is done in the case of unfavorable inspection reports?
    How many instances have there been of such unsatisfactory reports in recent years?
85. What is the extent of the educational program carried on among local dispensers of food?

The fight against communicable diseases has involved many skirmishes with disposal methods for garbage, sewage, and human excreta, which were found to be means of disease contagion. Close supervision of public and private disposal systems is especially necessary where people are crowded together in dense population concentrations. It is particularly important that the water supply be kept free from contamination by sewage and excreta disposal systems.

86. Is garbage and refuse collection a function of the local government? Which department?

[1] See *Ordinance and Code Regulating Eating and Drinking Establishments*, Public Health Service Publication No. 37, Government Printing Office, Washington, 1950.

If not, by whom and according to what arrangements with the municipality or individuals is it operated?

87. How often do collections of garbage and refuse take place?

88. Must garbage awaiting collection be kept in covered metal containers? Is it collected in covered vehicles?

89. What provisions of local ordinances relate to garbage and refuse collection and disposal?

90. Is the method of garbage and refuse disposal approved by state or local health officials?

91. Which parts of the community, if any, are not provided with garbage and refuse disposal services?

92. To what extent is each method of sewage disposal utilized in your community:

Public sewage system   Private
Disposal by sewage treatment   Septic tanks
Emptying into river,   Pit privies, chemical
  lake, or ocean   toilets, etc.

93. How many homes or establishments in your community are not connected with the public sewage system?

94. What provision is there for inspection of privies, septic tanks, or other private excreta disposal methods?

95. Are there any public comfort stations? How often are they inspected? Are they kept clean and orderly?

96. What ordinances govern sanitation in trailer camps? Are these ordinances adequate?

97. What provision is there for inspection of public sewage disposal facilities?

98. Have any local bathing beaches been condemned because of pollution?

Housing[1] and plumbing facilities are of definite public health concern. Poorly lighted or ventilated housing, housing in which there is overcrowding, or inadequate or faulty plumbing contributes more than its share to the diseases and general ill health of the community.

99. Which of the following provisions for building construction and inspection relating to public health does your community have (see Chapter 6):

Building code   Multiple dwelling law
Plumbing code   Other

100. How often and by whom are inspections made under each of these provisions?

101. How many cases of unsatisfactory conditions were found in each of the past five years? What was done in each case?

102. Have any surveys been made by the health department or other government or private agencies in recent years to determine the extent of un-

[1] See Chapter 6.

satisfactory sanitary conditions in institutions, places of employment, residences, and other buildings?

Particularly in large cities or where there are industrial concentrations, air and water pollution become important public health problems. In addition, many small communities pollute rivers, streams, and lakes with sewage disposal and industrial waste. Often these bodies of water are in turn the source of water supply for other communities farther along the lake, or farther downstream. Indeed, some communities pollute the very body of water which they utilize as a source of water. Moreover, bays and beaches which might otherwise be excellent for swimming are rendered public health menaces by unnecessary pollution through the disposal of sewage and industrial waste.[1]

A similar though perhaps less frequent hazard is caused by the pollution of the air we breathe. Carefully designed zoning laws may confine particularly noxious or otherwise offensive industries to sections far removed from residences. But frequently some type of processing of waste gases and fumes or soot is necessary if the air is not to be polluted.

103. Does your community zone industrial districts in such manner that industries producing noxious gases, soot, and so forth are kept far from residences? (See Chapter 5.)

104. Are there local ordinances governing the emission of soot and poisonous or unpleasant gases or fumes?

105. Does your state law make possible the protection of rivers and streams from pollution by communities along their course?

106. Are there any ordinances which govern the emptying of industrial waste products into rivers, lakes, or other bodies of water?

107. Does your state have a pollution control authority? Has your community investigated the aid which may be afforded by this body in solving its pollution problems?

The control of rodents, insects, and pollen is of frequent public health concern.

108. Is there a rat control program in the community?

109. Are refuse and litter kept from accumulating in places where rat growth and breeding would be encouraged?

110. Is there an insect control program?

111. Is any effort made to control the growth of ragweed on behalf of sufferers from asthma and hay fever?

[1] See *Washing Our Water:* Your Job and Mine by Helen B. Woodward, Public Affairs Pamphlet No. 193, New York, 1953; also *Let's Have Clean Water:* A Kit of Materials to Aid Community Leaders in Their Efforts to Solve Local Water Pollution Problems, Public Health Service Publication No. 264, Government Printing Office, Washington, 1952.

Laboratories. Essential to public health work is the laboratory analysis of various substances such as water, milk, and other foods in connection with sanitation measures as well as in connection with the diagnosis of various diseases.

112. What laboratory facilities exist in your community and are available for purposes of making analyses of various substances in connection with the sanitation program?

113. What facilities exist for laboratory analysis as an aid to diagnosis (blood tests, urinalysis, and so on)?

114. Is the laboratory a part of the health department, or connected with a hospital; or is some other type of laboratory facility used for public health work?

115. What types of analysis and diagnostic test can be performed by your local laboratory staff, and what types must be sent on to a more thoroughly equipped laboratory?

Health education. Public health education work must continue if the benefits of modern public health knowledge and techniques are to be widely applied. Such education is often directed at the nature of specific diseases, their prevention, treatment, after-care, and so on, as well as matters of nutrition, personal hygiene, and the rest. Recently, more comprehensive programs have come to be emphasized.[1] Such work is by no means the exclusive prerogative of the health department, although the health department usually participates in various aspects of health education work. Voluntary agencies are particularly active in this field, and considerable health education is provided for in the public school curriculum.

116. In what ways does your public health department participate in health education work?

117. Which agencies carry on educational work in the field of nutrition?

118. Which organizations, public, or private, engage in which of the following types of health education endeavor (see page 222):

Sponsor lectures	Organize displays, distribute posters
Show films	Give specific educational materials
Conduct institutes	to the newspapers
Distribute pamphlets	Sponsor radio programs
	Other

119. In what types of health education do the schools engage (see Chapter 7):

Courses in personal	Courses or units of
hygiene	study in nutrition
Courses in physical	Special lectures, films on
education	specific health topics

[1] See *Community Organization for Health Education,* American Public Health Association, New York, 1941.

120. How much time is allotted to such health instruction in the grade schools? High schools?

Public health nursing. One of the most widespread health services is public health nursing. Public health nurses perform a host of services, including home visiting and care of the sick, instructing families in care of their sick members, assisting at immunization and other clinics, conducting classes in maternal and infant care, planning or assisting in health education activities, and so on. There should be one such public health nurse, roughly, for every 5,000 persons. The National Organization for Public Health Nursing will supply you with standards for nurse personnel and services. Read Edith E. Wensley's *The Community and Public Health Nursing*[1] and *Public Health Nursing:* Responsibilities in a Community Health Program.[2]

121. Does your local municipal, county, or regional health department have a staff of public health nurses? How large is the staff?
122. Are public health nurses available for community work through the auspices of private health organizations such as visiting nurse associations? How many nurses?
123. How many people are there per public health nurse in your county or city?
124. What are the major duties of public health nurses in your community?
125. Are public health nurses included on boards and committees which plan health and welfare programs?

Maternal and child health. Special provisions for maternal and infant health care have long been recognized as a vital public health service.[3] In addition to state and local financing, the federal Children's Bureau is empowered to allot sums of money to states for improving maternal and child care programs.

126. What special health care is available to expectant mothers?
127. Is there a free prenatal clinic service? How many mothers make use of it in a year?
    Is there special instruction in nutrition?
128. What routine laboratory tests, such as the Wassermann, are administered to expectant mothers?
129. Are special classes available for expectant mothers? Fathers?
130. What percentage of babies are born in a hospital?
    What percentage are born under the care of a physician? Midwife?[4]

[1] Macmillan Co., New York, 1950.
[2] National League for Nursing, New York, 1949.
[3] See Schlesinger, Edward R., *Health Services for the Child*, McGraw-Hill Book Co., New York, 1953.
[4] See *Vital Statistics of the United States*, published annually by the Government Printing Office. This gives data for each state, county, and urban place of 10,000 or more. You can then compare your community with the rest of the United States, the rest of your state, or with other communities of approximately the same size.

131. How many deaths connected with pregnancy and childbirth occurred in your community in each of the past five years?
How does this number compare with other communities of similar size?
132. Do any clinics in your community give contraceptive advice?
133. What was the infant mortality rate during the past five years? How does this compare with that of other similar communities?[1]
134. What special public health services are available for children in the early years of life?
135. Does your local health department receive financial assistance from your state government in administering its maternal and child health programs?
136. What proportion of children are immunized against each of the following in the first year of life? During preschool years?[2]

Whooping cough	Polio
Diphtheria	Other
Smallpox	

137. Is there a special clinic for cardiac children, diabetic children, and so on? Children with orthopedic defects? Others?
138. Which agencies or organizations offer educational literature to mothers covering the problems of pregnancy and infant and child care?

Because of the special circumstances surrounding the birth of infants to unmarried mothers, special attention must be given to assure adequate health care.

139. What special safeguards are there to assure adequate health care to unmarried mothers and their offspring?

When you have finished with your survey of public health facilities and services, answer the following questions:

140. Are sufficient funds available in the community for adequate public health services?
141. Are there any glaring deficiencies in the public health program?
142. Are equal facilities available to people of different races?

Communicable Diseases[3]

The past half century has witnessed a heartening series of gains in the struggle against communicable diseases. Much of this progress has been the result of preventive medicine, sanitation, immunization, and the general rise in the level of living. A large part of it has been the direct result of outstanding medical developments of various types, including the development

[1] See the vital statistics reports published by your local health department or by your state health department, or consult *Vital Statistics of the United States*.
[2] For health services available in the schools, see Chapter 7.
[3] Communicable and chronic diseases are here treated separately from the public health section, although they both are a direct concern of public health work.

of mass x-ray programs, immunization techniques, penicillin and other "wonder drugs," and so on.

The President's Commission on the Health Needs of the Nation points out that in the past 50 years the death rate from tuberculosis per 100,000 has dropped from 194 to 27, diphtheria from 40 to fewer than one, influenza and pneumonia from 202 to 34. There has been an accompanying decline in typhoid fever, whooping cough, measles, diarrhea, and other infectious diseases. The death rate from all infectious diseases combined is a significant measure of modern progress. It has dropped from 676 per 100,000 in 1900 to 79 in 1949.[1] One should not assume that contagious diseases no longer constitute a problem. The case is simply that for many of them the methods of control are well known and therefore their prevalence in a community over a continued period of years indicates the possibility of deficient public health services. Public health measures must be rigorously maintained in order to sustain continued progress in the field of contagious diseases. For example, although the fight against tuberculosis has been dramatic, nevertheless there are an estimated 400,000 cases of active TB in this country of which an estimated 250,000 have been reported to health officials.[2]

Another problem which remains with great tenacity even though much progress has been made in prevention and treatment methods is the venereal diseases, of which over half a million known cases existed in 1949.[3]

143. What is the known number of cases of active tuberculosis in your community?

144. What was the death rate from tuberculosis in your community for the past five years?[4]

145. What public hospital facilities for the tuberculous serve patients requiring such hospitalization from your community?
Is there a charge for tuberculosis hospitalization, or is it free?

146. What mass x-ray or other mass screening devices are used to find new cases?

147. What follow-up is carried on in connection with active cases of tuberculosis uncovered by various mass screening programs?

148. What safeguards does the health law provide in order to prevent persons who are known to have active tuberculosis from spreading the disease?

[1] *Building America's Health*, p. 8.
[2] Dempsey, Mary, *Current Status of the Tuberculosis Problem*. National Tuberculosis Association, New York, 1952, mimeographed.
[3] See the American Social Hygiene Association's pamphlet entitled *In Defense of the Nation: Three Times in 33 Years*, New York, 1951. Read also *Challenge to Community Action*, Public Health Service, Government Printing Office, Washington. This is an excellent booklet on the community problems of prostitution, promiscuity, and venereal diseases.
[4] You may be able to get more detailed information by age, sex, occupation, race, etc. from your local tuberculosis or other health organization.

149. Have any persons with active tuberculosis been refused admission to the tuberculosis hospital because it was filled to capacity? What, if anything, is being done about expanding facilities?

150. How many cases of venereal diseases were reported to health authorities in your community during each of the past five years?

151. Is there a state or local ordinance making any type of medical care compulsory for persons who are found to have syphilis or gonorrhea? What types of public treatment facilities exist?

152. How many cases of stillbirth resulting from syphilis occurred in each of the past five years?
How many children were born with congenital syphilis?

153. Has the American Social Hygiene Association made a study of prostitution conditions in your community in recent years? What were the findings?

154. Is there an adequate law against prostitution in your community? Is the law systematically and efficiently enforced?

155. Must sex offenders, including prostitutes, undergo examination for venereal diseases, and submit to treatment if indicated?

156. What was the number of reported cases and what was the number of deaths from each of the following diseases in your community in each of the past five years:

Chicken pox	Poliomyelitis
Diphtheria	Streptococcal sore throat
Dysentery	(including scarlet fever)
Gonorrhea	Syphilis
Jaundice, infectious	Tuberculosis (all forms)
Measles	Typhoid fever
Mumps	Whooping cough[1]
Pneumonia (all forms)	

157. What were the morbidity rates (if available) for your community on the diseases listed above?[2]

158. How do these rates compare with those of other communities of similar size?

159. Are disability rates available for your community?

160. What was the frequency of reportable occupational diseases during the past five years?

161. What epidemics have occurred within the past five years, and what measures were taken to control them?

[1] In addition to these relatively common communicable diseases, there are others which often call for special consideration in various parts of the country. If yours is an area in which any of the following are present to any considerable extent, you will want to include them among those listed above: hookworm, malaria, Rocky Mountain spotted fever, tularemia, endemic typhus. The weekly public health reports of the U.S. Public Health Service give current data on reportable diseases.

[2] Morbidity rates give the number of cases of illness per year for a specific unit of people, such as 1,000 persons. Disability rates give the average number of days of disability per person per year.

162. Is there a plot map available in your health department or other health agency showing location of cases of tuberculosis, syphilis, or other communicable disease?

In what sections of your community is the number greatest?

How does this map compare with that of housing conditions, juvenile delinquency, and so on?

163. What ordinances or regulations give health authorities power to regulate the home care of various communicable diseases, and the carriers of such diseases?

Chronic Diseases

The problem of chronic diseases has increased as more people avoid the acute contagious diseases and survive many years longer, during which period they continue to be susceptible to one or another chronic disease. In addition, with the gradual "aging" of the population, more people are of the ages when chronic diseases are especially prevalent. This last point can be overdrawn, however, for over one-half of those with chronic illness are under 45 years of age.

Chronic illness involves illnesses which by their nature continue a long time, in some cases many years. Examples include heart disease and high blood pressure, cancer, rheumatism, and tuberculosis (contagious but also chronic). As can be seen from only these examples, one characteristic of many chronic diseases is their disabling effect. Thus, though these diseases in many cases may not be fatal, they nevertheless cause a great problem of disability, part of which, at least, is amenable to vocational and other types of rehabilitation treatment. Although estimates are difficult to make, two recent surveys indicate from three and one-half to four and one-half million people with disabling illness at any one time.[1]

Two groups of chronic diseases are particularly important for their high death rate as well. These are the cardiovascular-renal diseases and the various types of cancer, which together account for two-thirds of this country's deaths.

Chronic diseases vary in the extent to which they can be prevented or treated. Some 17 chronic diseases are largely controllable, including diabetes and pernicious anemia, while 27 others are in part controllable by already known preventive measures.

Two activities are particularly important in connection with prevention and early detection and treatment of chronic diseases. One is public education and the other is multiple screening. The latter is a device whereby

[1] See Woolsey, Theodore D., *Estimates of Disabling Illness Prevalence in the United States,* Public Health Monograph No. 4, Government Printing Office, Washington, 1952.

several diagnostic tests can be given to an individual practically simultaneously, thus extending diagnostic facilities to wide masses of people and reducing the cost per diagnosis. Individuals are given several tests which screen for many different illnesses in a very short while. While some of the tests are not decisive but rather yield only high probabilities, they are considered to be a great improvement, and, of course, further testing can verify diagnoses where such verification is called for.[1]

Another aspect of the approach to chronic illness has to do with rehabilitation. A recent survey estimates that there are approximately two million disabled persons in the United States who could be rehabilitated to employment or to more productive work than that in which they are now engaged. Many who need expensive care might be helped to the point where they can care for themselves. That such goals are possible is indicated by a rehabilitation study in West Virginia in which 376 families were rehabilitated at a cost of less than they were receiving annually in public assistance payments, and are now earning annually more than it cost to rehabilitate them.

Rehabilitation efforts are particularly effective where the physician, physical therapist, nurse, occupational therapist, medical social worker, and psychologist can function as a team. Such efforts are costly, yet not prohibitively so, when compared with what society already pays to support those who might be helped to self-support.[2]

For several decades, the federal government has made grants-in-aid available to states for vocational rehabilitation programs to provide medical and hospital services for persons whose disabilities give promise of yielding to rehabilitative procedures. A good program involves many services, some of which are free, others free in case of need: physical examination; medical, surgical, psychiatric, and hospital services where called for; artificial devices where called for; individual counsel and guidance in job training; vocational training; living expenses during rehabilitation where necessary; in some cases tools, equipment, and licenses; job placement and follow-up. Each state has a vocational rehabilitation program.[3]

164. Insofar as such information is available, what is the extent of each of the following diseases in your community:

Heart disease	Cancer	Diabetes
Cerebral palsy	Arthritis	Poliomyelitis
High blood pressure	Tuberculosis	Multiple sclerosis

---

[1] Read *The Multiple Screening Idea*, Health Information Foundation, New York, no date.

[2] In preparing the foregoing paragraphs, considerable use has been made of the sections on "Chronic Illness" and "Rehabilitation" in *Building America's Health*.

[3] For a practical pamphlet explaining how the plan works, see *Vocational Rehabilitation for Civilians*, Office of Vocational Rehabilitation, Government Printing Office, Washington, 1951.

165. What was the death rate from each of these diseases for the past five years?[1]
166. Do any of the hospitals have special sections for those with chronic illness? Are there any special hospitals for chronic illness?
167. Are there any hospital home care programs designed to enable the chronically ill to live outside the hospital?
168. Is casework by trained medical social workers available to help patients work out problems connected with chronic illness?
169. Are there adequate nursing homes for the chronically ill?
170. Do any institutions carry such depressing names as "home for the aged and infirm," "home for incurables," and so on?
171. Is there a program of selective job placement for the chronically ill who are able to do some work? Are there sheltered workshops?
172. How many people from your community are participating in the state vocational rehabilitation program?
173. Have any people been refused rehabilitation services because of lack of funds?
174. What other special provisions does your community have for those who are chronically ill?

An important and largely preventable cause of physical disability is accidents. According to the National Safety Council, approximately nine and one-half million disabling accidents occurred in 1951, of which some 350,000 resulted in permanent impairment. Accidents are the number one cause of death for the nation's children and youth. Increased use of safety devices in industrial production has been more than offset by the increase in motor vehicle accidents, which now account for more than a third of all fatal accidents. Another third of all accidents occur in the home. Other major categories of accidents are occupational accidents and public nonmotor vehicle accidents, such as railroad, air, fire, drowning, and so on. The National Safety Council can supply you with material on accident prevention, as well as material with which to study your community with respect to its safety provisions.

175. What has been the number of each of the following types of accident in your community in the past five years:

| Occupational | Motor vehicle |
| Home | Public nonmotor vehicle |

176. Is there an organization in your community which concerns itself primarily with accident prevention?

[1] "A chronic *disease* is an abnormal and persistent change in the structure or behavior of some part of the body. Chronic *illness* or disability may follow immediately or not for years." Quoted from Yahraes, Herbert, *Something Can Be Done About Chronic Illness*, Public Affairs Pamphlet No. 176, New York, 1951. This is a good popular presentation of methods for coping with the problems of chronic illness.

177. Is any trend in accident rates apparent in your community?
178. What departments of local or state government carry on inspection functions in industrial plants or elsewhere in order to prevent accidents?
179. What does your police department report as the most frequent causes of automobile accidents in your community?
180. Is there compulsory motor vehicle inspection in your community?
181. What special provisions are there to safeguard children on their way to and from school?
182. How well do street signs and traffic signals conform to standards available through the National Safety Council?
183. What steps have been suggested by governmental or other agencies to cut down the rate of various types of accident in your community?

Paying for Medical Care

Newer treatment methods and better medical facilities cost increasingly larger sums of money. The growing cost of medical care has resulted in part from the scientific developments which have lengthened the average span of life and improved the nation's health. Thus, although medical advances offer relief from illness and disabilities to many people who might not have been helped before, nevertheless there are millions of people in the United States who cannot afford to pay for adequate medical care.

Direct payment by the patient to his physician or his hospital is the traditional method of health care payment, but with the many complex changes in medical technology and in the organization of medical care, this has come to be only one way among many.

A familiar development in medical care payment has been the growth of voluntary nonprofit hospitalization and surgical expense insurance programs, notably the Blue Cross and Blue Shield organizations. It is estimated that in a recent year 44 per cent of the population had some degree of hospital insurance coverage, 27 per cent had some insurance against surgical cost, and 11 per cent had some insurance against nonsurgical services. About half of voluntary health insurance coverage is with nonprofit prepayment plans and about half is with commercial insurance companies. Together, the voluntary insurance plans accounted for slightly more than 8 per cent of all private expenditures for medical care in 1948.[1] Fraternal organizations and labor unions often maintain sickness funds to assist financially in case of illness. Some health services are offered within industry. Recent collective bargaining contracts have secured for millions of workers certain

---

[1] Klem, Margaret C., "Voluntary Medical Care Insurance," *The Annals of the American Academy of Political and Social Science*, vol. 273, January, 1951, p. 99.

"fringe benefits" connected with health care. In most cases, such health insurance is purchased from existing nonprofit plans or from commercial insurance companies.[1]

Although they represent only a small fraction of medical payments in the United States, there is a growing number of cooperative prepayment medical care plans under which people pay a stipulated amount and a staff of medical personnel retained by the cooperative organization provides comprehensive medical care.

Voluntary prepayment plans are growing, but there are nevertheless large groups of people who cannot afford them. Yet these are the ones who are most in need of medical care and who particularly need coverage. For this reason, national compulsory health insurance, somewhat analogous to such other insurance plans as workmen's compensation, and old-age and survivors insurance (see Chapter 10), has been suggested. Legislation in the form of the Wagner-Murray-Dingell bill was introduced in Congress, but was defeated.[2]

An important method of payment for medical care is through the public assistance programs of the country. This includes necessary health and medical care for those who are dependent on public assistance either in general relief or in one of the categories (see Chapter 10), and also the "medically indigent" people, who are just barely self-supporting but who cannot afford extraordinary medical or hospital expenditures. Recent changes in the Social Security Act which make it possible for public assistance departments to make direct payments to the providers of medical care have tended to increase the provision of necessary medical care for public assistance recipients. There is a growing interest expressed by welfare officials in prepayment plans for relief recipients.[3]

In addition to the public assistance program, private physicians and hospitals absorb a certain proportion of the cost of care through providing services either free or at a reduced rate to those who are in financial need, as well as in the services which are billed but never paid. Many hospitals have "endowed beds" or other endowment which enables them to charge less than the actual cost of care.

One of the major methods of financing medical care is through direct medical service in hospitals and other institutions for various disease groups,

[1] *Ibid.*, p. 101. See also *Management and Union Health and Medical Programs*, Government Printing Office, Washington, 1954.
[2] An interesting pamphlet giving both sides of this highly controversial issue a chance to explain their position is that by Oscar R. Ewing and George F. Lull, *How Shall We Pay for Health Care?* Public Affairs Pamphlet No. 152, New York, 1949.
[3] See Terris, Milton, "Medical Care for the Needy and Medically Needy," *The Annals of the American Academy of Political and Social Science*, vol. 273, January, 1951.

for the armed forces, veterans, and so on. Some indication of the extent of direct government care is given by hospital figures on bed capacity. Ninety-seven per cent of all beds in mental institutions are provided in public hospitals, as are 88 per cent of the beds in tuberculosis hospitals. And government institutions now provide 33 per cent of all beds in general and allied special hospitals. (These figures are exclusive of Army, Air Force, and Navy facilities.)[1] Add to this the extensive staffs maintained particularly by the armed forces and the Veterans Administration, and it is easy to realize how enormous is government's participation in direct medical care.[2] Another type of direct health service is offered through the schools.[3] Often this service is minimal. Many states make it mandatory for the schools to provide for physical examination of each pupil by a physician each year. Some school systems go much further in providing medical and nursing services.

184. Is there a Blue Cross type hospitalization organization which serves your community? Is there a Blue Shield type organization? Similar organization?

185. What percentage of people in your community are covered by each of these plans? How much are the monthly premiums?

186. What are the benefits and limitations under each type of policy?
Is there any coverage for nursing service? Provision for drugs, appliances, dental care?

187. What are the most widely needed services excluded under these policies?

188. What percentage of hospital charges is paid by nonprofit hospitalization insurance programs?

189. Can you get figures from insurance companies or agents as to the extent of coverage in commercial health expense policies for hospital expenses? Surgical expenses? Nonsurgical expenses?

190. What fraternal organizations or labor unions maintain sickness funds or help to pay health expenses of members?
How many are covered? What are the payments? Benefits?

191. Which industries in your community offer any type of medical coverage for their employees?

192. Are there any group practice cooperative prepayment medical care plans which serve people in your community?

[1] Figures from Hospital Number, *Journal of the American Medical Association*, May 12, 1951, tabulated in *Guide to Health Organization in the United States*, Public Health Service Publication No. 196, Government Printing Office, Washington, 1953, p. 92. This booklet is very helpful to the citizen who wants to familiarize himself with the organization of public health services, public and voluntary, at the federal, state, and local levels, respectively.
[2] See Stern, Bernhard J., *Medical Services by Government: Local, State, and Federal*, Commonwealth Fund, New York, 1946.
[3] See Chapter 7. A helpful pamphlet is *Priorities in Health Services for Children of School Age*, Federal Security Agency, Washington, no date.

What are the regular payments for this plan and what medical services are provided?

193. What provisions are there for those not receiving public assistance but who are medically indigent?

194. Are there any municipally operated general or chronic hospitals? Tuberculosis or mental hospitals?

195. Are there any statistics on the types and frequency of medical care offered at public expense to people who cannot pay?

196. Are there any statistics on similar care offered by voluntary agencies?

197. Can you procure an estimate of the annual value of medical care which is contributed by physicians and private hospitals free? At reduced charge? Through uncollected bills?

198. What forces in your community are working for or against national compulsory health insurance? What reasons do they give?

199. What medical services are offered to school children as part of the school program?

200. Is each school child given a physical examination by a physician at least once each year? How thorough are the examinations? How long do they take per child?
What follow-up is made where examinations indicate the need for medical attention?

201. Are immunization clinics held at the school?

202. Are preschool or school health clinics available for children?

203. Is there a dental hygiene program in the schools? What services are included in this program?
How often does each child receive a dental examination?

204. Do the schools schedule regular child health conferences?[1]

205. What other types of medical service or dental service do the schools provide?[2]

Voluntary Health Organizations

Perhaps in no other phase of community service is there such a proliferation of voluntary organization and effort as in the field of health. Voluntary organizations perform many functions, among which perhaps the most important and widespread is that of health education. They also raise money for facilities and research. Their role in pioneering in various types of health program is one of the most important. Health organizations often lead the way by demonstrating the effectiveness of a particular health facility, technique, or procedure, and then the new development, if proved satisfactory,

---

[1] See *The Child Health Conference:* Suggestions for Organization and Procedure, Federal Security Agency, Government Printing Office, Washington, 1949.

[2] See Chapters 7 and 13 for additional material relating to the schools' part in the community health effort.

gradually becomes absorbed into tax-supported health services or into other branches of the community's total health effort. Often, they work for new improvements and facilities, such as hospitals.[1]

Typically, health organizations in the local community are either locally established units of a state or national agency, or affiliated with one. Many national agencies can give great help in community health studies, particularly in those aspects of health with which they are respectively concerned. Although no listing for a chapter this size can include all the peripheral agencies, the following list may prove helpful.[2]

American Cancer Society
American Dental Association
American Diabetes Association
American Foundation for the Blind
American Hearing Society
American Heart Association
American Hospital Association
American Medical Association
American National Red Cross
American Nurses' Association
American Physical Therapy
  Association
American Psychiatric Association
American Public Health Association
American School Health Association
American Social Hygiene Association
Association for the Aid of Crippled
  Children
Association of State and Territorial
  Health Officers
Conference for Health Council Work
Maternity Center Association
Muscular Dystrophy Associations
  of America

National Association for Mental
  Health
National Association of the Deaf
National Epilepsy League
National Foundation for Infantile
  Paralysis
National Health Council
National League for Nursing
National Multiple Sclerosis Society
National Rehabilitation Association
National Safety Council
National Sanitation Foundation
National Society for Crippled
  Children and Adults
National Society for the Prevention
  of Blindness
National Tuberculosis Association
Planned Parenthood Federation of
  America
United Cerebral Palsy Association
U.S. Children's Bureau
U.S. Office of Vocational
  Rehabilitation
U.S. Public Health Service

Because of their great number and varying degrees of concentration on limited medical problems, health organizations are often plagued with lack of adequate coordination. Often the launching of a new organization on the local level seems to depend on the time which a particularly active citizen

[1] See Miller, Paul A., "400 Small Community Experiences with Health Improvement," *Sixth National Conference on Rural Health*, American Medical Association, Chicago, 1951.
[2] See List of Agencies appended to this book for the addresses of these and other related organizations.

has available to "start something" as much as it does on any real need for a separate organization of that particular type in that particular community. Nevertheless, it remains true that some people will collect money for cerebral palsy and show little concern for TB, or go all-out for polio but show no interest at all in muscular dystrophy. Occasionally health organizations hold onto functions in which they have long since been superseded by public health services. At times they do not gear their respective efforts with those of other similar organizations in the community or with those of the public health department. Nevertheless, they represent a tremendous force for health progress in this country, and show constant signs of changing their program to meet new needs.[1] Health organizations achieve some degree of coordination of effort within the health and welfare councils of the nation's cities. In addition, the health council movement has arisen to provide for coordination and planning in the health field.[2]

For further consideration of associations in the community, see Chapter 16 and for further material on coordination of effort among various organizations see Chapter 17.

206. Which of the following professional health organizations are there in your community:

Medical association   Hospital association
Dental association   Other
Nurse association

207. Is there any type of health coordinating organization in your community which is designed to coordinate the efforts of all public and private agencies and associations dealing with health:

Health council   Chamber of Commerce Health
Health division of the council   Committee
    of social agencies   Neighborhood health association
                                  Other

What are the member organizations?

208. Which voluntary citizen associations of each of the following types does your community have:

Joint coordinating and planning body for voluntary health effort
Organizations principally interested in a particular disease (heart, cancer, TB, and so on)
Hospital auxiliaries and similar organizations
Other

---

[1] See Gunn, Selskar M., and Philip S. Platt, *Voluntary Health Agencies:* An Interpretive Study, Ronald Press Co., New York, 1945. This is a definitive study of voluntary health organization in the United States. It reports more than 20,000 such organizations in existence.

[2] See *The Community Health Council:* Its Organization, Its Functions, and a Few Suggested Projects, American Medical Association, Chicago, 1949.

209. Which of the above agencies have paid executives on a full-time basis? Part-time?
210. Is there any type of health association for which your community has particular need?
211. Of the various health needs uncovered in your study, which are receiving attention from various voluntary or public agencies? Which ones are relatively neglected?

Mental Health and the Mentally Ill

It is estimated that about half of the people who visit their family physician, and about 30 per cent of those who occupy general hospital beds do so for complaints which are largely mental in nature. Difficulty in making the ordinary adjustments of life characterizes much juvenile delinquency, crime, divorce, drug addiction, and alcoholism. There are increasing indications that mental illness in varying degrees and forms accounts for many of our personal and social difficulties. Some 650,000 patients are in mental hospitals in the United States, and it is estimated that one out of every 12 children now being born will require hospitalization for mental illness sometime during his life. The problem of the nation's mental health was dramatized to American people by the experience with draft rejectees during and since World War II. During the war mental illness and other personality disturbances accounted for some 900,000 draft rejections.[1]

Mental health is the ability to face one's problems realistically, to make a wholesome emotional adjustment to oneself and other people, and to function adequately within one's social environment. Its close relation to physical health is studied in the discipline of psychosomatic medicine. Whatever philosophers have to say about the nature of mind and body, they are closely related in the functioning organism, and there is constant reciprocal stimulation between the two. Taking the World Health Organization's definition of health as "a state of complete physical, mental, and social well-being and not merely the absence of disease or infirmity," one can appreciate the increasing tendency to view man as an entity and to consider his mental as well as his physical health.

Similar statements can be made for both mental and physical health on the community level. Early detection and treatment are keynotes in both fields. Prevention is considered even preferable. Many mental as well as physical illnesses can be prevented. Mass screening techniques are helpful,

[1] These figures are taken from *Facts and Figures About Mental Illness and Other Personality Disturbances*, National Association for Mental Health, New York, 1952, as are other figures in these paragraphs unless a different source is given.

and they are now beginning to be developed in the mental health field. Public ignorance as to the cause of illness plagues the mental health movement as it plagued the public health movement. So does the attitude of social stigma attached to certain diseases, the hush-hush attitudes, only recently overcome in such physical diseases as tuberculosis, cancer, syphilis. Research is particularly important; new methods of treatment bring promise of greater advances. A whole host of circumstances of the physical environment as well as auxiliary personnel and facilities relate to the psychiatrist and his treatment as they relate to the general physician and his treatment. Above all, the need for public education in mental health principles is great. Current mental health practice in the communities of America is years, even decades, behind the advance of technical knowledge. We already *know* much more than we *do*.

Mental health conditions in your community. In studying mental health conditions in your community, you will, of course, want to know about special clinics, psychiatric services, mental hospitals and the rest, but you will also want to consider many agencies, services, and conditions which, although not primarily oriented to mental health, nevertheless have a great influence on it. In this respect, many of the chapters of this book raise questions about institutional facilities which have a bearing on mental health. Indeed, hardly any chapter is without its mental health implications. In the present section, only a few questions will be raised to point up some of the special aspects of such community services as they bear even more directly on mental health.

212. Are there counseling services or social casework services in connection with industrial companies?

213. To what extent do your labor leaders and industrial managers show a familiarity with and interest in newer knowledge of labor-management relations as brought out in the field of "human relations in industry"? (See Chapter 3.)

214. Do the criminal courts avail themselves of clinical facilities for the mental examination of prisoners, particularly habitual offenders?
Do other courts (family court, children's court) utilize the services of mental clinics or refer individuals to them where appropriate? (See Chapters 4 and 11.)

215. To what extent does your community's physical plan contribute to tensions and upset, as in constant traffic snarls, irritating delays in commuter service, and so on? (See Chapter 5.)

216. Which, if any, living sections are so squalid in appearance, or so overcrowded or unhygienic that they might be considered to constitute a hindrance to healthy mental and physical development?

217. Is the housing situation such that any sections of the community are being

"invaded" by people of different background, or under other circumstances which may lead to tension and friction between the groups? (See Chapters 6 and 15.)

218. To what extent are school teachers trained in mental health principles? What provision is made for their continued training in this field?

To what extent do classrooms have a permissive atmosphere rather than an autocratic one?

Are mental health principles taught as a regular part of the curriculum? Are libraries well supplied with books, pamphlets, and journals in the mental health field?

219. Are there counseling services, psychological services, and casework services available in connection with the schools for children who have difficulty in emotional adjustment?

To what extent do school personnel confer with parents on such matters? With other community agencies—clinics, and so on? (See Chapter 7.)

220. Are there wholesome recreational facilities?

Are recreation personnel familiar with mental health principles and do they help youngsters develop wholesome behavior responses? (See Chapter 8.)

221. To what extent are clergymen familiar with mental health principles? How much personal counseling do they give, and how well prepared are they for this delicate aspect of human relationships?

Do they refer persons who are in need of psychiatric help to a psychiatrist or clinic? (See Chapter 9.)

222. To what extent is the public assistance program carried out as a professional casework opportunity, or to what extent is it the perfunctory handing out of financial allotments to those who are proved to be legally eligible?

223. What provision is there for the in-service training of caseworkers in principles of social casework and mental health?

224. To what extent do welfare policies encourage a feeling of inadequacy and pauperism among relief recipients, as opposed to helping them rebuild their self-confidence and self-esteem and become wherever possible capable of self-support once more? (See Chapter 10.)

225. Are casework services available to families that have difficulty with family conflict or other problems?

Are casework services available for children with behavior problems?

226. Are the community's facilities with respect to juvenile delinquency such as to cause resentment and intensify the problem, or are they oriented toward the casework approach in the child's best interests?

Are psychiatric clinic services utilized freely where indicated? Is there a probation service which follows casework principles? (See Chapter 11.)

227. To what extent do physicians recognize mental health as an important part of their responsibility toward their patients?

Does the county medical society or other group promote continued mental health training opportunities for physicians?

Do physicians recommend psychiatric treatment where indicated? Do they refer people to the mental clinics that are available?

228. To what extent does the public health department recognize mental health as part of its concern? What activities does it carry on in this respect?

229. To what extent do the mental health facilities of the community accommodate such special groups as the physically handicapped and the aged? What counseling services are available to these persons when they face problems on which they need help in personal adjustment?

Are personnel who serve them well schooled in mental health principles? (See Chapter 13.)

230. Do newspapers, radio stations, and other media of public communication interpret the news in accordance with sound mental health principles, or do they tend to encourage outmoded concepts of "lunatics," "crazy people," and so on?

Has any mental health organization taken responsibility for helping to acquaint such people with mental health principles? (See Chapter 14.)

231. Do public communication media encourage community people to face their community problems in a constructive, problem-solving manner, or do they for purposes of circulation or sensationalism stir up misunderstandings, old hatreds, prejudices, and hostilities? (See Chapter 15.)

232. What intergroup misunderstandings in your community tend to prevent people from getting along with each other?

Are personnel working in the field of intergroup understanding adequately trained in existing knowledge from the social sciences?

233. To what extent is any racial, religious, nationality, or cultural group barred or hindered from access to community mental health facilities? (See Chapter 15.)

234. What associations in the community have mental health as one of their concerns?

Are professional group leaders adequately trained in principles of mental health? (See Chapter 16.)

If there is no mental health organization in your community, is there a need for one?

235. To what extent is the mental health effort of the community coordinated? Is there a committee within the health and welfare council which has primary responsibility for communitywide mental health organization?

If there is a mental health society, what is its relationship to the council? (See Chapter 17.) [1]

Mental health services and facilities. The more serious cases of mental

[1] For a more detailed set of questions about community mental health facilities, see *An Outline for Evaluation of a Community Program in Mental Hygiene*, Group for the Advancement of Psychiatry, Report No. 8, Topeka, Kans., 1949.

illness involving various psychoses and a few of the psychoneuroses require institutionalization. Less serious cases may be helped by the individual practicing psychiatrist or by the psychiatric team in the clinic, and do not need to be institutionalized. The psychiatrist and the clinical team of psychiatrist, psychologist, and (psychiatric) social worker are equipped to give treatment in mental illness. Supporting them in the community are many other facilities which may be important in preventive work, in early referral for psychiatric attention, or in aid with some of the less deeply rooted personality problems.

Some of these services have been alluded to in the immediately preceding pages. A list here may be helpful to you in outlining your study. The facilities enumerated are not so general as school, church, or family, and not so specifically oriented to mental health treatment as the psychiatric clinic, but somewhere between: family casework agency, marriage counseling service, child welfare casework agency, school guidance or counseling service, visiting teacher service, medical social work, probation and parole casework. Personnel in all these fields can be expected to have had formal training in mental health and to constitute resources in this respect. Another group of professional people may also be considered important resources, although one cannot be quite so confident of their training in mental health principles, or of their taking a "mental health point of view" in their professional work, although many of them do: physicians, teachers, clergymen, recreation workers, nurses, lawyers. You will perhaps know of other professional people in your community who should be added to such a group.

According to the National Association for Mental Health, approximately 200,000 persons, including children, are seen in psychiatric clinics each year. Nevertheless, clinical facilities require expansion. It is estimated that a community of 100,000 can support a full-time mental health clinic staffed by a full-time psychiatrist, a psychologist, and two psychiatric social workers, plus clerical staff. If clinical facilities were available according to this measure, there would be at least 1,500 such clinics in the United States. Actually there are far fewer. If to such full-time clinics are added the number of part-time clinics either fully or partially staffed, and traveling clinic service points (one traveling clinic may service a number of different communities, each one of which would be counted here), the total is only 1,228. Incidentally, in three states there were no such clinical facilities at all in 1950.

To help encourage and finance new psychiatric clinical facilities in the states, the National Mental Health Act makes available grants-in-aid to the states, and these in turn are matched by local funds. For every two dollars provided by federal funds, the state must match one dollar of state or local public funds.[1] Largely as a result of this program, clinical facilities are growing rapidly in this country.

236. How many psychiatrists are in private practice in your community or its vicinity?

237. How many clinical psychologists are available in an agency setting in your community?

238. Is there a mental health clinic (psychiatric clinic) available to adults in your community? If not, where is the nearest one?

239. Is your clinic located in your community, or of the traveling type?

240. Does it serve both adults and children?

241. How many full days of service per week does it give to the community?

242. How many of the following professional workers are on its staff, full time and part time:

Psychiatrists   Mental health nurses
Psychologists   Others
Psychiatric social workers

243. Is this service available to all?

244. What are the charges, if any?

245. Are services therapeutic as well as diagnostic?

246. How many men, women, and children were served by this clinic last year? Specify the number in each group.

247. Does the clinic sponsor public education work in mental health? How?

248. Do clinical personnel sponsor or participate in local conferences, institutes, workshops, or training courses in mental health?

249. Is there a separate psychiatric clinic especially for children (child guidance clinic)? If so, answer the preceding questions with respect to this clinic.

250. Do such clinics carry on active efforts to acquaint professional people such as clergymen, physicians, school officials, with their functions, so as to encourage referral when appropriate?

251. What facilities are there for the treatment of alcoholics and drug addicts in your community? Is the primary emphasis one of punishment or clinical treatment?

252. Is there any organization such as Alcoholics Anonymous in your community? What are its activities?

Increased realization of the importance of mental illness. as a problem and of the need for widespread education, research, and improvement of facilities, has led to the growth of a large number of community mental health associations across the nation. Spearheading this movement is the

[1] See *The National Mental Health Act and Your Community*, Public Health Service, Government Printing Office, Washington, 1948. See also the pamphlet *National Institute of Mental Health*, Public Health Publication Series No. 20, Government Printing Office, Washington, 1950.

National Association for Mental Health, with 29 state societies and more than 350 local associations.

253. Is there a mental health association in your community? Is it affiliated with the state branch of the National Association for Mental Health? Does it have a paid staff? What is its membership? Annual budget?
254. In what ways does it promote mental health education:

Distributes literature	Sponsors film showings
(number of pieces)	Conducts institutes, workshops
Provides speakers	Other

255. Does it ever bring together various professional personnel working in the field of mental health in order that they may collaborate more closely in your community?
256. How effective is its educational campaign?
257. Does it work for community improvements, such as a mental health clinic?

Mental hospitals. Many people with mental disorders can remain in their own communities, particularly if adequate clinical services are available. But others are so disturbed that they cannot function adequately in usual social situations, and must have special care in institutions.[1] About half of the new admissions to state mental hospitals each year are patients with schizophrenia (a mental disease largely of early adulthood) or senile psychosis or cerebral arteriosclerosis (diseases of old age). About 40 per cent of patients admitted to state hospitals are discharged within five years, about nine-tenths of these being improved or recovered.

There are 680 mental hospitals in the United States. About 97 per cent of mental hospital beds are public, the great bulk being in state institutions. Conditions in these institutions vary tremendously, but three out of four report being overcrowded, and for the most part, they are understaffed in physicians, nurses, attendants, social workers, and psychologists. Not a single one meets the standards for personnel set up by the American Psychiatric Association.[2] There is tremendous variation among states in the quality of their mental hospitals.[3]

258. What public mental hospitals serve people from your community?
259. How many people from your community are in mental hospitals at this time: Public? Private?
260. Under your state law, what are the procedures for voluntary commitment?

[1] Read *When Mental Illness Strikes Your Family* by Kathleen Doyle, Public Affairs Pamphlet No. 172, New York, 1951.
[2] See *Standards for Psychiatric Hospitals and Clinics*, rev. ed., American Psychiatric Association, Washington, 1951.
[3] See footnote on p. 225 for source of the foregoing facts. An interesting account of conditions in state mental hospitals is to be found in Albert Deutsch's *The Shame of the States*, Harcourt, Brace and Co., New York, 1948.

261. Under your state law, what is the procedure according to which a person may be committed to a mental hospital if he does not wish such commitment?
     Is such commitment made on the basis of a medical diagnosis rather than trial by jury?
262. What safeguards are there for the patient who is committed involuntarily?
263. How does the public mental hospital compare with the standards of the American Psychiatric Association as to the following personnel:

Physicians	Registered occupational
Clinical psychologists	therapists
Registered nurses	Other occupational therapists
Attendants	Social workers
Hydrotherapists	

264. Is there overcrowding in your public mental hospital? If overcrowded, how many more beds are needed?
265. Are any of the following newer types of facility available to your community's mentally ill persons:
     Day care programs
     Foster home placement of mental patients
     Intensive or "total push" treatment[1]
     Residential treatment centers for mentally disturbed children
266. Are there adequate follow-up services to discharged patients, including outpatient clinics, psychiatric social work service?
267. What private mental hospitals serve a substantial number of people from your community? Answer such of the preceding questions as apply to these institutions.

References for Further Study

An Inventory of Social and Economic Research in Health. Health Information Foundation, New York, 1953. This gives sufficient description of each project listed so that the reader is able to select those projects which have a bearing on his local health situation and follow them up for more detailed information.

Bachmeyer, Arthur C., *Hospital Care in the United States.* Commonwealth Fund, New York, 1947. Dr. Bachmeyer was the director of the study by the Commission on Hospital Care which is reported in this comprehensive description of hospital service in the United States.

Community Organization for Health: Selected References. Michigan State College, East Lansing, 1950. A report on projects and writings in various

---

[1] See Glover, Katherine, *Mental Health:* Everybody's Business, Public Affairs Pamphlet No. 196, New York, 1953.

branches of community organization work for health. It constitutes an annotated bibliography of various materials in this field.

Health Insurance Plans in the United States: Report of the Committee on Labor and Public Welfare, United States Senate. 82d Congress, 1st Session. Report No. 359, Part 1, Government Printing Office, Washington, 1951. This is a valuable source of information about the types and extensiveness of various health insurance plans in the United States.

Hiscock, Ira V., *Community Health Organization.* 4th ed. Commonwealth Fund, New York, 1950. A health organization which contains some of the best features of contemporary practice is suggested as a plan which can be used in organizing or modifying the health services, both public and private, of any community.

Leavell, Hugh R., and E. Gurney Clark, and others, *Textbook of Preventive Medicine.* McGraw-Hill Book Co., New York, 1953. As the title suggests, this collaborative effort by many authorities describes various aspects of preventive medicine. It seeks to present a clear view of community health activities.

"Medical Care for Americans," *The Annals of the American Academy of Political and Social Science,* vol. 273, January, 1951. This issue of *The Annals* includes articles by several leading authorities in each of the following fields: Prerequisites for Effective Organization, Methods of Organization, Public Medical Care, Medical Care Insurance, Specialized Programs, and Planning for the Future.

Mott, Frederick D., and Milton I. Roemer, *Rural Health and Medical Care.* McGraw-Hill Book Co., New York, 1948. This is a definitive work on the various ramifications of health and medical care in rural America.

Mustard, Harry S., *An Introduction to Public Health.* 2d ed. Macmillan Co., New York, 1952. This is a standard introductory text in public health. Well written, lucid, and comprehensive in scope, this book is good reading for the layman who wishes to familiarize himself with the scope of the public health field.

Mental Health

Deutsch, Albert, *The Mentally Ill in America:* A History of Their Care and Treatment from Colonial Times. 2d ed. Columbia University Press, New York, 1949. This is a definitive work on the development of modern treatment methods for the mentally ill.

Felix, R. H., *A Better Chance for Mental Health for Children in Smaller Communities.* Federal Security Agency, Government Printing Office, Washington, 1952. Written for smaller communities, this reprint of an article in *The Child* gives helpful suggestions to communities which do not have clinical facilities but which nevertheless want to do something about the mental health of their children.

Levinson, Abraham, *The Mentally Retarded Child:* A Guide for Parents. John Day Co., New York, 1952. This book helps to answer the many problems which may arise in connection with the mentally retarded child. Though designed primarily for parents, it is also of use to professional people.

Rennie, Thomas A. C., and Luther E. Woodward, *Mental Health in Modern Society.* Commonwealth Fund, New York, 1948. This is one of the best-known books on mental health.

Steiner, Lee R., *A Practical Guide for Troubled People.* Greenberg, New York, 1952. As its title indicates, this is a down-to-earth discussion of the resources available to a person who is mentally troubled.

13. Provision for Special Groups

THIS CHAPTER CONCERNS ITSELF with four groups of people who, because of their circumstances, require special consideration. They are the handicapped, the aging, migrant farm workers, and displaced persons.

The Handicapped

Residing in the various communities of America are a considerable number of persons who are sufficiently handicapped either physically or mentally to require special help if they are to maintain themselves outside of institutions as members of the community. A smaller number are so impaired by their handicap that they need the more specialized care which only an institution can offer.

We can study these handicapped people in the following groups: the deaf, the blind, those otherwise physically impaired, and the mentally handicapped. Many such handicapped persons are amenable to vocational rehabilitation, and material on this topic in the previous chapter should be considered in connection with the aforementioned types of handicaps.

1. What types of handicapped persons are eligible for vocational rehabilitation under your state's program:
    Victims of industrial accidents
    Victims of occupational diseases
    Nonindustrial orthopedically handicapped
    Handicapped but not orthopedically, such as the blind, the deaf, cardiacs, those with arrested tuberculosis
2. Are services for any one group of the handicapped more adequate than for others?
3. What services are provided?

The deaf. The American Hearing Society estimates that there are approximately 15 million hard-of-hearing persons in the United States. Of these, there are some three million children with defective hearing whose condition may be corrected through early detection and proper medical treatment. Screening and treatment programs in the public schools thus become an important part of a community's approach to the problem of the deaf and hard of hearing. Another need is for rehabilitative service for the deaf wherever possible. Community facilities for the deaf should include adequate diagnostic and treatment provisions, as well as services to alleviate the problems of those whose hearing cannot be improved.

There are many services which a community may provide for deaf or hard-of-hearing people. Hearing societies which are chapters of the American Hearing Society usually offer some or all of the following: scientific hearing tests, instruction in lipreading, auditory training, speech correction, assistance in the selection and use of hearing aids, instruction for preschool hard-of-hearing children and their parents, employment guidance, and group recreational activities. Similar services for the child of school age are also necessary, and in addition social services, psychiatric consultation and treatment, and special educational opportunity should all be available when needed.[1]

According to the American Hearing Society, school-age children with hearing difficulties can be classified into two groups. One includes the child who hears much of what is said but must be especially attentive and even so he often misses key words. Such a child should participate in regular classes but should have instruction in lipreading and should be seated advantageously for hearing. More serious is the plight of the child who cannot perceive ordinary speech unless he can see the speaker, and who otherwise can hear only what is said in a raised voice. Such children may also be educated in regular classes, provided they have lipreading instruction, auditory training, a hearing aid, and speech correction. The auditory training is to help them derive the most from what hearing they have; speech correction is needed because normal speech acquisition is difficult where hearing is impaired. But if they are found to lag behind because of their hearing loss, they should be placed in a special class or be sent to a special school. A standard reference on the deaf is Harry Best's *Deafness and the Deaf in the United States.*[2]

4. What is the estimated number of persons in your community with seriously impaired hearing?
5. How many children in the schools are reported with special hearing difficulties?
6. How many of your community's school-age children are in special schools for the hard of hearing, either in your community or elsewhere?
7. Does your state law require periodic hearing tests in the schools?

[1] See Lesser, Arthur J., *Services for the Child Who Is Hard of Hearing:* A Guide for the Development of Programs, Children's Bureau Publication No. 334, Government Printing Office, Washington, no date.
[2] Macmillan Co., New York, 1943.

8. Are hearing tests administered to each school child at least once every three years?
9. Which types of test are used:

Phonograph audiometer (group)	Pure tone audiometer (individual)
Sweep frequency (individual)	Speech reception test
	Other

10. What has been done with those children who were shown to have hearing deficiencies in each of the past five years?
11. What services are available through your school for children who are hard of hearing:
    Scientific hearing tests
    Instruction in lipreading
    Auditory training
    Speech correction
    Assistance in selecting and using hearing aids
    Instruction for preschool hard-of-hearing children and their parents
    Employment guidance
    Special educational facilities as needed
    Social services as needed
    Psychiatric consultation and treatment as needed
    Other
12. Which type of personnel is available to help hard-of-hearing children as needed:

Pediatrician	Teachers for special classes
Otologist	Pediatric nursing consultant
Conservation of hearing specialist	Medical social worker
Audiometer technician	Psychiatric consultant
Public health nurse	Mental hygiene consultant
Lipreading teacher	Vocational guidance consultant
	Other

13. Is there a hearing society in your community? What are its activities? Is it affiliated with the American Hearing Society?
14. Is there an organization of deaf people in your community? What are its activities?
15. What facilities are available in your community for adults who are hard of hearing? (Use list given above for school services.)
16. Is there a hearing center in your community, either in connection with a school, university, hearing society, or hospital?
17. What personnel are available in your community to help the hard of hearing? (Consult list of personnel in question 12 on school personnel.)
18. How many hard-of-hearing persons in your community are participating in your state vocational rehabilitation program?[1]

[1] See *Opportunities for the Deaf and the Hard of Hearing Through Vocational Rehabilitation*, rev. ed., an instructive leaflet issued by the Office of Vocational Rehabilita-

19. What estimate has your local employment service made as to the number of those who cannot find work largely because of hearing deficiency?
20. Is any special employment counsel or job placement help given the hard of hearing in the public employment service?

The blind. The American Foundation for the Blind estimates that in 1954 the blind population of the United States exceeded 322,000 persons. This estimate is based on the following definition of blindness, which is used by most of the states in defining eligibility for aid to the blind.[1] "Central visual acuity of 20/200 or less in the better eye, with correcting glasses; or central visual acuity of more than 20/200 if there is a field defect in which the peripheral field has contracted to such an extent that the widest diameter of visual field subtends an angular distance no greater than 20 degrees." There seem to be in this country more blind men than women, and a much higher rate of blindness among nonwhites than among whites. It is believed that at least half of the blind population are over 65, with only about one in 10 blind persons under 20 years of age.

Blindness is a particularly difficult problem since most blindness is caused by factors not yet controllable. However, much blindness, including industrial blindness and most blindness resulting from infectious diseases is now preventable.

21. Does your state Commission for the Blind or similar agency maintain a currently validated register of blind persons in the state? How many blind persons are there in your state? In your community?
22. How many persons in your community are receiving aid to the blind under the public assistance program? (See Chapter 10.)
23. Does your state have a law requiring prophylaxis to eyes of newborn infants?
24. How many school-age children are blind or visually impaired? How many such children are not in school?
25. What special facilities are there for blindness or visual impairment in the public school system:[2]

Preschool classes	Braille books and other equipment
Periodic screening examinations (How often? What type?)	"Talking books"
Sight-saving classes	Other

---

tion, Government Printing Office, Washington, 1949. See p. 218 for additional questions on vocational rehabilitation.

[1] For an explanation of the estimate underlying that for 1954, see the pamphlet issued by the American Foundation for the Blind, entitled *Estimated Prevalence of Blindness in the United States* by Ralph G. Hurlin, which contains estimates of the number of blind persons in each state in 1952.

[2] See Hathaway, Winifred, *Education and Health of the Partially Seeing Child*, rev. ed., Columbia University Press, New York, 1947.

26. Is there a residential school for the blind in your state? How many children from your community are in residence?
27. Which regional braille library acts as a distributing library in your region for braille and talking books from the Library of Congress?
28. What facilities are there in your community for the adjustment and reeducation of the large majority of blind persons who lose their sight after their twentieth birthday?
29. What provisions are made for the vocational rehabilitation of the blind in your state?[1]
30. How many blind persons in your community are enrolled in the state vocational rehabilitation program?
31. Is there a sheltered workshop for the blind in your community? If not, where in your region is the nearest one?
32. Is there any agency in your community that promotes work for the blind in their own homes? How does it help?
    Are there any means for providing vendors' stands in public places operated by blind people?
33. Are there vocational counseling services for the blind?
34. Is there an association which interests itself in the problems of the blind in your community? What is its program?
35. Is there a local organization of blind people? What are its activities?

Other physical handicaps. A large group of people have physical handicaps other than deafness or blindness. Some idea of the type and extent of physical impairment is given in the following list which was prepared for a study of the vocational capability of the various categories of handicapped people: orthopedic (loss of hand, arm, foot, leg, and so on, as well as deformities and abnormalities), vision, hearing, hernia, cardiac, ex-tuberculous, peptic ulcer, diabetic, epileptic, and multiple impairment. The last named involves people who have two or more impairments.[2] While many physical handicaps result from diseases, others result from a condition at birth or a disabling accident.

A recent statement gives some idea of the numbers involved in various types of physical disability: "Estimates by responsible organizations . . . indicate . . . 2,000,000 with diabetes, 500,000 with tuberculosis. There are more than 200,000 amputees who require artificial limbs. The National Multiple Sclerosis Society reports that from 50,000 to 100,000 persons

---

[1] See *Opportunities for the Blind and Visually Impaired*, a pamphlet prepared by the Office of Vocational Rehabilitation and distributed through the Government Printing Office. See also pp. 217ff.
[2] *The Performance of Physically Impaired Workers in Manufacturing Industries:* A Report Prepared by the Bureau of Labor Statistics for the Veterans Administration. Bulletin No. 923, Bureau of Labor Statistics, Government Printing Office, Washington, 1948, pp. 120–121.

are victims of this disease. More than 750,000 have epilepsy, and about 10,500 new cases of cerebral palsy appear each year. In poliomyelitis, 1952 was one of the worst years this country ever experienced, with 57,026 cases recorded for the 53-week period ended January 3, 1953."[1]

In addition, there are many other disabling illnesses, such as cancer and heart disease, and disabling accidents, which increase the total of the disabled to several millions. It is estimated that at least 2,000,000 of these can be rehabilitated. (For additional material on rehabilitation, see page 217.)

Although the community's facilities for the physically handicapped, both children and adults, should be regarded as a totality and should constitute an integrated program, nevertheless certain factors apply especially to the young child.[2] For one thing, many types of handicap can be corrected or modified if detected early and if proper treatment is instituted in childhood. Also, children who are physically handicapped have yet to experience many of their formative years during which time important personality and adjustment patterns are set. In the third place, there are the special requirements for assuring an optimum education to physically impaired children.[3]

The Children's Bureau administers a federal program of aid to states for diagnostic and treatment services to physically handicapped children. These services are provided by physicians and surgeons, nurses, psychologists, medical social workers, physical and occupational therapists, nutritionists, dentists and orthodontists, speech and hearing therapists, and other specialized personnel. The services are provided in rehabilitation centers, clinics, hospitals, convalescent homes, physicians' offices, or in the children's own homes.[4]

Your community may be one which has an agency conducting a program on behalf of the physically handicapped. If so, this agency will be able to supply you with many facts about the physically disabled in your community.

[1] Reprinted from Switzer, Mary E., and Howard A. Rusk, *Doing Something for the Disabled*, Public Affairs Pamphlet No. 197, New York, 1953. It should be noted that not all persons who have epilepsy or have had poliomyelitis are permanently handicapped. See also Linck, Lawrence J., "The Crippled," *Social Work Year Book, 1951*, American Association of Social Workers, New York, 1951. Reprints of this article are available through the National Society for Crippled Children and Adults.

[2] See Yahraes, Herbert, *Gains for Handicapped Children*, Public Affairs Pamphlet No. 212, New York, 1954.

[3] See *Education of Crippled Children in the United States*, Office of Education, Government Printing Office, 1949; and also, from the same source, *Some Problems in the Education of Handicapped Children*, 1952.

[4] See *One in Three Hundred:* Children Served by the Crippled Children's Program, in 1948, Children's Bureau Statistical Series No. 10, Government Printing Office, Washington, 1951.

36. Does your community have a voluntary organization or organizations which concern themselves with the problem of the physically handicapped? What are their activities?

Are they affiliated with the National Society for Crippled Children and Adults, with the National Rehabilitation Association, or with another of the national groups specializing in one or more of the handicapping diseases or conditions?

37. How many disabled persons are there in your community in each of the following categories:

Orthopedic	Hernia	Diabetic
Neuromuscular	Cardiac	Epileptic
Vision	Ex-tuberculous	Multiple impairment
Hearing	Peptic ulcer	

38. What was the incidence of each of the following types of diseases in your community in each of the past five years: [1]

Diabetes	Epilepsy and convulsive	Rheumatic fever
Tuberculosis	disorders	Other heart diseases
Multiple sclerosis	Poliomyelitis	
Cerebral palsy	Cancer	

39. Can you obtain estimates in your community as to how many cases of physical disability were caused by accidents in the past five years?

40. How many people in your community are receiving Aid to the Permanently and Totally Disabled under the public assistance program?

41. To what extent does your community offer or have access to any of the following services[2] for the physically handicapped:

Parent counseling	Speech therapy
Camping experience	Hearing service
Occupational therapy	Home therapy
Medical social service	Homebound work program
Convalescent care	Employment counseling
Physical therapy	

42. To what extent are special services and agencies coordinated, and to what extent do they plan together for a well-rounded community program?

43. What special services are available to your community through the state crippled children's program?

44. How many crippled children are known to be living in your community? How many of these need services for crippled children but are not receiving them? Why?

45. How many children in the school system have physical handicaps?

[1] Keep in mind that the diseases listed here do not lead to disability in all cases, and also that sometimes other diseases cause disability.

[2] See the pamphlet *The Problem and the Promise: A Brighter Future for the Crippled*, National Society for Crippled Children and Adults, Chicago, 1953. Such services are usually available at a rehabilitation center, a speech center, a diagnostic and evaluation clinic, and so on. There are many types of center, and even one type, such as a rehabilitation center, may offer a wide variety of services.

46. Is there a special school or are special classes conducted for handicapped children?
47. What special provision is made for children with physical handicaps:

Special classes	Home teaching
Special equipment	Speech correction
Modification of their program	Transportation
Physical therapy	Special vocational training

48. What efforts are made in your community to acquaint employers with the types of occupation at which handicapped workers have demonstrated their ability?[1]

The mentally handicapped. Mental deficiency is another type of disability which calls for special community consideration. It is difficult to estimate the number of mentally deficient, or feebleminded in the United States, because definitions and measuring instruments and standards of evaluation differ. There is fairly general agreement that those whose intelligence quotient is below 70 should be considered feebleminded, from the standpoint of intelligence. Practically speaking, however, feeblemindedness is not only a matter of I.Q. but also of social and economic inadequacy, the mental handicap being of such nature or taking such form that the individual is unable to make his way without special institutional care. Recent developments in psychology have indicated that inability to perform at a certain level of intelligence may be caused not only by basic deficiency in mental capacity, but also by poor training, poor motivation, emotional disturbances, and so on. Attitudes, habits, and home environment must all be evaluated in planning for the future of each individual. According to the National Association for Mental Health, there are approximately 120,000 persons in this country's institutions for the mentally deficient, and perhaps one and a half million mentally deficient people in the total population.

Of greater ability, but still needing special attention, are a large number of people who can make their way but who do not appear to be as "bright" as most people. Particularly in the schools, this group of children, variously classified as mentally retarded, dull-normal, borderline normal, and so on, often find school work dull, difficult, and discouraging. Yet, under favorable circumstances, these children can benefit by and need twelve years of schooling.[2] They represent a challenging problem to the schools, for much has still to be done in adapting school programs to

[1] Various studies indicate that physically handicapped workers, if suitably placed, do about as well if not better than nonhandicapped workers on such items as work performance, rates of injuries, average rates of absenteeism, and so on. See, for example, *The Performance of Physically Impaired Workers in Manufacturing Industries.*

[2] See *Curriculum Adjustments for the Mentally Retarded*, Office of Education, Government Printing Office, Washington, 1950.

their interests and abilities. In the absence of such adaptation, they often become discipline problems in the unappealing academic environment. Many times children appear to be mentally retarded who actually are capable of performance well within the rate of normality, but are hindered by illness, unrecognized defects such as partial deafness or poor vision, or a disturbing emotional environment.

49. How many persons from your community are now in public institutions for the mentally deficient?
50. What is the legal definition of feeblemindedness in your state?
51. To what state institution(s) are your community's feebleminded men, women, or children sent?
52. What is the procedure according to which a person is committed to such an institution? Returned to his own community?
53. Is there a "parole" system?
54. Is there a "colony" system by which groups of feebleminded people can "work out" under supervision, thus learning to adjust to living in the larger community?
55. Is there a separate institution for mentally deficient children?
56. Is special training in vocational and social adjustment given so that as many may return to their communities as possible?
57. What proportion of children committed are returned to their communities?
58. What intelligence tests are given in the school system, and in which grades? (See Chapter 7.)
59. What is done in cases where the child's first test indicates that he may be within the feebleminded range?
60. What special provision in the schools is made for those who are retarded but who are not sufficiently deficient to be institutionalized:

Special physical examinations	Special classes
Diagnostic services of mental clinic	Remedial reading where needed
	Other
Aptitude tests	

61. Does the guidance department or other agency help young people with mental handicaps find employment in jobs which are suited to their mental ability?
62. How well adapted is the school program, both curricular and extracurricular, for those children who are in the lower half of their class as far as mental ability is concerned?

A special and controversial question is that of whether feebleminded persons should be permitted to marry and have children, and whether and under what circumstances sterilization is morally or legally justifiable.

63. What restrictions does your state place on the marriage of feebleminded or legally insane persons?

64. Is there a sterilization law applying to such persons in your state? Is sterilization voluntary or compulsory?
How many have been sterilized under this program?

The Aging

The problem presented by the aging in the United States is twofold. First, the number of older people is increasing, as illustrated by the frequently cited comparison of the population over 65 as follows:

Year	Population over 65
1860	860,000
1945	9,920,000
1950	12,271,000
1970 (estimated)	16,000,000

More recent estimates indicate that the figure 16,000,000 may be reached by 1960. The aged population has been growing roughly twice as rapidly as the rest of the population, largely because of the successful combating of many diseases which would have otherwise caused many people to die in childhood or early adulthood.

The other part of the problem is that even as the aged become more numerous, their adjustment in community life becomes more difficult. It is increasingly harder for them to get employment. Modern living conditions make it harder for smaller families in urban circumstances to provide for the "old folks" to live with them. Older people are often in need of special medical care and frequently have not sufficient funds to pay for it. On the other hand, certain modern developments make it easier for older people to live alone. These include modern appliances like the vacuum cleaner, modern aids such as hearing aids, commercial services such as laundries, restaurants, and the rest.

It is important to note that the aged are not a separate class of people. There is nothing extraordinary about the sixtieth, sixty-fifth, and seventieth birthdays. Many people who have passed them lead happy, well-adjusted, self-sufficient lives and would be surprised to be told that they are a "problem." Others need special care even before they are sixty. Nor are the problems of the aged different in kind from those of any other group. Housing, social adjustment, health care, economic income—these problems characterize all age-groups. Among older people, however, they are encountered more often, or more intensely.[1]

It thus follows that many elderly people do not need special institutional

[1] Helpful pamphlets on the personal aspects of aging include: *When You Grow Older*, Public Affairs Pamphlet No. 131, New York, 1947; *Getting Ready to Retire*, Public Affairs Pamphlet No. 182, New York, 1952; and *Looking Forward to the Later Years*, Federal Security Agency, Government Printing Office, Washington, 1952.

or agency facilities so much as they need to be helped to remain or become again a part of the ongoing life of their community. While Golden Age clubs serve a useful purpose, the church, the grange, the lodge, and the civic club also provide opportunities for participation and expression by older people as well as younger. In appraising your community's facilities for older people, you will therefore want to consider not only the special facilities which may or may not exist, but also how adequately existing facilities are serving the needs and interests of older people and benefiting by their contributions.

A summary of basic statistical data on the aging is contained in *Fact Book on Aging*.[1] An informative book designed primarily for older people themselves but full of information of value to those making community studies is *The Best Is Yet to Be* by William G. Rose.[2] Among the best publications available for laymen on the subject of the aging are the annual publications of the New York State Joint Legislative Committee on Problems of the Aging in Albany. Two recent volumes are entitled *Age Is No Barrier* (1952) and *Enriching the Years* (1953).

65. How many persons 65 and over are in your community according to the most recent Census reports: Male? Female?
66. How many of these are employed either full time or part time:
    Farming   Other self-employment   Employment by someone else
67. How many persons in your community are receiving Old-Age and Survivors Insurance benefit payments under the Social Security program?
68. How many persons in your community are receiving Old-Age Assistance—a form of public assistance? (See Chapter 10.)
69. How many older people are receiving some other type of public assistance, such as Aid to the Disabled, general relief, county home care, and so on?
70. Answer the following questions for each of the principal sources of employment in your community:
    Is there a compulsory retirement system?
    Is there coverage under Old-Age and Survivors Insurance?
    Is there any other type of pension plan?
    If there are maximum age restrictions for hiring new workers, what are these restrictions?
    Has any study ever been made to determine the comparative performance at different jobs of people over 65 with younger people?
    How many people over 55 are now employed? Over 65?
    Is there a special preretirement counseling program?
    Is there any possibility for part-time work by older people who would prefer to work only part of a day?
    Are any special considerations extended to older people?

[1] Rev. ed., Federal Security Agency, Government Printing Office, Washington, 1952.
[2] Austin Phelps, New York, 1951.

71. Is there special employment counseling and placement service for older people in your community?

72. How many older people who are listed with the local public employment service are unable to find suitable work?

73. What special services are there in the community which might help older people to live in the community rather than in an institution:

    Visiting nurse service   Hospital home care programs
    Housekeeper service   Casework services by family
                                          agencies

74. Are there any special public or private housing developments part or all of which are specifically designed for the needs of older people?[1]

75. Is there any personal counseling service available to older people and especially designed to help them?

76. What institutional facilities are available for older people with various types of need in your community:[2]

    County or city "home" (Does it include an infirmary?)
    Chronic illness hospital
    Private home for the aged
        Boarding home
        Convalescent home (bedside care, not including medical or nursing)
        Nursing home (nursing care)

77. For each such institution, answer the following:

    What is the capacity?
    How many are now in residence?
    What are the charges, if any?
    Is there a resident or visiting physician?
    Are there any nurses on the staff? Trained social workers?
    What occasion or opportunity is there for recreation?
    What opportunity for religious ministration?
    Are visitors welcomed?
    Is the home pleasant and attractive?

78. What regulations govern such homes from the standpoint of sanitation, fire prevention, and so on?

79. Which homes are certified by your welfare department for the use of public assistance recipients?

80. Under what circumstances, if ever, do the needy aged have to sign over or otherwise dispose of their houses or other property before receiving public assistance?

---

[1] A helpful pamphlet on housing for older people, including institutional care, is *A Home in the Later Years: How to Meet the Needs of Older People for Housing and Supplementary Services.* New York State Association of Councils and Chests, 105 East 22d St., New York, 1953.

[2] See *Standards of Care for Older People in Institutions,* National Committee on the Aging, National Social Welfare Assembly, New York, 1953.

81. Has any thought been given to a foster care program as an alternative to institutionalization in the case of certain older people?

Health care of older people is little different in kind from that of younger ones. More facilities and services are needed in connection with chronic diseases, and there is a greater proportion who cannot pay for their health care. Health care for those in need is discussed in Chapter 10, and health as such is the topic of Chapter 12. Certain aspects of rehabilitation work, which often applies to the aged, are considered in Chapter 12 and earlier in the present chapter.

82. How many older persons in your community have received health or medical care during the past year which was paid for out of public assistance funds?

83. To what extent and under what circumstances is needed health care withheld from people over 65 who are unable to pay the full amount?

Because of retirement from active employment or because of confining physical conditions or for many other reasons, the aged often have considerable time to spend as they wish. All too often, this possible blessing of leisuretime becomes a depressing withdrawal from participation in various activities and resignation to a purely passive existence. Often former friends have moved away or died, existing organizations like the church, interest clubs, and the rest seem no longer to stimulate or to encourage the participation of the older person. Under such circumstances, it is little wonder that radio and television, both extremely passive forms of entertainment, have become a blessing to the aged for whiling away the long hours. Many of the considerations treated in Chapter 8, Recreation, apply to this part of your study and should be consulted. It should be kept in mind that much informal social participation is of a highly enjoyable type and should be considered here, although it is difficult to uncover by merely inventorying community facilities.

84. To what extent do each of the following types of organizations make a special effort to attract older people and utilize their services:

Churches	Interest groups
Fraternal and civic organizations	Economic groups

85. Do any of these organizations provide transportation to enable older people to attend services or meetings?

86. Is there any transportation program to help older people with their shopping?

87. Are there any groups in your community that are composed exclusively of older people?

88. In connection with any Golden Age, Oldsters, or other similar club, answer the following questions:
Where does it meet?
During what hours is the club open?
What physical facilities and equipment are there?
What organized activities?
Which organization sponsors it?
To what extent do older people themselves determine policy?
How many older people are served?
89. Is there an adult education program which offers activities particularly well adapted to the interests and capabilities of older people?
What courses or craft activities or discussion groups or other programs are included?
90. Is there a Committee on the Aging in your community, either within the health and welfare council or as a separate organization?
What groups send representatives to this committee?
What are its accomplishments, current activities, and plans for the future?[1]

Migrant Farm Workers

A group of people who are often in the greatest need of community attention are the migrants. Yet they often work in communities where great numbers of people are hardly aware of their existence. Migratory agricultural workers typically live out on the land, often not on the main roads. There are about a million of these persons in the United States, but half of them are foreign workers under contract or Mexicans who have entered this country illegally ("wetbacks"). Three large groups can be briefly described. On the West Coast are the white migrants from the dust-bowl area who migrated westward in the 1930's. Another group consists of Americans of Mexican ancestry who migrate northward, chiefly from Texas, every year. A third large group is composed of Negroes, chiefly from Florida, who follow the crops up the East Coast as far as New York and even Maine, and then return to the South each year.[2]

There are certain underlying conditions which contribute to the migrant problem. American agriculture uses migrants at special times during the year when certain crops, berries, fruits, or other produce are to be har-

[1] A good pamphlet designed for the use of such committees is *Community Action for the Aging*, available through the New York State Association of Councils and Chests, 105 East 22d St., New York. See also *Aging:* A Community Problem, Federal Security Agency, Government Printing Office, Washington, no date.
[2] See *Migratory Labor in American Agriculture:* Report of the President's Commission on Migratory Labor, Government Printing Office, Washington, 1951. This is an excellent summary of the migrant problem on the national level.

vested. The rest of the time they are not needed in that particular locality, so they go elsewhere. Being on the move so often, they frequently do not benefit from the strong community ties, community facilities, and informal community controls which operate in fixed communities where people have relatively stable residence. Temporary housing at the place of work is usually provided in "camps" supplied by the grower. These camps are in use only part of the year, a fact which does not encourage their upkeep. While larger camps are often structures of the barracks type, smaller camps may consist of old abandoned farmhouses, converted barns, shacks—in short, any building which has the semblance of affording shelter from the elements. Conditions in larger camps can be equally unsatisfactory. Nevertheless, there are many excellent camps of both the larger type and the smaller type. Many growers have found that the provision of attractive and wholesome housing can be economically feasible, for it attracts a better class of worker, makes for steadier work, and helps to avoid confusion or trouble.[1] Nevertheless, many growers neglect their housing, offering as an excuse that the workers do not appreciate good housing and are exceedingly destructive. It has been found that such destructiveness often arises from misunderstandings as to expectations, resentment of conditions, and so on. Sanitary provisions in the camps are often poor, and the laws in various states are not adequate for enforcing even a minimum of decency in these facilities, nor are the sanitation staffs large enough for adequate inspection.

Work is sporadic and undependable. Often migrants travel hundreds of miles only to find that the crop is a week late and they must be without work for a week, or that the crop has been ruined, or that for other reasons there is no work for them. They travel typically in large trucks provided by the labor contractor who procures them. Often these trucks are highly dangerous, to say nothing of being extremely uncomfortable, particularly for small children who often accompany their parents in the annual trek.

Under some circumstances, daily earnings are relatively high, but nevertheless the typical year's income is extremely meager. "In 1949, the average migratory farm worker of the United States, according to a survey of the United States Department of Agriculture, got 70 days of farm work and 31 days of nonfarm work, making a total for the year of 101 days. Aver-

---

[1] Two excellent bulletins on housing for migrant workers are Gallagher, Keith N., *Housing Seasonal Farm Labor*, Cornell Extension Bulletin 755, Ithaca, N.Y., 1949; and Loper, Ruby M., and Howard E. Thomas, *Housing for Migrant Farm Workers*, Cornell Miscellaneous Bulletin 15, 1953.

age annual earnings of the individual migratory farm worker from both types of employment were $514."[1]

91. Are migrant seasonal farm workers employed in the vicinity of your community?

92. What estimates of their number are made by the health department, department of labor, growers' association, or other agency?

93. What are the state regulations governing the employment of migrant labor?

94. Do migrant workers come under any of the following programs:

Minimum wage law   Unemployment insurance

Workmen's compensation system   Guaranteed minimum earnings

95. How often must migrants be paid?

96. What were the rates last season (per bushel, basket, peck, pound) for migrant farm work?

97. What are the chief crops which migrants help to harvest?

98. How long is the season during which farm work is available for the bulk of migrants in your community?

99. How many different migrant camps are there in your vicinity?[2]

100. How many are there of each of the following types of camp:

Barracks

Converted farmhouse

Buildings not originally designed for human occupancy

101. How many camps were specifically designed and built to house migrant labor? How many were converted from other purposes?

102. For each camp, answer the following questions:

What is its stated capacity?

How many occupied it last year?

Is there electricity? Heat, if needed? Running water?

What provisions for bath or shower? Laundering clothes?

How many people per cook stove?

How many people per room?

What furniture is provided, if any?

What type of toilet facilities? Are they sanitary?

In what condition is the structure?

In what condition is the interior? Are the walls painted; is the plaster intact, and so on?

Are there fire escapes from the second story, where appropriate?

Is the building weatherproof? Are there any leaks in the roof, window-panes missing, or open cracks in the walls?

---

[1] *Migratory Labor in American Agriculture*, p. 125. See also Fuller, Varden, *No Work Today!* The Plight of America's Migrants, Public Affairs Pamphlet No. 190, New York, 1953. This is a summary of the Report of the President's Commission.

[2] In some states, this information is available through the local or district or state health department, which enforces those provisions of the sanitary code applying to such camps. In others, the law applies only to camps housing more than a certain number of people.

Community facilities. The health conditions under which migrants live and work are often unsatisfactory. Poor facilities for cooking and for food storage as well as long hours in the field both contribute to a tendency to "eat out of cans" and to discourage a well-rounded diet. Exposure to climate, poor living quarters, and other conditions add to the problem. Many migrants, particularly Negroes, find difficulty in securing proper medical care, even when they can pay for it. In addition, the fact that many migrants are not able to pay for the medical and surgical care they need often makes them unwelcome patients. Welfare policies in some states make them ineligible for public assistance because they cannot meet the residence requirements.

Other community facilities, likewise, are available to migrants often in only a grudging manner. Thus, many stores, restaurants, and other establishments either do not serve them or charge them higher prices. They are unwelcome at many public recreation places, motion picture houses, and so on. In some communities, only the bars welcome the migrants, and not even all of them do. In the absence of adequate community recreation facilities, living in unpleasant accommodations, some migrants engage in disorderly conduct, fights, and other excesses.

103. Are facilities for food storage in migrant camps adequate?
104. Are cooking facilities adequate and such as can be easily maintained in sanitary condition?
105. Is the water supply in migrant camps inspected regularly by health authorities?
106. What other items are inspected by the health department?
107. How often do these inspections take place?
108. Are needy migrants eligible for public assistance benefits?
109. Can health expenses be paid through public assistance for migrants who cannot pay such extraordinary expenses but are otherwise not on public assistance rolls?
110. Is public health nursing service available in the migrant camps?
111. Are migrants discriminated against in any of the following types of establishments:

| Restaurants | Other stores | Motion picture houses |
| Grocery stores | Taverns, bars, etc. | Others |

112. Answer the following questions pertaining to recreational facilities that are available to migrants at the camps:
Is there an organized recreational program?
Is there a large room or building which can be used for recreational purposes?
Are dances held? Films shown?
Are church services held at any camps?

Is there equipment and space for games such as softball?

Is there a phonograph or radio?

Other recreational facilities?

113. What recreational opportunities are available to migrants in nearby villages or cities:

Public recreational facilities   Commercial facilities

Private agency facilities   Other

114. In what types of offense are migrants most often involved in your community, according to local police officials?

115. Do local police officials maintain a prejudiced attitude with regard to migrants?

116. From police and court records, can you make a comparison between migrant and resident persons arrested or held on similar charges as to their:

Arrest   Hearing   Release on bail   Sentence

117. Is any local organization carrying on a program on behalf of migrants in your community?

118. Of what does the program consist:

Providing recreational opportunities at the migrant camps

Sponsoring a "migrant chaplain" program

Providing recreational opportunities for migrants at the community center

Establishing personal contacts between residents and migrants

Carrying on a group fellowship program for residents and migrants

Helping to interpret the migrant situation sympathetically to the community

Helping to promote clearer understanding between migrants and growers

Providing counseling or other services for migrants

Migrant children. One of the most severe handicaps of the average migrant is lack of education. Many migrants cannot even write their own name. While great strides have been made in the education of the rest of the nation's children, the children of migrant laborers are receiving scarcely any better education than their parents had. One reason is inherent in the nature of their migratory life—they move so often from place to place. But even in communities where they remain for months at a time during the school season, many migrant children are excluded from the schools, either through explicit laws or through lax enforcement of existing legislation. The problems to small community schools of the coming and going of migrant children are great. Yet most Americans will not assent to a condition in which "a new generation of persons, inherently as competent as other Americans, . . . will be compelled to spend their lives in poverty because the communities in which they spend their childhood do not provide them with even the rudiments of an education."[1]

[1] *Migratory Labor in American Agriculture*, p. 171.

Part of the reason the children are not in the schools is their labor is wanted in the fields. Often children from the youngest ages upward work at "stoop labor" in the fields with their parents. In October, 1950, the Bureau of the Census estimated that there were 150,000 children in the 10 to 13 age-group working in the fields, 40,000 of whom were not even enrolled in school.[1] In some states, child labor laws do not apply to migrant workers. In others, the law applies, but enforcement is difficult. The chief pressure toward child labor is the economic need of the migrants themselves. But a negative pressure is the absence of any constructive alternative to the children working in the fields. Sometimes infants are left in baskets at the ends of the rows while the parents pick. Older children, if they are not working in the fields, are left at the camp, sometimes locked in, sometimes locked out. There is a great need for day care centers for children of migrant workers.[2]

Some communities which are alert to the welfare needs of their own children remain either ignorant of or oblivious to the equal or greater needs of the migrant children in their midst. Yet in most instances child welfare facilities are not available to children of migrant workers as they are to local children. Not only casework services, but also public health nursing services, immunization clinics, and other facilities, are all likely to miss the migrant children.

119. Are local child welfare services available to migrant children in your vicinity?
120. Specifically, how many children of migrants were listed as receiving such services during the past year? (See Chapter 11.)
121. Is any mass immunization work done with migrant children in your vicinity regularly? Under what auspices?
122. Are there any day care facilities available for children of migrants in your vicinity? Under what auspices? Are there any charges for this service? What proportion of migrant children do they reach? What is the nature of their program?
123. Are there migrant children in your vicinity while school is in session?
124. What proportion of migrant children attend school?
125. What provisions are made to enforce their attendance?
126. Are they segregated in special classes? If so, do you think segregation results from genuine concern for their special needs, or from discriminatory attitudes?
Are any other attempts made to meet their special needs?

---

[1] *Ibid.*, p. 161.
[2] For information on the organization of day care centers for children of migrant workers, write to the National Council of Churches of Christ, Home Missions Division, which has had considerable experience in this field, as have various state councils of churches.

127. What does your state education law say with respect to migrant children and their attendance at school?
128. What does your state child labor law say with respect to children of migrant laborers?
  Are they considered under the same provisions as other children, or are provisions relaxed for them?
129. Which groups in your state are most in favor of allowing migrant children to work in the fields?
130. If there are provisions which exclude certain children from labor in the fields, by what department of the state government are they enforced?
131. How often are inspections made? What are the penalties?
  Have there been any violations in your community in recent years? What disposition was made?
132. Are inspections made at regular intervals, thus permitting anticipation, or are they unannounced?

Displaced Persons

The number of immigrants entering the United States has been reduced to a relative trickle in recent decades. As the proportion of the foreign born has decreased in the population, the great need which earlier existed for mass programs of what was then called "Americanization" has lessened. Nevertheless, economic change and international disruption have resulted in a series of acts of emergency legislation in recent years to permit and encourage the immigration of a limited number of displaced persons, aside from the usual immigration policy under the controversial "quota system."

Displaced persons almost by definition must be people whose experience is such as to have disrupted their lives, and often their family relations. All have suffered such disruptions, many of them in extreme. Thus, they are in need of special help, particularly in the direction of agency assistance to help them get here and to help them secure employment and housing; to help them establish themselves; to promote community understanding; and to provide opportunity, where desired, for formal classes in the English language, in American society, and so on.

Since laws governing the immigration of displaced persons have repeatedly specified that they cannot be admitted under situations where they will displace an American from employment or housing, these problems are not an issue, although there is widespread misunderstanding on these points. Special preference is given to types of employment skill needed in this country. Indeed the economic and cultural contributions of recent immigrants, like those of earlier immigrants, have been great.[1]

[1] See Crawford, W. Rex, editor, *The Cultural Migration:* The European Scholar in America, University of Pennsylvania Press, Philadelphia, 1953. For a comprehensive re-

While the number of displaced persons has not been large, many communities have had experience with such persons coming into their midst whose backgrounds and circumstances have been so varying that no organized effort on their behalf seemed feasible. On the other hand, in larger communities there are often large enough groups of displaced persons to make feasible the setting up of special agency programs in their behalf.

Since there are many agencies dealing with the immigration of displaced persons, and since there is, of course, no limit on their place of residence in this country, it is extremely difficult to get up-to-date figures on displaced persons in your community. Nevertheless, various church groups and social agencies can put you in touch with organizations which have been instrumental in locating displaced persons in your region, and which can supply you with such current information as they have.

133. According to any estimates which may be available, how many immigrants have settled in your community in recent years:
    Regular "quota" immigrants   Displaced persons
134. What social agencies have helped such immigrants settle?
135. What follow-up services are performed by these agencies?
136. Has your community an agency which specializes in services to recent immigrants? What is its program?
137. What can you learn about the vocational placement of recent immigrants?
138. Is there any organization which seeks to better the conditions of all the foreign-born in your community?
139. Are there any courses or study groups offered especially for immigrants:
    English language   Citizenship courses   Other courses
140. To what extent are immigrants made aware of the general adult educational facilities which exist in the community for vocational training or other purposes?
141. What special nationality organizations, brotherhoods, fraternities, or mutual benefit societies, exist for people of various nationality backgrounds?
142. Is there a foreign language newspaper or radio station serving numbers of foreign-born people in your community?
143. Is there any group of immigrants toward whom there has been hostility shown in recent years? What were the circumstances?
144. What agency offers help to the foreign-born in acquiring citizenship?
145. How many applications for first papers and full citizenship were granted or denied last year by the courts serving your community?

---

port of recent experience with displaced persons, see *The DP Story:* The Final Report of the United States Displaced Persons Commission, Government Printing Office, Washington, 1952.

146. What public assistance or social security benefits are not available to non-citizens on the same basis as citizens?

References for Further Study
The Handicapped

Bindt, Juliet, *A Handbook for the Blind*. Macmillan Co., New York, 1952. Written by a blind author who is a home teacher for the blind under the California State Library, this book is a practical guide for the problems the blind face in everyday living. It includes a section consisting of five chapters written specifically for sighted people to help them deal with blind people.

Stern, Edith M., and Elsa Castendyck, *The Handicapped Child:* A Guide for Parents. A. A. Wyn, Inc., New York, 1950. Specific chapters are devoted to the crippled child, cerebral palsy, epilepsy, the blind or partially sighted, retarded and speech handicapped, rheumatic fever or other long illnesses. The entire book is written in a friendly and sympathetic manner and should be a great aid to parents of handicapped children.

The Aging

Aging. A bimonthly publication of the U.S. Department of Health, Education, and Welfare designed as "a medium for sharing information about programs and activities among agencies and organizations in the field. . . ." Government Printing Office, Washington.

Breckinridge, Elizabeth, *Community Services for Older People:* The Chicago Plan. Wilcox and Follett Co., Chicago, 1952. This report is the result of four years of study by the Chicago Community Project for the Aged. On this basis, a plan is offered for a comprehensive program of community services for older people.

Kaplan, Jerome, *A Social Program for Older People*. University of Minnesota Press, Minneapolis, 1953. Chapters include, among others, The Social Group Worker, The Volunteer, To Organize a Group, What to Do for Program, To Increase Participation, The Role of Homes for the Aged. This is a helpful book for persons interested in community programs.

Tibbitts, Clark, editor, "Social Contribution of the Aging," special issue of *The Annals of the American Academy of Political and Social Science*, vol. 279, January, 1952. It is devoted to articles by authorities in various aspects of the aging.

Migrant Farm Workers

Children in Migratory Agricultural Families. Federal Security Agency and U.S. Department of Labor, Government Printing Office, Washington, 1946. This pamphlet brings together several articles giving information on child labor, day care, educational conditions, and health services for migrant children, all written by Ione L. Clinton and appearing in *The Child* during 1945 and 1946.

McWilliams, Carey, *Ill Fares the Land:* Migrants and Migratory Labor in the United States. Little, Brown and Co., Boston, 1942.

Sweatshops in the Sun. Consumers League of New York, 1952. This illustrated and instructive pamphlet is based on an extensive study of conditions of migrant workers in New York State. It helps to give a picture of the day-in and day-out life and problems of migrant workers who come to New York State each summer, mostly from Florida.

Displaced Persons

Humphrey, Hubert H., Jr., *The Stranger at Our Gate:* America's Immigration Policy. Public Affairs Pamphlet No. 202, New York, 1954.

14. Communication

IF COMMUNITY SCHOOLS, churches, governments, businesses, and organizations of various types are to adapt to new conditions as they arise, it is important that they have access to new ideas and approaches from other communities. American communities are fed by a complex network of mass communication media which diffuse new knowledge, ideas, and opinions from one place to another. Through such mass communication media as newspapers, radio and TV stations, and motion picture theaters, ideas are introduced into the communities of America in fairly regular, predictable, and patterned fashion. We have already considered such other means of cultural diffusion as schools, libraries, and various citizens' organizations connected with the topics of the various chapters.

Another aspect of communication is the means by which ideas are circulated from person to person within each community. These means vary all the way from informal "gossip" to organized educational campaigns by citizens' groups, newspaper reports, forums, and discussion groups. It is important that there be some medium by which important occasions, dates, programs, or other local events can be announced to the people in a community. The newspapers and broadcasting stations are important media for announcing such items of community interest.

Occasionally there are groups in the community between whom there is poor communication, little exchange of information and points of view. This is frequently the case where racial or cultural "islands" of diverse people exist in the community. (See Chapter 15.) Community workers today are concerned about improving the means by which information is circulated through the community, about reaching the roughly half of community people who participate in no organized social activity, and about furthering an interchange of opinions and values which would help groups having different points of view to come to mutual understanding and agreement.

Completing the circle would be the various means by which ideas are disseminated from one's own community to other communities throughout the region, state, or nation.[1]

In practically every aspect of our social living, we "know better than we do"; that is, new and better methods or professional practices or social patterns are available but not yet in wide use because people do not know enough about them, or they do not find them to their liking, or they are not sufficiently interested to do anything about them. From this standpoint, whether the idea be concerned with early diagnosis of cancer, the importance of voting in the primaries, the need for adequate probation services for juvenile delinquents, or a satisfactory ordinance governing the construction of multiple dwellings, it is important that the means for spreading such ideas be adequate, and that they be kept open. Hence, the question arises not only as to the extensiveness of communication facilities, but the extent to which they are kept free for the circulation of ideas, whether they be those of the majority or of the minority. Censorship is the attempt to limit or curtail the communication of an idea. Propaganda, on the other hand, is the attempt to utilize the means of communication to further a particular point of view, usually through both distortion of the truth and emotional appeal.[2]

Good background reading at this point would be *Public Opinion and Propaganda* by Leonard W. Doob,[3] and *The Making of Public Opinion* by Emory S. Bogardus.[4] It is not widely recognized that the advertisements in newspapers, magazines, radio and TV, and other media are an important method of communicating ideas. They not only instruct people in the merits, uses, and principles involved in their products, but also occasionally venture into the field of political and social issues attempting to influence attitudes, and thus becoming propaganda. Regardless of one's appraisal of the objectivity and veracity of advertisements, they are an important means of transmitting ideas.

The Press

Newspapers are an important means of disseminating information and influencing opinion. For background read *The Daily Newspaper in America*

[1] For a more extensive discussion of the communication of ideas in a community, see Chapter 3, The Business of Communication, in *The Public Library in the United States* by Robert D. Leigh, Columbia University Press, New York, 1950.
[2] Propaganda differs from ordinary attempts at persuasion chiefly in the degree to which it involves a conscious distortion or falsification of facts.
[3] Henry Holt and Co., New York, 1948.
[4] Association Press, New York, 1951.

by Alfred McClung Lee.[1] There are some 1,700 daily English language newspapers in the United States and close to 9,000 weeklies. The weeklies ordinarily have smaller circulation and tend to limit themselves more to local news and issues. An important trend is toward a smaller number of daily newspapers, with newspaper mergings or shutdowns leaving all but the larger cities with only one daily newspaper. Another important development has been the increasing use of the writings of syndicated columnists. Where such columns are carefully chosen, this practice may enrich the editorial offerings of the newspaper by presenting various points of view. Often, however, it serves to discourage the editorial responsibility of the local newspaper as the local editor withdraws from competition with the "big name" columnists. Communities differ in the extent to which they are fortunate enough to have newspapers which take an active and constructive interest in civic improvement and in the encouragement of citizens' efforts in various fields.

Where the following questions call for an analysis of content, all issues of dailies for an entire week should be studied, and all issues of weeklies for at least a month:

1. What local newspapers serve your community?

For each such newspaper, answer the following questions:

2. What is its average circulation per issue? Is it published daily or weekly? Does it publish a Sunday edition?
3. Is it owned locally? Is it part of a chain? Is its viewpoint Democratic, Republican, Independent, or other?
4. To what wire services does it belong?
5. What syndicated columns does it run? Do they represent a variety of different social and political viewpoints?
   If not, do they tend to lean toward the "liberal" or "conservative" point of view on national, state, and local politics?
6. Does political or other bias affect reporting or editorial treatment of local issues such as health, education, the community's economic basis, and so on? Does the newspaper have a "sacred cow"; that is, is there some subject which it either suppresses or deals with in a particular way because of its affiliation or the interests of its owner?
7. Are there ever any articles in which names or pictures of such persons as the following are given humiliating publicity:
   Relief recipients   Children awaiting foster home   Other
   Juvenile delinquents   placement
8. Is it a "crusading" paper? What campaigns or programs has it sponsored and with what results?

[1] Macmillan Co., New York, 1937.

9. Does it run regular columns or features devoted to education, health, government, and so on, in the local community?

10. Does it welcome announcements of meetings of various civic organizations and reports of their activities?

Particularly in smaller communities, local newspapers often concern themselves chiefly with local events, leaving the wider coverage for larger daily newspapers from nearby cities. If outside newspapers serve your community, you will want to answer for them such of the preceding questions as are appropriate.

11. Which "outside" newspapers have extensive circulation in your community?

The following questions apply to the aggregate of newspapers serving your community.

12. Do your newspapers represent diverse editorial viewpoints?

13. Do your newspapers actively and carefully report developments in the field of local government and in agency activity?

14. To what extent do your newspapers function as a "community bulletin board" for letting people know of coming events?

15. What community achievements can be attributed to interest stimulated largely by newspapers?

16. Do your newspapers give intelligent editorial comment on local events and issues as well as those on the national and international scene?

17. What educational features, such as columns, special stories, special departments, are conducted by your newspapers in such fields as health, nutrition, recreation, and so on?

18. Has any newspaper run a "know your community" series comprised of the type of material treated in this book?

Also important as a source of ideas and information flowing into the community are the hundreds of different periodicals which are published in the United States. A number of these have a circulation going into the millions, and as such are an important influence on national thinking. From local magazine stores and from the circulation department of various periodicals, you may be able to get information on the number of sales or paid subscriptions in your community.

Books constitute another important means of communication. Local bookstores may be able to give you an indication of which books have been bought with greatest frequency in recent years. An additional source of books is the "book club" type of membership. Perhaps you can get information from various book clubs as to the number of people from your community who belong. Public libraries are considered in Chapter 7.

19. Which periodicals have the greatest newsstand circulation in your community? The greatest subscription circulation?
20. Which books have sold the greatest number of copies in your community in the past year: Fiction? Nonfiction?

Radio and Television

Radio and television stations function not only as sources of news and entertainment, but often present programs of definite local community value.[1] This practice is encouraged by the Federal Communications Commission policy providing that a portion of the time of each station must be devoted to public service features. In addition to programs on current national or international issues, there are occasionally fine programs acquainting citizens with one or another aspect of the local community. Spot announcements and regular calendars of activities often keep citizens informed of important meetings or other civic or cultural events.

21. What radio and television stations are there in your community?
22. In addition, what other stations are most frequently listened to by people in your community?
23. Do these stations make free broadcast time available for educational programs of a civic nature?
24. Which regular programs, if any, are devoted to familiarizing people with their local community?
25. Do local stations announce forthcoming events of community interest?
26. Do they, through spot announcements, publicize worthwhile campaigns such as community chest drives, hospital campaigns, and so on?
27. List the regular programs which are of an "educational" or "cultural" type as opposed to pure entertainment.
28. What is the estimated "audience" of your radio station for various programs of an educational or cultural nature?
29. Do local study groups listen to and discuss local or national programs? On which topics?

Motion Pictures

Motion pictures are not only an important source of entertainment; in addition, whether deliberately or not, they influence attitudes toward various groups of people and toward various social issues. They are an important source of education about people and customs in other coun-

---

[1] Read *Radio, Television, and Society* by Charles A. Siepmann, Oxford University Press, New York, 1951.

tries, other times, other occupations, cultural backgrounds, and so on. Motion pictures like *Good Bye, Mr. Chips* or the *Dr. Kildare* series are effective in constructing or perpetuating stereotypes of teachers, doctors, and other groups.

Legitimate theater productions, where available, are an important "cultural" offering as well as a medium for introducing new ideas and attitudes.

30. How many motion picture theaters are there in your community?
31. In each case on what basis does the manager select the films which are to be shown?
    To what extent is his choice limited by agreements with a distributing company?
32. How often during the past year have special brief films been shown on material of an educational or civic nature or in connection with fund-raising campaigns or community chest drives?
33. Do any of the theaters show "art" films? How often?
    Has the community a documentary film library or access to one?[1]
34. What stage productions have been available in your community during the past year by professional groups? A little theater group? Local organizations such as schools or churches?

Other Media of Communication

Such mass communication media as the press, radio and TV, and motion pictures are not the only means of diffusing information and opinion. Others are considered in various chapters of this book. The schools (see Chapter 7), both through their regular educational program for children and through their adult education activity have an important function of diffusing ideas and stimulating an interchange of viewpoints. Libraries (Chapter 7) are deliberately organized to serve as centers of distribution of ideas in books or periodicals most of which come from outside any particular community. Religious organizations (Chapter 9), through sermons, Sunday school classes, printed tracts, and other means are important in the diffusing of ideas and the forming of opinion. Citizens' groups of various sorts (Chapter 16 and others) often have as a primary function an educational program designed to acquaint more citizens with the importance of new developments, procedures, and needs in their respective areas of interest. Forums, study groups, institutes, and conferences (Chapter

[1] See Starr, Cecile, editor, *Ideas on Film:* A Handbook for the 16 mm. Film User, Funk and Wagnalls Co., New York, 1951; or Waldron, Gloria, and Starr, Cecile, *The Information Film*, Columbia University Press, New York, 1949.

7) all similarly constitute avenues for the interchange of facts and opinions. Finally, the informal "word-of-mouth" communication which takes place in the informal group network of the community (Chapter 20) is particularly important in "getting the word passed around" and in the formation of public opinion.

Propaganda and Censorship

The media of public communication are the constant targets of propaganda efforts by various interest groups.[1] Propaganda is the attempt to influence attitudes on controversial matters, and is generally characterized by distortion of truth and by emotional appeal. Of the two principal ways of combating propaganda, censorship and counterpropaganda, the latter is generally considered to be more appropriate in this country. Counterpropaganda is the answering of propaganda by pointing out its distortions and omissions and by giving the "other side of the picture." Propaganda becomes particularly effective when it is disguised as straight "news" or as part of the "facts" which are taught in the schools. For this reason, various interests are constantly attempting to get their own propaganda into the news columns disguised as "straight" news stories and into the school curriculum disguised as "straight" education.

Freedom of speech and the press are articles of faith which are constantly affirmed and as constantly threatened.[2] Particularly on controversial matters, strong opinions are formed. Believing that their own opinions are right and that the opposing opinions must therefore be wrong, many people wish to prevent the opposing "fallacious" opinions from circulating. This basic attitude underlies censorship in the field of ideological controversy. Another area of censorship activity concerns standards of decency and morality, and what should be done when publications, plays, motion pictures, and so on, allegedly violate them.[3] The question of censorship, which includes any attempt to impose a barrier to the communication of ideas, is a knotty one. The point that free speech and press are specifically set up to guarantee the right to circulate ideas which someone may brand as immoral, subversive, or heretical, is often countered with the argument that circulation of such undesirable material is a violation of the spirit of free speech, or that free speech was never set up to safe-

[1] Read Lee, Alfred McClung, *How to Understand Propaganda*, Rinehart and Co., New York, 1952.
[2] See Cushman, Robert E., *New Threats to American Freedoms*, Public Affairs Pamphlet No. 143, New York, 1948.
[3] Read Inglis, Ruth A., *Freedom of the Movies*, University of Chicago Press, Chicago, 1947.

guard such undesirable items, but rather only the desirable ones. The would-be censors at this point fill in their own particular conception of desirability, "decency," "Americanism," and so on.

In governmental censorship, some official or board is empowered to suppress, refuse a license to, or otherwise deal with, certain classes of material, whether they be books, magazines, motion pictures, dramatic productions or other media of communication. In censorship by private organizations, pressure may be brought to bear on publishers, theatrical producers, or lecturers either to withhold or to revise objectionable material. In private self-censorship, material may be reviewed by an industrial or company board or official to see if it is acceptable according to some voluntarily accepted "code," such as that of the motion picture producers, or of a particular newspaper, radio station, or periodical. A special type of censorship is involved in the occasional case where an auditorium or other meeting place is denied to some group or individual by the organization, governmental or private, which operates the facility.

A national organization of great help in studying censorship activities is the American Civil Liberties Union, which has various regional branches and organizations throughout the country. Its policy is to defend the legal right of people to circulate ideas, even though the ideas involved may be objectionable to some people.[1]

The media of mass communication, including newspapers, magazines, books and pamphlets, radio broadcasting, motion pictures, and comic books, are censored in various ways and to different degrees. In a study of censorship activities, it is also important to watch for restrictions on material to be discussed in the school curriculum, the refusal of meeting places and lecture halls to people who represent unpopular or "controversial" viewpoints, and the arrest of unpopular speakers on public nuisance charges or on grounds of not having a proper permit.

35. What state laws restrict in any way the free expression of opinion or communication of ideas or of artistic expression?[2]

36. What local units of government, if any, are charged with enforcement of decency laws as they affect communication media?

---

[1] See *Freedom, Justice, Equality:* Report on Civil Liberties January, 1951 to June, 1953, American Civil Liberties Union, New York, 1953. For another survey of the field of civil rights, see "Civil Rights in America," the May, 1951, issue of *The Annals of the American Academy of Political and Social Science,* vol. 275, edited by Robert K. Carr.

[2] Certain laws are designed to prevent practices which are widely recognized to be abuses of freedom of expression. These include laws against libel and slander, incitement to riot, and attempts to overthrow the government by violence. Laws establishing some basis for prevention of obscene public performances or publications are also widespread, but more controversial. In any case. there is always a possible threat that in the enforcement of such laws which afford desirable protections, limits of authority will be overstepped.

37. What subjects, movements, or organizations are restricted from the use of such facilities as newspaper advertising space, public meeting places, radio time, and so on?[1]

38. If local newspapers, broadcasting stations, auditoriums, or other facilities have a written "code" or statement of policy as to what types of expression they will exclude, what are its provisions?

39. What instances of censorship activity have arisen in your community in regard to preventing any of the following items:
    Showing of a motion picture film
    Showing of a stage play
    Appearance of a particular speaker or performer
    Presentation of a particular radio program
    Public discussion of a particular topic
    Inclusion of certain books or periodicals in the school or community library
    Sale of certain books, periodicals, or comic books
    Discussion of certain topics in the schools
    Other instances of censorship

40. In each case, what was the nature of the material which people were censoring or attempting to censor?

41. What was the principal method of attempted censorship; that is, refusal of license or permit, order to desist, picketing, boycotts, public attacks on the presentation of the objectionable material, intimidation, and so on?

42. What organizations were involved in the censoring activity?

43. What organizations' activities were the target of censorship?

44. Did the attempted censorship succeed?

45. If the censorship was by a governmental agency, was an appeal made by the publishers, producers, or other persons? With what results?

46. What groups supported the censorship and what groups opposed it, and on what grounds?

47. Which organizations in the community are particularly concerned with keeping open the channels of communication against attempts to bar the communication of ideas which are not politically or religiously orthodox, or which are "controversial"?

After you have finished this section of your study, ask yourself this question:

---

[1] It is often difficult to ferret out such information without raising specific questions. For example, in 1953 the Central Committee for Conscientious Objectors sought to buy advertising space in several of the country's leading newspapers in order to acquaint young men with their legal right to conscientious objection on religious grounds under the Selective Service Law. Almost without exception, the newspapers refused the advertisement. Yet it is doubtful whether most newspaper officials, in answer to a general question of what types of material they censor, would have been prepared to supply a definite policy statement on this matter.

48. Is this community a place where people are free to present opinions, however unpopular?

What are the most important threats to freedom of expression in this community?

References for Further Study

A Free and Responsible Press: Report of the Commission on Freedom of the Press. University of Chicago Press, Chicago, 1947. This is a general report on mass communication in newspapers, radio, motion pictures, magazines, and books.

Berelson, Bernard, and Morris Janowitz, *Reader in Public Opinion and Communication.* The Free Press, Glencoe, Ill., 1950. An extensive collection of writings by experts in the fields indicated.

Chafee, Zechariah, *Free Speech in the United States.* Harvard University Press, Cambridge, 1946. This is a basic reference work on censorship.

Walpole, Hugh R., *Semantics:* The Nature of Words and Their Meanings, W. W. Norton and Co., New York, 1941. The way in which words, themselves, often become a barrier to adequate communication is studied in the science of semantics. This is a widely used elementary book in the field.

A large number of books are available on civil liberties particularly as affected by the nervousness about "subversion" arising out of the cold war. Here are four that are especially helpful:

Barth, Alan, *The Loyalty of Free Men.* Viking Press, New York, 1951.

Biddle, Francis B., *The Fear of Freedom.* Doubleday and Co., New York, 1951.

Davis, Elmer H., *But We Were Born Free.* Bobbs-Merrill Co., New York, 1954.

Thomas, Norman, *The Test of Freedom.* W. W. Norton and Co., New York, 1954.

15. Intergroup Relations

AMERICAN SOCIETY IS COMPRISED of many different types of people with diverse interests, religious affiliations, racial and nationality backgrounds, occupations, and ways of doing things. The special characteristics which numerous people may have in common are sometimes ignored, sometimes made the center of great interest. Persons who share certain characteristics may or may not associate with each other, feel a common bond of unity, and constitute an actual sociological group. Other persons may come to look upon them as a group, or on the other hand seldom think of them in that way. If they are looked upon as a group, they may be regarded with favor or disfavor.

Such social groupings on the basis of race, nationality, or religion have been particularly important in the United States, not only as a source of common loyalty within each group but often as a source of friction, misunderstanding, and discrimination among groups. The process is sustained by the ease with which people generalize about those they do not know very well, and think of them as being all the same. Often the worst characteristics which have been observed in individual members of the group are taken as the norm for the group. Such stereotyped thinking persists despite experience which would belie it and facts which would disprove it.[1]

As a result, people are often prejudged, not on the basis of the way they behave but on the basis of the alleged characteristics of the group to which they belong. Such prejudice is often a disturbing factor preventing harmonious relations between various groups.

In addition to attitudes of prejudice there may be actual discriminatory behavior against members of a particular group. They are treated in a different way from other people. They may not be allowed access to certain public accommodations; they may be segregated into certain neighborhoods; they may be barred from membership in various organizations, or from the patronage of various establishments.

[1] See *What Is Race?* A UNESCO publication distributed in the United States by Columbia University Press, New York.

The problem of the contrast between such discriminatory behavior and American ideals of justice and equality of opportunity has been called *An American Dilemma* in one of the most definitive works to date in the field of race relations.[1]

While race, religion, and nationality are important sources of intergroup discord, they are not the only ones. Many communities are torn by friction, misunderstanding, and conflict between groups on entirely other lines. The traditional suspicion between farmer and villager may constitute the greatest source of intergroup misunderstanding in some communities. A bitter history of labor-management feuding may result in important group cleavages. In some college communities, the town-gown controversy is an abiding focus of suspicion and recrimination. In resort areas, considerable hostility may prevail in the relations between "natives" and the "summer people." Many suburban communities experience a three-way pull as farmers, villagers, and commuters clash over different wishes in respect to local government or the local school. Nevertheless, the area of behavior toward racial, religious, and nationality groups constitutes the most important source of intergroup tension.

Your Community's Social Groups

This section of your study is devoted to ascertaining the principal areas of intergroup misunderstanding in your community. It takes up the various types of groups of persons among whom there is a possibility of serious misunderstanding, the number involved in each group, and the quality of the relationships which exist between the various groups.

Racial, religious, nationality, or other groups whose members are often objects of prejudice and discrimination are called "minority" groups. Although this is for various reasons not a completely satisfactory term, it is preferable to any other term for designating the groups treated in this chapter. At this point it might be well to read a standard text in the field of minority groups, such as *One America* by Francis J. Brown and Joseph S. Roucek,[2] *These Our People* by R. A. Schermerhorn,[3] or *Racial and Cultural Minorities:* An Analysis of Prejudice and Discrimination by George E. Simpson and John M. Yinger.[4] Sometimes still other factors influence attitudes toward racial, religious, or nationality groups. For example, new immigrants as well as various groups of longer tenure in this

[1] Myrdal, Gunnar, *An American Dilemma.* Harper and Bros., New York, 1944.
[2] 3d ed. Prentice-Hall, Inc., New York, 1952.
[3] D.C. Heath and Co., Boston, 1949.
[4] Harper and Bros., New York, 1953.

country often have access to only relatively low-status occupations. This low occupational status in turn reinforces the low status attributed to the group. In the case of Negro migrant agricultural workers, there is the racial difference, the fact that the migrants are strangers in the community, and the low status of their occupation. Likewise, the hostility toward commuters on the part of older residents is often a product not only of the fact that they are newcomers, but also that they are associated, occupationally, with the "city," toward which there may exist suspicion and hostility.

1. What is the number of each of the following types of people in your community:

White	Indian	Japanese
Negro	Chinese	Other races

2. How many foreign-born whites are in your community?
3. How many foreign-born whites come from each country of birth?
4. How many white persons with Spanish surname are living in your community: Native-born? Foreign-born?
5. How many foreign-born persons in your community are naturalized? Alien?[1]
6. Has there been a considerable influx of refugees, displaced persons, or "quota" immigrants into your community in recent years?
7. What has been the attitude of older residents toward these newcomers?[2]
8. From the preceding questions, make a list of the racial or nationality groups which constitute a significant factor in intergroup relations in your community.
9. Has there been hostility with respect to any of these racial or nationality groups in recent years?
10. What specific instances of hostile behavior have there been?
11. If various racial and nationality groups tend to cluster in certain residential neighborhoods in the community, make a careful plot map of the different residential sections.
12. Do you find that types of occupation tend to be divided along racial or nationality lines?
    Which such groups tend to be disproportionately represented in which types of occupation?[3]
13. What is the approximate number of members of each of the major religious affiliations in your community?[4]

[1] Answers to the preceding questions can be obtained from the Census, vol. 2, chap. B. Some of the information is available for urban communities of 2,500 or more, while some of it is available only for larger cities and counties, or only in regions where there are large numbers of people of the category listed.
[2] See Chapter 13 for other questions about immigrants and displaced persons.
[3] For an occupational classification used by the Census, see p. 21.
[4] For questions about church membership and other religious considerations, including interchurch hostility and cooperation, see Chapter 9.

14. Are there any religious groups that are discriminated against or "looked down upon" by other groups in the community?
15. What form does this discrimination take?
16. Of the following types of social grouping, which are relatively ignored or given little importance and which are given special interest and "really make a difference" in your community:

Racial (specify)	Native-summer people
Nationality	Older generation-younger
Religious	generation
Occupational	Labor-management
Farmer-townspeople	Town-gown
Oldtimer-commuter	Others

17. From the groups listed above, which are objects of hostility, discrimination, or segregation? In each case, what form does the hostile behavior take?

Discrimination Against Minority Groups

Discrimination involves the unequal treatment of people according to the group to which they belong or are alleged to belong. It is widely denied and widely practiced, although often in subtle forms. As we shall see, it applies to various aspects of living, including employment, housing, education, health facilities, community services, voting and holding office, law enforcement, and social participation.

Discrimination is an important problem in American communities for many reasons. It is against the professed American creed of the brotherhood of men under God and of ideals of justice and equality of opportunity. It is a constant source of resentment by groups that are the targets of such discrimination. It is extremely costly, particularly where overcrowding in segregated areas breeds slum conditions with their cost in human and financial values[1] or where educational segregation necessitates a highly uneconomical duplication of public school facilities.[2] It involves as well an uneconomical utilization of the nation's manpower when competent individuals are barred from employment in jobs for which they are qualified, and must take only simpler or more menial work. Of increasing importance is the international embarrassment which the country suffers in its attempt to win the hearts of the peoples of the world to a democratic way of life.

Although discrimination remains a difficult problem which will require

[1] See Chapter 6.
[2] Racial segregation in the public school systems of the nation was declared unconstitutional by the Supreme Court decision of May 17, 1954. Considerable time will probably elapse before this decision is fully implemented in all the states.

decades to overcome fully, there are important signs of achievement in this aspect of intergroup relations. In its report on civil rights, the special President's Committee stated:. "But we have seen nothing to shake our conviction that the civil rights of the American people—all of them— can be strengthened quickly and effectively by the normal processes of democratic, constitutional government. That strengthening, we believe, will make our daily life more and more consonant with the spirit of the American heritage of freedom."[1]

Discrimination in employment, housing, and education. Occupational discrimination takes many forms. It is involved in cases where race, religion, or national origin make it difficult, if not impossible, for an individual to obtain a particular position, even though he may be as well or better qualified than others; or where individuals do not receive equal pay for equal work. Some states have laws which prohibit discrimination in employment in private industry, while others do not. In some instances, cities have similar laws. Legislation barring discrimination in employment is often flaunted, however, and little is done about the existing conditions. Sometimes the enforcing authorities, although they are empowered by law to take definite action, prefer the slower method of "persuasion," which may become an excuse for inaction. Nevertheless, such laws have been generally effective, despite dire predictions which were made as to their unenforceability.[2] In states where no such law exists, however, there is nothing illegal about rejecting an application for employment on the basis of the applicant's race, religion, nationality, or any other arbitrary basis selected.

18. Does your state or city have legislation prohibiting discrimination in private employment?[3]

19. How many complaints regarding discrimination in employment have been reported to the anti-discrimination board from your vicinity during the past year?
   What disposition was made of these cases?

20. Can you procure informed opinions as to how effectively the anti-discrimination law is enforced?

---

[1] *To Secure These Rights:* Report of the President's Committee on Civil Rights. Simon and Schuster, New York, 1947, p. 10. This report is highly recommended as a survey of the status of civil rights in general and those of minority groups in particular.
[2] Read Berger, Morroe, *Equality by Statute:* Legal Controls over Group Discrimination. Columbia University Press, New York, 1952. See also Burma. John H., "Race Relations and Antidiscriminatory Legislation," *American Journal of Sociology,* vol. 56, March, 1951.
[3] See *State and Municipal Fair Employment Legislation,* Government Printing Office. Washington, 1953

21. If your state does not have such a law, is there a movement underway to pass one?
    What organizations are working for or against such action?
22. Which companies discriminate in their employment policies in the following ways:
    Refuse to hire people of certain minority groups
    Pay different wages to minority group for essentially the same work
    Restrict job openings for minority group members chiefly to unskilled labor
    Other
23. Which unions discriminate in their membership policies, and which do not?
24. In what occupations do various minority groups tend to be disproportionately represented?
25. From which occupations in your community is any particular minority group virtually barred?
26. If there are segregated washroom and toilet facilities for minority groups in various companies or public offices, how do the facilities compare?

A frequent type of discrimination involves housing. In federally subsidized housing where there must by law be equal treatment of all citizens, many states follow the "separate but equal" policy, denying that segregation (with equivalent facilities) is a form of discrimination. This position is now widely controverted. On the other hand, many states and cities maintain a policy of nondiscrimination and nonsegregation, or "integration" in public housing.[1] The recent Supreme Court decision has weakened the old "separate but equal" principle, according to which segregation in public housing was earlier considered constitutional.

Years ago, segregated residential neighborhoods were facilitated by zoning ordinances specifying such segregation. These have since been declared unconstitutional. Nevertheless, residential segregation existed before such ordinances, and it persists even today.[2] Negroes in the South and in many cities of the North are confined to certain residential areas, where overcrowding, excessively high rents, poor community facilities, and general slum conditions often prevail. The same often applies to people of Japanese or Mexican origin and Puerto Ricans, where they are numerous, as well as to certain other minorities in various places. Such residential segregation is effected through restrictive covenants (declared unenforceable but not illegal by the United States Supreme Court), collusion among real estate dealers, refusal to rent or sell to certain people, intimidation, and so on.

[1] See Chapter 6 for questions on discrimination in public and limited dividend housing.
[2] See, for example, *In These Ten Cities:* Discrimination in Housing, Public Affairs Committee, New York, 1951.

Often, there is a fear that the influx of minority group members, particularly Negroes, into a residential section will cause land values to depreciate. This fear is frequently played upon by unscrupulous real estate dealers who stand to benefit by buying at low prices properties whose owners are apprehensive, later to resell them, either to whites or Negroes, at much higher prices.

Segregated residential neighborhoods constitute a particularly critical problem where the segregated group is increasing rapidly in population. This adds to the overcrowding which already usually exists in such neighborhoods, and makes it necessary for persons to seek residence elsewhere. With the invasion of formerly minority-free neighborhoods by the segregated group, friction arises, sometimes so bitter as to cause rioting.[1]

27. What sections of your community are characterized by substandard housing, as indicated by some of the questions in Chapter 6?
28. Which minority groups are disproportionately represented in these areas?
29. To what extent is there residential segregation of minority groups in your community, as indicated by a disproportionately high or low number of members of such groups in any neighborhood, good or bad?[2]
30. How do the rentals paid by Negroes for various types of housing accommodation compare with rentals for similar accommodations by whites?
31. Are there groups of people other than Negroes who must pay inordinately high rents for various types of housing?
32. In which groups is housing a particularly critical problem?
33. To what extent are restrictive covenants used to prevent members of various minority groups from occupancy of privately owned dwellings?[3]
34. In what other ways are minority group members kept out of certain residential areas?
35. Have any incidents involving intergroup hostility arisen in connection with housing in the past few years?
36. Is there any organized group working to preserve or strengthen residential segregation?
37. Is there any organized group working to eliminate residential segregation?
38. Is there any minority group that tends to be restricted to segregated housing but that is growing rapidly in numbers? What plans are being made to accommodate this need?
39. To what extent do hotels, tourist cabins, and other establishments offering lodging to travelers refuse to serve members of any minority group?

[1] See Lee, Alfred McClung, *Race Riots Aren't Necessary*, Public Affairs Pamphlet No. 107, New York, 1945.
[2] The assumption here is that if segregation were not operating, various groups would be distributed in various neighborhoods in approximate proportion to their number in the population. Large deviation from these proportions would indicate segregation.
[3] At your local registry of deeds, you can study the deeds themselves and determine how many include restrictive covenants.

Educational discrimination dates back to the days when it was illegal to teach a slave to read or write. In the past century enormous strides have been made toward enhancing the educational opportunities of Negroes and other minority groups, but discrimination at the time of writing was still widely prevalent. In many southern jurisdictions prior to May 17, 1954, when racial segregation in the public school systems of the nation was declared unconstitutional by the Supreme Court of the United States, segregation was mandatory in the public schools and in some private schools as well. Under the Fourteenth Amendment, all citizens are entitled to equal access to public services, but this was circumvented by the "separate but equal" policy in educational and other facilities. The facilities for the segregated group seldom were equal in fact, however. Nevertheless, important gains had been achieved in improving segregated facilities and large breaches in the "separate but equal" doctrine had occurred at all levels of education, particularly in the graduate schools, where the lack of "equal" facilities had necessitated admitting Negroes. Racial and religious discrimination still existed, however, to some extent on the college level, both in public and private institutions throughout the country.[1]

Some states had no laws directly dealing with educational segregation. Others made it obligatory, while still others prohibited it. Different provisions were sometimes made for education on different levels. Even where it is explicitly prohibited by law, segregation often exists, supported by unofficial practices, intimidation, public opinion, "custom," and so on.

Some years will elapse before the full impact of the Supreme Court decision has permeated the nation's public schools. As cities and states begin to respond, of course, many of the following questions will lose their relevancy.

40. Prior to May, 1954, did your state have a law dealing with educational segregation?
   Did the law prohibit segregation? Permit segregation but not require it? Require segregation?
41. On what educational levels did the law operate:
   Elementary   High school   College or other post-secondary institutions
42. What provisions of the law, if any, applied to private as well as to public schools and colleges?
43. What agency was charged with enforcing this law? What action has been taken with regard to reported violations in the past three years?

[1] See Ashmore, Harry S., *The Negro and the Schools*, University of North Carolina Press, Chapel Hill, 1954; and *Segregation and the Schools*, Public Affairs Pamphlet No. 209, New York, 1954.

44. If your state practiced segregation in its public schools, what steps have been taken in response to the Supreme Court decision of May, 1954, making such segregation unconstitutional?

45. Aside from the statutory law, what are the actual conditions with respect to educational discrimination in your community?

46. Do all children have equal access to the public schools?

47. If your school system is segregated how do the facilities, teaching staff, and other items compare with those for whites? (See Chapter 7 for questions on which comparisons can be made.)

48. If you do not have a segregated school system, how does the proportion of teachers who are Negroes or members of other minority groups compare with the proportion of such persons in the general population?

49. Do the private schools discriminate in their admissions policies, either deliberately or by subterfuge?

50. Do the private colleges discriminate in their admissions policies?

51. If there is an anti-discrimination law, does this law make it illegal to inquire as to a person's race, nationality background, or religion for use as a possible condition of admission?

52. Do private schools or colleges ask apparently innocuous questions which nevertheless supply them with information they can use in discrimination, such as mother's maiden name, parents' place of birth, and so on?

Discrimination in public services, civil rights, and associations. Discriminatory treatment of minority groups takes place in varying degrees along a broad front of community services and public accommodations. There is often differential treatment in the services provided by government, including public assistance, public health work, public recreation facilities, public transportation, public washroom and toilet facilities, and similar matters. Likewise, in private or commercial facilities, there is much segregation. Some youth groups maintain segregated recreational facilities for boys' or girls' clubs. Commercial establishments such as theaters, restaurants, bowling alleys, department and other stores often discourage or bar minority groups from their patronage.

53. Can you find out if there is differential treatment of minority groups in public assistance, regardless of state law or stated policy?
   For example, do Negroes in similar circumstances receive the same allotments as whites?

54. Are there other forms of differential treatment in the public welfare program?

55. Do minority groups receive equal treatment with respect to such public health services as:

Public health nursing	Immunization clinics
Enforcement of sanitary code	Other

56. Are public or private clinic and hospital facilities open to all who need them?
   Is there segregation of racial or other minority groups in the use of such facilities? If so, are the segregated facilities "equal" to the others?
57. Are Negro physicians and nurses admitted to the staff of hospitals?
58. Are public recreational facilities such as parks, playgrounds, civic auditoriums, and swimming pools restricted in any way for certain minority groups?
59. If segregation is the declared policy, are there "equal" facilities for the segregated group?
60. Is segregation permitted or required on local transportation facilities? On railroads and bus lines?
61. Make a list of different types of recreational facilities (see Chapter 8) and for each type indicate whether minority discrimination is nonexistent, occasional, or widely prevalent.
62. Make a list of types of stores and service establishments (see Chapter 3) and in the case of each type indicate whether minority discrimination is nonexistent, occasional, or widely prevalent.
63. What developments in the past few years indicate a tendency toward less discrimination in the availability of public facilities?

Although the right of all citizens to equal protection of the laws and their right to vote are assured by the Fourteenth and Fifteenth Amendments to the Constitution, nevertheless there is considerable discrimination in law enforcement and in the exercise of the right to vote and hold office. Although discrimination in voting behavior is difficult to detect, nevertheless there are many instances where the race, religion, or nationality background of a candidate has operated in his favor or against him. In many northern cities and states, the important political power of many minority groups has encouraged a practice involving a type of "reverse discrimination," in which each party deliberately sprinkles its slate with representatives of each of the important minorities in order to attract their vote. Where minority group status, rather than qualifications, becomes the important issue, discrimination is involved just as much as when it operates to the individual's disadvantage.

However, this practice constitutes far less of a problem than the deprivation or enfringement of the right to vote. Historically, this has been effected in the case of southern Negroes through a variety of different and sometimes ingenious devices, including "literacy" tests, intimidation, "grandfather" clauses, and so on. Poll taxes have operated against the Negro in two ways. First, they are often overlooked or paid for by other parties in the case of whites but not Negroes; second, Negroes, being usually poorer, are less able to pay the tax. In addition, restriction of Negroes from voting in party primaries has been effective, because traditionally the Democratic primary determines who will ultimately be elected. This practice has been declared unconstitutional by the Supreme Court.

Another area of infringement of civic rights is discrimination in law enforcement. Considerable leeway must be permitted to law enforcement officials such as policemen, sheriffs, district attorneys, and judges. Often they discriminate against members of different races or other minority groups. They may enforce the law rigorously in the case of the minority group, only loosely if at all in the case of the others. Or witnesses may refuse to testify against persons indicted for a crime against a member of a minority group; or brutal police methods, search without warrant, intimidation, and so on, may be employed. In instances where some people can rely on law enforcement officials being helpful and cooperative if they get in trouble, while others can expect only hostility and harsh treatment, the discrimination problem is serious.

64. Does your state have a law prohibiting racial intermarriage? What races are specified? What are the penalties?
65. Can you get estimates from party or election officials as to what percentage of the eligible voters in significant minority groups actually voted in the last two elections?
66. How does this compare with the percentage of all eligible voters who vote?
67. Does your state have a poll tax?
68. In what ways, if at all, are pressures applied to minority groups not to exercise their right to vote?
69. Are minority groups encouraged or discouraged from participating in political party activities, primaries, and so on?
70. To what extent have minority group problems become political issues in recent local elections?
71. How closely do political campaign slates reflect the relative strength of various minority groups in the electorate?
72. Are there any Negroes occupying elective or appointive office in your local government?
73. Do various law enforcement officials give evidence of prejudiced attitude toward certain minority groups?
74. Does a check of court records and sentences indicate that people convicted of similar offenses receive similar sentences, regardless of race, creed, or nationality?
75. Has there been any indication of such discrimination in law enforcement as:
    Police brutality and "third degree" methods against members of minority groups who are arrested
    Intimidation of members of minority groups by law enforcement officials

> Refusal to prosecute or to testify against persons accused of crimes against minority group members
>
> Failure of police to give adequate protection to minority group members who need it
>
> Unequal enforcement of certain laws

Discrimination in voluntary organizations and informal groupings is sometimes easy, sometimes extremely difficult to detect. Some organizations have specific clauses in their constitution or charter which exclude membership by certain racial, nationality, or religious groups. Others, while they have no such written provisions, just as effectively bar such persons. The absence of minority group membership in a particular organization may have only a most indirect bearing on discrimination, if any. Certain organizations by their very nature are selective. Religious organizations may confine themselves to membership in a particular denomination, other organizations may be centered around people of interests and qualifications which are not widespread among certain minority groups. Thus, the local historical society may have no foreign-born merely because it is composed, for other reasons, of well-established families whose forebears have been in the community for centuries. This may be snobbishness, but not necessarily discrimination against minorities.

The right of people to associate together voluntarily on any legal basis of common interests is an important right. For this reason, many people who regret the snobbishness, exclusiveness, or downright prejudice of certain voluntary organizations which deliberately discriminate in membership, nevertheless oppose any move to force them to admit to membership anyone whom they do not want. At the same time they may regret that such policies prevent people from being considered according to their own individual personality, merit, likeability, or whatever, and instead place them in artificial categories of undesirability according to race, religion, or nationality.

76. List the organizations in your community, or if they are too numerous, list the types of organization. (See Chapter 16.)

77. Which organizations have in their constitution a clause barring membership to members of a particular race, religion, nationality background, or the like?[1]

78. Which organizations, regardless of whether or not they have a membership clause, actually do discourage or prevent membership by members of any minority group?

[1] In answering this question, try to differentiate between membership specifications which have to do with bona fide similarity of interest, rather than the avoidance of membership by members of minority groups thought to be "undesirable."

79. In the case of organizations with restrictive membership clauses, has any move been made in recent years to get rid of these provisions?
80. Are there any organizations whose program includes promotion of ethnic or racial antagonism, such as anti-Semitism, opposition to Negroes, Mexicans, Puerto Ricans, various Oriental groups?

Programs to Improve Intergroup Relations

Substantial progress in the field of intergroup relations has been made in the past few years, particularly with regard to removing discrimination and otherwise implementing the civil rights of minorities. Some of the most notable gains have been in the opening up of new vocational opportunities to groups which formerly were effectively barred from them; the opening of housing projects for mixed occupancy; the declaration of segregation in the public schools to be unconstitutional; the withdrawal of discriminatory membership provisions in labor unions, fraternities, and other organizations, and the implementing of the Negroes' constitutional right to vote and hold office. Large areas of discrimination and hostility remain. Particularly in the field of housing, serious outbreaks still occur, and in all of the items mentioned above much progress remains to be made.

The improvement of intergroup relations takes place on different levels. Many recent gains against discrimination have been made through Supreme Court decisions which have declared unconstitutional various laws restricting the rights of different groups of American citizens, particularly Negroes. At the other extreme, perhaps, there is the gradual, unorganized attrition against discriminatory practices which are not in accord with basic professed American ideals of justice and equality. More directly pertinent for our purposes, there is the deliberate, planned activity of various organizations working in the field of race relations. They conduct continuous programs of education, promote intergroup fellowship programs, bring to court cases where statutory rights have been violated, and in other ways work to improve intergroup relations. While some of these organizations confine their efforts to one particular minority group, others direct themselves to a much wider field. Most of them recognize that poor intergroup relations arise out of complex social and individual contexts. A few organizations are particularly noteworthy in the scope of their activities, the size of their staff, or the number of people connected with them. These are the Common Council for American Unity, National Association for the Advancement of Colored People, National Urban League, National Conference of Christians and Jews, and the Anti-Defamation League of B'nai B'rith.[1]

[1] For addresses, see List of Agencies, pp. 363ff.

Although studies of the effectiveness of various types of program in intergroup relations have only recently come to be made in any great number, the following principles are accepted as widely applicable:

It is easier to combat discrimination than prejudice.

In most situations, close association on the basis of equal status reduces prejudice.

Where discrimination is removed, therefore, a reduction in prejudice often results.

Legislation against certain forms of discrimination has been found to be effective, but not a cure-all. People are generally willing to obey reasonable laws which are in accordance with basic American ideals of justice and equality.

In removing segregation, the dire predictions made by the advocates of segregation usually do not occur. Apparently, in many instances, it is easier to get objectors to go along with a nonsegregated policy after it is put into effect than before.

Prejudice is related to the personality organization of the individual, but is also related to the structure of the social system.

Intergroup relations constitute not an isolated problem but one closely interwoven with such others as economic well-being, housing, recreational facilities, and so on.

"One-shot" educational measures, such as an individual film, lecture, or pamphlet have little measurable effectiveness. A broad, many-pronged approach is required, including education, appeals to American ideals, pressure by organized groups, legislation, court cases, and other methods.

Efforts, to be effective, should persist over a period of time and be part of a continuous program.

Educational efforts are most effective when directed to people who are in situations where the new learnings can be applied: workers or managers in industry, children in mixed schools, police who confront problems of intergroup relations, for example.

Fellowship programs, by whatever name, within which people of different groups work, play, go to school, worship, or otherwise participate with equal status are usually effective in reducing prejudice and fostering improved understanding.[1]

81. What organizations in your community are active in the field of intergroup relations as their major concern? As a regular part of their program?

82. What courses or study units in the school curriculum give particular attention to the subject of intergroup tensions and improved intergroup relations?

---

[1] The following books or booklets contain summaries of research and experience in the field with different types of program: Watson, Goodwin, *Action for Unity*, Harper and Bros., New York, 1947; Allport, Gordon W., *The Nature of Prejudice*, Addison-Wesley Publishing Co., Cambridge, Mass., 1954; and Williams, Robin M., Jr., *The Reduction of Intergroup Tensions: A Survey of Research on Problems of Ethnic, Racial, and Religious Group Relations*, Social Science Research Council, New York, 1947.

83. In such courses, or when such units are studied, what is the nature of the factual knowledge taught?
    What is the nature of the· moral or other admonition of the teachers?
84. In schools which are interracial or which are attended by children of various minority groups, what is the general tenor of the intergroup relations?
    Have there been any incidents of friction in recent years?
85. How extensive is the literature in the school or public library dealing with intergroup relations?
86. What adult education programs have involved courses, units, projects, or discussions on intergroup relations in the public school system? In programs by other organizations?[1]
87. What organizations in your community distribute pamphlets, leaflets, posters, and other educational material in the field of intergroup relations?
88. To what extent do newspapers, radio, and other mass communication media carry educational features on intergroup relations, and what is the general tenor of such features?
89. Do newspapers and radio accentuate minority group divisions by emphasizing, in connection with crime stories, the race, religion, or nationality of the individuals involved?
90. What conferences or institutes have been held in the past two years in your community on some aspect of intergroup relations?
91. Has your community ever held an intergroup or interracial clinic in which leaders from various racial, religious, or nationality groups have met to discuss freely intergroup problems in such fields as education, housing, recreation, and so on, with a view to developing programs of improvement?
92. Do the churches and other organizations in your community celebrate Brotherhood Week?[2]
93. Are organizations working in the field of intergroup relations themselves composed of people who represent various minority groups in the community?
94. Have any organizations made a "community self-survey" of minority group relations following the methods developed by the Commission on Community Interrelations of the American Jewish Congress?[3]
95. Have there been any neighborhood organizations formed to welcome new-

---

[1] The National Conference of Christians and Jews publishes an outline for a short course on intergroup relations designed for clubs, labor unions, business firms, and similar organizations. Write for *America's Number One Problem:* Group Relations. For discussion groups within industry, see this organization's pamphlet entitled *Industry Looks Ahead.*

[2] See the pamphlet *Brotherhood Week in Your Community*, National Conference of Christians and Jews. 1953.

[3] See Wormser, Margot H., and Claire Selltiz, *How to Conduct a Community Self-Survey of Civil Rights*, Association Press, New York, 1951; and *Community Self-Surveys: An Approach to Social Change*, the Spring, 1949, issue of the *Journal of Social Issues*, vol. 5.

comers of different racial or religious groups and work toward preventing or easing any tensions which might arise?[1]

96. Have there, on the other hand, been organizations of people formed to keep out members of any minority groups from any particular residential neighborhood, public recreation facility, school, and so on?

97. Have there been any programs to open up new employment opportunities for members of minority groups, particularly Negroes?[2]

98. How many unions now have no official policy of discrimination against admitting members of any minority group to full participating status?

99. Of these, how many unions have opened their doors in the past five years?

100. Are there particular occupations or industries in which notable advances in opening employment opportunities to minority groups have been made within the past rive years?

101. To what extent do opportunities for close association exist between groups which previously have been segregated in:

Public schools   Religious organizations
Private schools   Industry
Summer camps   Housing projects
Public recreational facilities Other situations
  (specify)

102. Do the police in your community receive special training in intergroup relations?[3]

103. Has your local municipality a Mayor's Committee on Race Relations or on Civil Rights, however titled?

104. What are its functions? Powers? Accomplishments?[4]

105. Does your police department or other agency maintain a "barometer" of race relations?[5]

106. Have any intergroup festivals involving characteristic music, folk dances, costumes, and other cultural characteristics been held in your community in recent years?

[1] See the pamphlet *Are You Getting Good Neighbors?* Community Relations Service, 386 Fourth Ave., New York 16.

[2] Two national organizations carry on extensive programs in helping business firms and industrial companies expand their employment opportunities for minority groups in such a manner as to avoid unnecessary friction and improve intergroup relations: The National Urban League and the American Friends Service Committee. Read *Ever Widening Horizons*, a pamphlet published by the former organization in 1951.

[3] See *A Guide to Race Relations for Police Officers*, American Council on Race Relations, Chicago, 1945; and *The Police and Minority Groups*, International City Managers' Association, Chicago, 1944.

[4] See *Manual for Official Committees*, American Council on Race Relations, Chicago, 1945. This is an excellent manual for such committees.

[5] Such a "barometer" consists of a systematic listing of incidents of hostility which occur, including information on the minority groups involved, the place of occurrence, the type of incident, and similar matters. This allows officials to keep a check on such incidents and to notice when they grow in frequency, and take prompt preventive action where indicated.

107. Has any anti-discriminatory legislation, ordinance, or executive order been enacted in your community in recent years in any of the following fields:

Education   Anti-lynching law   Employment   Housing
Poll tax   Anti-defamation law   Transportation   Other

What are its provisions?
108. If no anti-discriminatory legislation has been enacted in these fields, is any attempt being made to pass such legislation?

References for Further Study

Berry, Brewton, *Race Relations:* The Interaction of Ethnic and Racial Groups. Houghton Mifflin Co., Boston, 1951. Although minority group relations are involved, this book concerns itself more broadly with the patterns of interaction which arise wherever racially or culturally diverse groups meet.

Community Relations Manual. American Council on Race Relations, Chicago, 1945. This attempts to outline activities in the intergroup relations field, for both official and unofficial organizations.

Ellison, Jerome, *These Rights Are Ours to Keep.* Public Affairs Pamphlet No. 140, New York, 1948. This is a summary of the findings of the President's Committee on Civil Rights (see page 272) presented in popular form.

Forster, Arnold, *A Measure of Freedom.* Doubleday and Co., Garden City, N.Y., 1950. Lest the reader think that anti-Semitism is a dead issue, this book documents concerted anti-Semitic movements in recent years.

Group Tensions in the United States: An Outline for Community Study. American Association of University Women, Washington, D.C., 1948. This pamphlet discusses briefly the nature of the problem, then inventories some of the things which have been done by various AAUW branches, and then makes suggestions for a community study of the problem.

Let's Look at Ourselves: A Brief Guide for Conducting A Community Audit. Community Relations Service, New York, no date. This brief pamphlet includes many practical suggestions for making a survey of discriminatory practices in your community.

Stewart, Maxwell S., *The Negro in America.* Public Affairs Pamphlet No. 95, New York, 1944. This is a popularly written summary of Gunnar Myrdal's *An American Dilemma,* which in turn is a comprehensive review of the Negro situation in the United States.

"To Secure These Rights" in Your *Community:* A Manual for Discussion, Fact-Finding, and Action in State and Local Communities. American Council on Race Relations, Chicago, 1948. This booklet was designed to be a practical follow-up to the report of the President's Committee on Civil Rights. It is a useful guide to action.

16. Associations

ONE OF THE OUTSTANDING CHARACTERISTICS of American community living is the great number and variety of clubs, organizations, societies, leagues, and similar associations into which people group themselves and through which they pursue their interests. They are usually characterized by a definite membership, a formal structure including assigned positions for leaders, officers, and other workers in the organization, regular meetings, and a name. Often they are affiliated with larger, more inclusive groups. A century ago, a great European observer reported: "Wherever, at the head of some new undertaking, you see the government in France, or a man of rank in England, in the United States you will be sure to find an association."[1] Undoubtedly one of the reasons for this plethora of associations lies in the nature of our society, in which large areas of important activities have been left for action outside the official channels of government. But even in fields where government is active, associations abound to perform additional functions, to pioneer with new developments, to conduct educational programs, and to influence governmental policy.

Thus, a whole series of associations parallels the various branches and activities of government and extends into many areas where government is relatively inactive. The outline of different types of associations offered below repeats, with few changes, the chapter outline of this book. In every significant aspect of community living, organizations abound. We have seen these organizations operating in connection with studying the various topics considered in the different chapters. The present chapter is designed to pull much of this material together for purposes of comparison and summary, and to examine primarily the organizations themselves rather than the topics with which they are concerned.

Although organizations are plentiful, they do not reach all elements of the population equally. Various studies have indicated that only about half of the people of the country are actively associated with any type of

[1] de Tocqueville, Alexis, *Democracy in America*. Oxford University Press, New York, 1947, p. 319.

organization.[1] These studies indicate that in general it is the people in the higher-income brackets, the better-educated, those having high prestige who are most active in organizations, and that most of those at the opposite end of the scale are largely inactive. There is considerable indication that those in lower-income brackets tend to associate more with people in informal groups than in formal ones, particularly with relatives. This fact indicates that large numbers of the persons who need it most are not being reached through membership in health, recreational, and other types of organizations. It also indicates the importance of the informal network of the community in ordinary day-to-day association among community members, particularly those with lower incomes. (See Chapter 20.)

Types of Associations

For our purposes, the most useful outline of different types of association is one based on the principal function of the organization, such as recreation, religion, and so on. It has the additional advantage of permitting a fairly close correspondence to the chapter outline of this book. Nevertheless, in working with any outline for classifying different organizations, one finds considerable overlapping caused by the fact that most organizations are multi-functional. For example, a young people's church club is usually both religious and recreational, the local grange usually has recreational, vocational, and religious functions. For this reason, associations are best classified according to their primary function, with other functions being given due consideration.

Another word of caution with regard to organizational functions concerns the difference between stated and actual functions. A "service club" may be more important for its function of developing the business "contacts" of the individual member than in rendering service to the community. The principal decisions on community developments may be made at the country club rather than in the council of social agencies, even though the stated classification of the country club might be "recreational."

In this part of your study you will be in an advantageous position if you can procure a list of associations. The council of social agencies, a federation

[1] See especially Komarovsky, Mirra, "The Voluntary Associations of Urban Dwellers," *American Sociological Review*, vol. 11, December, 1946; Knupfer, Genevieve, "Portrait of the Underdog," *Public Opinion Quarterly*, vol. 12, Spring, 1947; Dotson, Floyd, "Patterns of Voluntary Association Among Urban Working-Class Families," *American Sociological Review*, vol. 16, October, 1951; Freedman, Ronald, and Morris Axelrod, "Who Belongs to What in a Great Metropolis?" *Adult Leadership*, vol. 1, November, 1952; and Kaufman, Harold F., *Participation in Organized Activities in Selected Kentucky Localities*, Kentucky Agricultural Experiment Station Bulletin 528, Lexington, 1949.

of women's clubs, community council, chamber of commerce, or some similar organization may have compiled such a list. If there is a city directory, you may find a separate listing of various organizations. In none of these cases should the list be relied on exclusively, for such lists are seldom complete. Indeed, some of these very organizations may want to make use of your list when you have finished this part of your study. The local newspaper may also be able to supply you with a list, and if not, a perusal of a month's issues of the newspaper at two different times during the year should give you an extensive list to use as a nucleus. If you examine newspaper files for club notices, you will often be able to pick up additional information which will be useful in connection with the material outlined in the second section of this chapter.

1. List the organizations in your community under the appropriate headings in the following outline:[1]

a. *Economic groups*
   Service clubs
   Chamber of commerce
   Vocational groups
     Unions
     Retail merchants association
     Farmers association
     Boards of banks, corporations
     Professional associations

b. *Government groups*
   Political party organizations
   Good government leagues
   Patriotic and veterans associations
   Taxpayers associations

c. *Planning groups*
   Neighborhood planning associations
   Community planning associations
   Community councils

d. *Housing groups*
   Real estate associations
   Housing associations

e. *Education groups*
   Better schools groups
   Parent-teacher organizations
   Adult education groups

f. *Fraternal groups*
   Nationality group fraternal associations
   Other fraternities, lodges, secret societies

g. *Recreation groups*
   Athletic teams
   Athletic clubs
   Hobby clubs
   Social enjoyment groups

h. *Religious groups*
   Churches and synagogues
   Groups associated with churches and synagogues
     Primarily religious (Bible study groups, worship groups)
     Other (clubs, teams, social groups)

i. *"Cultural" groups*
   Concert societies
   Study and forum groups
   Art societies
   Dramatic groups
   Literary societies

[1] In most cases, an entire chapter of this book is devoted to the topic of each major heading.

j. *Welfare groups*
  Charitable organizations
  Boards of social agencies
  Welfare or humane associations

k. *Groups for children and youth*
  Child welfare organizations
  Big brother movement
  Police athletic league
  Youth organizations

l. *Health groups*
  General community health groups
  Groups on specific diseases (cancer
    society, heart society, etc.)
  Safety council

m. *Intergroup relations groups*
  General groups
  Groups serving one particular
    minority

n. *Community organization groups*
  Chests
  Councils
  Coordinating committees
  Federations of clubs
  Other intergroup agencies or
    organizations

Characteristics of Individual Associations

The extent to which you gather detailed material on each organization will depend on the purposes of your study. If a simple listing of different organizations will suffice, there is little need of gathering some of the detailed information listed below. Or you may be interested only in those organizations having a bearing on your special field of study. If, on the other hand, an intensive study is being made, you may want to expand some questions or add still others. If you go into any detail, it will probably be necessary to duplicate the following list and supply data for each organization with the help of one of the officers or active members. Care in standardizing the manner of recording the material will enable you to make analyses of the pattern of associational life of your community as indicated in the following section.

In connection with membership limitations, stated or actual, you may want to be alert to discrimination against minority groups, where present. (See Chapter 15.) In the same connection, and in view of the fact that much organizational activity does not encompass people from the lowest socioeconomic groups, you may want to consider how representative of the interests and needs of *all* the citizens your community organizations actually are.

Functions and activities vary greatly, even among organizations listed under the same classification. Some organizations may confine their activities to passive listening or other perfunctory attention to their field of interest. On the other hand, organizations may perform volunteer services, campaign for progressive legislation, promote community projects, present

forum programs and workshops, run demonstration programs, and in other
ways be extremely active.

2. For each organization listed in the previous section, supply the following
   information:

Name	Meeting time and place
Principal function	Address (if different from
Other functions	meeting place)

   Is the organization for males, females, or both?

Number of members	Age of members
Male	Adults
Female	Teen-agers
	Children

3. Is membership by families or individuals? If by families, how many families
   are members?
4. Are the membership provisions or limitations as to age, sex, religious or
   other limitations[1] stated? Actual but "unwritten"?
5. To what extent is the membership representative of all income groups,
   minority groups, residential neighborhoods, and so on?
6. General description of the type of people who belong, as to income, residence,
   cultural group, education.
7. Average attendance.
8. What special physical facilities does the organization have to offer?
9. What special services on community matters is it capable of performing?
10. What is its program? What are its accomplishments as to:
    Educational work
    Cultural achievements
    Community improvement projects
    Successful campaigns for needed legislation
    Other
11. List of present officers and offices they hold.
12. List, if desired, of other outstanding workers in the organization.
13. Is there a paid executive or staff? If so, describe.
14. Is it geographically a local (neighborhood) group? Communitywide group?
    County or regional group?
15. With which organizations in the community does it cooperate? In what
    ways?
16. Is it affiliated with another group in the community? List only the more-
    inclusive groups of which it is a part, not the smaller groups which are a
    part of it.
17. Is it affiliated with an organization outside the community as an autonomous
    unit in a loose federation with policy determined locally? As a branch of
    a larger organization with policy determined elsewhere?

[1] See Chapter 15.

The Pattern of Associations in Your Community

If you have carefully recorded the information listed in the previous section for each organization in your community, you will be able to make many interesting analyses which will help you understand the structure and operation of associations in your community. A few additional questions may be answered from personal observation or from interviews with people who are close to the organizations involved.

18. How many groups are primarily concerned with each of the functions listed in the first section—economic, government, planning, and so on?
19. How many groups are exclusively for males? Females? How many groups are mixed?
20. How many are for specific age-groups? How many for those of all ages?
21. Which groups are based on family membership?
22. In what type of organization do you find various types of membership restrictions?
23. In what type of association do you find very unbalanced membership as to income, residence, cultural group, and so on?
24. What organizations have been most effective in accomplishments of communitywide importance?
25. Make a list of the people who are officers or important workers in more than one organization.
26. What paid professional organization workers does your community have?
27. What neighborhoods seem to be highly organized, poorly organized with respect to associations?
28. What outside organizations have affiliates or branches in your community?
29. What percentage of the total organizations are affiliated with local religious groups?
30. Which groups are most influential in "getting things done" in the community? Which are the high-prestige groups?
31. Which groups are the most exclusive?
32. What income groups, minority groups, or other groups are not being reached through membership in various types of community associations?
33. Do any groups constitute problems to the further harmonious development of the community—groups spreading hostility toward minorities, or obstructing needed community improvements for selfish reasons?
34. What rivalries exist between the various organizations of the community? Are any of these harmful to the community?
35. Are there "too many organizations"? In which particular type of activity?
36. Is there a community calendar?
37. Which organizations are the most important in "reaching" various publics, or groups of people? That is to say, if you want to get something done that depends on the cooperation of these respective groups, which organizations would be in the best position to help you:

Housewives	Minority groups
Wage-earners	Businessmen
Professional people	People from various neighborhoods
Consumers	

References for Further Study

Adult Leadership. This periodical is published monthly by the Adult Education Association of the United States of America. Each issue is devoted to a specific theme, such as getting and keeping members, programs, leadership, and so on. It applies the newer approaches from the field of "group dynamics" to the problems of voluntary groups.

Brown, Ann C., and Sally B. Geis, *Handbook for Group Leaders.* Woman's Press, New York, 1952. This guidebook for clubwomen has to do chiefly with the internal activities of committees and clubs. It is a useful handbook for people who are active in the various organizations.

Gunn, Selskar M., and Philip S. Platt, *Voluntary Health Agencies:* An Interpretive Study. Ronald Press Co., New York, 1945. Devoted particularly to health organizations, this book is basic reading for anyone seeking knowledge on the structure and function of voluntary organizations in American life.

Lindeman, Eduard C., *Motivations of Volunteers in Community Service.* Community Chests and Councils of America, Inc., and National Social Welfare Assembly, 1949. An interesting study of the motivations of volunteers in various communities in different parts of the country, reported in simple language, with actual tabulations of answers to each of the questions asked in the questionnaire.

Read, Charles R., and Samuel Marble, *Guide to Public Affairs Organizations:* With Notes on Public Affairs Informational Materials. Public Affairs Press, Washington, D.C., 1946. A useful handbook of various national and international agencies devoted to various fields of organizational activity, with descriptions of their services.

Sanders, Irwin T., *Making Good Communities Better:* A Handbook for Civic-Minded Men and Women. rev. ed. University of Kentucky Press, Lexington, 1953. An extremely useful handbook for those interested in working through organizations for community betterment. It includes a section on guides to various activities in which organizations may enter, with advice by numerous authorities.

17. Community Organization

IF THE READER will make a quick mental review of the content of this book thus far, he will note that it has stressed community institutions, agencies, associations, laws, procedures, all directed more or less clearly at meeting human needs. If we think of these organizations as resources which enable the community to meet its needs, we may ask how well they are doing it, what areas tend to be neglected, what older areas of service are no longer needed, what is being done to avoid duplication of services, and what methods are used to continue to adapt resources to needs. This, broadly speaking, is the field of community organization.

Chapter 3 dealt with certain aspects of community organization, particularly those centering around the economic basis of the community. Chapter 5 discussed the activity which has grown up around planning commissions, with their primary historical concern for the physical aspects of the community but with their continually expanding interests. The present chapter considers, but does not confine itself to, that area of coordination and planning which centers around health, welfare, and recreational services. This is the area of "community organization" which forms one of the major established divisions of the social work field, others being social casework and social groupwork. Here, too, there is an expanding area of interest as coordinating and planning work among the social agencies involves wider and wider circles of community institutions, facilities, and organizations. Whether one starts with economic activities, or with physical planning, or with welfare agencies, one soon sees how vital to his primary interest are these other aspects of the community. Nevertheless, perhaps more as a result of historical development than of logic, these three fields of coordinating and planning activity persist relatively independently of each other in most communities.

Because the term "community organization" has a broader reference than is usually denoted when it is applied to coordination and planning in the field of health and welfare, the term "community welfare organization" has been used by some to denote this limited area of community organization,[1] and we shall employ it when we wish to confine the discussion to this field. Community organization as considered in this chapter includes the activities, organizations, and processes through which, by concerted action, a community secures the services and facilities it desires. Community welfare organization, community physical planning, and community industrial planning are all parts of community organization in this sense, as are other activities which will be discussed.

In some communities, no formal coordinating and planning agency exists, and yet planning functions are carried on by various groups. In other communities where formal agencies exist, the extent of actual coordination and planning may be slight. Most important of all is the function which is performed, whether by a city planning commission, a community welfare council, a Chamber of Commerce, or adult education group, church group, county health or welfare department, or other agency.

Particularly in smaller communities, which are less likely to have one or all of the three major types of coordinating and planning organization, a wide variety of different organizational structures are employed to perform the corresponding functions. In the developing or acquiring of new services, resources, facilities, and so on, there is no fixed organizational pattern in small communities. Suggested references at this point for a person who is interested in small communities are such books as *Small Communities in Action:* Stories of Citizen Programs at Work by Jean and Jesse Ogden,[2] *The Small Community Looks Ahead* by Wayland J. Hayes,[3] and *Kentucky on the March* by Harry W. Schacter.[4]

In larger communities with their multiplicity of agencies and organizations, various types of coordinating and planning agencies exist. They are characterized by fairly close adherence to the following well-established principles. The important agencies in the field of interest are all represented by delegates to the organization, and in some cases there may be additional memberships by individuals. These agencies themselves do not ordinarily engage in direct service, such as operating a hospital, placing children for adoption, and so on; rather, they are made up of agencies which do. Another important principle is closely allied. They work through exist-

[1] See Stroup, Herbert H., *Community Welfare Organization,* Harper and Bros., New York, 1952. This text is highly recommended as an introduction to the field. Another excellent book on an introductory level is *Community Organization and Agency Responsibility,* which includes several chapters describing the field in general, as well as a number describing a special study of interagency relations. It is written by Ray Johns and David F. DeMarche and published by the Association Press, New York, 1951.

[2] Harper and Bros., New York, 1946.

[3] Harcourt, Brace and Co., New York, 1947.

[4] Harper and Bros., New York, 1949.

ing organizations wherever possible, rather than starting new agencies, and they delegate functions as soon as practicable, so that they are free to consider other projects. Such organizations will be considered in detail later in this chapter.

Community Organization Functions

We turn now to functions relevant to community organization in the broad sense in which we have defined it. Many of these functions are appropriate to communities of all sizes. Others are appropriate only to communities large enough to have a relatively full complement of professional social agencies.

1. List some of the more important community betterment projects which have been carried out in the past five years:

    New facilities, such as hospitals, social agencies, playgrounds, and so on
    New agencies or organizations, such as health and welfare agencies, civic associations, various community interest groups
    New government services, desirable social legislation, and so on[1]
    Other
2. What agencies or organizations were instrumental in achieving each of the improvements listed above?
3. Are there any agencies or organizations specifically designed for community organization work?
4. If not, what organizations help to "get groups together" to work for common goals?
5. Have there been any studies of community needs and resources in recent years in health and welfare or in other fields?
6. By what group was each study sponsored? Conducted?
7. What action, if any, was taken on the basis of the study?

The functions mentioned in the questions which follow are often performed by special community organization agencies. However, in the absence of such an agency, they may also be performed by other organizations or agencies.

8. Is there any concerted program in which two or more agencies or organizations combine in helping the community to understand the nature and importance of their work?
9. What is done to avoid overlapping in the services provided by different agencies?
10. Are there methods by which various agencies and organizations can take

---

[1] See Bond, Elsie M., *Methods of Securing Social Welfare Legislation*, State Charities Aid Association, New York, 1941.

joint action in influencing legislation, initiating new services, working on various community projects?
What patterns of joint action can be found in your community?

11. Is there any organization which is primarily concerned with long-range community planning in the field of health and welfare, planning the physical community, or industrial development, or all three?
12. What planning activities have been carried out by such organizations? What is the current status of the plans which were developed?
13. Is there a community calendar?
14. Is there a community directory which describes social agencies and perhaps other facilities of the community?
15. If there is no community chest, is any attempt made by fund-raising organizations to coordinate their appeals or to avoid bunching them in one season of the year, or in other ways to facilitate the process?
16. Is there any agency or organization which issues permits to solicit funds, gives approval, or in other ways helps to safeguard the community against unscrupulous fund-raisers and "charity racketeers"?
17. Is there any plan according to which Christmas, Thanksgiving, and other gifts or baskets to the poor are coordinated, thus avoiding duplication of gifts, and the families most in need selected?
18. Is there any organization which helps to recruit volunteers and makes known to them the various opportunities for service with different agencies in the community?

Many of the activities referred to in the preceding questions are conducted in communities which have no specialized coordinating and planning agencies. Where the latter are present, they are often active in such endeavors. There are still other important functions which arise out of the multiplicity of agencies and needs in large communities, and which frequently, if not always, are carried on by chests or councils.

19. What has your welfare council achieved in the past five years in improving standards of service by social agencies?
20. What services or agencies have been discontinued, initiated, or consolidated as a result of studies or recommendations or agreements made by or within the welfare council?
21. What special studies of community need or of agency services have been made by one division or another of the welfare council, or by a special study group set up for the purpose, or by outside survey specialists engaged to do the research?
22. How is your local chest or council related to state or national organizations in the community welfare organization field or in particular fields of council interest such as health, family and child welfare, and recreation?

23. Is your chest or council affiliated with Community Chests and Councils of America?
24. Is there a social service exchange in your community?
25. What is its relationship to the welfare council? Is it operated by the council? Another voluntary agency? A government department?
26. What agencies participate in the social service exchange?
27. What information is listed on the index cards?
28. What safeguards are there to protect the anonymity of the client?
29. What organizations or agencies, if any, have been refused access to the social service exchange service in the past five years? Why?
30. What public or private agencies whose participation in the social service exchange is desired by other agencies nevertheless refuse to participate? Why?
31. Is there a "community trust" in your community which administers gifts and bequests for the community and permits donors to give large sums without unnecessarily restricting their use to existing services which may become obsolete?
32. Is there an information and referral bureau which individuals can consult to ascertain what agency in the community is best suited to serve their particular need?
33. Is there a common social agency building in which a large number of agency offices are concentrated, thus facilitating interchange between them, and ready referral of clients?
34. Are there other types of collaboration among social agencies, such as central bookkeeping, or joint insurance or purchasing programs?
35. What other coordinating or planning functions are carried on in your community by the welfare council, community chest, or other such agency?

Types of Community Organization Agency

There are several different types of structure through which the various organizations and agencies in the community work together for community improvement. They differ largely in size, in the extent to which they carry on direct activities themselves or delegate them to member agencies, and in the inclusiveness of their concern.

Community councils. One of the simplest organizations is a neighborhood or community council. Such an organization has as a geographic base a small community or a neighborhood of a large city.[1] In either case, it is usually composed of delegates from as many as possible of the different organizations and agencies in the area, including not only the usual social agencies but also church groups, service clubs, study clubs, labor unions,

---

[1] See Dillick, Sydney, *Community Organization for Neighborhood Development—Past and Present*, Woman's Press, New York, 1953.

and so on. It may also have members-at-large. Its purpose is community improvement in any or all of its aspects, and its method is to work through member organizations wherever possible, devoting itself to coordinating and planning, and performing only those functions which cannot be handled adequately by any existing organization. Such community councils, although they may deal with virtually any problem, not being restricted to health and welfare, nevertheless often concern themselves with limited and rather isolated projects which may need doing but which do not necessarily add up to a balanced program of coordination and planning, such as is usually carried on by a community welfare council. Neighborhood councils are often organized into a citywide association of such autonomous councils, sometimes under the wing of the community welfare council from which they may receive staff service and leadership, or sometimes under the welfare department or some other governmental auspices. Community councils may be organized on a statewide basis, as well. Such councils go by many names, including that of citizens' council, neighborhood association, and the like.[1]

Coordinating councils, originally developed in California as primarily delinquency prevention agencies, follow a similar pattern of organization. In most communities their concern with delinquency prevention has encompassed broad areas of related interest, such as housing, recreation, education, and so on, while in some communities the program is so broad as to fit the description of a community council.

36. Is there a local community organization of the community council type, such as a neighborhood council, citizens' council, coordinating council, neighborhood association, and so on?
37. If so, what organizations are members of this council?
38. Does the council also have as members-at-large individual citizens who are members in their own right?
39. Does its membership include practically all the socially significant organizations in your community, or only a small portion?
40. What branches, divisions, standing committees does the community council have?
41. In what projects is it now engaged?
42. What have been the principal accomplishments of the community council in the past five years?
43. Is the council affiliated with an association of such councils in the city, in the county, or in the state?

[1] For procedure in organizing community councils, as well as further material on their structure and functions, see such pamphlets as *Community Council Handbook*, Association of Community Councils, Pittsburgh, 1950; *Teamwork in the Community:* The Why and How of Community Councils, Wisconsin Community Organization Committee, Madison, 1951; and *Organizing A Community Council*, Michigan Council on Adult Education, Lansing, 1953.

Organization Chart for a Typical Council

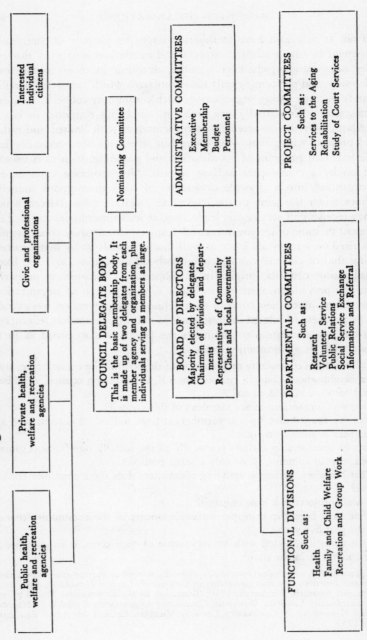

Suggested administrative structures can be simply but clearly illustrated through organization charts such as this, depicting the structure of a typical community welfare council recommended by Community Chests and Councils of America.

SOURCE: *Teamwork in Our Town: Through a Community Welfare Council*, Community Chests and Councils of America, 1954.

44. Would you conclude that the council is largely a "paper" organization, or is it carrying on a vital program in your community?

In the smaller communities, where no specific community organization agency exists, many of its functions, particularly those having to do with initiating projects, programs, or activities of communitywide value, are carried on by civic-minded organizations. The difference is that these organizations are composed directly of members, rather than being composed of member organizations. Thus, a church group, a chamber of commerce, service club, grange, or other group may perform important community organization functions, even though it is not a composite "organization of organizations," the usual distinguishing characteristic of special agencies in the community organization field.

45. In the absence of a community council or other community organization agency, which groups or organizations are particularly active in promoting programs for civic improvement, initiating new services, or carrying on activities of broad community interest?

46. What specific accomplishments of the past five years can be accredited to the efforts of one or more such groups?

Community welfare councils. Another type of agency is the community welfare council (health and welfare council, council of social agencies, and the like), which is made up of as many as possible public and voluntary agencies in the field of health,[1] welfare and recreation, in addition to other groups which have an interest in its activities, such as labor unions, women's clubs, and so on. Although its membership and interests may not be so broad as those of the typical community council, it is more likely to have a full and balanced program within its area of interest. In addition to professional and lay board member delegates from the various agencies, it also may have members-at-large. It is usually organized into such functional divisions as health, family and child welfare, and recreation, and frequently performs certain common services for the various agencies, such as social service exchange, volunteer service committee, central information service, community calendar, Christmas Bureau, and so forth.[2] There are six fairly well-established areas of program for these councils: (1) coordination, (2) fact-finding, (3) joint action, (4) improving quality of service, (5) providing common services, and (6) developing public understanding.[3] According to Community Chests and Councils of America, which is the national agency serving these councils and whose symbol is the red feather, there

---

[1] Sometimes health agencies and hospitals are not included.
[2] See chart on p. 298.
[3] *Teamwork in Our Town:* Through a Community Welfare Council. Community Chests and Councils of America, Inc., New York, 1950.

are now more than 450 communities in the United States and Canada that have a specialized agency such as a community welfare council devoted to health and welfare planning.

47. Does your community have a community welfare council (health and welfare council, council of social agencies, etc.) which coordinates effort and carries on planning in the health, welfare, and recreational fields?

48. Is the welfare council comprised of agencies in the city or town, or is it countywide? Is it affiliated with Community Chests and Councils of America?

49. List its members in each of the following classes:
   Public health, welfare, and recreation agencies
   Voluntary health, welfare, and recreation agencies
   Civic and professional organizations
   Individual citizens

50. To what extent are labor and other general community groups encouraged to cooperate through "labor participation committees" or other means?

51. Are there any important health and welfare agencies in the community which are not members? Why?

52. What regular departments does the council maintain:

Social service exchange	Christmas bureau
Information and reference bureau	Public relations department
	Research department
Volunteer service bureau[1]	

53. To what extent are the main projects of the council carried on by separate functional committees in such fields as health, family and child welfare, and recreation; or by the board of directors; or by the delegate body?

54. Does membership in the council constitute approval of program by the council, or does membership carry no such implication?

55. To what extent does the council exercise authority, either direct or indirect, over the member agencies as regards their standards, activities, quality of personnel, budget, and so forth?

56. List the principal functions of the council. (See questions on pages 294 to 296.)

57. What have been the outstanding accomplishments of the welfare council during the past few years?

58. What is the relation of the council to the community chest?

59. How many are on the paid professional staff of the council? What is their professional preparation?
How many clerks and other nonprofessional personnel are there on the staff?

60. In the opinion of informed persons, to what extent is the council dominated by professional personnel from member agencies, or by lay personnel from member agency boards and members-at-large?

[1] See *Handbook on the Organization and Operation of a Volunteer Service Bureau,* Community Chests and Councils of America, Inc., New York, 1946.

An important function of a council is to promote cooperative understanding and agreements between public and voluntary agencies.

61. In each of the major functional fields represented in the council what agreements are in effect between public and voluntary agencies in regard to:
Respective functions of each
Types of problems each will accept on transfer from the other
Types of problems on which the agencies will work jointly
Other matters of mutual relationship

Community chests and united funds. A coordinating agency concerned primarily with joint financial campaigns is the community chest. There are nearly two thousand chests in the country today which are known to Community Chests and Councils of America, and an unknown number of additional campaigns which are not affiliated with this organization. Community chests vary all the way from relatively small efforts of local organizations to unite their fund-raising campaigns, without any professional help, to large organizations staffed with many workers employed on a year-round basis. Community chests are organizations whose membership is representative of contributors, community groups, and social agencies. In addition to providing for efficiency, adequacy, and continuity in fund-raising, they also facilitate budgeting according to community needs and sound fiscal principles, and promote public understanding, coordination of efforts, and coordinated planning.[1] In some communities the community chest is combined with the community welfare council, while in others the organizations are separately administered. Close collaboration is, of course, always desirable, particularly in the field of budgeting and public relations.[2]

Many state and national organizations do not participate in the community chest, preferring to conduct their own campaigns. Since the community chest is based on the idea of united fund-raising, separate campaigns constitute a problem.[3] In some instances, employee groups have organized federated funds, according to which a particular group, perhaps the workers in a plant, combine all plant contributions for all campaigns, including the community chest, into a single inclusive campaign effort. In a growing number of instances, a communitywide united fund has been able to gain the participation of the local community chest as well as state and national agencies which raise money in the community.

[1] Ford, Lyman S., "Community Chests," *Social Work Year Book, 1951.* American Association of Social Workers, New York, 1951.
[2] Community Chests and Councils will supply model constitutions for a separate chest and a separate council, or a combined chest and council.
[3] See *Recommendation for Local and State Action to Bring About More Orderly Methods of Raising and Allocating Funds for Voluntary Health and Welfare Agencies,* Community Chests and Councils of America, Inc., New York, 1949, mimeographed.

There are separate fund-raising federations for Protestant, Jewish, or Catholic agencies in some communities. If this is the case in your community, many of the following questions will apply to them also.

62. Is there a community chest in your community? Is it affiliated with Community Chests and Councils of America?

63. How is the governing board appointed? What proportion are:
    Members of agency boards
    Agency executives
    Individual contributors without agency connection
    Representatives of labor, business, and other general community groups
    Representatives of the large number of "small contributors"

64. What was its budget last year?

65. What agencies receive funds from the community chest? How much was each agency's share last year?

66. During the past ten years, what changes have occurred in the following:
    Number of agencies participating
    Total amount allocated to local agencies
    Amount of campaign goal
    Number of contributors
    Amount pledged
    Percentage of pledges collected

67. How does your community compare with others of similar size and resources, according to figures published annually in *Community*, the news bulletin of Community Chests and Councils of America?

68. What organizations cooperate with the work of the community chest?

69. Are only local agencies listed in the community chest or are there any state or national agencies?

70. Which local, state, or national agencies refuse to participate in the community chest, preferring to carry out their own separate drives?

71. What is the relation of the community chest to the community welfare council, if there is such a council?

72. How many workers are on the paid staff of the community chest the year-round? What is the number of seasonal workers? Professional? Clerical or other?

73. If there is no community welfare council, which functions usually performed by such a council are performed by the community chest:
    Joint planning and coordination   Research
    Public relations   Other

74. Under what conditions may member agencies conduct independent appeals for funds?

75. Does the community chest have anything to do with the capital financing (as opposed to current financing) programs of agency members?

76. Are any moves being made to incorporate some of the nonparticipating

agencies into the chest, so as to reduce the number of separate financial campaigns?

77. Are there any "federated funds" in your community?

78. Does your community chest maintain an "open door" policy, being willing to admit any *bona fide* local, state, or national agency which might otherwise conduct a separate campaign in the community?

79. Is there an over-all communitywide "united fund" combining local, state and national agency campaigns in your community?

80. Is there a county or state fund which performs functions similar to a community chest on a county or state level?

Is the campaign geared to that of the local chest, or separate from it?

Other coordinating groups. Particularly in the larger cities, the various divisions of the welfare council may be more or less autonomous councils in their own right, such as a health council, recreation council, and so on. Best practice calls for a close functional relationship between such councils, since so many matters are of mutual concern.

Certain other groups, treated elsewhere in this book, may be affiliated on a communitywide basis, particularly in large cities. These may include organizations in various degrees of relationship to the welfare council, some of them being an organic part, others not even closely related. Included here would be denominational federations of welfare agencies, hospital councils, youth councils, councils of churches, city planning and housing groups, economic development groups, and federations of clubwomen.

The pattern of public and voluntary agencies and citizens' associations in a large city is extremely complex, and often some degree of communitywide coordination in the relatively independent areas of community welfare organization, city planning, and economic development is all that can be expected. Some large communities have gone a step beyond this in the attempt to relate all of these types of activity—governmental, voluntary agency, and citizens' association. The result is a communitywide development organization, an over-all planning body, such as the Syracuse and Onondaga County Post-War Planning Committee, the Allegheny Conference on Community Development, and various other conferences and councils in different large cities or metropolitan counties.

81. Aside from a community council or community welfare council, what other federations of organizations or agencies on a topical or geographic basis exist in your community:

Health council	Association of neighborhood
Hospital council	councils
Recreation council	Association of planning and
Youth council	housing organizations

Association of business or   Denominational federations of
industrial groups   welfare agencies
Federation of women's clubs   Other
Council of churches

82. In what relation does each of these associations stand to the community welfare council:
Structural part
Provision for overlapping board membership
Other formal provision for close relationship
Joint membership or office by leading citizens or leading agencies
Other

83. Is there a post-war planning council or metropolitan development association, however titled, which provides a top-level basis for coordination and planning of all significant groups and agencies, public and voluntary, including community welfare councils, community chests, industrial development groups, and city planning and housing groups?

84. Make or secure a chart of this organization's structure.

85. What are its outstanding accomplishments during the past five years?

86. What is its present program?

87. In the opinion of informed persons, is this largely a paper organization or a vital, functioning agency of your community with strong citizen support?

References for Further Study

Alinsky, Saul D., *Reveille for Radicals*. University of Chicago Press, Chicago, 1946. This extremely stimulating and controversial book describes the work of the author and his "people's organizations," which are noteworthy for their seeking out of informal leaders, their grass-roots support, and their occasional use of unorthodox methods of community action.

Buell, Bradley, and associates, *Community Planning for Human Services*. Columbia University Press, New York, 1952. Based on the famous St. Paul study, this book demonstrates the need for a more coordinated approach to dependency, ill-health, maladjustment, and recreational need.

Dunham, Arthur, editor, *Bibliography on Community Welfare Organization*. Association Press, New York, 1951. An annotated bibliography of various reading materials in community organization.

Hillman, Arthur, *Community Organization and Planning*. Macmillan Co., New York, 1950. This book is unique as a text which seeks to do justice to community planning, housing, and welfare organization.

King, Clarence, *Organizing for Community Action*. Harper and Bros., New York, 1948. A popularly written casebook of stories illustrating basic principles of community organization work in many different agencies and settings.

McMillen, Wayne, *Community Organization for Social Welfare*. University of Chicago Press, Chicago, 1945. This is the most comprehensive and authoritative text in its field. It is designed primarily for professional workers or those training for professional work, but should be intelligible to the careful layman.

Proceedings of the National Conference of Social Work. Published annually by Columbia University Press, New York. These annual proceedings contain papers delivered at the national conference. Included usually is a section on community organization.

Sanderson, Ezra D., and Robert A. Polson, *Rural Community Organization*. John Wiley and Sons, New York, 1939. Although there have been several more recent books in this field, none outlines it in so careful and balanced a fashion.

Social Work Year Book. American Association of Social Workers, New York. This is a most useful reference book on current practices in the social work field. It includes many articles bearing on community organization.

The following books depict numerous instances of constructive community endeavor by way of community improvement, community projects, planning activities, and similar matters in many communities:

Dahir, James, *Communities for Better Living:* Citizen Achievement in Organization, Design and Development. Harper and Bros., New York, 1950.

Hitch, Earle, *Rebuilding Rural America:* New Designs for Community Life. Harper and Bros., New York, 1950.

Ogden, Jean, and Jesse Ogden, *These Things We Tried*. University of Virginia, Extension Division, Charlottesville, 1947.

Poston, Richard W., *Small Town Renaissance:* A Story of the Montana Study. Harper and Bros., New York, 1950.

18. Organizing a Community Survey

OFTEN DURING THE DISCUSSION of a community problem, someone suggests, "Let's have a survey," and the other members of the group, perhaps knowing no other positive course of action, give their assent. A survey may or may not be indicated for the type of program you have in mind. We present below some considerations which might be weighed before reaching a decision.

1. Are the facts you need already available in usable form? If so, the time and money and energy spent in making a survey might possibly be put to better use in an action program, that is, in doing something to improve the existing conditions.

2. Is the survey likely to be a substitute for action? Often a survey is merely a mode of temporizing about a problem which everyone knows exists and about which there is adequate factual information to form a basis for an action program. People sometimes choose a survey so as to postpone or avoid action. Occasionally the survey is undertaken with a view toward action, but so much time and effort are spent in making an exhaustive survey that there is little energy remaining to do anything about the results.

3. Is your group an "action group"? If it wants to see definite results and to work hard in a constructive program of community action, then perhaps it should confine itself to a brief survey. In one type the procedure is simply to ask the people of a community to fill out slips stating what they think are the worst things about the community, and what they think might be done to improve it. This simple procedure often yields interesting suggestions and indicates how widely held are some of the viewpoints expressed. The suggestions received are often sufficient to keep an active group occupied for years in community improvement projects, although there may be a need for modifying the program to meet changing situations.

If your group is eager to go into action, it is important that the action be carefully thought out. Often more extensive study of the situation is required than is at first apparent. For example, some people may suggest the need for a local mental health clinic. It may be unwise to embark immediately upon a campaign to raise the necessary funds, for a survey may show that there is not a large enough population to support such a clinic, or that the clinic would actually cost many times more than was originally supposed. It may be possible to join forces with some other community and share a clinic, or there may be other ways of securing the needed services. The point here is that premature action in carrying out suggestions may be highly wasteful and inopportune.

The survey is not, and should not be, an end in itself. If the purpose is merely to assemble useful information for referral by anyone who cares to consult it, then the survey should be so planned and conducted. If it is to be part of an action program, then it should be so oriented, and only the material necessary should be solicited. Knowledge about the community has value if it is used only as an aid in the normal discharge of the duties of citizenship; or it may lead to more definite, enterprising action toward community betterment. In any case, the survey is not the end product; it is a tool to work with. The end product is a healthy, vital, growing community whose citizens are alert to its needs and possibilities and active in building the type of community they want.

Different Kinds and Uses of Surveys

The term "survey" is used with a variety of meanings. It can denote an extensive study of the needs and resources of a large community involving a large staff and extending over many months' duration, or it can denote a brief and superficial study of the "situation" of a particular organization or agency. Between these extremes lie a multitude of possibilities, and the person who is interested in making a survey will want to have a clear idea of just what he hopes to accomplish.

Experience has shown that surveys usually involve much more work and time than is anticipated. Even surveys of relatively small communities often occasion surprise on the part of laymen when they learn that their community is so complicated, or that it supports so many organizations, business establishments, and so on. And a survey of a metropolitan community may involve scores of volunteer workers headed by a professional staff of survey consultants over a period of months and even years.

The reader may want to consider some of the possibilities in survey work. He can thus measure his own or his group's resources against the size of the community and breadth of the proposed survey, and make a reasonable disposition of effort.

Surveys can be primarily for information or for action. Surveys are often conducted with no particular end in view. Groups of high-school or college students in social studies classes occasionally study their local community as a sort of social laboratory. Or members of a women's club may set out to study the local community to inform themselves on its government or some other aspect.

Such surveys have definite value. They provide learning experience for the participants, stimulate awareness of community conditions and problems, and afford a useful body of factual knowledge for those interested in learning more about their community. It is not at all unusual for such studies to lead to action as needs are uncovered and possibilities for remedial measures present themselves. Indeed, some survey chairmen find that their survey committees have become so absorbed in a particular problem which they have uncovered that they prefer to remedy this problem than to complete the survey. There is no reason why a survey group must refrain from action completely, but, of course, care should be taken that the energies of the participants do not become diffused with every new problem which presents itself.

Usually the purpose of surveys of any size is to stimulate remedial programs to correct such serious deficiencies in the community structure as are found to exist. A long history of social surveys indicates that if action is considered a primary objective of the survey, early planning is necessary. It is not essential to foresee the survey results, but it *is* important to develop citizen interest that will bring about action. Many excellent factual surveys gather dust because the broad base of citizen support, or the organizational and agency base for action programs, was not developed. One of the best ways to avoid this is to involve in the survey process the people and agencies that will be called upon later to support and implement the survey findings.

Sometimes a community survey is one of the first activities of a new community betterment organization. Although the survey has no specific end in view, the thought is that from it will come definite programs of action which the new organization can stimulate. Community councils have a long record of such stimulation. One such organization in Kentucky reported a list of 115 different activities, large and small, which were initiated as citizens organized, surveyed their needs, and took action.[1]

A term which is often applied to a somewhat different type of survey-action program is the "community self-survey." Used in this narrower sense, the term denotes a study of discriminatory practices in the community with

[1] The London-Laurel County Development Association. See *Start Now . . . A Community Development Program*, 2d ed., Kentucky Chamber of Commerce, Louisville, 1951.

remedial action as an integral part of the program. Because it is confined largely to discrimination, it has been considered in Chapter 15, Intergroup Relations. Of course, the term is also used in its broader meaning to denote any community self-study activity.

There is a continuous line of possibilities between two extreme types of survey activity. At the one extremity is a survey conducted by outside experts, which is scientifically accurate and reliable, but is destined only for the library shelves. At the other, is an unscientific, hastily put-together survey of community needs; a survey short on facts and long on generalizations but enthusiastically carried into action by a well-organized, high-spirited citizens' group. But there is no reason why widespread, interested participation and support should be separated from scientific accuracy, and no reason why an enthusiastic desire for action should militate against the validity of the study.

Surveys can cover the whole community or merely one aspect of it. A decision will have to be made as to whether the community is to be studied in its manifold aspects or whether the survey is to be confined to only one area of community activity, such as economic conditions, welfare, or education.

It is well to keep in mind that the more extensive the survey is, the more people or time will be needed. Also, generally speaking, the larger the community, the more time-consuming is the survey task. If the purpose is simply to help the surveyors learn more about their community, they may choose between an extensive but somewhat superficial survey and a more intensive survey limited to one particular field. However, if the material gathered is to be used as a valuable source of facts about the community, if important decisions are to be made on the basis of the survey findings, or if the desire is to become thoroughly familiar with some aspect of the community, a limited but intensive survey may be indicated. In any case, a certain amount of general data about the community will have to be gathered.

Many surveys which are thought to be comprehensive are actually somewhat limited in scope. They may comprise data which are chiefly of an economic nature, or they may be limited to needs and resources in the health, welfare, recreation, and education fields, omitting important economic or physical aspects of the community.

Even a single aspect of the community, such as health, may be too broad as a survey topic. If so, the effort may be confined to a study of public health facilities, or hospitals, or medical care, or facilities for and care of the chronically ill, or children. Obviously such limited topics can be studied adequately only by considering their setting in the whole health picture, and indeed in the whole community picture. It is simply a question of emphasis and the degree of intensiveness desired.

Surveys can be designed to canvass a particular need. Some surveys arise as part of the program of an interested group to improve the community's facilities in one or another of its aspects. A women's group may be interested in determining whether it should go ahead in promoting a child day care center, or a citizens' organization may be studying the desirability of a new school building program, or another group may be studying the problem of juvenile delinquency with a view toward improving the probation system. Early determination of the specific purpose of the survey can be of great help in formulating the survey plan so that it will yield the type of information desired without needless excursions into by-roads which are not relevant to the problem. However, in perhaps no other type of survey is there greater possibility of inaccurate information or biased conclusions. The temptation is to be like the club president who said, "We want to make an objective study and prove why we need a new clinic!" Such studies should always be undertaken tentatively, with the strong possibility that as the study progresses those interested may find that their earlier conception of what the community needed is not warranted by the facts.

One of the chief advantages of such a study, over and above the information gathered, is that the study itself often becomes part of an action program. That is to say, the interested participation of many citizens in ferreting out the facts, their experience in "seeing the conditions with their own eyes," and the publicity given to the problem by the study procedure itself, may all contribute to stimulating public interest in the needs and assuring that action will result from the study.

Surveys can be made by volunteers or professionals. The advantages of volunteer surveys are that they are generally less expensive; many citizens have an opportunity to learn more about their community; the results may be more readily accepted because they are not the work of "outsiders who don't understand that this community is different"; and enthusiasm and interest may be generated during the course of the survey which will help carry over into action.

The advantages of the professional survey are that there is less waste of time, much more likelihood of getting the type of information which is available and needed without overlooking important sources of relevant data, and above all, scientific validity. Professional survey personnel are usually well equipped for fact-gathering and making analyses. This fact of itself does not assure their competence in *evaluation* of services in any particular field such as child welfare or education. Some professional survey specialists are, of course, well qualified for evaluation in specific fields of community services.

Where a survey is to be made in a community of any considerable size, a large number of workers will be needed unless the work is to be extremely superficial. A growing practice is to have the survey conducted by local people, with an outside survey specialist giving expert advice. Such a professional consultant can help the survey group formulate its plans and organize for the undertaking, assure that the data gathered will be objective and in usable form, and also help in evaluating the findings. In addition to the help given by the consultant the fact that he is an "outsider" fosters confidence generally in the impartiality of the survey and reassures the survey group itself. Nevertheless, there are limitations to what the consultant can accomplish. The bulk of the work must still be done by local people. Caution should be exercised in regard to accepting "package plans" for surveys, plans made up in advance and utilized elsewhere, which may or may not be feasible for the local community.

Since nationally affiliated organizations often conduct larger surveys, they may be able to obtain professional consulting service from their national headquarters. Examples would be a local welfare council, which could get help through any number of national organizations, or a local league of women voters or chamber of commerce. If there is no such national affiliation involved, it is possible, depending on the type of survey, to get help from the appropriate department or agency of the state government. This is particularly true of the state or agricultural college, or the state department of commerce. Various state or national private organizations may be willing to lend a hand. The survey conducted by volunteer citizens with professional leadership often combines the advantages of the volunteer survey with those afforded by the professional research team.

There are three aspects of the community in which the gathering of facts for planning is widespread. They are: (a) industrial development, (b) planning the physical aspects of the community, and (c) health and welfare planning. These are considered in Chapters 3, 5, and 17 respectively. In all such activity, community survey work is called for.

The existence of the three types of planning described above is important for several reasons. First, much information about one of these aspects of the community may be available through the local industrial development commission, city planning commission, or health and welfare council. Second, an organization in one or all of these three fields may, itself, be the appropriate body to carry out the particular survey in which the reader is interested. At least, the organization exists, and presumably it is equipped for fact-gathering in its field. It should not be ignored. Third, the reader should keep in mind that each of these organizations is typically concerned with only a limited aspect of the community, so that in a sense there is no assurance that any of them represents a communitywide point of view. With this in mind, the reader is less likely to be deflected into following the conventional pattern of community study carried on under any of these auspices unless it suits his purpose.

Steps in a Citizens' Survey

This section is designed for readers in small or medium-sized communities or in neighborhoods or districts of large communities who want to survey the whole community in comprehensive fashion with a view toward making recommendations and encouraging community action on such recommendations. The plan given here should be considered merely as a series of suggestions based on experience. Considerable modification may be advisable in adapting it to any particular community.

Determining the scope and size. Here are some of the questions you will want to consider:

What is the size of the "community" you want to study? (See Chapter 19.)
How many people can you count on to help with the work of the survey?
How much time do you want to devote to the survey?
How thorough do you want it to be?

An intensive survey of even a small community, say, a village of 1,500 people and its surrounding area, should keep many people occupied over a period of several months. If your survey seems too extensive a task for your group, you can expand the group, get additional help, study a smaller geographic area, or narrow the topic of your survey.

The sponsorship of the survey. It is important that some organization sponsor the survey, for the following reasons:

1. To lend the survey prestige and give it some standing in the community;
2. To organize and launch the survey committee;
3. As a source of volunteer workers;
4. To provide funds for survey expenses and to provide for possible publication and distribution of the survey report.

The sponsoring organization can be a local service club, the local chamber of commerce, or a church, women's club, farm bureau, or like organization. Frequently the question of who will sponsor the survey answers itself because the idea develops within a particular organization which more or less automatically comes to be the sponsor. Sometimes the organization which develops the idea may not be the proper one to sponsor the survey, for it may be too small or insufficiently representative of the community, or it may not have sufficient prestige, or it may be without adequate funds to undertake the responsibility, and so on. Careful thought should be given to the sponsoring organization, for community attitudes toward the organization may be transferred to the survey. Is the organization considered to represent only one particular economic group? Is it considered to prefer its own selfish interests to those of the larger community? If this organization is sponsor, will large segments of the community feel alienated? Can this organization act as sponsor without "taking over" the survey and using it merely for its own aggrandizement or to promote the special economic interests of its members?

Sometimes no organization exists which adequately reflects the various interests and groups in the community and which can act for the community because it is broadly representative of it. As a result, it may seem wise to form an organization along the lines of a "community council." (See Chapter 17.) Such an organization, whatever it is called in the local community, is a logical sponsor for a community survey, and indeed the survey committee may be a committee of this community council. If such an organization does not exist, it is often formed as part of the process of organizing a survey.

The cost of the survey. Surveys of small communities conducted by groups of local volunteers need not be costly. Two major items should be kept in mind. Even though the services of a survey consultant may be given free by a national agency or the extension service of the state university or a department of the state government, it may be necessary to pay the consultant's expenses, which may be considerable over a period of time. This matter should be ascertained, and plans should be made accordingly. Another sizable item may be the publication of the survey report. If the survey findings are to be given wide attention, it is definitely advisable to plan for a mimeographed or printed report.

Below is an outline suggested for use in estimating the expenses of the small survey:

Postage, paper, and other supplies
Secretarial work, such as typing, mimeographing, filing, mailing, unless such service is to be donated
Travel, perhaps to gather data at the county seat, or to canvass farmers within the trade area, or for other reasons
Expenses or fees for a survey consultant

Expenses, if any, of renting meeting halls for such communitywide meetings as may be held

Expenses of publishing and mailing the survey report

Other expenses

Organizing the survey committee. Certain principles should be kept in
mind in organizing the survey committee itself.

First, it should be comprised of persons who represent different groups in
the community, and who, if possible, are familiar with the general aspect
of the community under study.

Second, the survey committee should be divided into subcommittees
according to the major outlines of the study. Thus, there may be one subcommittee for the economic aspects of the community, another for government, another for health, another for welfare, another for education, and so
on. Perhaps six or seven such topical categories would be a good number.
The chapter topics of the present book can be combined into the number desired. If the study is limited to one of these topics, the subcommittees can
each be responsible for one aspect of the topic.

Each subcommittee may consist of several persons, with one acting as
chairman. In larger communities, it may be judicious to turn over each
separate topic to an appropriate organization within the community,
and let it take responsibility for gathering the information. Thus, the topic
of health may be assigned to a health organization; the topic of economic
activities, to the chamber of commerce or a service club; the topic of education, to a parent-teacher association; and so on. In this process, care
must be taken to safeguard the accuracy and objectivity of the survey, and
to avoid any distortion of it by groups who want to promote their own
objectives. In smaller communities an individual, rather than a subcommittee, may be charged with gathering the facts in each branch of the
survey.

The survey chairman. The chairman of the survey should see that each
committee has clearly in mind the purpose and procedure of the whole
study and its own part in it, ascertain that the various subcommittees are
assembling their information according to schedule, help to iron out
any personality clashes, bolster up any branch of the survey that bogs
down, and, finally, assemble the results and perhaps draft the final report,
subject to the approval of the whole committee. Needless to say, it is advisable that the chairman of the survey committee should be someone experienced in survey work or at least in some field of endeavor where
objectivity and accuracy are called for, someone whose point of view is

broad rather than that of some special group, and one who commands wide respect and is skillful in human relations.

A professional survey expert may be called in to direct the survey, or such a person may be engaged as a consultant. Where a special expert is asked to direct the entire study, he will take over the direction of the actual mechanics of the survey, while the local chairman of the survey committee will function administratively as committee chairman.

Preparing the survey forms. The survey forms list the questions which are to be answered and the information which is to be filled in. These forms should be prepared in advance of the actual field work. Each subcommittee chairman should have a complete set of forms to be filled out by his subcommittee, in such quantities as are needed. For example, the subcommittee on churches will solicit certain information from each church. All the kinds of information to be solicited from each church should be assembled in question form and then sufficient copies made so that a worker can fill one out for each church. The effort spent in planning these forms to facilitate tabulation will be well rewarded. Care should be taken that a suitable amount of space is provided for the answers.

It is probably needless for any community to start completely from scratch in making up its forms. There are many different survey outlines available for certain aspects of the community, such as health, recreation, delinquency, and so on. The questions in the present book are devised for use as a survey outline, requiring only that the questions which must be asked of each of many different agencies or organizations in the community, such as schools, churches, associations, and so on, be transferred to separate forms and duplicated in the quantities desired.

Unevenness of intensity in the survey should be avoided, unless there is special reason for studying one aspect of the community more thoroughly than others. Since all of the data will be gathered according to the forms which are prepared, the survey committee can assure itself even before the field work commences that it is covering each aspect of the community with the appropriate degree of intensity.

Conducting the field work. If adequate time and care have been devoted to preparation and to getting the various parts of the community behind the survey effort, the field work will be facilitated. Organization of the survey around the principle of joint participation by various organizations in the community should assure the cordial reception of the field workers as they go from one center of information to another.[1] Nevertheless, it is important

---

[1] See Chapter 19 for "Some Hints in Interviewing."

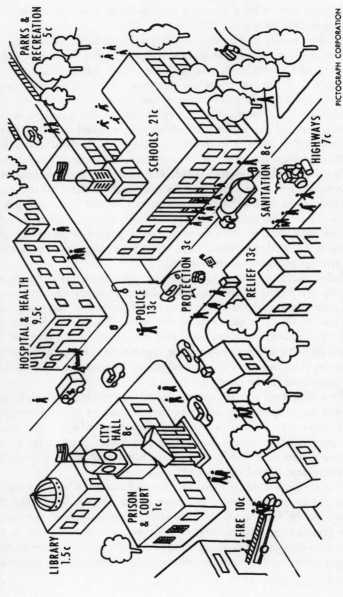

YOUR CITY TAX DOLLAR PAYS FOR MANY SERVICES

PARKS & RECREATION 5c

SCHOOLS 21c

HOSPITAL & HEALTH 9.5c

LIBRARY 1.5c

POLICE 13c

PROTECTION 3c

SANITATION 8c

HIGHWAYS 7c

RELIEF 13c

CITY HALL 8c

PRISON & COURT 1c

FIRE 10c

PICTOGRAPH CORPORATION

HOW THE COMMUNITY TAX DOLLAR IS SPENT

This "picture story" type of chart makes the various expenditures of tax money meaningful by picturing the types of service provided. Such illustrations help to interest the reader in the findings of a community survey. Compare the pie chart of educational expenditures on page 95.

SOURCE: Modley, Rudolf, and Dyno Lowenstein, *Pictographs and Graphs: How to Make and Use Them.* Harper and Bros., New York, 1952.

that the field workers be given careful instructions as to how to conduct their work. Sources of information already compiled should first be combed and the available material recorded insofar as possible before the field interviews commence. This will enable the interviewers to be reasonably well informed and will avoid bothering busy people unnecessarily. Material gathered in interviews should be recorded as precisely as possible. This will be easier if most of the survey forms are of such a nature as to request definite answers to specific questions, rather than requiring extensive comment and interpretation. However, care should be taken not to record purely categorical answers, such as "yes" or "no," when they are misleading unless qualified.

It should be impressed upon the field workers that accuracy is not only desirable but necessary if the survey results are to be worthwhile.

The matter of neatness in the recording of data is much more important than it may seem. Frequently the temptation is to scribble so as not to prolong the interview, or to copy figures too rapidly so as to speed up the tedious job of extracting material from official records. Illegibility makes for wasted time in retraced steps, and militates against accuracy. All material should be labeled sufficiently so that any member of the survey group can identify and use it. Unidentified data are a menace to the accuracy of the survey and a constant source of frustration to all concerned. All figures and facts should be checked against the original source after they have been recorded.

When all the forms which will require tabulation are completed, the work of tabulation can begin. Tables should be clearly labeled. They should be checked when completed, and any individual item on which there was a question concerning the way it should be classified should be marked and indication given as to how it actually was tabulated. When the statistical work has been completed, the total amounts, averages, and other statistical measures can be incorporated into the report, along with such tables as are thought desirable to reproduce.

Writing the survey report. In the case of a small survey, the survey director or someone who has been directly connected with the entire survey process should write the report. In larger surveys, each subcommittee chairman may draft the report of the work of his subcommittee. The report should be written in a simple, direct style without the use of technical jargon but also without "talking down" to the reader. Charts and other illustrations often help to clarify important points.[1] Documentary photo-

---

[1] See Modley, Rudolf, and Dyno Lowenstein, *Pictographs and Graphs: How to Make and Use Them*, Harper and Bros., New York, 1952.

graphs are particularly effective in presenting to the reader some of the conditions which the report seeks to emphasize. The various charts in this book are designed to furnish the reader with suggestions for graphic illustration of the survey report. The numerous plot maps which have been suggested in connection with various chapters may in some cases become a valuable graphic supplement to the verbal report.

Presumably, the facts gathered will be much more voluminous than can be handled in a summary report; therefore careful selection of data should be made so as not to obscure any of the important findings.

Depending on the purposes and nature of the survey, there may be a section on "chief findings" or "recommendations," or both. One possibility would be to put a brief section on "chief findings" at the beginning, right after the acknowledgments, and a section on "recommendations" at the end. Some prefer to start out with the recommendations, then give the supporting data as the body of the report. Another possibility is to have a section on appropriate recommendations at the end of each topic covered in the report. Sometimes both "findings" and "recommendations" are briefly summarized at the beginning of the report.

Whatever acknowledgments of help and cooperation are appropriate should be made at the beginning of the report. Mention may be made of the participating organizations, the survey committee, the field workers and other helpers, the government officials and agency heads on whom great demands for help were made, any outside agency which lent aid, and so on.

It is highly desirable that all major findings and recommendations be reviewed by the officials and organization or agency heads to whose work they pertain, and that they approve of the manner in which these findings and recommendations are presented. Sometimes this desirable result cannot be brought about, but it should be sought earnestly.

Publicity and follow-up. Publicity is important particularly at the beginning of the survey process and at the end. At the beginning, publicity will aid in achieving communitywide support or participation. It will prepare the way for the field workers, in that their informants will already know about the survey and will receive them graciously.

During the survey, publicity can serve to sustain interest, to give credit to individuals and organizations that are actively helping in one phase or another, and to prepare the community for the report. Publicity should not be thought of only in terms of newspapers, but also radio, TV, letters and speeches to organizations, and so on.

As the survey is brought to a conclusion, sometimes a meeting or a series of meetings is held to acquaint the interested individuals and organizations in the community with the findings and recommendations.

A plan to be recommended is the holding of a communitywide meeting to coincide with the distribution of copies of the survey report. This makes an occasion of the distribution of the reports, and brings together the people and organizations that are most interested, for it is upon them that follow-through depends. Such a meeting may be a dinner meeting. In any case, the chairman of the survey committee or some other appropriate person can give a speech reviewing briefly the history of the survey and then the major findings and recommendations can be presented. Copies of the report itself can be distributed. The press should be invited to this meeting.

If the sponsoring agency or the survey committee intends to follow through and try to stimulate action on the recommendations, this meeting can be part of the initial stages of the follow-up. Whatever organizational steps are indicated may be taken. The survey committee may be terminated at this point, and a follow-up organization activated. The survey committee and the sponsoring organization may see their job only as one of fact-finding. In this case the carrying out of the recommendations will be left to the appropriate community agencies and organizations.

Plans should be made to mail the report to certain persons who did not attend the meeting but should be apprised of the survey findings, and to publicize the fact that copies of the report are available on request.

If it is possible to interest the newspapers or radio or TV stations in publicizing different aspects of the findings and recommendations over a period of time, this will do much to get the findings before the people who might not otherwise be informed. Copies of the report should be displayed, if possible, in schools, libraries, and other places where they may be consulted.

Human Relations in Survey Work

Whether intentionally or not, community surveys are all ventures in human relations, an aspect of survey work which can be ignored only at the surveyor's peril. This section will give some suggestions on human relations specifically related to the survey task. They are derived from generally accepted principles of human relations which have arisen out of the experience of countless community workers. They are merely applications of certain basic truths about human beings, in our culture at least. We all like a little praise; we all want to keep and enhance our self-respect; we have our own group loyalties and cultural values; we like to have the situation fully explained to us; and we usually respond when we feel our contribution is really wanted.

Obtain broad representation on the survey committee. Most communities show broad groupings of interest and association. They should not be ignored. For example, in a rural community it is easy to forget the farmers. Be sure the Grange, Farm Bureau, Home Bureau, and such organizations are represented. Similarly, do not let your committee be composed exclusively of any particular income or education group.

Use the principle of participation. People usually throw themselves into a project when they have made a contribution to it that is considered important. Let it be their survey, let them help plan it, determine its goals, carry out the procedures, review the findings, consider the recommendations, and they will be more likely to support it actively.

Understand the role of leaders. Try to put the "natural" leaders in positions of actual leadership. Avoid "cliquishness" if possible. Don't assign someone to leadership who is not capable of fulfilling the task. Not all people take leadership naturally. Avoid people who antagonize their associates by being domineering. Democratic leadership does not involve doing things for people who are able to do these things for themselves. On the other hand, democratic leadership does not demand chaos. There is often a tendency to equate ineffectiveness with democracy. People in a group need clarity of purpose, a common "definition of the situation." In this, the leader must take responsibility.

Be patient in encountering resistance. You may find people who do not want to cooperate, who want to withhold the required information, who deprecate the study, or who in other ways show resistance. Patience and forbearance in doing what is called for will often win their support. They may need reassurance that no one is out to "get" them or their department. They may simply be taking their own way of showing their resentment at having been ignored in the planning stages, or at this intrusion on their time. Straightforward and patient interpretation of what is being done, acknowledgment of any affronts, and willingness to see the other fellow's point of view will usually be rewarded.

Observe the informal groupings in your own committee and in the community. On your own committee, see that people who are congenial to each other are assigned as members. In the community, work through the natural "networks" of informal groupings (see Chapter 20). Very likely many of the official leaders will be on your committee. Also, win the support of people of prestige. These may or may not be the same persons as the official leaders. See that you get the backing of some of the unofficial leaders as well. The local groceryman may wield more influence than the president of the women's club. Natural leaders are found in every neighborhood, and their influence is often wider than that of the official leaders.

Use people where they can help the most. Some people are especially clever at drawing. They can make maps, posters, or charts. Some people have a tremendous enthusiasm for one little segment of the community's activities. They will ring doorbells for cancer but not for juvenile delinquency. Some people will make excellent interviewers, others will not. Often, the latter can perform valuable service in noninterview activities.

Be sure everybody knows where his task fits in with that of other workers. The subcommittee chairman should have a clear picture of what his group is responsible for accomplishing. Individual field workers are entitled to definite and clear assignments. Leaders should have a clear idea of the problems that can be settled on the level of their own group and of which ones should be referred back to the larger group for a decision. Instruction sheets can be drawn up, particularly for the field workers, who will want to know where they stand and what is expected of them.

Keep open the channels of communication. People like to know what is happening. Field workers should report significant events to subcommittee chairmen, and so on. Developments may call for modifications which should be known by other people taking part in the survey. New decisions reached in the course of administering the survey should be relayed to those who should know of them. People are rightfully resentful when they discover, sometimes under embarrassing circumstances, that they have been acting according to a procedure which was changed two weeks ago without their being informed. Similarly, the community should be informed of the progress of the survey. People who will be interviewed should have some idea when to expect a call. Suggestions made for improving methods should be communicated to those who are charged with that part of the survey.

Conduct meetings effectively. Among other things, this means preparing carefully the agenda for the meeting and holding the meeting in as informal a manner as is consistent with the accomplishment of the business at hand. Generally speaking, the larger the group, the more formally must the meeting be conducted. Parliamentary procedure can be used as an aid; it should not become a straitjacket.

Adapt to your own community. In one sense, every community *is* different. Each community has its own "flavor." It differs slightly in what is accepted as "the thing to do" and who are "the people to know" if you want to get things done, and whose approval has to be given to a project if it is to receive wide acceptance in certain groups. Some communities are not used to working together; others have a long history of intergroup cooperation. Some are conservative; others are ready for anything that sounds reasonable. Some will "go for" a clam bake; others will have nothing to do with it. In some, the political party officials are more important than governmental officials; in others, it is the other way around. In one community, it is a particular church which "runs" things; in another it is the "Garden Club"; and in still another it is the Volunteer Fire Department. Flexibility of approach is important. No hard and fast "system" can be applied to every community with equal success. Adapt your program to the organization and tone and general climate of your community.[1]

References for Further Study

Examples of extremely brief "community score cards" which form an outline for a rapid check and evaluation of the small community as a basis for an action program are the following:

Scoreboard for Your Town. New York State Citizens' Council, Syracuse, 1948. Reprinted in *Adult Leadership,* vol. 1, October, 1952.

Town Telescope: A Community Scorecard. Department of Community Adult Education, Extension Service, University of Michigan, Ann Arbor.

A somewhat more extensive community score card is used by the Agricultural Extension Service of West Virginia University, which is revised from time to time. See Rapking, A. H., *Education Through Organized Community Activities,* 2d ed., College of Agriculture, West Virginia University, Morgantown, 1935.

An 11-point community profile for appraising the rural community, with considerable commentary as to how it may be used, is contained in Ensminger, Douglas, *Measuring the Effectiveness of Your Community:* Diagnosing Rural Community Organization. Cornell Extension Bulletin 444, Ithaca, 1940.

Booklets outlining procedures for community development plans where the survey activity is either minimized or confined to specific "suggestions for bettering this community" include:

Community Survival. Extension Service in Agriculture and Home Economics, College of Agriculture, University of Illinois, Urbana, 1949.

Community Development in Georgia. Georgia Agricultural Extension Service, University of Georgia College of Agriculture, Athens, 1951.

Rural Communities of Wisconsin: Getting Ready for Tomorrow. Extension Service of the College of Agriculture, University of Wisconsin, Madison, 1945.

[1] An excellent guide to this and other aspects of community betterment work is Irwin T. Sanders' *Making Good Communities Better,* 2d ed., University of Kentucky Press, Lexington, 1953.

Your Community: Organizing for Action. League of Minnesota Municipalities and State Department of Business Research and Development, 1950.

The following publications combine the idea of self-study for community betterment with a survey effort of more comprehensive scope:

A Community Looks at Itself. University of Nebraska Press, Lincoln, 1952.

A Handbook in Community Development. The Southeastern Workshop, Greenville, South Carolina, 1941.

Atchley, Mell H., *Community Study Guide.* Department of Sociology and Anthropology, University of Florida, Gainesville, 1951.

Your Community Looks at Itself: A Manual for the Home Town Self-Survey. Southern Regional Council, Inc., Atlanta, Georgia, no date.

Lippincott, Earle, *Our Home Town.* Association Press, New York, 1949.

Preparing a Community Profile: The Methodology of a Social Reconnaissance. Kentucky Community Series No. 7, Bureau of Community Service, University of Kentucky, Lexington, 1952.

Further readings on neighborhood and community councils are suggested in Chapter 17.

For a detailed guide to the organization of a community study and betterment program, including both the organization and functions of various committees and an outline for collecting facts for the study itself, see Poston, Richard W., *Democracy Is You:* A Guide to Citizen Action, Harper and Bros., New York, 1953.

Two pamphlets of the Hogg Foundation, University of Texas, Austin, are aimed more or less directly at the process of organization for survey efforts: *Family, Community and Mental Health:* Profiles of Community Action, 1950; and *So You Want to Make a Community Study?* A Self-Study Guide for Communities, 1950.

See also the chapter "Surveying the Community" by Wilbur C. Hallenbeck in Bingham, Florence C., editor, *Community Life in a Democracy,* National Congress of Parents and Teachers, Chicago, 1942.

19. Aids to the Survey

IN MAKING A COMMUNITY STUDY the reader who is so engaged may wish to utilize various reports of the federal Bureau of the Census or avail himself of certain methods of gathering data, such as interviews and questionnaires. The present chapter consists of a series of aids which the survey worker may find helpful in demarcating his community and in procuring the detailed information he needs.

Choosing the Geographic Area for Study

What set of boundaries will you choose to demarcate your community for purposes of your survey? In order to help decide, let us examine the interrelation of communities of different sizes. We can begin with a rural neighborhood, perhaps consisting of a score of families, perhaps with a one-room school or church or service agency, but not large enough to support the many services and institutions of a full-fledged community. This neighborhood, along with other such neighborhoods including a village center, forms a village-farm community. This community, along with several others, is served by a small city for various wholesale, professional, department store, and other needs. This small city, in turn, is within the service area of a city of considerable size, say from 50,000 to several hundred thousand, which provides even more specialized services. A relatively small number of such cities, with their service areas, are served by a large metropolis, which, with them, makes up a metropolitan region that may extend across several state lines. Somewhere in this network will be found the reader's community: neighborhood—village-farm community—small city and trade area—medium-sized city and trade area—metropolitan region.

Looked at from the standpoint of a resident of a metropolis, the "community" which he wishes to study could be the whole metropolitan region, or the metropolitan area, or the city, or a large community within the city, or his local neighborhood. Even if he chooses his neighborhood as the

324

study unit, he must still see it in its relation to the rest of the city, and see the city in relation to the whole region which it serves.[1]

Although villages and cities have definite boundaries prescribed more or less arbitrarily in their charter, communities typically disregard such artificial political boundaries. They extend outward from the center as far as there are people who are served principally by the institutions and agencies, stores, schools, banks, of the community center.

This means that if you live in a small village or town, very likely you will want to study not only this municipal unit but also the territory which forms part of the community, although it lies beyond village or town limits. If your home is in a city of some size, you may want to study not only this municipal unit but also its "trade area," the area of farms, villages, and other municipalities served by your city. On the other hand, you may feel that such a large "community" is too big for your survey purpose, and you may decide to confine yourself to a particular neighborhood within the city, and pay only secondary attention to the surrounding city and its larger trade area.

Below are some of the geographical units which form the base for the tabulation of various types of factual data by the Bureau of the Census and many other agencies. The selection of one of these geographical units as the "community" you are to study will facilitate the gathering of already available data, but the unit in question may not actually constitute a "real" community in the sociological sense. In the case of some of the smaller units, they can perhaps be combined to constitute the geographic area in which you are interested. Even if you find no convenient geographic enumeration area which coincides with the community you want to study, you can make use of material collected for these various enumeration areas to give a background. For example, if you choose the village-farm community, that is, the village and the surrounding area of farm land and farm people which it serves, you may find that it corresponds neither to a township nor to a county. Nevertheless, you may be able to combine figures from certain townships which constitute, roughly, the trade area of your village, or you may want to use county figures as being representative of the type of countryside which forms the setting and background of your community.

Places under 2,500. Some Census material is published for places under 2,500 population, but not a great deal. Such places are included in tables

[1] For a brief somewhat technical guide to using Census material for city neighborhoods, see *Population Analysis of Small Areas*, Business Information Service, U.S. Department of Commerce, Government Printing Office, Washington, 1950.

which list enumerations for "incorporated places and unincorporated places of 1,000 or more." In other words, if your little village has fewer than 1,000 population, it will not be listed separately in the Census unless it is incorporated. If more than 1,000, it will be listed whether or not it is incorporated.

Places of 2,500 to 10,000. Considerably more material is available in the Census for urban places of 2,500 to 10,000, whether or not incorporated.

Urban places of 10,000 or more. There is fairly complete listing of Census data for urban places of 10,000 or more. This means that if your "community" is a village or city of 10,000 or more, just about all the figures which the Census gives for specific localities will be listed separately for your community. This applies to the largest cities as well.

Standard metropolitan areas. "Except in New England, a standard metropolitan area is a county or group of contiguous counties which contains at least one city of 50,000 inhabitants or more." Contiguous counties are included "if according to certain criteria they are essentially metropolitan in character and socially and economically integrated with the central city."[1] In New England, towns and cities, not counties, are the units used in defining standard metropolitan areas. The idea of the standard metropolitan area is to include not only the metropolis itself but also "the entire population in and around the city whose activities form an integrated social and economic system." Thus, through the metropolitan area, you can get figures for the whole metropolitan community, rather than for just the principal city. Practically everything which is published for other enumeration areas is published for the standard metropolitan areas.

Urbanized areas. "The urbanized area can be characterized as the physical city as distinguished from both the legal city and the metropolitan community. In general, urbanized areas represent the thickly settled urban core of the standard metropolitan areas. Urbanized areas are smaller than standard metropolitan areas and in most cases are contained in them."[2] Thus, if you use an "urbanized area" as the "community" you are studying, you will have the central city and the surrounding thickly settled "urban fringe." Identical information is published for such units as is published for standard metropolitan areas.

Census tracts and block statistics. If you are choosing only part of a large city as your study "community," you may find that one or more Census tracts or blocks may coincide with the area you are interested in studying. (See pages 330–331.) In other cities, some information is usually available

---

[1] Bureau of the Census, *U.S. Census of Population: 1950.* Preprint of vol. 2, part 32, chap. B. Government Printing Office, Washington, 1952, p. v.
[2] *Ibid.,* p. vi.

by wards. Even if your study area is a small neighborhood within a city, however, you will probably also want citywide data of many types to show the "setting" of your neighborhood.

Counties. If you choose a county as your study community, a vast assortment of collected data will be available to you from the Census and other sources. The Census publishes for counties all the material that it publishes for any other area. Generally speaking, a county is a fairly large unit for study, although some counties are small enough to be surveyed by a small group of volunteers. This is particularly true since so many data are already available on a county basis. At any rate, you will probably want to make use of county data if you are studying either a village-farm community or small city. In the case of the large city, one or more counties may constitute its metropolitan area.

Minor civil divisions. Some material is available in the Census according to minor civil divisions. These are "the primary political divisions into which counties are divided." In the 1950 Census, "the most numerous of the minor civil divisions were the civil and judicial townships, which numbered 20,879 and were found in 20 states. The total also included 8,708 precincts, 6,739 districts, and 4,326 independent municipalities, and 3,599 towns. The remaining minor civil divisions are known as beats, gores, grants, islands, purchases, surveyed townships, and so on, some of which are found only in a single state."[1] One or more minor civil divisions may be combined to make up the study area for a rural community, so far as Census material is concerned.

Should you include the trade area? In many ways, a large village or small city is integrated with its retail and wholesale trade areas, and the political boundaries which separate it from the surrounding countryside are rather artificial and arbitrary. Usually, the wholesale trade area is larger than the retail trade area, for it may include other communities as well. The retail trade area is confined to the area surrounding the trade center from which people come for ordinary retail purchases. People in nearby communities would patronize their own trade centers for ordinary retail purchases. However, a large trade center might serve several such communities for wholesale purposes and for specialized stores like department stores, furniture stores, and so on, as well as radio stations, daily newspapers, cultural facilities, hospitals and such establishments.

You may decide to study only your own town, or you may include its retail trade area, or its wholesale trade area. Only you can decide that. How-

[1] Bureau of the Census, *U.S. Census of Population: 1950. Number of Inhabitants: U.S. Summary.* Government Printing Office, Washington, 1952, vol. PA 1, p. xxviii.

ever, if you confine your study to the political boundaries of your town, you should at least realize that you are studying only one section of a highly interrelated entity—your town and the people and communities it serves.

Using the Census

The Censuses of Population and Housing. The following plan of the 1950 Censuses of Population and Housing will help the reader to orient himself:

Population

Volume 1. Number of Inhabitants (Population Series P-A Bulletins)
Volume 2. Characteristics of the Population
Chapter A. Number of Inhabitants (Population Series P-A Bulletins)
Chapter B. General Characteristics (Population Series P-B Bulletins)
Chapter C. Detailed Characteristics (Population Series P-C Bulletins)
Chapter D. Tracted Areas (Population Series P-D Bulletins)
Succeeding volumes covering the following subjects:
Nativity and Parentage, Nonwhite Population by Race, Persons of Spanish Surname, Institutional Population, Differential Fertility, Labor Force Characteristics, Occupation, Industry, Income, Internal Migration, Education, Characteristics of Families and Households.

Housing

Volume 1. General Characteristics (Housing Series H-A Bulletins)
Volume 2. Nonfarm Housing Characteristics (Housing Series H-B Bulletins)
Volume 3. Farm Housing Characteristics
Volume 4. Residential Financing
Volume 5. Block Statistics Bulletins

In general, the Bulletin Series are preprints of the individual parts of the Census volume with which they are listed above. For example, the population Series P-B Bulletins are 54 in number, including a U.S. Summary, one for each of the 48 states, and one each for Washington, D.C., Alaska, Hawaii, Puerto Rico, and Minor Possessions. They give general characteristics of the population, including the material listed in the population questions in Chapter 2 of this book. Altogether, including the P-A, P-C, and P-D Series, they comprise Volume 2 of the Census of Population. If you want only material for your own state, order the Bulletin Series, for the cost is less.

Similarly, the Housing Series B Bulletins (H-B Bulletins) are preprints of the separate chapters of Volume 2 of the 1950 Census of Housing. There are 162 in the series. They include a U.S. Summary, one for each of the major geographical divisions of the United States, and one for each of the standard metropolitan areas of the United States. Notice that these bulletins are not by states. If your city is in one of the standard metropolitan areas, much Census material is so classified, and one of these H-B bulletins which describes its housing characteristics is available. The individual H-B bulletin for your locality costs less than the full Housing Volume 2 and will serve your purpose.

The most important volumes for most communities are Population Volumes 1 and 2 (the material given in Volume 1 is incorporated in Volume 2, along with much more material) and Housing Volume 1. Both of these give data for such small areas as places between 1,000 and 2,500, 2,500 and 10,000, and over 10,000, as well as counties and other divisions. With the exception of Housing Volume 5 most of the other volumes concern themselves with figures for the United States, for geographical divisions, states, metropolitan areas, urban, rural nonfarm, rural farm, and so on.

"In general, identical information is published for counties, standard metropolitan areas, urbanized areas, and urban places of 10,000 population or more. For these areas nearly all of the tabulated data are published. Some items are less detailed and others are omitted in the publication of information for rural-nonfarm and rural-farm portions of the county, urban places of 2,500 to 10,000, and Census tracts."[1]

No matter what size community you are studying, the Housing Volumes of the 1950 Census, particularly Volume 1, will interest you.

Housing Volume 1 presents statistics on the general characteristics of housing. The state chapters contain state statistics by residence (urban, rural nonfarm, and rural farm), standard metropolitan areas, urbanized areas, counties, urban places, places of 1,000 to 2,500 inhabitants, and the rural-nonfarm and rural-farm portions of counties. More detailed information is presented for states, standard metropolitan areas and their constituent counties, urbanized areas, and urban places of 10,000 inhabitants or more, than for the other areas.

The following subjects are covered:

Occupancy Characteristics of the Dwelling Unit

Occupancy and tenure
Population per occupied dwelling unit

[1] Bureau of the Census, *U.S. Censuses of Population and Housing, 1950:* Key to Published and Tabulated Data for Small Areas. Government Printing Office, Washington, 1951, p. 3.

Race or color of occupants
Number of persons
Persons per room

Structural Characteristics of the Dwelling Unit

Type of structure
Number of rooms
Year built

Condition and Plumbing Facilities

Condition and plumbing facilities (in combination)
Water supply
Toilet facilities
Bathing facilities

Equipment and Fuels

Electric lighting   Kitchen sink
Heating equipment   Radio
Heating fuel   Refrigeration equipment
Cooking fuel   Television

Financial Characteristics of Nonfarm Dwelling Units

Contract monthly rent
Gross monthly rent
Value
Mortgage status

If you are studying part of one of the 209 cities with a 1940 population of 50,000 or more for which block statistics are available, you will be able to gather together block by block the statistics which are so tabulated. The following is a list of such statistical topics tabulated by blocks in the Housing Series H-E Bulletins:

Number of dwelling units classified by occupancy and tenure
Condition and plumbing facilities
Persons per room
Color of occupants
Average contract monthly rent
    Renter-occupied units
    Selected vacant units
Average value of one-dwelling unit
    Owner-occupied
    Selected vacant structures

These data are also tabulated for the city as a whole and for Census tracts or wards. They are available in Housing Volume 5 of the 1950 Censuses of Population and Housing. The 213 Block Statistics Bulletins are available separately. Together, they constitute Housing Volume 5. You can find out whether or not your city is included in Volume 5, thus having the information described above, by writing to the Superintendent of Documents for the following free leaflet: *1950 Censuses of Population and Housing, Announcement 2, Final Reports, Block Statistics Bulletins* (Housing Volume 5), September, 1951, U.S. Department of Commerce, Bureau of the Census.

You may be studying one of the more than 60 cities for which Census tract bulletins are available. You can determine this by writing to the Superintendent of Documents for a free copy of the leaflet *1950 Censuses of Population and Housing, Announcement 4, Final Reports, Census Tract Bulletins, 1951.* Census tracts are small areas into which various cities have been divided for purposes of tabulating population and housing data. An attempt is made to keep them roughly the same size and to keep them fairly homogeneous. In this way, different sections of the city can be compared with one another. As units of study, they are greatly preferable to the use of the traditional "wards."

The tables included in Census Tract Bulletins are as follows:

1. Characteristics of the Population, by Census Tracts (includes 1949 income)
2. Age, Marital Status, and Economic Characteristics, by Sex, by Census Tracts
3. Characteristics of Dwelling Units, by Census Tracts

The Census of Agriculture. Most communities serve a considerable population of widely dispersed farm people as well as the people who live in the community center and in the rural nonfarm population. The condition of these farm families affects the communities to which they sell goods and from which they buy them.

The major source of information about farmers is the *U.S. Census of Agriculture*, which is published every five years. This Census gives information for geographic areas as small as the county, but no smaller. On the county level there is a wealth of information about farms and farm activities under the following major headings:

Farms, acreage, value, and farm operators	86 items
Farms by size and by color and tenure of operator	100 items
Facilities and equipment, farm labor and farm expenditures	85 items
Livestock and livestock products	165 items

Specified crops harvested   375 items

Farms and farm characteristics for commercial farms and
other farms   79 items

Farms classified by total value of farm products sold, by type of
farm, and by economic class; and value of products sold   60 items

The number of items of information under each heading indicates the tremendous scope of information. However, these headings only hint at the wealth of detail available about the farms of each county.

Just a few items will illustrate the appropriateness of some of this material. From the first table you can find the number of farms in your county, their average size, the value of the land and buildings, and many other basic facts about the number and size of farms and type of land use. You can also get the number of farm families whose income from other sources exceeds the value of agricultural products sold. This represents a significant group of farm families who depend more on other sources for an income than they do on their farms. The proportion of this group to the total number of farms can be found and compared with other counties or with your state in general. The number of farmers working off their farm 100 days or more will give an index of part-time farming.

The above items constitute only five of the 86 items in Table 1. Table 2 will give you the type of farm tenure, how many farm operators are full owners, part owners, managers, all tenants, and many more items. Table 3 indicates how many farms have various types of facilities like the telephone, electricity, tractors, automobiles, and so on; this table also indicates the farmers' relation to the trading center, type of roads they must travel, farm labor, and farm expenditures for various purposes. Each of these topics has several detailed items. And so on through the various tables.

All the foregoing material is contained in Volume 1. This volume is divided into 34 parts, each part of which reports on one state or group of states. The five volumes of the *Census of Agriculture* are as follows:

Volume 1. Counties and State Economic Areas
Volume 2. General Report—Statistics by Subjects
Volume 3. Irrigation of Agricultural Lands
Volume 4. Drainage of Agricultural Lands
Volume 5. Special Reports

Volume 1 includes data for counties, as explained above, and thus may be of use in local surveys. Volumes 3 and 4 include data for counties only in the states affected.

The Census of Manufactures. Manufacturing is a vital activity for many communities, whether they are large or small. The growth of light manufacturing activities in small towns and villages, coupled with the increasing tendency for farm people to supplement their income with nonfarm employment, makes the manufacturing industries of a village, city, county, or metropolitan area important for most community surveys.

The *Census of Manufactures* is published in the following four volumes:

Volume 1. General Summary
Volume 2. Statistics by Industry
Volume 3. Statistics by States
Product Supplement

Volume 3 is of most interest to those engaged in community surveys, for it gives statistics not only for individual states, but also for standard metropolitan areas, counties, and urban places of over 10,000. Particularly important are Tables 2 and 7 for each state. Table 2 gives for each standard metropolitan area, county, and urban place of 10,000 or more population the following data: population, number of establishments, average number of employees, total salaries and wages, average number of production workers, total wages, value added by manufacture. There is also a comparison of some of these items with an earlier year.

Table 7 gives for each county the total number of establishments and also the number of establishments for each of 20 major industry groups, with a breakdown of establishments within each major industry group according to whether they have 1–19 employees, 20–99 employees, or 100 employees and over. This table gives an excellent picture of the industrial effort in each county, both as to number and size of establishments in each of the 20 occupational groups.

Tables 6 and 9 give additional details for highly industrial counties and (Table 9) for metropolitan areas.

In Volume 1 several tables give general statistics for standard metropolitan areas and selected counties.

The Census of Business. The *U.S. Census of Business* is a valuable source of information about retail, wholesale, and service trade in your locality. Roughly, it covers the business activity up and down "Main Street." In it, data are available for counties as well as for cities above a minimum size, the minimum size varying with the type of material presented.

Volumes 1, 2, and 4 are not particularly helpful for community surveys, since they deal with various activities on a national, state or regional basis. The other volumes contain material on a county or city basis as follows:

Volume 3 gives area statistics for retail trade. It contains 50 chapters (48 states, the District of Columbia, and Territories). Within each chapter, one of the tables gives retail trade statistics for counties and cities of 2,500 inhabitants or more.

Volume 5 gives statistics for wholesale trade, and one of the tables in this volume gives area statistics for counties and cities of 5,000 inhabitants or more.

Volume 6, Chapter 7, gives figures for certain service trades for cities above a specific size. Some of the figures are given for all cities above 10,000 in size, while others are only for cities above 100,000 in size. In other words, if your city is approximately 25,000 it will be included in some of the tabulations but not all of them.

Volume 7 contains three tables giving service trade figures for counties and cities of 2,500 or more. One of these tabulates personal, business, and repair services; another tabulates figures for amusements, and still another tabulates figures for hotels. By looking up one's city or county in the tables described above, one can obtain valuable figures on the number and volume of business of the retail, wholesale, and service establishments in his locality.

An extensive Census of Business was to be taken in 1953, with certain expanded features, but Congress did not appropriate sufficient funds for a thorough Census such as that of 1948. It later reversed itself and scheduled a Census of Business, a Census of Manufactures, and a Census of Mineral Industries for 1955 to cover 1954 activities.

Local or state agencies, such as the chamber of commerce, board of trade, or state department of commerce, may be able to furnish supplementary figures.

Useful Reference Books

Publications related to the Census. "The *Statistical Abstract of the United States,* published annually since 1878, is the standard summary of statistics on the industrial, social, political, and economic organization of the United States. It includes a selection of data from most of the important statistical publications, both governmental and private. Of necessity, it is limited primarily to the presentation of data for the country as a whole, and, to a much lesser extent, to data for regions and individual states. Data for cities or other small geographic units are shown only in a small number of instances."[1]

This book will give you various national statistics with which one may compare his own community. It is widely available, and may be consulted for certain very general Census figures if the individual volumes of the

[1] Quoted from the Preface to the *Statistical Abstract.*

Census are not available. It lists numerous tables under each of the following headings:

Area and population
Vital statistics, health, and nutrition
Immigration, emigration, and naturalization
Education
Law enforcement and federal courts
Climate
Public lands and national park system
Labor force, employment, and earnings
Military services and veterans' affairs
Social security and related programs
Income and expenditures
Prices
Elections
Federal government finances and employment
Banking and finance
Business enterprise
Communications
Power
Roads and motor vehicles
Transportation, air and land
Waterways, water traffic, and shipping
Irrigation, drainage, and soil conservation
Agriculture—general statistics
Agriculture—production and related subjects
Forests and forest products
Fisheries
Mining and mineral products
Construction and housing
Manufactures
Foreign commerce (including international accounts and aid)
Commerce of territories and possessions
Distribution and services (including advertising)
Comparative international statistics

The *County and City Data Book* is particularly valuable, for it combines in one volume material on a county and city basis which is otherwise available only in many different sources. It is a "small area" supplement for the *Statistical Abstract*. The 1952 edition gives 128 statistical items for each county and 133 items for cities of 25,000 or more. It also gives total population for each of these areas, based on 1950 Census figures.

Below is a list of some of the major items taken from the county table; many of these items have a further breakdown which lack of space prevents showing here.

Retail trade

Wholesale trade

Personal, business, and repair services

Tourist courts and camps

Amusements

Bank deposits

Savings and loan figures

Automobiles

Manufacturing establishments

Agriculture (many items from the current Census of Agriculture)

Vital statistics

Area and population

Labor force

Educational attainment of the population

The *County and City Data Book* first appeared in 1949 as a "revision and consolidation" of the *County Data Book* (last issued 1947) and the *Cities Supplement,* (last issued 1944) both of which are out of print. It contains 51 full-page maps showing county boundaries and standard metropolitan areas. The 1952 edition is the second one to be made available.

If you do not have available the individual publications for the Census of Business, Census of Manufactures, Census of Agriculture, and so on, this book will give you the most essential information about your county or city from all of these sources.

Other useful reference books. The *Municipal Year Book*[1] is the authoritative reference work on the activities of municipal governments. It includes extensive descriptive and interpretive material on the phases of municipal governments and on recent developments in the municipal field. It is particularly valuable for the many tables which list in some detail various facts and figures about one branch or another of the activities of municipal governments of different sizes. Most of the tables apply to cities of 10,000 or more, but some include cities of 5,000 to 10,000. Since city government has many branches, the book is, in a way, a compilation of facts about the role of city governments in the various branches of community endeavor, including education, housing, welfare, health, and so on. This *Year Book* makes it possible to compare any city with other cities on literally hundreds of items. If you live in a city, you will find in this book information about your city's activities which would take days and days to ferret out by yourself. Not all the material is presented in each annual edition, so it is worthwhile to consult editions for different years.

The usual, commercial type of *city directory* is an invaluable source of information for the community survey. Its most valuable part is probably

[1] International City Managers' Association, Chicago, published each year since 1934.

the alphabetical list of persons, usually obtained by actual house-to-house canvass. It typically lists the occupation of each adult, as well as the address. Another useful feature is the numerical street directory, which lists the residents for each street according to street number, and indicates whether the occupant is the owner or not, as well as whether he has a telephone. Another useful feature is the classified business directory, which will give a fairly accurate listing of the business and industrial enterprises of the community, as well as a partial list of associations, clubs, and societies. Some directories list rural routes by number, and list alphabetically the names of the people who are served by each rural delivery route. In addition, various items of information are given about the features and history of the city, and while much of it will duplicate what has perhaps already been gathered for the survey, some may suggest new avenues of inquiry or list items not yet ascertained. An inquiry at the chamber of commerce or similar organization will usually be sufficient to determine whether or not your community has such a directory.

What You Can Do with Maps

Maps can serve the survey in two ways. They can be used to illustrate various relationships which have been found, and they can be used to uncover additional relationships. Once you have procured a satisfactory map of the outlines of your community, various trace maps can be made from it, and each trace map may be used to illustrate a different thing, or combination of things. Many types of information can well be put on such maps for study. Here are some examples:

Different land-use zones
Location of "blighted" areas
Various "social resources" (see below)
Addresses of people arrested, or indicted, or convicted for a crime
Location of traffic accidents
Density of population
Movement of people (traffic flow)
Location of schools, parks, and playgrounds in relation to the number of people, or of children
Location of various types of industries
Location of various neighborhoods within the rural or urban community
Sections which are losing population and those which are gaining

Much will depend on the purposes of the survey. However, the above examples show some of the types of information which are suitable for the use of maps, and indicate that the comparison of certain maps with other related maps may show interesting relationships. This is true of the various plot maps suggested in different chapters of this book.

Sometimes it is desirable to plot on a map of a large village, small city, or section of a larger city, the location of various "social resources" such as fire stations, schools, churches, settlement houses, children's homes, hospitals, clubs of one sort or another, recreation facilities, business establishments, railroad stations, and so on. For this purpose, the Social Map Symbols designed and published by Russell Sage Foundation may be used. There are more than 100 such symbols, which come on a cut-out sheet, each symbol being 3/8 of an inch in diameter. A sample may be obtained free of charge and additional sheets at 5 cents a sheet. (See the accompanying Social Base Map of Part of Central Harlem, New York City.)

Sources of city maps. It should not be difficult to obtain maps of cities on almost any scale desired. The official city directory may have a map which is suitable. Often good maps are published by the chamber of commerce or various trade associations, banks, service clubs, and similar organizations. Official city zoning maps may be available. The council of social agencies may have developed maps for its purposes, or may be able to put the reader in touch with resources of maps. The various departments of the municipal government, such as the highway department, will have maps which may be procured. Atlases often contain maps of large cities. The usual motor highway maps procured at gasoline stations are not readily adaptable for local survey purposes.

If the "community" being studied is a section of a large city, it may be fairly easy to develop one's own map, particularly if the streets are on the conventional gridiron pattern. In many instances, complete accuracy of scale is not important.

Sources of rural maps. Geological Survey Maps are particularly good in that they show the topography of the land. Not all parts of the country are mapped in this series. The reader can obtain a circular which describes the areas in his state which are mapped from the Director, Geological Survey, Washington 25, D.C. The most common scales for these maps range from two miles to one-half mile to the inch. If for certain purposes the topographic lines are not desired, trace maps can be made.

Another possible source of excellent maps are the blueprint maps of rural postal routes obtainable from the Post Office Department, Washington, D.C., at a nominal cost. They are excellent in that they show individual houses and other buildings.

Soil survey maps are available for many individual counties. The county agricultural agent should be able to put the reader in touch with these maps,

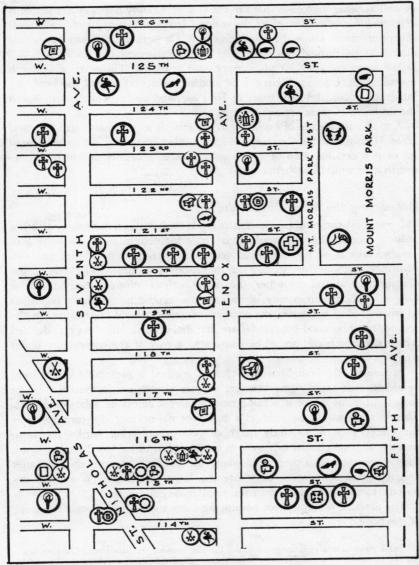

Data, Courtesy of the Mayor's Committee on City Planning

SOCIAL BASE MAP OF PART OF CENTRAL HARLEM, NEW YORK CITY

as well as other sources of maps in the county. County highway departments often publish official maps of the county. If not, they may have individual blueprint maps which they will give you. Or perhaps you can get school district maps through your local or state department of education.

For many counties, air photographs are available. These are well worth investigating, for with them can be studied the actual face of the land, the buildings, roads, different types of land use, and so on. Your county agent should know if these are available to you.

A map with a scale of one inch to the mile is a convenient size for rural areas. If names of farmhouses in thickly settled farm land are to be written in, or if a detailed map of a village is desired, probably one inch to one-fourth mile would be a better scale.

Delineating the Rural Community

Since rural communities seldom coincide with village, township, or other political boundaries, the need often arises for determining just what geographic area is to be considered part of the community. There are two principal methods for delineating the rural community. The first is the Galpin method and the other, the "neighborhood cluster" method. In the Galpin method, community boundaries are determined without regard as to whether they cut across the constituent neighborhood boundaries. In the second, neighborhood boundaries are first determined, and then it is decided which neighborhoods are to be considered a part of the community under study.

In general, the "neighborhood cluster" method is preferable where local neighborhoods seem to be stronger centers of group life than the larger communities, or where it is important not to cut across neighborhood lines. This method would be used as a basis for delineating the community if the intention were to study neighborhood organization within the community, or if neighborhoods were to be treated as units. On the other hand, the Galpin method is preferable where there is little concern about smaller neighborhood boundaries, or where the larger community is a more important focus of activities than the smaller neighborhood.

The detailed procedure for employing these methods is beyond the scope of this book.[1]

[1] For a more extensive description of the Galpin method, see Sanderson, Dwight, *Locating the Rural Community*, New York State College of Agriculture, Ithaca, 1939; and for the "neighborhood cluster" method, see Sanders, Irwin T., and Douglas Ensminger, *Alabama Rural Communities:* A Study of Chilton County, *Quarterly Bulletin* No. 136, Alabama College, Montevallo, 1940.

How to Delineate the Urban Neighborhood

Earlier in the present chapter it was suggested that the urban reader who is interested in a modest area within the city may want to choose a particular neighborhood of the city as his "community" for study. Several factors will be of help in determining the boundaries of the neighborhood to be studied:

1. Natural or artificial barriers often form the boundaries of neighborhoods. Such a barrier can be a river, large traffic artery, railroad track, hill, or park.

2. Neighborhoods often have names, and often their boundaries are well established by custom, so that a few inquiries will yield consistent answers as to where the neighborhood boundaries lie in the understanding of those who live there.

3. Often organizations of one type or another have neighborhood branches, with more or less clear conceptions as to where the service areas of these neighborhoods are. Sometimes there are neighborhood organizations such as citizens' associations or taxpayers' associations and it is possible to get from them their idea of neighborhood boundaries.

4. Neighborhoods are often though not always characterized by small service centers. The local trade area of stores and other local service institutions may be the area within which people cluster for other purposes.

5. Both in urban and rural settings, the neighborhood is sometimes thought of as the area served by the elementary school and the larger community or district by the high school.

6. Neighborhoods are often characterized by the "same type of people," and land is put to much the same type of use. In other words, the most important clue to a particular neighborhood may be a homogeneous area made up of the same kind of people and the same kind of activity.

7. In choosing neighborhood boundaries it is often wise to take into consideration the areas which have been used for former studies by other groups. This would be particularly true of Census tracts in tracted cities (see page 331). In some instances, such tracts, themselves, may serve as the neighborhood to be studied. In other cases, the neighborhood will consist of several tracts. Much the same can be said for block statistics, where these are available.

8. The section of the city in which the reader is interested may show itself to be no such homogeneous, easily defined district as is indicated above. There may be overlapping neighborhood boundaries depending on whether one is considering the schools or the type of people or the service institutions or some other item. In such a case, the important thing is to determine the boundaries of the neighborhood with the specific purpose of the survey

in mind, and with an eye toward blocks, tracts, wards, or other Census enumeration districts.

Some Hints in Interviewing

1. Select tactful people for interviewers. While it is possible and desirable to train interviewers, there is no substitute for common sense and tact in dealing with people. Choose as interviewers people who get along well with other people, and who can be trusted to be tactful and circumspect. Gossipy, vindictive, or garrulous people are to be avoided like the plague.

2. Train your interviewers. At the least, there should be a brief instruction sheet, perhaps incorporating some of the considerations in these paragraphs plus those which you think should be added. This can be gone over with the interviewers. In addition, it is often helpful to have each one "rehearse" an interview. Send him out of the room and ask him to come in as though he were approaching a home, or an office, where he wishes an interview. Have him proceed with it, using someone to act out the part of the housewife or official to be interviewed. Experience has shown that by presenting various interview situations and letting the interviewers act out the interview within these situations, great confidence is gained, and defective interview techniques may be attended to.

3. Make an appointment, where possible, particularly if you wish to interview an official, who is likely to grant you more time if you come at his convenience. Otherwise he may feel rushed and the interview may fail simply because the timing was not right. A busy official may rightfully resent encroachment on his "free" time. See him during the working day, if at all possible. Sometimes it is helpful to have some mutual friend approach the official to be interviewed and make the appointment. It is often wise to indicate in advance any material which will be requested during the interview, so that the official may gather appropriate facts and figures beforehand, if these are called for. Interviewers should respect the chain of command and approach administrators on matters that concern them, rather than going over their heads to their superiors.

4. It is important that the interviewer have a clear idea of the nature and purpose of the survey and be able to communicate it to the person interviewed. The latter is entitled to know, and is likely to respond favorably to a clear, frank statement of the nature of the survey and the part which this interview plays in it. The interviewer should be fairly conversant with the scope of the topic under study, but he should be careful not to demonstrate his erudition.

5. Establish "rapport." "A state of rapport exists between interviewer and respondent when the latter has accepted the research goals of the interviewer, and actively seeks to help him in obtaining the necessary information. Although the best way to achieve this result may usually be a warm and sympathetic approach, mere friendliness between respondent and interviewer is not sufficient in all cases."[1]

6. It is important that the field worker not give the impression that he is out on an "investigation" or "exposé." Informants should understand that their data will be used in the spirit and with the safeguards of a bona-fide survey, rather than to produce sensational charges or headlines.

7. Assure anonymity where appropriate, and respect the confidences granted you. Where material is not of a confidential nature, obviously there is little point to assuring that it will be kept in confidence and that anonymity will be preserved. However, where various comments or factual information of a confidential nature are given, these should be respected. Some caution should be exercised in promising confidentiality where the material solicited is such that all citizens have a right to know. Where confidentiality is involved, the respondent is entitled to know which material will be kept confidential and which will be published, and he should have a chance to check the final draft in this regard and to make comments or suggestions, but not necessarily exercise a veto.

8. Begin the interview with easy questions which do not ask for confidential material and about which there is unlikely to be any negative reaction. Tactful questioning will help to build confidence on the part of the respondent, and the more confidential questions, or those on controversial subjects, may be introduced after such confidence has been established.

9. Don't ask "loaded" questions. It is possible, by phrasing questions in certain ways, to deflect the response in the direction which the interviewer desires. Obviously, such questioning is likely to destroy rapport and militate against the objectivity of the survey. The best rule of thumb is to ask questions in such a manner that the respondent does not know what particular answer would be most favored by the interviewer. The interviewer should appear to be a "neutral" person.

10. Guard against using the interview as an educational device. It is often true that the process of thinking about and answering the questions may be a desirable educational experience for the informant. Nevertheless, if this effect is sought too deliberately, the informant is likely to feel that he is being "preached to," however subtly, and resent it. Presumably, the

[1] Goode, William J., and Paul K. Hatt, *Methods in Social Research*. McGraw-Hill Book Co., New York, 1952, p. 190.

primary goal of the interview will be to gain information, however much "education" may feature in the long-run purposes of the survey effort.

11. The interview should be tapered off gradually. The informant should not be given the impression that once the last question has been asked, the interviewer has no more use for him. Particularly where a cordial rapport has been built up, or where confidences have been given, it is important that the interview be ended in a casual and friendly manner rather than too abruptly. It is good not to close the interview at a point of confidential response. Appreciation should be expressed, and perhaps the interviewer can pass the time of day for a minute or so with "small talk." This is simply a way of demonstrating a sympathetic attitude rather than an exploitative one.

12. Careful notes should be taken of the interview. Notes may be jotted down during the interview, thus assuring immediate transfer to the record in the interest of accuracy. However, if this seems to inhibit the respondent, or to be too time-consuming, it may be well to delay the note-taking until immediately after the interview. Experience has shown that trained interviewers can record the chief points of the interview with remarkable accuracy, if this is done soon after the interview. The longer the interval, the more hazy the recall. On particularly complicated answers, the respondent can be asked to help the interviewer record his answer correctly.

Using Questionnaires and Schedules

Questionnaires consist of a series of questions to be answered on a prepared form by the respondent. They do not require an interview, and can be handled by mail. Schedules consist of questions to be filled in by the interviewer. The advantage of questionnaires and schedules is that they assure that each respondent supplies information on the same items, and in a comparable form. They can usually be filled out in less time than an ordinary interview requires, and if properly constructed they are easy to tabulate.

In choosing between questionnaires and schedules, it may be well to keep in mind that people like to talk to you but they often dislike filling out a questionnaire. If the group is small like that composed of the clergymen of a neighborhood or small community, the schedule will almost invariably assure more complete returns. In addition, the schedule has the advantage that questions can be interpreted, and the interviewer can be sure that all questions are answered.

Unfortunately, the construction of sound questionnaires or schedules is not an easy matter. If possible, enlist the aid of someone, perhaps from a nearby college department of sociology or psychology or from a marketing concern, who has had experience in questionnaire and schedule construction.

The following points, if carefully followed, should help to avoid the most obvious pitfalls of the questionnaire technique. But it would be well to study the chapter or chapters on questionnaires and schedules in a book on social research methods.[1]

1. First, determine as precisely as possible what you want to know. This is important, for you can thus avoid catch-all questionnaires which are needlessly long and which may fail to yield the type of information required.

2. Plan in advance the way in which you are going to tabulate your material. This is possible through the use of "dummy tables."[2] Actually construct models of the tables with which you want to end up. These can be used as a basis for planning the questions you will wish to ask in order to get the necessary information for these tables.

3. Ask yourself whether, on the basis of the dummy tables, you will actually have the answers to the questions you are seeking after you have made all the tabulations.

4. Draft the individual questions for the questionnaire. In general, it is extremely helpful if these can be in a form which requires only check marks, or "yes" or "no," or a specific figure for an answer. In order to do this, it is necessary to anticipate the types of answers which will be given. Then list the possible answers, plus one for "undecided," or "other," or "don't know," where appropriate, so that to answer the question the respondent need only place a check mark next to the answer which indicates what he wants to say. This has the advantage of rapid administration of the questionnaire and rapid tabulation.

However, there are some types of questions on which you should solicit individual comment and opinion. For these, you may want to use "open-end" questions, that is, questions where the respondent does not check one or more of a number of answers which are listed for him, but rather supplies the answer in his own words. This procedure has two advantages. It enables the respondent to answer in a way which may yield fresh insight into the matter being investigated, and it enables him to use his own words. The disadvantage here is that such questions are difficult to tabulate. However, a little practice with tabulating open-end questions will train the tabulator to classify the individual answers into a series of categories which seem to be appropriate. Nevertheless, the process is somewhat time-consuming.

[1] For instance, Lundberg, George A., *Social Research*, Longmans, Green and Co., New York, 1942; and Young, Pauline V., *Scientific Social Surveys and Research*, 2d ed., Prentice-Hall, Inc., New York, 1949.

[2] George A. Lundberg, *Op. cit.*, pp. 166–167.

5. Exercise care in wording the individual questions. Use language which is sufficiently simple for the intellectual level of the respondents. Avoid ambiguity in the wording. Guard against questions which are actually "double-barreled" and which ask for a yes or no answer when it is possible that the answer to one-half of the question would be "yes" and to the other half "no." As in interviewing, don't ask loaded questions. In general, ask a question which is neutral in tone and clear to the respondent.

6. Try to keep the questionnaire short. A long questionnaire is particularly discouraging to the potential respondent. The schedule can usually be longer than the questionnaire and still get good response.

7. Carefully explain special terms or categories used in the questionnaire so as to avoid possible misunderstandings of meaning. Prepare an instruction sheet for the schedule which defines possibly ambiguous terms (for example, if you are counting family units, define "family") and gives instructions as to how to mark for "no answer," or "question not applicable to respondent," and so on. Such instructions assure valid answers and facilitate accurate tabulation. The instruction sheet can be worked up in advance, then modified as a result of the pretest.

8. Test the questionnaire in advance of mailing it by getting a small group of people to fill it out. As a result of the pretest experience you will discover difficulties in administering the questionnaire, discover questions that cannot be answered in their present form, and find other "kinks" that can be corrected. This pretest is often overlooked but is very important, for it is desirable to find the deficiencies before rather than after the questionnaires have all been filled out. At this time, the instruction sheet can also be revised. Tabulate the answers to the pretest questionnaires just as you will tabulate the final answers, for in the process you may find that changes are indicated.

9. Mail the questionnaires, or send the interviewers around with the schedules. In the case of mailed questionnaires, follow-up letters may be important. Unless there is special interest in your survey by the people who are to fill out the questionnaires, a return of 20 per cent is to be regarded as good. You should consider whether those who return the questionnaire are truly representative of the whole group. Often they are better educated and have a higher income than the average. You should send a covering letter and enclose a stamped, self-addressed envelope. If confidential information is requested, you stand a better chance of getting it if the name of the respondent or other identifying data are not requested on the questionnaire.

10. Tally the answers to the questions and prepare the statistical tables.

If no cross-tabulations are to be used, the easiest way is to take a separate sheet of paper for each question and list the various categories of answers with ample space for tallying. The tally sheet is filled in according to the way the individual questions are answered. By adding the number of tallies for each type of answer, you will have a summary answer for each question. Where numerical data are requested, like number of years of schooling, you may want to use averages, or other statistical measures.

A footnote on "sampling." If you have a questionnaire to be filled out by school teachers, it may be practicable to get all the school teachers to fill it out. In a large city, however, this may be not only time-consuming but unnecessary. If, for example, there are a thousand such teachers, it may be that questionnaires filled out by one hundred of them will be sufficient to give you the information you need, *provided they are sufficiently representative of the larger group.* The use of sample studies is economical and feasible in many instances, but is fraught with difficulty for the amateur. The chief cause of the difficulty is the problem of assuring that the sample is sufficiently representative of the population which it purports to describe. Thus, if you distribute your school teacher questionnaire at PTA meetings, you will get only teachers who attend such meetings, and the responses may not be truly representative of teachers who usually avoid such meetings. You want to be sure, therefore, that the sample you select is like the total population you are studying in all significant respects.

The best advice for those who propose to make use of sample studies is to get the expert consultation of someone thoroughly familiar with the sampling process, who can help you draw a sample. This person may be a social scientist at a university, a field representative of a state or national association, a market analyst, and so on. If it is not possible to secure such help, consider using some other method. A helpful pamphlet entitled *Sampling:* Elementary Principles has been written by Philip J. McCarthy.[1] Standard works on social research, such as those cited earlier in this chapter, usually include material on sampling.

[1] Bulletin No. 15, New York State School of Industrial and Labor Relations, Cornell University, Ithaca, N.Y., 1951.

20. Some Important Aspects of the Community

THE PURPOSE OF THIS CHAPTER is to call the reader's attention to certain important aspects of the community which are especially related to community surveys. No systematic description of community life is attempted, but rather a selection has been made of some of the conditions or trends in American community living which may only partially be reflected in the answers to the questions in the relevant chapters.

Your Community: Rural or Urban?

"The city" and "the country" used to be thought of as two extreme ways of living, but the difference between them is becoming more and more blurred. It has been thought that cities are more likely to emphasize the individual as the social unit, while rural areas emphasize the family. It has also been considered that cities are characterized by the importance of secondary groups, decline of many functions of the family, great specialization of labor, and heterogeneity of population, while rural areas tend toward the opposite. But while these distinctions hold perhaps in extreme cases, the contrast is in all instances one of degree rather than kind.

Unless the reader lives in the midst of a large metropolis on the one hand or in a small, relatively isolated village or farm on the other, his community will have many characteristics usually considered to be urban in nature, and many which are rural. Several important developments make this likely.

City ways are being diffused to the country. Television sets, washing machines, electric refrigerators, complete plumbing and electrical facilities, and other conveniences usually associated with city living are becoming increasingly prevalent in many rural districts, along with such social facilities as large schools, supermarkets, child welfare services, and concert series.

Country people move to the cities. Roughly half of the rural youth migrate to the cities. Since the cities normally do not have sufficiently high birth rates, this influx of rural people is necessary for cities to maintain their number or to grow. But the result is that many "city people" are not so far away from the "country" as one might suppose.

City workers are moving to the suburbs. The commuting area surrounding cities continues to grow larger and larger. The countryside, which was formerly devoted to farming and small village life, is being invaded by suburban commuters. Suburban communities, made up as they are of older residents and newcomers, develop interesting community patterns which are neither wholly rural nor wholly urban.

Small industries are locating outside the large cities. Electric power and truck and rail transportation have made it possible for many small industries to establish themselves in relatively small communities, thus affording a partial industrial base to the economy of the rural community and joining it with larger communities for sources of raw materials and markets.

Many farmers are engaged in only part-time farming. In 1951 nearly three out of every ten dollars of farmers' incomes came from nonfarm sources. Work on the roads, or in local industries, or elsewhere, is becoming an increasingly important source of income for farmers. Far from being an isolated group of "rugged individualists" tucked away on scattered farms, an increasing number of farm people are as much at home with typewriters or turret lathes as they are with crop and livestock production. The Twentieth Century Fund reports that one out of every seven employed persons who lived on farms had a nonfarm job in 1930. By 1940 this had become one out of five; and in 1949 it was one out of three.

Country ways and city ways are therefore growing closer together. Somewhere between the extreme of the largest metropolis and the smallest, most isolated rural community, you will find your community, with its own peculiar mixture of city ways and country ways, a mixture which is determined in part by the trends listed above.

People and Their Environment

Each community has its own internal spatial pattern and is related in space to adjacent communities. These spatial arrangements arise out of, and in turn help to determine, the types of social activity carried on.

If you live in a rural area, it will be interesting to notice: how roads often follow along river valleys; how natural obstacles tend to divert people and activities; how time, rather than distance, often determines which route traffic will take; the clustering of service establishments in a relatively small space at the service center of the community; the surrounding closely settled homes and the more widely dispersed farms outside the village; the influence of the highway or railroad or river on the location of small industries and business establishments; the appearance of the buildings and the use which is made of the land bordering on the railroad tracks; new housing developments at the edges of the village or even outside the village limits (suburbanization on a modest scale).

If you live in a city, you will be interested in the effects of the gradual growth of the city center, the downtown district which is characteristic of so many large and small American cities. You may find evidences of a transitional zone surrounding the central business district, a zone in which business and industrial use is made of land and buildings which earlier were for residence only. There may be centralization of certain establishments, like department stores, theaters, or hotels, in certain areas. You may find slums in the zone of transition, where physical blight and social blight go hand in hand. There will likely be different "natural areas" of the city, each with its own characteristic pattern of people, social activity, and land use. You will be interested in the islands of various cultural and ethnic groups. Notice the change in types of residential dwelling from the hotels near the city center, through the slum areas to the apartment houses and semi-detached residences, and out to the suburbs with their new realty developments of single family houses and often mammoth apartments. The areas at the fringe of the city will often show a typical pattern found in many sections of the United States, a mixture of hot-dog stands, used-car lots, drive-in theaters, truck farms, golf courses, cabarets, new realty developments, junk yards. The movement of people to the suburbs will be of interest, as will other changes of land use within the city. Particularly interesting as an example of changing land use is the typical broad street with large formerly sumptuous single family homes which are now used for doctors' offices, tearooms, funeral parlors, and so on.[1]

Social Classes in the Community

Community people often tell the surveyor, "We don't have social classes in our community. Everybody's equal here." Yet various community studies in different parts of the country indicate that people are usually divided into

[1] The study of the spatial distribution of people in relation to their geographic environment on the one hand and their social behavior on the other is called "human ecology." For further reading in human ecology, see Quinn, James A., *Human Ecology*, Prentice-Hall, Inc., New York, 1950; or Hawley, Amos H., *Human Ecology:* A Theory of Community Structure, Ronald Press Co., New York, 1950. There are chapters on the ecology of the city in most textbooks in urban sociology and in many general sociology texts. Textbooks in rural sociology usually include chapters on neighborhood and community structure which deal with some of the ecological factors in rural communities.

different social "layers," or groups with different degrees of prestige, income, and access to the products of society.[1] They are often called socioeconomic groups, or social classes. These social classes have the following characteristics: They are unorganized groups. People are born into them, marry into them, or otherwise enter them from adjacent social classes. Within them, people tend to associate with each other more than with people outside their social class. An individual's social class position is determined to a large extent by such factors as the social class position of the family he was born into, amount and type of education, amount and type of income, residence, associations, such symbols of class as etiquette, dress, and mannerisms, language idiosyncracies, type of recreational activity.

On the average, people of different social classes vary in esthetic tastes, in the type of books and magazines they read, the way they vote, the size of their families, the way they spend their leisuretime, and even in their sex morality.

You will most likely find that people near the top of the social class structure receive more income, have more influence and prestige in the community, live in the more desirable residential sections, belong to more social and community organizations, and are more widely educated than people in the lower socioeconomic strata.[2]

The actual rating of the social status of individual people is beyond the scope of this book, but there are books available which give extensive descriptions of methods which can be used in discovering social classes and in assigning people to their social classes.[3]

The consideration of the social class structure of your community is important because people vary considerably in so many aspects of daily living on the basis of their social class position. Nevertheless, although the reader should be aware of the importance of social class, he probably would do better to avoid studying this complex aspect of his community, or else turn it over to an expert.

[1] See for example Warner, W. Lloyd, and Paul S. Lunt, *The Social Life of a Modern Community*, Yale University Press, New Haven, 1941; Hollingshead, August B., *Elmtown's Youth*, John Wiley and Sons, New York, 1949; Davis, Allison, Burleigh B. Gardner, and Mary R. Gardner, *Deep South*, University of Chicago Press, Chicago, 1941; and Kaufman, Harold F., *Prestige Classes in a New York Rural Community*, Cornell Agricultural Experiment Station, Ithaca, N.Y., 1944.

[2] These statements have been proved true again and again in different communities. Nevertheless, it is an extremely difficult theoretical problem to determine where the investigator should draw the lines between different social classes; or whether there are two, three, four, or six such classes; or if there is merely a gradual continuum of prestige and income from the lowest to the highest, without definite groups which can be called "classes."

[3] See Warner, W. Lloyd, and others, *Social Class in America:* A Manual of Procedure for the Measurement of Social Status, Science Research Associates, Chicago, 1949, and Hollingshead, August B., *Op. cit.*

The Community's Informal Structure

Extensive studies have indicated that alongside the formal structure of any social system, such as a factory, an army unit, a housing project, or a community, there is always an informal structure. People group themselves into little cliques or friendship groups which are not formally organized with charters or constitutions and do not have officers with carefully prescribed duties. For this very reason, such groups are difficult to investigate, but at the same time they are vital in the social life of the community.

A brief listing of points of difference between formal groups and informal groups will help the reader gain a clearer picture of informal structures:

Formal group	Informal group
Has charter, constitution, or other formal pattern according to which it is structured	Has no formal pattern to follow
Has name	Usually has no name
Has officers with prescribed rights and duties and methods of selection	Has no officers
Usually meets at regular intervals	Meets casually
Has definite membership status	Membership status not clearly defined
Interaction largely according to established patterns of procedure	Interaction involves a freer interplay of personalities
Is formed through a definite act of organization or incorporation	Arises gradually out of the free interplay of personalities
Controls members' actions through rules and regulations	Controls members' actions through informal sanctions like gossip, praise and blame

Informal groups may form among students in the same college course, among people who drift into "getting together" to eat lunch, among particular people or families in a neighborhood, among workers on the factory floor, among commuters riding the same train, within formal associations (especially the women's auxiliary), among children at school, and so on. They are variously called cliques, friendship groups, informal groups, autonomous groups, congeniality groups, and so on.

Put any number of people who are strangers to each other into a new environment and these informal groups will begin to form. Apparently propinquity is the chief guiding factor at the outset, as to who will associate with whom, but as things become more settled and people have an opportunity to make wider acquaintances, congeniality of interest and mutual compatability of personality come into play, with nearness becoming less important. The reasons why people everywhere and in various social situations form these little knots of intimate association have not as yet been fully explored, but certain possible contributing factors suggest themselves:

1. Through such association, people tend to be linked with the social system around them, whether it is the organization of a factory, or the formal organization of a military unit. They feel more secure in the social system as they share with other participants on intimate terms a feeling of mutual support.

2. These informal groups serve as channels of communication. Through them, one "gets the word." Without them, one is relatively isolated from the interesting and vital information which passes along the "grapevine" rather than through the pages of the community or company newspaper.

3. Informal groups affect the attitude of their members on the subjects which are discussed or communicated within the group. As such, they become little cells within which public opinion is formed. Apparently, people feel a need to talk over some new development with other people to determine what it means and how they should react. Informal groups serve this purpose of helping the individual arrive at a "definition of the situation."

4. Important satisfactions are involved in sharing with people in a fairly intimate way the common experiences of daily living: eating lunch, riding on the train, taking time out for a smoke or a cup of coffee, griping about the state of affairs, talking shop. This type of thing goes on within families where families are strong functioning units. In addition, when people are away from their families, they seek congenial people with whom to share these experiences.

Sometimes informal group association may be on a family basis, and at other times on an individual basis. Considerable attention has been given the informal visiting patterns of rural families. Perhaps not enough study has been given to the individual visiting patterns of family members. Nevertheless, it has been found in various parts of the United States and also in other countries that the question: With which families does your family visit most frequently? is a meaningful one, and that the families have little difficulty in calling to mind the families whom they visit regularly.

A whole series of research studies of social participation in both urban and rural environments has pointed out that lower-income people tend to belong to a minimum number of organizations if any. It is only now coming to be realized that membership in formal organizations is a measure of only one type of social participation, and that nonmembership in formal voluntary organizations need not be an indication of social isolation. The individual or family may be satisfying the desire for social participation through informal group participation rather than through formal groups.

In studying informal groups in your community, it might be well to keep in mind that they do not correspond exactly to the local "neighborhood."[1] The network of informal group participation may well cluster within the immediate neighborhood, but usually such visiting cliques are smaller than the neighborhood. In addition, people may go outside their immediate neighborhood for such informal social participation.

Warner and associates have found that most informal participation takes place among people of approximately the same social status.

With a knowledge of the informal structure of your community, your survey should be easier to conduct and more useful for various community purposes.

1. Your survey will contain information about the informal structure of the community, an aspect of the community which is often neglected in survey work.

2. Knowledge of the informal relationships may give important clues in interpreting the formal structure. Koos found, for example, that families in the Yorkville section of New York were making more use of the local druggist and bartender for counseling purposes, than they were of the many social agencies which existed in the vicinity.[2]

3. The informal structure serves as an intricate but effective communication network. If you are interested in learning what people are thinking, or in disseminating certain types of information, the informal network, "the grapevine," is highly effective. Loomis found that when relatively few of the informal group leaders in a rural community were carefully selected and invited to a farm demonstration meeting, everyone in the community with whom he talked the next day knew about the demonstration which had taken place.[3]

4. The people in a key position to help in the survey or action program are those who are in key positions in the informal network. They form a

[1] Loomis, Charles P., and J. Allan Beegle, *Rural Social Systems*. Prentice-Hall, Inc., New York, 1950, chap. 5.

[2] Koos, Earl L., *Families in Trouble*. King's Crown Press, New York, 1946.

[3] Loomis, Charles P., "Tapping Human Power Lines," *Adult Leadership*, vol. 1, February, 1953.

bridge between the various groups to which they are related; they see many people in a more or less intimate relationship of friendship. People tend to cluster naturally around them.

5. In the formal organization of larger communities, there are often people in key spots who have great "power" in that a word from them can decide the fate of a community project. Mustering support within the formal organizational structure may lead to failure if it does not take into account the informal relationships of kinship or friendship which exist among people in key spots in the formal structure.

To make local opinion and interests felt it is necessary to know where the important decisions regarding the community are made. Do you know where and by whom these decisions are made for your community? I do not mean the "front" man; I mean the man or group from whom he takes his orders. Not until you know that will you be able to direct local sentiments, opinions, interest, and collective movements in the proper direction to give them force.[1]

6. The people who "set the tone" in the community and who exercise crucial influence in the development of public opinion are not always the formal leaders. Loomis concludes that "many individuals who occupy key positions in networks of relationships are not formal leaders and do not recognize themselves as leaders. Those who will carry their programs to the people must relate such individuals both to the accepted formal leaders of organizations and to the informal 'grass roots' leaders."[2]

Primary, Secondary, and Mass Relations in the Community

There are three levels on which social activity takes place within the community. They are vital in determining the nature of community life. Most communities show activity on all three levels, in various combinations. How is your community organized with relation to these three levels of social activity?

Primary activity. Primary activity is carried on in "face-to-face" groups, the "primary groups" first described and so named by Charles Horton Cooley.[3] These groups consist of persons who see each other face-to-face;

[1] Wirth, Louis, and others, *Community Planning for Peacetime Living.* Stanford University Press, Stanford, 1946, p. 42. See also Hunter, Floyd, *Community Power Structure: A Study of Decision Makers,* University of North Carolina Press, Chapel Hill, 1953; Chapter 3, The X Family: A Pattern of Business-Class Control, in Lynd, Robert S., and Helen M. Lynd, *Middletown in Transition,* Harcourt, Brace and Co., New York, 1937; and Warner, W. Lloyd, and Paul S. Lunt, *The Social Life of a Modern Community,* Yale University Press, New Haven, 1941.

[2] Loomis, Charles P., and J. Allan Beegle, *Op. cit.,* p. 171.

[3] Cooley, Charles Horton, *Social Organization.* Charles Scribner's Sons, New York, 1909.

they are of some degree of permanence, and relatively intimate. Examples of primary groups are the family, play group, and small neighborhood. Friendship groups such as have just been described are also largely primary in nature.

Primary activity is carried on by and within such groups. Recreation may consist of informal, more or less spontaneous visiting, conversation, games, and so on. Much educational activity is engaged in by such groups, particularly within the family, as children learn to take on the ways of those around them. Often, economic functions are performed by such groups. The family farm is such a primary economic activity, but so is the cooperative teamwork of several farmers who trade labor in connection with threshing activities. Such face-to-face groups exert a strong influence in regulating the behavior of their members. Devices like ridicule, praise and blame, gossip, and ostracism play a crucial role in making individual members conform to group standards. Within such groups there is considerable mutual aid in time of sickness, economic difficulty, or family tragedy. The intimate group of friends and neighbors thus exercises many health and welfare functions.

To sum up, primary activities are carried on within face-to-face groups that are informal in structure, characterized by relatively intimate relationships, and governed by custom more than by law. Such types of activity go on in countless instances every day, even in the large metropolis, but they are thought to be more characteristic of the smaller, rural communities.

Secondary activity. Secondary activity takes place under more formal auspices. The people involved often meet face-to-face, but do not have such intimate contact. They see each other as persons in certain categories, customer-storekeeper, lawyer-client, doctor-patient, and so on. For this reason, these contacts are often called "categorical."

Most of the agencies and organizations in the community are of this secondary nature. Examples would be the recreational activity at the large church, the local bowling alley, or the lodge. The organized recreational program at the community recreation center, park, or playground, is another example, as contrasted with the spontaneous activities of the primary groups. Educational activities of a formalized nature are conducted through the local school. Economic activities such as stores, small manufacturing establishments, or service trades such as automobile repair shops are good examples. Health and welfare activities on this level are carried on by the social agencies, the family societies, hospitals, clinics, neighborhood centers, and community chests.

Secondary activity is more formal in that it tends to be organized according to professional codes, "rules of the game," charters, constitutions, regulations, law, and so on. Activities of the participants are governed more by these formal rules than by informal pressures, and as a result these relations are sometimes called "contract" relations.

Mass activity. Mass activity is even more impersonal, and the people between whom such mass relations exist may never converse with each other or become acquainted personally. The relationship is often heavily weighted on one side and the flow of communication is often in one direction, as in the relation of a popular columnist to his reading public, or of a television performer to his audience. This need not always be the case, however, for mass relations exist likewise among the people who crowd into the subway car or who pass each other hurriedly on the sidewalks during rush hours in a large city. These people do not usually know each other, do not speak with each other, and their relationship is highly impersonal.

Mass activity is carried on in such depersonalized relationships. Recreation may consist in going to a movie or watching television or reading the funny sheet, all through the mediation of instruments of mass communication—motion picture projection, radio, television, or printing press. Educational processes occur within such mass activity. The funny sheet helps to mold the child's stereotype of his teacher or of the members of a different ethnic group; the movies instill attitudes toward the many situations, ideas, and people that they portray. The newspaper or radio columnist brings new information before his audience. Mass activity in the economic line is exemplified by mass advertising campaigns, mass production of standardized goods, and mass supplying of certain services, such as telephone or water supply. But they are also exemplified in the large, impersonal labor union, or the mass of stockholders who "own" a corporation.

Health and welfare activity on this level involves the national educational "campaigns" against one disease or another, the observance of "Mental Health Week," the state and national legislation activating social security programs, and health and hospital grants-in-aid.

Mass activity has its own characteristic ways of controlling behavior. It does so by means of the influence which mass communication media have on attitudes and opinions. Many people can remember the campaign which the cigarette companies launched to persuade the American public to accept female smoking. Advertising, propaganda, "public relations" work, national political campaigns, all are directed in part at least to the mass audience, to get people whom they do not know to think or behave in a certain way.

The trend toward mass activity. As society becomes more complex, social activity tends to move from the primary type to the secondary and mass type. The national brand product supplants the local product, which in turn had supplanted grandmother's home preserving. The motion picture and television program supplant the playground and settlement house, which in turn had supplanted the spontaneous visiting, game-playing, and other unorganized activity of the primary groups. Federal health and welfare programs supplement the efforts of local agencies, which in turn had largely taken the place of neighborly help in time of sickness, dependency, and other kinds of trouble.

Generally speaking, the more rural and isolated the area, the more likely are social activities to be preponderantly of the primary type. The more urban and metropolitan the area, the more likely are mass relationships to predominate. There are many rural neighborhoods in which primary activities predominate in the recreational, educational, economic, and health and welfare fields. Nevertheless, the syndicated column is likely to appear in the local newspaper, the radio is likely to be tuned in to add to the mass audience of a commentator, the federal social security program will probably reach right into the home of an elderly couple who receive an Old-Age and Survivors check.

Typically, social activity shifts toward impersonality of organization either where new satisfactions are desired which cannot be provided through the primary group, or where needs arise which the primary group can no longer take care of. Thus, the television program may seem more appealing than a game of croquet, a spot on the high-school basketball team may be more challenging than simply playing with "the kids in the neighborhood." In another vein, modern facilities in medical care may be beyond the abilities of the small locality group to provide. Under modern conditions of industrial, urban, highly mobile life in small family units, it may no longer be feasible for married couples with children to take care of their aging parents. Local communities, and indeed entire states, may be at an economic disadvantage in providing for those who are without work or who for other reasons are economically dependent.

Social Functions and Social Agencies

In survey work it is advisable to consider functions as the most important thing, and agencies as the means for fulfilling these functions. In smaller communities, there may be few secondary agencies, such as family societies, youth centers, child guidance clinics, and social service exchanges. Never-

theless, they may be very much needed. On the other hand, it may be that their functions are already being carried out satisfactorily by such primary groups as family, friends, and neighborhood. As more impersonal, urban ways spread to rural communities, there is perhaps greater need for secondary agencies to fill recreational, welfare, and other functions which earlier were filled within the local face-to-face group. Some rural communities woefully lack adequate recreational facilities and programs, for example. Others, conceivably, may not have many special formalized recreational programs, and they may not need them because ample recreational activities already exist on an informal basis.

In larger communities, many specialized agencies are needed, and the population base is large enough to support them. The various social agencies considered in this book are highly desirable, perhaps necessary adjuncts of an urban, industrial society such as that in which so many Americans live. Yet two questions arise. One has to do with whether social agencies can entirely supply the type of face-to-face relationship which seems to be conducive to a rich community life. The other concerns the relevance of urban agencies in rural communities.

Regarding the first question, most people agree that the satisfactions available on the mass level, such as good radio programs, symphony concerts, and national publications, are highly desirable and can hardly be supplied except on a mass basis. Similarly, there is agreement on the value of supervised recreation programs and the varied activities of other local social agencies on the secondary level. Yet it need hardly be pointed out that these are designed to supplement, rather than supplant, the activities of local family, friendship, neighborhood, and other community groups of a more primary nature. For example, the availability of excellent symphonic programs by nationally known orchestras should not deter local community groups from forming civic orchestras, summer band concerts, or smaller ensemble groups, and such activity, in turn, need not preclude pleasant evenings of "making music" in the family home.

The second question suggests that readers consider carefully, where an agency program is thought to be needed, whether the small community's answer should necessarily be a miniature edition of the large city agency. A Golden Age Club may be highly appropriate in a community of 50,000. Is it equally appropriate or feasible in a community of 1,000? The question implies a need, which professional personnel are increasingly recognizing, to develop agency patterns for the small community out of the needs, resources, and values of the small community rather than the big city.

Thus, to sum up, the basic question would seem to be: How do people meet their needs and derive their satisfactions? The presence or absence of various agencies is certainly relevant to the answer to this question, but it does not constitute the answer. There is little point in looking for a secondary or mass agency when primary groups are adequately fulfilling the functions which such agencies perform. Even in the impersonal metropolitan community, mass activity rests on secondary group activity, which in turn rests on the way people treat each other in their daily dealings. Many of the most vital functions of community living—the rearing of the young, the formation of opinion, the care of the neighbor across the way, the walk to the store for an ice cream cone, the game of bridge, the control through gossip—go on in the metropolitan community under the auspices of primary activity. Such vital activities of the community are not reflected in the agency program, and the agency program cannot completely substitute for them. But it is easier to locate a family society or a settlement house and record the functions listed in its annual report than it is to uncover or count or otherwise determine the extent to which primary activity prevails in the different aspects of community living, and for this reason the surveyor must redouble his efforts if he is to observe, record, and report this activity.

Social Change and Your Community's Problems

Many of the problems which you will find in your community are largely the result of vast social changes which have swept the western world, the United States, and your community as well. While each problem has its own peculiar configuration of circumstances, most of them are related to the fact that economic and technological changes have brought about a type of social living which can best be described as predominantly urban, specialized, industrial, and individualistic. In the process great aggregations of population have become concentrated in small areas. Man who throughout his history has been accustomed to living in small, face-to-face groups which met his major needs, is confronted in modern times with the problems of getting along side by side with people whom he does not know. The basic social controls of the primary group on individual behavior have lost much of their effectiveness. We now have the problem of keeping in balance a highly specialized and complex, interdependent network of different people who are no longer largely self-sufficient, but take part in only one minute aspect of economic production. We have the problems of people who exercise little control over their own economic future; problems of avoiding social chaos in a society which places a premium on individualism; problems of adapting an agrarian, preindustrial type of family life to the needs and changed conditions of the city; problems of finding some constructive activity for children who in former generations would have been busy with useful farm and household chores; problems of finding a substitute for primary group functions where these have broken down.

These underlying problem situations resolve themselves into the type of specific problem which your study is likely to uncover: How do we arrange for off-street parking in the downtown area? What shall we do about juvenile delinquency? Do we need a mental health clinic? How can we improve the quality of instruction in our schools? What shall we do to get adequate sanitary inspection of eating places? Can our community support a youth center? How can social agencies better pool their efforts to give service to the whole community? How can we attract new industry and what kind should it be? What happens to children who are given up for adoption in our community? What can be done about sorely needed low-cost housing? How can we make our Main Street a more attractive place to shop? What about vocational opportunities for our youth?

It is well to search for the background factors underlying your community's particular problems, for sometimes their causes are deeply rooted in the structure of our society, while at other times they are more susceptible to amelioration. This sort of study will help your community people decide in any particular case whether they want to take a course of action which consists of easing the trouble and grief caused by the problem (free meals for the unemployed), or trying to remedy the problem (family clinics to help restore families at the point of breakdown), or planning ahead for a type of community situation in which the problem does not arise.

In the present period of rapid social change, new problems arise constantly. Communities differ in their alertness to these problems and in their ability to tackle them. In some communities, problems are largely ignored until the situation has become so critical as to threaten a large number of people directly. Then action is taken, but only enough to patch things up for a while until another similar crisis comes along. On the other hand, some communities are alert to the problems as they arise, and are capable of mustering concerted action to confront them. Indeed, they are purposefully building the type of social situation in which wholesome community living does not produce the same problems all over again. The reader will want to keep in mind, as he studies his community, how his community measures up in the way it confronts its problems. Which problems does it confront merely with missions of mercy to those whose lives have already been blighted? Which problems does it tackle through effective action to correct the difficulty? Which problems does it avoid by positive planning for wholesome conditions?

References for Further Study

The following textbooks in rural sociology are examples of the way in which rural community living is portrayed in this field:

Kolb, John H., and Edmund DeS. Brunner, *A Study of Rural Society*. 4th ed. Houghton Mifflin Co., Boston, 1952.

Lindstrom, David E., *American Rural Life*. Ronald Press Co., New York, 1948.

Smith, T. Lynn, *The Sociology of Rural Life*. 3d ed. Harper and Bros., New York, 1953.

Taylor, Carl C., and others, *Rural Life in the United States*. Alfred A. Knopf, New York, 1949.

Similarly, community living under urban conditions is described from the sociological standpoint in such standard works as the following:

Gist, Noel P., and L. A. Halbert, *Urban Society*. 3d ed. Thomas Y. Crowell Co., New York, 1950.

Hallenbeck, Wilbur C., *American Urban Communities*. Harper and Bros., New York, 1951.

Hatt, Paul K., and Albert J. Reiss, Jr., *Reader in Urban Sociology*. The Free Press, Glencoe, Illinois, 1951.

Queen, Stuart A., and David B. Carpenter, *The American City*. McGraw-Hill Book Co., Inc., New York, 1953.

Riemer, Svend, *The Modern City*. Prentice-Hall, Inc., New York, 1952.

The following books emphasize especially the community approach:

Kinneman, John A., *The Community in American Society*. Appleton-Century-Crofts, Inc., New York, 1947.

Zimmerman, Carle C., *The Changing Community*. Harper and Bros., New York, 1938.

List of Agencies

Governmental—Washington 25, D.C.

Bureau of the Census, Department of Commerce
Bureau of Indian Affairs, Department of the Interior
Bureau of Labor Statistics, Department of Labor
Children's Bureau, Social Security Administration, Department of Health, Education, and Welfare
Department of Agriculture
Department of Health, Education, and Welfare
Department of Labor
Farm Credit Administration
Farmers Home Administration, Department of Agriculture
Federal Extension Service, Department of Agriculture
Federal Housing Administration, Housing and Home Finance Agency
Food and Drug Administration, Department of Health, Education, and Welfare
Geological Survey, Department of the Interior
Housing and Home Finance Agency
Immigration and Naturalization Service, Department of Justice
Internal Revenue Service, Department of the Treasury
National Labor Relations Board
Office of Defense Mobilization, Executive Office of the President
Office of Education, Department of Health, Education, and Welfare
Office of Vocational Rehabilitation, Department of Health, Education, and Welfare
Public Health Service, Department of Health, Education, and Welfare
Public Housing Administration, Housing and Home Finance Agency
Small Business Administration
Social Security Administration, Department of Health, Education, and Welfare
Veterans' Administration
Women's Bureau, Department of Labor

Voluntary

Adult Education Association of the U.S.A., 743 North Wabash Avenue, Chicago 11, Illinois

Alcoholics Anonymous, P.O. Box 459, Grand Central Annex, New York 17, New York

American Association of Social Workers, One Park Avenue, New York 16, New York[1]

American Association of University Women, 1634 I Street, NW., Washington 6, D.C.

American Association on Mental Deficiency, Mansfield Training School, Mansfield Depot, Connecticut

American Cancer Society, 47 Beaver Street, New York 4, New York

American Civil Liberties Union, 170 Fifth Avenue, New York 10, New York

American Country Life Association, 1201 Sixteenth Street, NW., Washington 6, D.C.

American Dental Association, 222 East Superior Street, Chicago 11, Illinois

American Diabetes Association, 11 West 42d Street, New York 18, New York

American Federation of Labor, American Federation of Labor Building, Washington 1, D.C.

American Foundation for the Blind, 15 West 16th Street, New York 11, New York

American Friends Service Committee, 20 South 12th Street, Philadelphia 7, Pennsylvania

American Hearing Society, 817 Fourteenth Street, NW., Washington 5, D.C.

American Heart Association, 44 East 23d Street, New York 10, New York

American Hospital Association, 18 East Division Street, Chicago 10, Illinois

American Medical Association, 535 North Dearborn Street, Chicago 10, Illinois

American Municipal Association, 1625 H Street, NW., Washington 6, D.C.

American National Red Cross, 17th and D Streets, Washington 13, D.C.

American Nurses' Association, 2 Park Avenue, New York 16, New York

American Physical Therapy Association, 1790 Broadway, New York 19, New York

American Planning and Civic Association, 901 Union Trust Building, Washington 5, D.C.

[1] To become part of National Association of Social Workers during 1955.

American Prison Association, 135 East 15th Street, New York 3, New York

American Psychiatric Association, Room 310, 1270 Avenue of the Americas, New York 20, New York

American Public Health Association, 1790 Broadway, New York 19, New York

American Public Welfare Association, 1313 East 60th Street, Chicago 37, Illinois

American School Health Association, Kent State University, Kent, Ohio

American Social Hygiene Association, 1790 Broadway, New York 19, New York

American Society of Planning Officials, 1313 East 60th Street, Chicago 37, Illinois

American Sociological Society, New York University, Washington Square, New York 3, New York

Anti-Defamation League of B'nai B'rith, 212 Fifth Avenue, New York 10, New York

Association for the Aid of Crippled Children, 345 East 46th Street, New York 17, New York

Association for the Study of Community Organization, Room 810, One Park Avenue, New York 16, New York

Association of the Junior Leagues of America, 305 Park Avenue, New York 22, New York

Association of State and Territorial Health Officers, State Department of Health, State Office Building, Cheyenne, Wyoming

Boy Scouts of America, National Council, New Brunswick, New Jersey

Boys' Clubs of America, 381 Fourth Avenue, New York 16, New York

Braille Institute of America, 741 North Vermont Avenue, Los Angeles 29, California

Camp Fire Girls, 16 East 48th Street, New York 17, New York

Chamber of Commerce of the United States of America, 1615 H Street, NW., Washington 6, D.C.

Child Study Association of America, 132 East 74th Street, New York 21, New York

Child Welfare League of America, 345 East 46th Street, New York 17, New York

Christian Social Welfare Associates, 297 Fourth Avenue, New York 10, New York

Common Council for American Unity, 20 West 40th Street, New York 18, New York

Commonwealth Fund, One East 75th Street, New York 21, New York

Community Chests and Councils of America, 345 East 46th Street, New York 17, New York

Community Service, Box 243, Yellow Springs, Ohio

Conference for Health Council Work, 505 North Seventh Street, St. Louis 1, Missouri

Congress of Industrial Organizations, 718 Jackson Place, NW., Washington 6, D.C.

Council of Jewish Federations and Welfare Funds, 165 West 46th Street, New York 36, New York

Family Service Association of America, 192 Lexington Avenue, New York 16, New York

Foreign Policy Association, 345 East 46th Street, New York 17, New York

General Federation of Women's Clubs, 1734 N Street, NW., Washington 6, D.C.

Girl Scouts of the U.S.A., 155 East 44th Street, New York 17, New York

Goodwill Industries of America, 1222 New Hampshire Avenue, NW., Washington, D.C.

Institute of Public Administration, 684 Park Avenue, New York 21, New York

International City Managers' Association, 1313 East 60th Street, Chicago 37, Illinois

International Social Service, American Branch, 345 East 46th Street, New York 17, New York

League of Women Voters of the United States, 1026 Seventeenth Street, NW., Washington 6, D.C.

Maternity Center Association, 48 East 92d Street, New York 28, New York

Muscular Dystrophy Associations of America, 39 Broadway, New York 4, New York

National Association for the Advancement of Colored People, 20 West 40th Street, New York 18, New York

National Association for Mental Health, 1790 Broadway, New York 19, New York

National Association of the Deaf, 2495 Shattuck Avenue, Berkeley 4, California

National Association of Housing and Redevelopment Officials, 1313 East 60th Street, Chicago 37, Illinois

National Association of Social Workers. *See* American Association of Social Workers

National Catholic Welfare Conference, 1312 Massachusetts Avenue, NW., Washington 5, D.C.

National Child Labor Committee, 419 Fourth Avenue, New York 16, New York

National Committee on Boys and Girls Club Work, 59 East Van Buren Street, Chicago 5, Illinois

National Conference of Catholic Charities, 1346 Connecticut Avenue, NW., Washington 6, D.C.

National Conference of Christians and Jews, 381 Fourth Avenue, New York 16, New York

National Conference of Jewish Communal Service, 1841 Broadway, New York 23, New York

National Conference of Social Work, 22 West Gay Street, Columbus 15, Ohio

National Congress of Parents and Teachers, 600 South Michigan Boulevard, Chicago 5, Illinois

National Consumers League, 348 Engineers Building, Cleveland 14, Ohio

National Council of the Churches of Christ in the U.S.A., 297 Fourth Avenue, New York 10, New York

National Council on Family Relations, 5757 South Drexel Avenue, Chicago 37, Illinois

National Education Association of the United States, 1201 Sixteenth Street, NW., Washington 6, D.C.

National Epilepsy League, 130 North Wells Street, Chicago 6, Illinois

National Federation of Settlements and Neighborhood Centers, 129 East 52d Street, New York 22, New York

National Foundation for Infantile Paralysis, 120 Broadway, New York 5, New York

National Health Council, 1790 Broadway, New York 19, New York

National Housing Conference, 1129 Vermont Avenue, NW., Washington 5, D.C.

National Jewish Welfare Board, 145 East 32d Street, New York 16, New York

National League for Nursing, 2 Park Avenue, New York 16, New York

National Legal Aid Association, 328 Main Street East, Rochester 4, New York

National Multiple Sclerosis Society, 270 Park Avenue, New York 17, New York

National Municipal League, 542 Fifth Avenue, New York 36, New York

National Planning Association, 1606 New Hampshire Avenue, NW., Washington 9, D.C.

National Probation and Parole Association, 1790 Broadway, New York 19, New York

National Publicity Council for Health and Welfare Services, 257 Fourth Avenue, New York 10, New York

National Recreation Association, 8 West Eighth Street, New York 11, New York

National Rehabilitation Association, Room 615, 1025 Vermont Avenue, NW., Washington 5, D.C.

National Safety Council, 425 North Michigan Avenue, Chicago 11, Illinois

National Sanitation Foundation, Headquarters—School of Public Health, University of Michigan, Ann Arbor, Michigan

National Social Welfare Assembly, 345 East 46th Street, New York 17, New York

National Society for Crippled Children and Adults, 11 South LaSalle Street, Chicago 3, Illinois

National Society for the Prevention of Blindness, 1790 Broadway, New York 19, New York

National Travelers Aid Association, 425 Fourth Avenue, New York 16, New York

National Tuberculosis Association, 1790 Broadway, New York 19, New York

National Urban League, 1133 Broadway, New York 10, New York

Planned Parenthood Federation of America, 501 Madison Avenue, New York 22, New York

Public Administration Service, 1313 East 60th Street, Chicago 37, Illinois

Public Education Association, 20 West 40th Street, New York 18, New York

Regional Plan Association, 205 East 42d Street, New York 17, New York

Rural Life Association, Quaker Hill, Route 28, Richmond, Indiana

Russell Sage Foundation, 505 Park Avenue, New York 22, New York

Salvation Army, 120 West 14th Street, New York 11, New York

Social Legislation Information Service, 1346 Connecticut Avenue, NW., Washington 6, D.C.

Southern Regional Council, 63 Auburn Avenue, NE., Room 432, Atlanta 3, Georgia

United Cerebral Palsy Association, 50 West 57th Street, New York 19, New York

United Community Defense Services, 345 East 46th Street, New York 17, New York

United Hias Service, 425 Lafayette Street, New York 3, New York

United Housing Foundation, 345 East 46th Street, New York 17, New York

United States Conference of Mayors, 730 Jackson Place, NW., Washington 6, D.C.

Volunteers of America, 340 West 85th Street, New York 24, New York

Young Men's Christian Association, National Council, 291 Broadway, New York 7, New York

Young Men's Hebrew Association, National Council, 145 East 32d Street, New York 16, New York

Young Women's Christian Association of the U.S. of America, National Board, 600 Lexington Avenue, New York 22, New York

Young Women's Hebrew Association, National Office, 145 East 32d Street, New York 16, New York

Index

Index

373

This book is to be returned on or before
the last date stamped below.